Bilingual Higher Education in the Legal Context

Studies in International Minority and Group Rights

VOLUME 2

The titles published in this series are listed at brill.nl/imgr

Bilingual Higher Education in the Legal Context

Group Rights, State Policies and Globalisation

Edited by
Xabier Arzoz

MARTINUS
NIJHOFF
PUBLISHERS

LEIDEN • BOSTON
2012

Library of Congress Cataloging-in-Publication Data

Bilingual higher education in the legal context : group rights, state policies and globalisation / edited by Xabier Arzoz.
p. cm. -- (Studies in international minority and group rights ; v. 2)
Includes bibliographical references and index.
ISBN 978-90-04-20925-1 (hardback : alk. paper) 1. Education, Bilingual--Law and legislation. 2. Universities and colleges--Law and legislation. 3. Law schools. I. Arzoz, Xabier.
K3259.B55 2012
340.071'1--dc23

2011051427

ISSN 2210-2132
ISBN 978 90 04 20925 1 (hardback)
ISBN 978 90 04 22806 1 (e-book)

This book is printed on acid-free paper.

TABLE OF CONTENTS

NOTES ON CONTRIBUTORS

Elisabeth Alber is Senior Researcher at the Institute for Studies on Federalism and Regionalism at the European Academy (EURAC), Bolzano/Bozen. Her main research fields include multinational federalism, minorities and autonomies, multilevel governance and participatory democracy.

Xabier Arzoz is Associate Professor of Administrative and EU Law at the University of the Basque Country, Bilbao. Currently, he clerks for one of the Spanish constitutional judges. He has authored over sixty works in various languages on Spanish and European administrative law, linguistic diversity and language rights, fundamental rights, and federalism and autonomy.

André Braën is Professor of Law and former dean and associate dean at the Faculty of Law of the University of Ottawa, Civil Law Section. He began his academic career at the Faculty of Law of the University of Moncton in 1979. He has been a visiting professor in several foreign institutions. His main areas of expertise are language rights and maritime law. Mr Braën is a member of the Bar of Quebec.

Bethan Sarah Davies is a PhD student within the Department of Law and Criminology at Aberystwyth University. Her research is focused upon minority language provision within higher education, focusing specifically upon Welsh medium education. To that effect, she has been awarded a Welsh medium scholarship from Y Coelg Cymraeg Cenedlaethol.

Gyula Fábián is Public Prosecutor at the Court of Appeal Cluj, Romania and Associate Professor at the Babeş-Bolyai University, Cluj-Napoca, Romania, where he coordinates the "European Private Law" LLM Programm. He is author of several books and studies in several languages in the fields of European law, minority law, international law and criminal law.

Nicole Kornet is Assistant Professor of Commercial Law at the Faculty of Law of Maastricht University. She is a member of the steering comittee for the European Law School English Track bachelor. She is a fellow at the Maastricht European Private Law Institute and the Institute for Globalisation and International Regulation. Her research focuses on the impact of globalisation on international commercial contract law and practice.

Alba Nogueira López is Associate Professor of Administrative Law at the University of Santiago de Compostela. She is the author of many contributions about language rights, environmental law and administrative economic law, and the editor of a commentary on the ECRML to be published by the Council of Europe. She is member of the Scientific Board of the specialised journal *Llengua i Dret*.

Francesco Palermo is Professor for Comparative Constitutional Law in the Faculty of Law, University of Verona and Director of the Institute for Studies on Federalism and Regionalism at EURAC, Bolzano/Bozen. Main research areas include comparative federalism, minority rights and European integration.

R. Gwynedd Parry is Professor of Law and Legal History at Swansea University. He is also Director of the Hywel Dda Research Institute at the university. His main research interests are in the fields of criminal justice, modern legal and social history and law and minority languages. He is also a qualified barrister, and in 2010 he was elected Fellow of the Royal Historical Society.

Eva Pons is Associate Professor of Constitutional Law at the University of Barcelona, Spain. She is the author of many contributions in the field of public law, comparative law, language rights in international and European legal systems, and the regulation of the Catalan language. She is member of the Board of Directors of the specialised journal *Llengua i Dret*.

Sophie Weerts is a PhD student and a member of the Research Centre on State and Constitution (CRECO) at the Faculty of Law of the University of Louvain. She has been attorney at Law and expert for the Federal Minister for Civil Service during the linguistic reform of the federal administration (1999–2004). Her main research interests are in the field of comparative constitutional law and international human rights law with a particular focus on democracy and language policies.

Nicolas Schmitt is Senior Researcher at the Institute for Federalism of the University of Fribourg since its foundation in 1985. He has been working worldwide on many topics ranging from local authorities to comparative federalism and policy analysis. He was a former secretary/treasurer of the IACFS, is current vice-president of Fondation Emile Chanoux (Aosta) and has written extensively on federalism and decentralisation.

Markku Suksi is Professor of Public Law at the Department of Law, Åbo Akademi University, in Finland. He has published, *inter alia*, the following books and edited volumes: Markku Suksi (ed.), *Autonomy: Applications and Implications* (Kluwer 1998), Markku Suksi, *Finlands statsrätt* (2002), Markku Suksi, *Ålands konstitution* (2005), and Markku Suksi, *Sub-State Governance through Territorial Autonomy* (Springer 2011).

ACKNOWLEDGEMENTS

The origins of this book lie in a workshop on Bilingual Higher Education in the Legal Context held on 24–25 May 2010 in the International Institute for the Sociology of Law, Oñati, Basque Country. The workshop was supported by the International Institute for the Sociology of Law and by the Vice-Rectorship for Basque and Multilingualism of the University of the Basque Country, under whose auspices the workshop was held. First of all, I would like to thank the participants in the Oñati workshop and especially the authors for their contributions. I am grateful for the support given by Malen Gordoa during the preparation phase for the workshop. I would also like to express my gratitude to Patrick Carlin (Cardiff University) who commented on and checked parts of the book. Thanks are also due to Bea Timmer, at Brill Publishers, for her kind assistance in the process of preparing the manuscript for publication.

This book aspires to contribute to our understanding of the challenges arising in bilingual higher education in the legal context for the implementation of language rights and ultimately for the preservation of linguistic diversity. Its thematic focus is on legal education, but it is relevant for scholars working on the implications of linguistic diversity in the fields of law, education, political science and sociolinguistics.

September 2011

INTRODUCTION

CHAPTER ONE

LEGAL EDUCATION IN BILINGUAL CONTEXTS: A CONCEPTUAL, HISTORICAL AND COMPARATIVE INTRODUCTION

Xabier Arzoz

The social sciences have explored the relevance of language policy for state construction and for the reproduction of linguistic groups. Yet there is one issue of language policy which has received relatively little attention from the perspective of either law, political theory or bilingualism: that of higher education. To my knowledge, there has been no single monograph or edited volume which examines the issue of higher education language policy from those perspectives.

This is a striking gap when compared with the many important volumes by legal scholars and social scientists dedicated to issues of minority language rights,[1] languages, constitutionalism and governance,[2] languages and nationalism,[3] minority language education,[4] language rights and political theory,[5] linguistic diversity and globalisation,[6]

[1] Fernand de Varennes, *Language, Minorities and Human Rights* (Kluwer Law International 1996); Stephen May, *Language and Minority Rights* (Longman/Pearson Education 2001); Snezana Trifunovska and Fernand de Varennes (eds.), *Minority Rights in Europe: European Minorities and Languages* (T.C.M. Asser Press 2001); Jean-Marie Woehrling, *The European Charter for Regional or Minority Languages* (Council of Europe Publishing 2005); Marc Weller (ed.), *The Rights of Minorities. A Commentary on the European Framework Convention for the Protection of National Minorities* (Oxford University Press 2005); Marc Weller (ed.), *Universal Minority Rights. A Commentary on the Jurisprudence of International Courts and Treaty Bodies* (Oxford University Press 2007); Tawhida Ahmed, *The Impact of EU Law on Minority Rights* (Hart 2010).

[2] André Braën, Pierre Foucher & Yves Le Bouthillier (eds.), *Languages, Constitutionalism and Minorities* (LexisNevis 2006); Colin Wiliams, *Language and governance* (University of Wales Press 2007).

[3] Stephen Barbour and Cathie Carmichael (eds.), *Language and nationalism in Europe* (Oxford University Press 2000).

[4] Barbara Elaine Wilson, *La liberté de la langue des minorités dans l'enseignement: étude de droit international et de droit suisse* (Basilea 1999).

[5] Will Kymlicka and Alan Patten (eds.), *Language Rights and Political Theory* (Oxford University Press 2003); Pierre A. Coulombe, *Language Rights in French Canada* (Peter Lang 1997).

[6] Louis-Jean Calvet, *Le marché aux langues – Les effets linguistiques de la mondialisation* (Plon 2002); Jacques Maurais and Michael M. Morris (eds.), *Languages in a*

and linguistic diversity in the European Union.[7] By contrast, one would be hard-pressed to know where to look to find studies reflecting on experiences of bilingual higher education. Even in officially bilingual or multilingual states it is difficult to address the issue of bilingual higher education. In the hundreds of publications on issues of higher education and legal education, even in the many important volumes dedicated to legal education in comparative terms or related to the challenges of globalisation and Europeanisation, the issue of bilingual academic education seems to be absent.

Some recent publications attempt to remedy this surprising gap. A UNESCO-CEPES Seminar held in Bucharest on 16–17 March 2000 was devoted to the bilingual university as a unique formal structure.[8] This Seminar focused on European experiences (the Free University of Bozen/Bolzano in Italy;[9] Åbo Akademi University in Finland;[10] the University of Fribourg in Switzerland;[11] and Belarus[12]), although it also included presentations on the Universities of Ottawa[13] and Puerto Rico.[14] Papers on other European and non-European experiences are rather scattered in specialised journals (the Babeş-Bolyai University in

Globalising World (Cambridge University Press 2003); Claude Truchot, *Europe: l' enjeu linguistique* (La documentation française 2008).

[7] Dario Castiglione and Chris Longman (eds.), *The language question in Europe and diverse societies* (Hart 2007); Xabier Arzoz (ed.), *Respecting Linguistic Diversity in the European Union* (John Benjamins 2008); Peter A. Kraus, *A Union of Diversity. Language, Identity and Polity-Building in Europe* (Cambridge University Press 2008); Anne Lise Kjær and Silvia Adamo (eds.), *Linguistic Diversity and European Democracy* (Ashgate 2010).

[8] For an introduction, see Lewis Purser, 'The Bilingual University—General Reflections on its Origins, Mission, and Functioning', XXV *Higher Education in Europe* (2000) p. 451–459; Lewis Purser, 'L'université bilingue – Réflexions générales sur ses origins, sa mission et son fonctionnement', in Sjur Bergan (ed.), *Les politiques linguistiques dans l'enseignment supérieur* (Council of Europe Publishing 2003) p. 25–35.

[9] Sandra Campisi, 'Case Study on the Free University of Bozen/Bolzano, Italy', XXV *Higher Education in Europe* (2000) p. 477–486.

[10] Olle Anckar, 'University Education in a Bilingual Country: The Case of Finland', XXV *Higher Education in Europe* (2000) p. 499–506.

[11] Michael Langner and Rüdi Imbach, 'The University of Freiburg: A Model for a Bilingual University', XXV *Higher Education in Europe* (2000) p. 461–468.

[12] Irina Konchitis, 'Bilingual and multilingual universities in the Republic of Belarus', XXV *Higher Education in Europe* (2000) p. 507–509.

[13] Jean-Michel Beillard, 'Bilingualism in a Canadian Context: The Case of the University of Ottawa', XXV *Higher Education in Europe* (2000) p. 469–476.

[14] Norman I. Maldonado, 'The Teaching of English in Puerto Rico: One Hundred Years of Degrees of Bilingualism', XXV *Higher Education in Europe* (2000) p. 487–497.

Romania,[15] Hong Kong,[16] Macau,[17] South Africa,[18] Lebanon[19]). On the other hand, the past years have witnessed the publication of several volumes on the issue of *lingua francas*, especially in the academic field.[20]

The aim in this volume is to document the experiences of institutions and states that are implementing bilingual higher education policies in the legal context, to identify the different approaches and to suggest some of the likely areas for future theoretical development. It examines the role of higher education language policies (medium-of-instruction policies in higher education) in mediating the tension between on the one hand the centralising forces of state-mandated policies and globalisation and demands for language rights by ethnic and linguistic minorities on the other. As Tsu and Tollefson observe, the medium-of-instruction policy is central in socio-political processes: "All too often, policy makers put forward an educational agenda that justifies policy decisions regarding the use and/or the prohibition of a particular language or languages. Yet, behind the educational agenda are political, social, and economic agendas that serve to protect the interests of particular political and social groups".[21]

[15] Wolfgang W. Breckner, 'The Multicultural Babeş-Bolyai University of Cluj-Napoca', XXVI *Higher Education in Europe* (2001) p. 391–398.

[16] Natalia Li, Doris Y.P. Leung and David Kember, 'Medium of instruction in Hong Kong universities: the mis-match between espoused theory and theory in use', 14 *Higher Education Policy* (2001) p. 293–312.

[17] Mark Bray and Ora Kwo, 'Higher Education in Small Territories: Political Transition and Development in Macau', 16 *Higher Education Policy* (2003) p. 413–432.

[18] Andrew Foley, 'Language policy for higher education in South Africa: implications and complications', 18 *South African Journal of Higher Education* (2004) p. 57–71; Christa Van der Walt, 'The challenge of multilingualism: in response to the language policy for higher education', 18 *South African Journal of Higher Education* (2004) p. 140–152; Theo Du Plessis, 'From monolingual to bilingual higher education: The repositioning of historically Africaans-medium universities in South Africa', 5 *Language Policy* (2006) p. 87–113.

[19] Tamara El Khoury, 'Encrucijada de tradiciones: sobre el desarrollo de la enseñanza del Derecho en Líbano', 11 *Cuadernos del Instituto Antonio de Nebrija* (2008) p. 87–100.

[20] Ulrich Ammon (ed.), *The Dominance of English as a Language of Science: Effects on Other Languages and Language Communities* (Mouton de Gruyter 2001); Ulrich Ammon and Grant McConnell, *English as an Academic Language in Europe* (Peter Lang 2002); David Crystal, *English as a Global Language* (Cambridge University Press 2003, 2nd edition); Robert Phillipson, *English-Only Europe? Challenging Language Policy* (Routledge 2003); Ute Smit, *English as a lingua franca in higher education: a longitudinal study of classroom discourse* (Mouton de Gruyter 2010).

[21] Amy Tsu and James W. Tollefson, 'The Centrality of Medium-of-Instruction Policy in Sociopolitical Processes', in James W. Tollefson and Amy Tsu (eds.), *Medium of Instruction Policies: Which Agenda? Whose Agenda?* (Lawrence Erlbaum Associates 2004) p. 2.

This volume's focus on bilingual higher education in the legal context is not arbitrary. On the one side, law is one of the most symbolic domains of the state. Certainly many public services may be offered to some extent in various languages, with a view to accommodate linguistic diversity existing within the state borders. Nevertheless, one of the testers of the seriousness of the constitutional commitment to language equality and linguistic diversity is the extent to which the legal system effectively operates in more than one language. In bilingual or multilingual states, law must be created and administered bilingually or multilingually. A range of institutional and personal arrangements needs to be adopted to that effect. But, in the end, no legal system can duly operate in more than one language if legal higher education is not guaranteed and provided for through the medium of those languages and if enough members of the legal professions are not linguistically competent in all recognised languages. On the other hand, law is also a discipline that needs to be taught and learnt. There are likely to be greater differences in the teaching of law than in physics. Apart from the many divides (the civil and common law divide, the boundaries between university and non-university education, and the different legal cultures) that separate Western legal systems, academic and professional legal writings cater mostly to the corresponding national community. For the work of, say, a French-speaking Swiss scholar or lawyer, it is much more important to know the relevant German-language Swiss law publications concerning the problem that needs to be solved, than to know the corresponding bibliography published in French in France or in Belgium. Despite the international and European Union dimensions of law, legal studies are traditionally less exposed to a transnational dialogue than other academic disciplines, particularly in the sciences.

This volume is devoted to complex questions of building and developing legal education in more than one language, through two state languages (French and Dutch in Belgium, German and French in Switzerland, English and French in Canada, Finnish and Swedish in Finland) and/or through the medium of minority or lesser used languages (Basque, Galician, Catalan, Hungarian, Welsh). Some states have a long and well-established tradition of bilingual legal education; others have only recently started to develop a legal education system through non-dominant languages; finally, in some other cases only partial bilingual legal education obtains, rather than a fuller model.

The volume purports to examine best practices and to draw useful lessons from the experiences of other bilingual societies.

In this introduction, I begin by exploring the notion of bilingual higher education and the issue of bilingual higher education in historical perspective. I then survey the need for bilingual higher education in general, before turning to the need for bilingual legal education in particular. Finally, the pressures towards, and the tensions between vernacularisation, internationalisation and Europeanisation on academic legal education will be analysed. I hope that this will give the reader a sense of to what extent bilingual higher education exists, what it consists of, and what the challenges are. This will help situate the more detailed presentations developed in subsequent chapters.

A. The Meanings of Bilingual Higher Education

There are between 6,000 and 7,000 languages in the world. However,the number of languages that have detailed grammar books, dictionaries and textbooks is much more reduced. Alfred Majewicz[22] estimates that only 350 languages belong to that category. This is the first and most relevant filter: without standardisation and basic reference books it is difficult for a language to have access to universities as a medium of instruction. In practice, the number of languages used in higher education seems more reduced. Some authors estimate that the number of languages used in higher education can be slightly over 100.[23]

Use of a language in higher education can, however, mean very different things, since there are many ways to structure a bilingual or multilingual higher education system and to provide higher education in more than one language in a given higher education institution. The issue of bilingual or multilingual higher education can be analysed from the perspective of either each individual institution or the higher education system as a whole. As a matter of fact, bilingual universities as formal institutions are very rare. For the purpose of this volume a

[22] Quoted by Jean Laponce, *Loi de Babel et autres régularités des rapports entre langue et politique* (Presses Universitaires de Laval 2006) p. 26.

[23] Laponce, *supra* n. 22, p. 27. The author suggests that the number of languages used in international social sciences conferences is not more than fifty (at p. 9).

broad approach has been taken and both abovementioned perspectives have been included, that of the system as a whole (which can be categorised as a bilingual one) and that of a given institution. The main reason is that a bilingual or multilingual state can structure higher education in different ways. A higher education system may offer bilingual or multilingual higher education through separate monolingual institutions, through bilingual institutions or through a combination of both. It does not necessarily mean that all degrees are offered through the medium of all recognised languages, but that there is a reasonable offer of higher education given the circumstances in all recognised languages. Yet many bilingual or multilingual states resort principally to monolingual higher education institutions, while bilingual institutions are rare.

For the purpose of this volume it is the language of instruction which matters. Other forms of institutional bilingualism may be relevant in other contexts. A university's administration may conduct its business bilingually or multilingually, especially in its relationships with third persons, as far as language legislation requires it to do so, but that does not necessarily mean that it will provide education in more than one language.

Types and variations of bilingual education have been analysed in detail with regard to primary and secondary education.[24] However, those rich typologies can be applied to higher education in a restricted sense only. A much more reduced offer of bilingual higher education exists in practice.

Bilingualism with regard to a given institution can have different meanings and degrees. At the lowest level, the use of a language can be limited to certain courses or to certain degrees. Many lesser-used languages are used as media of higher education instruction only in philology departments and/or in teacher training schools. Similarly, in some states the study of a second or third language may be a compulsory element of the curriculum, even in legal studies.[25] However, the type of bilingual higher education that this volume aspires to document and analyse goes beyond that.

[24] Colin Baker, *Foundations of Bilingual Education and Bilingualism* (Multilingual Matters 2001); Ofelia García, *Bilingual Education in the 21st century: A global perspective* (Wiley-Blackwell 2009).

[25] Julian Webb, 'Academic legal education in Europe: convergence and diversity', 9 *International Journal of the Legal Profession* (2002) p. 139–156 at p. 151.

Some institutions are bilingual in the sense that students can register for tuition in two languages. This tends to be the case when both are official languages of the state, the canton or the region where the university is located. Students from both linguistic tracks do not need to mix themselves for academic purposes. There is a strict separation between languages. This kind of bilingualism has been called 'parallel-medium' or 'double monolingual education'.[26] It can be found at the University of Ottawa, the University of the Basque Country and the Welsh universities. Starting from that general model, subsequent distinctions or variations can be made in the level of bilingualism.[27] On the one side, strong and weak parallel-medium education can be considered. Strong parallel-medium education refers to the availability of tuition, course materials and textbooks in both media of instruction. In the case of weak parallel-medium education only the instruction and perhaps some of the study materials are provided in both languages. The former applies to majority languages of the state or the region, while the latter to languages that are minority or lesser-used languages. On the other side, not all courses or degrees may be provided for in both languages. For example, at the University of the Basque Country all undergraduate courses and degrees must be and are in fact provided for in Spanish and Basque (with some minor de facto exceptions such as medicine), but postgraduate instruction tends to be monolingual in Spanish.

An institution can also be considered as being bilingual when the students are required to receive tuition in the two (or more) recognised languages. The proportion of courses that will be taught in each language can vary according to different factors (availability of staff, historic reasons, etc.), although a minimum of tuition in each language may be required. There are here three possibilities according to who has the choice of establishing the language of instruction for each course. The first option is that the education authority or, by delegation, the higher education institution itself determines what and/or how many courses will be offered to students in what language. All students will take the same courses, regardless of their preference or their first language. A second option exists to my knowledge only in Catalonia: the choice of the medium of instruction resides with the

[26] Du Plessis, *supra* n. 18, p. 89.
[27] Du Plessis, *supra* n. 18, p. 91.

lecturer, who may offer a course either in Catalan or Spanish. When the same course is taught by more than two lecturers in different languages, students can opt for his or her preferred language of instruction in that particular subject: this possibility, however, is limited to those degrees with a large number of students, such as business and law, which allows for different linguistic tracks. In practice, students receive tuition in two languages, some subjects in one language and others in the other language, but the exact combination of them depends on the sum of individual lecturers' decisions and on the available resources, and it varies from faculty to faculty and from university to university. The Catalan system is also bilingual in a second sense. Lecturers have the right to choose the language of instruction, but students have the correlative right to ask questions and write exams in both languages, the result may be a kind of 'code-switching': according to students' multiple identities and language proficiencies, both languages may be used concurrently in the classroom, in exercises and in tutorials, although this does not mean that they are used symmetrically or in equal proportion. In general terms, the 'Catalan' model sets the individual bilingualism of students and lecturers as a requirement (which lies within the responsibility of the primary and secondary school on the one side and of the university appointment system on the other), and it is facilitated by the proximity between the two languages of instruction.

The third option is that the institution organises the offer according to both official languages and the student is free to choose which courses in which language to take, provided that a minimum is taken in the second language of the student, at least if the student wants to get a bilingual mention for his or her studies program and/or degree. This type of bilingual program has the mission of fostering individual bilingualism: it is each individual who stays at the centre of the higher education system. For instance, at the University of Fribourg in Switzerland, tuition is offered both in French and German and students have to take at least 25 percent of their credits in the second language.

B. Bilingual Higher Education in Historical Perspective

Bilingual higher education within a given state is quite unique and seems to run against the main trend in contemporary history.

The main instrument of nation-building is the imposition of a common state language. Initially, the focus was on primary education, with the aim of making illiterate peasants often speaking different languages and dialects into loyal citizens.[28] The extension of the 'educating state' involved the imposition of a common identity through the supremacy of a common language. The nationalisation of education included also higher education, even if Latin – the lingua franca of higher learning from older times – continued to be used in certain domains (e.g., the writing of doctoral theses) in the nineteenth century. The nation-state had profound consequences for the patterns of control and administration in the university world: the university was at the apex of those institutions defining national identity.[29]

It is no surprise that the first bilingual universities were established in the nineteenth century only in the rare openly bilingual or multilingual states of the time that did not endorse the nation-state triad of a language, a culture and a nation. For bilingual higher education institutions are the exceptions to the rule of monolingual higher education within given nation-states in contemporary history. The University of Ottawa was established in 1848, and the University of Fribourg/Freiburg was established in 1889. However, the biggest repertoire of languages of instruction in higher education in the nineteenth century is to be found in Austria-Hungary.

During the nineteenth century, most of the ethnolinguistic groups in Central Europe went through periods of national awakening or revival. New or renewed universities became or were from the outset national institutions, even if the corresponding ethnolinguistic group had not its own state. Among the Poles in the Russian Empire, older establishments in Warsaw (1816–69) and Vilnius/Wilno (1803–30) functioned for a while as Polish universities, while in Warsaw a new one was opened in 1906.[30] In Austria-Hungary, German, Hungarian,

---

[28] Eugen Weber, *Peasants into Frenchmen: The Modernization of Rural France* (Stanford University Press 1976).

[29] Guy Neave, 'The European Dimension in Higher Education: An Excursion into the Modern Use of Historical Analogues', in Jeroen Huisman, Peter Maasen and Guy Neave (eds.), *Higher Education and the Nation State – The International Dimension of Higher Education* (Emerald 2007) p. 13–73 at p. 26 et seq.; Märtha Norrback and Kristina Ranki (eds.), *University and Nation – The University and the Making of the Nation in Northern Europe in the 19th and 20th Centuries* (Finish Historical Society 1996).

[30] Paul Peter Magosci, *Historical Atlas of Central Europe* (Thames & Hudson 2002, 2nd revised ed.) p. 102.

Italian, Czech and Polish were languages of instruction in higher education, apart from Latin traditionally used for the teaching of theology. One of the demands of the Prague students' petition in March 1848 was for the equality of the Czech and German languages in teaching and examinations. This was unanimously accepted by Czech and German professors; the emperor accepted it and the bilingual period in the history of Prague University began. Nevertheless, the rights of both languages in the lecture room were equal, but their real role was not the same because the overwhelming majority of the professors did not speak Czech.[31] This bilingual period did not last very much. In 1882, the Prague University was divided into two halves, German and Czech, according to the language of instruction: most of the old professors went to the German one, and mostly young scholars with greater ambitions went to the Czech stream.[32] In addition, in 1899 a Czech-medium Superior Technical School was founded in Brünn/Brno. After 1867, the Vienna government changed the language of instruction in two universities from German to Polish. The older institutions of Lemberg/L'viv/Lwów (Galizia) and the Jagiellonian University of Cracow became polonised respectively in 1873 and 1879: a total of 9,620 students were enrolled only in the Lemberg High Technical School in 1909/10, many of them from Prussia and Russia. Since 1869, Italians citizens from Trentino and from the whole Austria could study law at the University of Innsbruck integrally through the medium of Italian, apart from taking some Italian-medium philosophy and medicine courses. Also the University of Graz offered Italian-medium law courses as well as the possibility of obtaining a law degree through the medium of Italian. Professors had to be always Italian native speakers, and a number of them were recruited in Italy by the Austrian ministry of education. The opening of a law school in Trieste, foreseen for 1915/16, was made impossible because of the world war and, later, the collapse of Austria-Hungary. Other languages such as Slovenian and Ruthenian had a more limited presence in higher education.[33] In the Hungarian half of Austria-Hungary, however,

[31] J. Havránek, 'The Czech, Slovak and Polish Intellectuals in the Habsburg Monarchy between the State and the Nations', in M. Norrback and K. Ranki (eds.), *University and Nation – The University and the Making of the Nation in Northern Europe in the 19th and 20th Centuries* (Finnish Historical Society 1996) p. 133.

[32] Havránek, *supra* n. 31, p. 136.

[33] Gustav Otruba, 'Die Universitäten in der Hochschulorganisation der Donaumonarchie – nationale Erziehungsstätten im Vielvölkerreich 1850–1914', in

Hungarian was the only language of instruction in higher education, with the only exception of a university established in Zagreb for the Croats (1874).

However, there need not always be a strong correspondence between the choice for the language of instruction and the foundation of national identity. From the 1770s, all inhabitants of the Duchies of Schleswig and Holstein who wanted to serve in an official position in one of the two duchies had to study at least two years at the University of Kiel in Holstein, where the official language was German, even though the popular language in Schleswig was mostly Danish.[34] This was an effective, *avant-la-letre* way of promoting the bilingualism of future government officials. In Dorpat/Tartu, Livonia, a German-speaking university founded in 1632 by the Swedes and reopened in 1802, catered for a multinational studentship from the Russian Empire.[35] Unlike the rest of existing or requested Austria-Hungarian universities, which were conceived primarily as national higher education institutions, the German-speaking University of Czernowitz (1875–1919) was grounded in Czernowitz/Chernivtsi at the bequest of the principal regional nationalities, Ukrainian and Romanian, and it was designed as a university open to all nationalities of the autonomous territory of Bucovina. It included the first European Greek-Orthodox Theology Faculty, following the modern Catholic theology faculty model, which used Ukrainian and Romanian as languages of instruction.[36]

C. Helfer and M. Rassem (eds.), *Student und Hochschule im 19. Jahrhundert* (Vandenhoeck und Ruprecht 1975) p. 75–158; Theodor Veiter, *Die Italiener in der österreichisch-ungarischen Monarchie* (Verlag für Geschichte und Politik 1965) p. 76.

[34] The Duchies of Schleswig and Holstein belonged to the Kingdom of Denmark, but were governed by a separate administrative body in Copenhagen. *See* D. Tamm, 'Professors and Politics – an outline', in M. Norrback and K. Ranki (eds.), *University and Nation – The University and the Making of the Nation in Northern Europe in the 19th and 20th Centuries* (Finnish Historical Society 1996) p. 22.

[35] H. Tankler, 'Dorpat, a German-speaking International University in the Russian Empire', in M. Norrback and K. Ranki (eds.), *University and Nation – The University and the Making of the Nation in Northern Europe in the 19th and 20th Centuries* (Finnish Historical Society 1996) p. 91–100; G. Von Rauch, *Die Universität Dorpat und das Eindringen der frühen Aufklärung in Livland 1690–1710* (Olms 1969, reprint).

[36] Franz Hieronymus Riedl, 'Die Universität Czernowitz als völkerverbindende Institution 1875–1919', in Rudolf Wagner (ed.), *Alma Mater Francisco Josephina. Die deutschsprachige Nationalitäten-Universität in Czernowitz – Festschrift zum 100. Jahrestag ihrer Eröffnung 1875* (Hans Meschendörfer 1975) p. 375–393 at p. 382; Magosci, *supra* n. 30, p. 102.

After the First World War, newly formed states created "national" universities that would teach in the new official language and assist in creating administrative and cultural cadres for the state.[37] Therefore, it was only in 1919 that the following institutions were created in Central Europe: the Masaryk University in Brno, the Lithuanian State University in Kaunas, the Polish Mickiewicz University in Poznan, the Slovak Comenius University in Bratislava and the Slovenian University of Ljubjana. Similarly, existing states that acquired territories also established new national higher education institutions in those territories: for instance, the Romanian Babeş University in Cluj-Napoca (1919) and the Italian University of Trieste (1924). Bilingual higher education was reproduced in some of the new states or the existing states that had acquired more territory, in addition to the already existing institutions. Finland, Czechoslovakia and Romania were conditioned both by the pre-existence of prestigious Swedish, German and Hungarian higher education institutions and by the demographic and/or cultural significance of the relevant minorities.

From today's positive assessment on the richness of multiculturalism and multilingualism, one can regret the many historical opportunities of transforming pre-existing monolingual universities into bilingual universities, with a view to bridge linguistic and ethnic communities in many border or multinational regions, that were lost, for instance, after the First World War, in Strasbourg (formerly Germany, then France) or in Czernowitz (formerly the Austrian half of Austria-Hungary, then Romania, now Ukraine),[38] which were respectively German-speaking universities of 1914 located most westwards and eastwards.[39] Many Central and Eastern European universities have changed the language of instruction several times along the years to adapt themselves to the new political circumstances (for instance, the universities of Dorpat/Tartu in Estonia, Cluj-Napoca in Romania, etc.).

---

[37] Magosci, *supra* n. 30, p. 58

[38] Until 1919 the area was part of Austria-Hungary and the main language of instruction at the university was German, but Ukrainian and Romanian were also used as media of instruction. Between 1919 and 1940, the area became part of Romania and the language of instruction at the university was Romanian. Between late 1944 and 1991, the university operated within the Soviet academic system. Since 1991, the university has been acting within the Ukrainian higher education system.

[39] As to the University of Strasbourg, it must be noted that, in 1918, only ten per cent of the Alsace population could speak French. This circumstance, its old German tradition and its vicinity with Germany could have allowed for creating a pioneer bilingual French-German institution in Strasbourg.

In contrast with the occasions that were lost in the interwar period, after the Second World War the French military government administered the Saar territory as a protectorate until 1955. They created several higher education institutions: the first, on 8 March 1947, was named "Institut d'Études Supérieures de l'Université de Nancy en territoire sarrois', which, in February 1948, was renamed 'Institut Supérieur de Homburg' (a medicine and a sciences faculty), whose administrative board included an equal number of French and German members; later a philosophy and a legal and economics faculty followed, as well as a pioneer European Studies Centre. Although those initiatives were still conceived mainly in the traditional terms of power and influence,[40] the grounding of the new bilingual *Université de la Sarre/Universität des Saarlandes*, with its European orientation and its international character, was an important contribution to European integration. Nevertheless, the population of the Saar territory voted in the referendum of 23 October 1955 against the creation of a special status for the Saar territory and for a return to the Federal Republic of Germany. In October 1956, the university had its first German rector, and many French professors and lecturers left the institution.[41] Although the university became fully German in organisation and curricula, the French-German Legal Centre, a unique higher education co-operation institution founded in 1955 that has full professorships on French public and private law and is integrated in the law department of the University of Saarland, continues awarding jointly with the University of Metz (France) a double law degree that attracts many French students.

The new multinational empire emerging from the First World War, the Soviet Union, fostered initially the creation of alphabets for previously unwritten languages, the standardisation (grammar books, dictionaries, orthography) of lesser-used languages and mother-tongue education through many minority, until then marginalised languages. Yet its later language policy aimed at squeezing out the non-Russian languages and limiting the development of important functional styles of absolutely all languages other than Russian. According

[40] France had plans for the establishment of the headquarters of the European institutions within the Saar territory, provided that it preserved its internationalised regime.

[41] Wolfgang Müller, *Die Universität des Saarlandes. Impressionen aus über 50 Jahren* (Sutton 2002) p. 9, 19.

to Bruchis,[42] in the 1980s 'in the overwhelming majority of higher educational institutions of all national republics, both union and autonomous, the basic teaching language (except in pedagogical institutes and university philology departments) [wa]s Russian'. To what extent higher education was offered in the non-Russian languages is not clear, but it seems that at least in some republics of the Soviet Union such as Georgia or the Baltic republics there was some higher education teaching through the medium of non-Russian languages.

With the independence of the non-Russian speaking republics of the Soviet Union, most of the universities have become monolingual in the new state language. In the Russian Federation, Russian is the official language of instruction in all higher education institutions with the exception of the autonomous republics (Tartastan, Mordovia, Chuvashia, Bashkortostan), where certain courses are imparted in the minority languages.[43] Nevertheless, those states that have recognised the bilingual character of the state (the national language plus Russian), such as Belarus or Kazakhstan, have bilingual higher education and possess bilingual institutions, as is the case of the Belarusian State Pedagogical University. Others limit themselves to provide some courses in Russian in certain institutions, as is the case with the Technical University of Tallin and the University of Tartu in Estonia. The originally bilingual University of Priština in the Serbian province of Kosovo became resolutely monolingual in Serbian after the withdrawal of the Kosovan autonomy in 1989 and later, after the collapse of the Serbian administration, de facto monolingual in Albanian.[44] A second University of Priština was created in Mitrovica with the assistance of the Serbian government, as it considered Kosovo a Serbian province.

Today, India would seem to possess the largest repertoire of higher education languages in the world. The state official language or languages (there are sixteen full official languages at the state and national level and four partial official languages at the state level) and English are the media of instruction in higher education, with two caveats:

---

[42] Michael Bruchis, *One step back, two steps forward: On the language policy of the Communist Party of the Soviet Union in the national republics (Moldavian: A look back, a survey, and perspectives, 1924–1980)* (East European Monographs 1982) p. 16.

[43] Vera Zabotkina, 'Les politiques linguistiques dans les établissements d'enseignement supérieur russes', in Sjur Bergan (ed.), *Les politiques linguistiques dans l'enseignement supérieur* (Council of Europe Publishing 2003) p. 43–47 at p. 43.

[44] Purser 2000, *supra* n. 8, p. 452.

English is sought after by the majority of students, particularly in the sciences; in professional education like medicine, engineering, law, business administration and finance, the medium is mostly English.[45] It is noteworthy that, as of 1990, forty-three languages were offered as medium of instruction during primary education (out of about 100 categorised languages self-reported).

In general, the development of regional co-operation in higher education in border areas had to wait until the more favourable times of the 1990s: the European University Viadrina along the German-Polish border in Frankfurt Oder[46] and the Duna-Maros-Tisza Regional Cooperation Unit involving eight contiguous Romanian and Hungarian counties and the neighbouring Serbian autonomous region of Voivodina, including three university towns, Szeged, Timisoara and Novi Sad,[47] were unconceivable before the fall of the iron wall.

As we have seen, bilingual universities have existed and exist today in many states. And probably the trend will be for its number to increase. The focus in this section was on historical experiences or current cases that cannot be covered by the chapters of this volume. In any case, bilingual universities also exist in other states (Cameroon, Rwanda, etc.).

C. The Need for Bilingual Universities

One might believe that bilingual universities exist mainly because they are embedded in bilingual or multilingual states. Since some states happen to be officially bilingual or multilingual, their universities should follow that pattern. This is only partially true. There is a close relationship between the language policies of bilingual or multilingual states on the one side and the existence of bilingual universities on the other, but this is not always the case.

On the one hand, actual or purported changes in status and in language policy have of course influenced the language of instruction in

---

[45] E. Annamalai, *Managing Multilingualism in India* (Sage 2001) p. 136.

[46] Thomas Vogel, 'Internationalization, Interculturality, and the Role of Foreign Languages in Higher Education', XXVI *Higher Education in Europe* (2001) p. 381–389.

[47] Tamás Kozma and Imre Radácsi, 'Should We Become More International or More Regional? Aspects of Minority Higher Education in Europe', XXV *Higher Education in Europe* (2000) p. 41–45.

higher education. In the Maghreb area, both French and Arabic have been traditionally used in higher education although in different proportions, and the university language policy has been always sensitive to changes in national and international politics. According to an Act of 1990, French had to be replaced in Algeria by Arabic as the language of instruction in higher education by 1997.[48] Similarly, the University of Puerto Rico has vacillated several times between Spanish and English before settling for both.[49] In South Africa, the end of apartheid brought a sociolinguistic metamorphosis of the historically Afrikaans-medium universities, from monolingual higher education to bilingual higher education, which coexists with English-medium universities.[50] In Lebanon a law degree can be taken both in Arabic and in French, although in different public and private institutions.[51]

Bilingual or dual medium higher education can also be 'tolerated' in a postcolonial scenario, as an interim measure until the national language has developed enough resources. In post independent Malaysia, a bilingual system was established in 1965 at the University of Malaya, which had been created in the 1960s as an English medium university: the Bahasa Malaysia was to be used for arts subjects and English for science and technology. This bilingual system was used as an interim measure before converting into a monolingual system, in order to allow time for the non-Malay speaking academic staff to adjust themselves to Bahasa Malaysia, the national and official language of the country. By 1983, all subjects, including the sciences, were taught in Bahasa Malaysia in all public universities. Ironically only two decades later, however, English came back to higher education this time not for postcolonial reasons, but for the sake of the country's internationalisation and competitiveness. Patriotic intellectuals opposed the introduction of English as a language of higher education in public universities. Nevertheless, the government decided to liberalise higher education as a way to promote the knowledge economy. The liberalisation of higher education lead to the bifurcation of higher education in Malaysia, whereby public institutions of higher education retained the national and official language as the medium of instruction, and

[48] Roland Kühnel, *Die sprachliche Situation an Hochschulen des Maghreb und die offizielle Sprachpolitik – Eine soziolinguistische Untersuchung* (Peter Lang 1995).
[49] Maldonado, *supra* n. 14.
[50] Du Plessis, *supra* n. 18.
[51] El Khoury, *supra* n. 19.

private institutions of higher education were given the freedom to use English as a medium of instruction.[52]

In Pakistan there is a similar conflict between the ideological goal to promote Urdu as the national language and maintaining English as the second official language of the state on a temporary basis, 'until arrangements are made for its replacement by Urdu' (Art. 251(2) of the 1973 Constitution). The long-term policy is to have Urdu as the sole national and educational language, but English continues for all practical purposes as the official language of Pakistan, in higher education in particular under the argument or the excuse that adequate materials in Urdu to cope with higher education still need to be developed. Despite the constitutional provisions, since no significant advance has been made to implement the declared policy of developing textbooks and teaching materials in Urdu, this has led to prolonging a dual medium policy in higher education, where the public sector students study mainly in Urdu and the private sector students in English. Nevertheless, a 'mix' of languages (Urdu and English) is prevalent in most public and private higher education institutions, both to supplement the English lectures and to take examinations, this being indicative of students' and teachers' difficulties in using the English language. It must be noted that English is not a vernacular language in Pakistan and that Urdu is the mother tongue of only 7.5 percent of the population according to the 1998 Census. The role of the vernacular languages—Punjabi, Sindhi, Pushto, Balochi, Saraiki and others—in secondary and higher education is practically negligible; Sindh is the only province where the regional language is being used for higher levels of schooling.[53]

On the other hand, as we will see, bilingual or multilingual states universities do not need to reflect the bilingual or multilingual character of the state as a whole. As a matter of fact, most territories within a bilingual or multilingual state basically follow the principle of territoriality: territories are preferably monolingual, and all citizens must conform to that. Finland, Switzerland, Belgium and Canada all have a

---

[52] Saran Kaur Gill, 'Medium-of-Instruction Policy in Higher Education in Malaysia: Nationalism Versus Internationalization', in James W. Tollefson and Amy Tsu (eds.), *Medium of Instruction Policies: Which Agenda? Whose Agenda?* (Lawrence Erlbaum Associates 2004) p. 135–152.

[53] Sabiha Mansoor, *Language Planning in Higher Education – A Case Study of Pakistan* (Karachi: Oxford University Press 2005).

majority of administrative districts, regions, cantons or provinces in which only one official language is recognised. Accordingly, all or most universities are monolingual: each uses the official language of the territory in which it is based as the language of instruction. Even in officially bilingual territories, monolingualism can be regarded as the easiest solution for organising higher education. Therefore, the bilingual character of all or some of its universities does not necessarily derive from the bilingual character of a state or of a region. Moreover, the splitting into two monolingual sections or even two separate monolingual institutions of the previously bilingual universities of Prague (1882) in Austria-Hungary and of Brussels and Louvain in Belgium (1970–1979) points to the political complexity of running a bilingual institution when the two linguistic groups of the state or the region are in serious contestation with each other and academic life becomes unbearable.

Then, why should a university or higher education in general work and/or offer tuition in more than one language? Here, only political reasons can be considered. As Purser has argued, the linguistic policies of bilingual universities are 'never simply an accident, but rather the results of deliberate decisions involving more than simply the academic community'.[54] Each experience is closely linked to its specific function and regional needs. Drawing from the presentations to the abovementioned Bucharest seminar of 2000, Purser elaborated five missions of bilingual universities: promoting participation by a linguistic minority in the life of the country, the region, or the city; promoting the coherence of a city, region or country, often in a situation in which few other institutions bridge the linguistic and cultural divides between different populations; promoting a wider outlook for the university and its graduates; promoting bilingualism as an objective rather than as a condition; and encouraging students to stay in the region.

The promotion of participation and coherence—in Purser's terms—is determining in many cases. Although a bilingual higher education institution (as any other bilingual institution such as a parliament or a broadcasting service) is more expensive and complex, there can be a national interest in creating an instrument of cohesion between two otherwise separate linguistic groups. For the sake of national

---

[54] Purser 2000, *supra* n. 8, p. 452.

understanding and cohesion, some states may maintain an interest in forming and recruiting a bilingual elite and/or promoting individual bilingualism. A bilingual state cannot survive without a bilingual elite that is fluent in both official languages. Other times, it is not merely instrumental, but a national imperative: it is politically wiser to create a bilingual university than two separate monolingual universities that could give expression to linguistic rivalries and generate two separate communities within the same state.

The preservation or development of a minority language and culture may also be a strong motivation for establishing a bilingual or a minority-language-medium university.[55] Minority-language-medium provision at university level is key for the long-term sustainability of minority-language-medium primary and secondary education: not only because it is instrumental for the codification and modernisation of the language, the pre- and in-service training of qualified primary and secondary teachers, the development of a literate environment and literate culture, etc., but also because it is crucial for the continuity of mother tongue education itself and for the self-confidence of speakers of those languages. In Wales, the paucity of Welsh-medium provision at university level and in further education institutions is one of the reasons why fluent speakers of Welsh, educated through the medium of Welsh at nursery and primary levels, opt predominantly for English-medium tuition at secondary level.[56]

Recognising the connection between the provision of minority-language-medium higher education and the vitality of a minority language community, the European Charter for Regional or Minority Languages includes university and other higher education in regional or minority languages among the measures to promote the use of regional or minority languages in public life in the field of education (Article 8.1.e[57]). Only Finland (with regard to Swedish) and Slovakia (with regard to Hungarian), however, have ratified the strongest

[55] Sjur Bergan, 'Les politiques linguistiques dans l'enseignment supérieur – Introduction à un débat', in Sjur Bergan (ed.), *Les politiques linguistiques dans l'enseignment supérieur* (Council of Europe Publishing 2003) p. 11–23 at p. 18–21; Du Plessis, *supra* n. 18, p. 93.

[56] Dylan V. Jones and Marilyn Martin-Jones, 'Bilingual Education and Language Revitalization in Wales: Past Achievements and Current Issues', in James W. Tollefson & Amy Tsu (eds.), *Medium of Instruction Policies: Which Agenda? Whose Agenda?* (Lawrence Erlbaum Associates 2004) p. 21–41 at p. 55.

[57] See Woehrling, *supra* n. 1, p. 154–155.

obligation in this regard: the obligation 'to make available university and other higher education in regional or minority languages'.[58] This does not mean that these are the only European states that actually provide for bilingual higher education, including minority language higher education. For instance, Spain provides for Basque-medium higher education, Switzerland for Italian-medium higher education,[59] Romania for Hungarian-medium education and Norway has a Sámi-medium higher education institution.[60]

The Council of Europe's Committee of Experts has interpreted that the so-called "structured bilingual model" (dual-medium primary and secondary education) followed in some Spanish bilingual autonomous communities (Balearic Islands, Valencia and Galicia) does not comply with the requirements of the European Charter for Regional or Minority Languages, because the Charter recognises a right to receive education fully through the medium of the relevant regional or minority language.[61] It is not clear whether the same approach should also be applied to higher education. In any case, Article 8.1.e does not oblige states to provide *separate* minority language higher education institutions. Here, different policies are conceivable at the discretion of the Contract Parties: separate vs. integrate higher education institutions. A relevant strategy for the sustainability of minority language higher education seems to be in certain cases the creation of bilingual higher education institutions, in which minority language tuition will be offered with regard to certain studies or courses, which may be

---

[58] This higher education provision must be differentiated from the basic and further training of teachers, to which another provision (Article 8.1.h) is specifically devoted. For the lack of obligations in this field concerning the Welsh language, see Richard Gwynedd Parry, 'Higher Education and Article 8.1.e of the European Charter for Regional or Minority Languages: a Welsh "opportunity avoided"?', in *The European Charter for Regional or Minority Languages: Legal Challenges and Opportunities* (Council of Europe Publishing 2008) p. 253–275.

[59] Switzerland does not consider German and French as minority or regional languages to the European Charter's effects, but only Italian and Romansh.

[60] Kirsti Koch Christensen, 'Les politiques linguistiques dans l'enseignement supérieur – L'exemple de la Norvège', in Sjur Bergan (ed.), *Les politiques linguistiques dans l' enseignment supérieur* (Council of Europe Publishing 2003) p. 37–41 at p. 41.

[61] Report of the Committee of Experts on the Charter for Regional or Minority Languages and Recommendation of the Committee of Ministers of the Council of Europe 2008, Application of the Charter in Spain (Initial monitoring cycle), Doc. ECMRL (2005) 4 of Sept. 21, Strasbourg: Council of Europe, point L of the findings, p. 160.

gradually extended to more studies if there is a significant demand or it is reasonable in the circumstances. While the members of some linguistic minorities may go to a university of their kin-state to obtain higher education in their mother tongue (for instance, Hungarian-speaking Romanians to Hungary or German-speaking Italians to Austria), the members of many linguistic minorities have no kin-state and they have to create higher education institutions for themselves if they want to develop their minority languages as vehicles of modern science and technology, law, commerce, education and government.

The third strong motivation to create a bilingual university is the role accorded not to a national language or to a minority language, but to a major international language. The development of multilingualism at European universities is a general trend. Many efforts address themselves to facilitating and improving the language learning process of as many languages as possible, for instance through new or expanded linguistic university services, but also through the incorporation of second languages as languages of instruction. Here, two kinds of objectives may be considered at the same time: on the one hand, strengthening individual bilingualism or multilingualism of national students, since linguistic skills are crucial for employability and professional performance and for further higher education; on the other hand, tuition must be offered in international languages if a university wants to attract international students and talented researchers. In a globalising world, the role and importance of multilingual higher education institutions will increase. In the past languages such as French, German, Russian or Japanese have been international academic languages. Today, English seems unrivalled in this regard. English is being introduced as a medium of instruction in many universities, although at different degrees and speeds. Of course, there are different strategies to achieve or strengthen the individual bilingualism or multilingualism of students: they go from foreign language programmes having optional tuition in English for some courses or studies to shifting completely to English as the primary medium of instruction, through imposing tuition in English for some courses.[62] In certain European universities, for instance in the Netherlands and the Scandinavian countries, the national language is more and more confined to some

[62] For experiences at the European University Viadrina, see Vogel, *supra* n. 46.

courses and seminars, provided that no foreign student is attending. The trend will be for the number of available bilingual (English and the state language) or trilingual (English, the state language and the minority or regional language) course programmes to increase.

Initiatives with a strong international focus include always English as, at least, one of the languages of instruction. Very virtuously, the relatively young Free University of Bozen/Bolzano in Italy aims at satisfying both the regional needs and the demands of internationalisation: it has a trilingual approach (English, German and Italian) in many studies as well as a separate German, Italian and Ladin-medium education for teacher students. At the University of Central Asia, which, although still on development, will have campuses in Kazakhstan, Tajikistan, and Kyrgyzstan, English will be the language of instruction for all degree courses, while non-degree courses will be in Russian or in Kazakh, Kyrgyz or Tajik, depending on where they are offered.

D. The Need for Bilingual Legal Education

The motivations for bilingual legal education are more specific. Law is the most linguistic of all social institutions. It cannot exist outside of language: it is drafted, approved, proclaimed, administered, interpreted and repealed through acts of language. In a number of states law and justice are administered in more than one language. The official status of a language has enormous consequences for the different branches of government. When the equal status of official languages is constitutionally entrenched, two (or more) language versions of the same statutory text are signed by the relevant authority and published in the corresponding official statute book and all those versions are equally authentic. Even if the statutory texts are simply translated from one language to another, legal experts as well as translators need to be involved. By contrast, if a more ambitious technique of drafting bilingual legislation such as co-drafting is adopted, the text is simultaneously drafted and co-ordinated by two (or more) people, provision by provision, in the two (or more) official languages at all stages of the drafting process. This implies basically that legal drafters conversant with all official languages as well as translators from all official languages should be involved at all states of the drafting process.

The implications of official-language or minority language rights[63] for the justice system are particularly strong. Access to justice in a recognised language is one of the most relevant but also delicate of language rights. This right not only concerns individuals, but the entire system of justice. Important consequences flow from the constitutional or legal right of access to justice in more than one official language.[64] Firstly, obviously, for the members of the public. The judicial process starts with a comprehension of one's rights and recourses through the availability of all statutory legislation and accompanying regulations in the recognised languages, and continues with the availability of counsel who can communicate easily in the relevant languages, the freedom to have proceedings drafted in those languages, and the ability to present one's case before the courts, both orally and in writing, in those languages. It also means receiving judgment or a translation in the preferred language. It also implies the availability of the necessary legal forms and bilingual or multilingual personnel in the court houses in order to inform, to advise and generally to guide speakers of all recognised languages. Secondly, consequences also flow for members of the bar. Lawyers speaking the recognised non-dominant language should be able to find meaningful employment and carry on a productive practice provided they are functionally bilingual, because the other party will be free to choose any recognised language of his or her choice. Thirdly, members of the judiciary and other judicial staff (prosecutors, registrars, etc.) should be bilingual. In some countries (Finland, Switzerland, Belgium), there is indeed a legal obligation for judges and other personnel to be bilingual, whatever this means in the particular context.

To be able to enforce law and administer justice in more than one language, the state must count on a sufficient number of legally educated bilinguals and/or bilingually educated lawyers. The best way to guarantee a proper administering of justice in more than one language is providing legal education through all or the main official languages. But this may not be sufficient. Bi- or multilingualism in the twenty-first century must be more than the knowledge of two or more

---

[63] On the distinction between official-language and minority language rights, see Xabier Arzoz, 'Accommodating Linguistic Difference: Five Normative Models of Language Rights', 6 *European Constitutional Law Review* (2010) p. 102–122.

[64] C. M. Bloom, 'Access to Justice in English in the Judicial District of Montréal – A Unique Experience', in A. Braën, P. Foucher and Y. Le Bouthiller (eds.), *Languages, Constitutionalism and Minorities* (LexisNexis 2006) p. 433–438 at p. 434.

languages. Lawyers working within a legal system that operates in two or more languages require an extra formation. Abilities such as translation, language switching and designing information bilingually will be increasingly important.[65] The manner in which this is achieved may be some form of bilingual legal education.

E. Academic Legal Education between Vernacularisation, Internationalisation and Europeanisation

Academic legal education in bilingual or multilingual European states is facing several challenges: the challenge of vernacularisation that is peculiar to bilingual and multilingual states and regions, the pressure towards the convergence of higher education systems that is common to European states, and the challenge of internationalisation that is a more general trend.

1. *Vernacularisation*

Education always has been an important element of the nation-state, crucial for its consolidation and continuation.[66] Newly formed states created or reconstituted universities (often qualified as 'national') that would teach in the newly adopted official language and assist in creating administrative and cultural cadres for the state.[67] On the other hand, the nation-state brought with it the nationalisation of higher education: the state gained control of certification, accreditation, financing and academic appointments.

In the last fifty years, universities have been created or expanded to democratise access to higher education, but also as a way to foster regional development and cohesion. That higher education institutions have an impact upon the economic development of a region is not a new idea. However, there is a basic conceptual dichotomy here between local provision and regionalisation: on the one hand, a certain portion of the national provision of higher education can be decentralised to a particular region because of arguments of opportunity and for

[65] García, *supra* n. 24, p. 297.
[66] Tsu and Tollefson, *supra* n. 21, p. 1–18.
[67] Norrback and Ranki, *supra* n. 29.

a distributional purpose; on the other hand, an explicit formal mandate to serve regional stakeholders may be recognised as part of the mission of higher education.[68] Even if the impact of the first approach should not be underestimated,[69] it is certain that only the second approach involves conferring upon the university a specific regional responsibility. This regional responsibility might include the mission to promote, sustain and develop the local culture and language. Nineteenth century nationalism and the homogeneous view of national identity have given way to a new understanding of the multiple layers of culture and identity. In very specific cases, the regional dimension has led to the expansion of higher education as a minority language sector.

From an international perspective, both revival of languages and decentralisation have brought a new role to local higher education institutions as promoters of regional wellbeing and cultural development. In particular, change in the status of languages has had an impact on the language of higher education. Where ethno-linguistic groups have succeeded in resisting linguistic domination and thereby gained political autonomy or even independence, educational and medium-of-instruction state policies have been adjusted or new policies have been established to accommodate demands from ethno-linguistic groups.

The link between the creation of public universities and devolution is evident in the Spanish case. In the bilingual autonomous communities of Spain, new or renewed universities have the mission of contributing not only to the economic, cultural and social development of the surrounding region, but also to the development of all functional styles of regional or minority languages. This commitment

---

[68] Guy Neave, 'On Flies in Amber – Some Eccentric Thoughts on Universities and Regions from an International Perspective', in *Expanding Colleges and New Universities* (University of Uppsala 1996) p. 175–184 at p. 179.

[69] For instance, the creation of a Basque studies department at the multidisciplinary Faculty of Bayonne (attached to the University of Pau) goes back to 1985/86 and is part of a decentralisation of the national provision of higher education in France. Students can write all their research works, including doctoral theses, in Basque and within the Basque region. See Xarles Bidegain, 'Euskararen egoera Baionako Unibertsitatean (Xarles Bidegaini elkarrizketa)', 50 *Bat. Soziolinguistikako aldizkaria* (2004) p. 77–82. It must be noted that the demand for a Basque department in France often goes hand in hand with demands for a Basque university, i.e., with demands for the regionalisation of higher education.

to regional development and cultural identity is entrenched in the Catalan, Basque and Galician university constitutions.[70]

In other bilingual regions such as Wales and Scotland, the vernacular language is struggling to find its role within the university system, either in existing institutions or in specific institutions to be grounded. The plans to create a Welsh-medium 'federal college' in Wales or to foster Gaelic-medium education at the University of the Highlands and the Islands in Scotland go in that direction. It must be stressed that the pressure for vernacularisation of higher education does not dissolve the close ties that exist between higher education and the nation-state. Catalan, Basque and Galician universities and Welsh universities have to operate and to compete within the Spanish and British legal framework, respectively. Yet in economically and demographically powerful regions such as Catalonia there is the aspiration and the critical mass too, to develop a quality and coherent Catalan-medium higher education system.[71]

In South Africa, a change in the status of languages took place at the end of apartheid. The Constitution of 1996 declares eleven official languages (Afrikaans, English, plus nine indigenous languages) that should be accorded 'parity of esteem and must be treated equitably' and recognises the special needs of promotion and development of indigenous languages according to their 'historically diminished use and status' (section 6). As regards education, section 29(2) reads: 'Everyone has the right to receive education in the official language or languages of their choice in public educational institutions where that education is reasonably practicable. In order to ensure the effective access to, and implementation of, this right, the state must consider all reasonable educational alternatives, including single medium institutions, taking into account equity; practicability; and the need to redress the results of past racially discriminatory laws and practices'. The development of a language policy for higher education was postponed

---

[70] Xabier Arzoz, 'Universidad y pluralismo lingüístico', in Julio V. González Garcia (ed.), *Comentario a la Ley Orgánica de Universidades* (Civitas 2009) p. 1125–1192; Iñaki Agirreazkuenaga, 'Universidad y lengua: Universidades multilingües para una Europa multilingüe', 86 (II) *Revista Vasca de Administración Pública* (2010) p. 17–45.

[71] See Catalonia's Regional Steering Committee (2010). *The Autonomous Region of Catalonia, Spain: Self-Evaluation Report*, OECD Reviews of Higher Education in Regional and City Development, IMHE, <www.oecd.org/edu/imhe/regional development>, visited June 27, 2011.

for years because of the problematic nature of such a policy. In November 2002, the Minister of Education released a policy document entitled *Language policy for higher education*. The two main thrusts of that document were the need to develop South African languages as academic/scientific languages for use in instruction, and the need to develop student proficiency in the currently designated language(s) of tuition, namely, English and, to a lesser extent, Afrikaans. All higher education institutions were required to develop their own language policy subject to that document's policy framework. The University of the Witwatersrand, for instance, aims at having seSotho elaborated into a language of tuition within ten years to be used alongside English in a bilingual-medium of instruction policy.[72] As the South African languages recognised by the Constitution as official languages are many (nine), they are not standardised but divided in many dialects and they do not rely on any kind of fierce ethno-cultural nationalism behind them, the development of all or, at least, several indigenous languages as languages of instruction in higher education, alongside English and Afrikaans, constitutes a very ambitious objective: some commentators consider that it is not practicable even in the medium to long term.[73] In any case, the level of standardisation and modernisation of the different African languages will depend primarily upon the language policies which African governments are willing to pursue, not on their inherent inability.[74]

2. *Internationalisation*

The other pressure facing academic legal education is internationalisation. The term 'internationalisation' has been used with regard to higher education since the early 1980s. Nevertheless, the implications of the concept have evolved enormously since the environment in

[72] Foley, *supra* n. 18.

[73] Foley, *supra* n. 18; but see van der Walt, *supra* n. 18, and Vic Webb, 'Language Policy in Post-Apartheid South Africa', in James W. Tollefson and Amy Tsu (eds.), *Medium of Instruction Policies: Which Agenda? Whose Agenda?* (Lawrence Erlbaum Associates 2004) p. 217–239.

[74] Hassana Alidou, 'Medium of Instruction in Post-Colonial Africa', in James W. Tollefson and Amy Tsu (eds.), *Medium of Instruction Policies: Which Agenda? Whose Agenda?* (Lawrence Erlbaum Associates 2004) p. 195–214; Catherine Griefenow-Mewis, 'Are African languages fit for use in education, science and technology?', in Catherine Griefenow-Mewis (ed.), *On Results of the Reform in Ethiopia's Language and Education Policies* (Harrosowitz 2009) p. 11–20.

which higher education is operating has also been changing.[75] Internationalisation can be defined as 'the process of integrating an international, intercultural or global dimension into the purpose, functions or delivery of postsecondary education'.[76] Internationalisation of legal education includes many aspects:[77] competition among law schools and among different systems of legal education to design attractive programmes and catch international lecturers and graduate and postgraduate students for them, the internationalisation and convergence of academic curricula, and the cooperation between higher education institutions at various levels (mobility of researchers, lecturers and students, creation of cooperative law programmes aiming at joint/double international degrees, creation of networks to carry out many different tasks, etc.). These processes are pushed mainly by two connected arguments: the relevance of highly educated and trained labour forced for the state's competitiveness as a whole; and the neo-liberal idea that universities provide for a service of economic value that, as other economic activities, must respond to the choices and the needs of 'consumers' and has to assess its competitiveness and quality standards through quality assurance. Even states that resist adopting the strongest neo-liberal vision do not reject removing final obstacles and facilitating the free movement of students in the area of higher education.

The consequences of the 'market' vision of higher education on the use of minority languages as media of teaching and learning are controversial. Some positive consequences can be considered. Firstly, the responsibility for providing higher education shifts away from the state and towards the market. State language policy has often restricted the use of minority languages. By contrast, if education is conceptualised as a commodity to be traded on global markets, it is up to the provider to decide which kind of service must be offered and how. If barriers to the provision of, say, English-medium higher education are removed, the same should apply to other foreign suppliers by virtue of the most favoured nation treatment.[78] And if there is not enough offer in the local market, cross-border services from kin-states might cater for the

---

[75] See Jane Knight, 'Internationalization: concepts, complexities and challenges', in James J.F. Forest and Phillip G. Altbach (eds.), *International Handbook of Higher Education* (Springer 2007) p. 207–227 at p. 208–211.

[76] Knight, *supra* n. 75, p. 214.

[77] For a repertoire of internationalisation strategies, programmes and policies, see Knight, *supra* n. 75, p. 221–224.

[78] The most favoured nation treatment is one of the unconditional obligations under the General Agreements on Trade in Services (GATS).

local linguistic minority. For instance, the Slovenian linguistic community which is divided into three neighbouring nation-states (Slovenia, Italy and Austria) but concentrated in the same historic region could benefit from the four modes of supply included in the GATS: cross-border supply (distance education, e-learning, virtual universities), consumption abroad (students who go to Slovenia to study), commercial presence (opening of local branches or satellite campuses, twinning partnerships, etc.), and presence of natural persons (professors, teachers, researchers working abroad). The same could apply to other border regions[79] or cross-border linguistic communities of demographic relevance, such as Hungarian speakers in Slovakia and Romania. Since some of the European minority languages are at the same time state languages of kin-states, the liberalisation of trade in education services may contribute to the elimination of trade barriers, state language policy obstacles and, therefore, to the increasing cross-border use of some middle-sized languages.

Secondly, one might also consider that cross-border higher education services will create new opportunities, since modern technologies (e-learning, virtual universities, distance universities, etc.) will allow for creating and providing new and more diversified services in ever more languages.[80] In some areas (business, IT technologies, adult education, popular science, etc.), for-profit universities and education companies will standardise their products in order to offer them in as many languages as is profitable, as it is now the case with many cultural products (books, DVDs, television programmes, films, applications for iphones and ipads, etc.). Consumers will have access to a bigger range of education services in many languages, in the same way as they can choose among hundreds of cable or online television programmes in many languages.

However, as regards traditional higher education (i.e., physical colleges and campuses), the trend appears to be rather the reduction, not the expansion, of languages of tuition. In spite of occasional beneficial aspects, the impression seems to be that, in general, the rise of

[79] Kozma and Radácsi, *supra* n. 47.

[80] It must be noted that open universities exist since the 19th century in Britain, and that tuition by correspondence is a rather old affair. British universities catered for individuals living in Britain and overseas. On the University of London as an archetypal global institution see Malcolm Tight, 'Re-writing history: The University of London as a global institution in the nineteenth, twentieth and twenty-first centuries', in *International Relations* (=International Perspectives on Higher Education Research vol. 3) (Elsevier 2005) p. 89–306.

'for-profit' higher education[81] will be detrimental to the use of minority languages and to state languages as well. The conceptualisation of the aims of higher education will shift away from obtaining personal and social development benefits to the purely economic aspects: university degrees as the way to achieve a better job and a higher standard of living. In particular if higher education is traded on a high price, the consumer will seek to optimise the money he or she is paying. More mobility of students and more competition between higher education institutions to catch students will be the consequence. Since international skills and degrees will be very much appreciated and rewarded by the job market, the demand for education in international or world languages will increase, above all if more and more opportunities are given over to the liberalisation of trade in higher education.

It must be noted that lecturers and students speaking minority languages are all bilingual, and their second language is in some cases an international one (English or Spanish). Firstly, bilingual or minority language education is more expensive and economically less rewarding for institutions, university managers and lecturers than courses in international languages (English and Spanish). In particular, public institutions, caught in the squeeze of decreased public funding and increased operational costs, may increasingly look for internationalisation activities as a way to generate alternative sources of income.[82] Secondly, lecturers have legitimate expectations of professional status and accreditation, which seem to be facilitated for those enrolling in the internationalisation agenda of higher education (through mobility, teaching and publishing in international languages, developing links with international institutions, etc.). The same is applicable to the use of national languages as academic/scientific languages. The exclusive focus on publishing in English in many European states assumes that writing for an 'international' journal implies better quality than in a national one. In Norway, a system of performance pay for university staff was introduced in the 1990s: a book written in a 'international language' triggers a bonus of 15,000 crowns, whereas one in Norwegian gests 7,000; an article in English in a refereed journal is rewarded by a

[81] Richard S. Ruch, *The Rise of the For-Profit University* (John Hopkins University Press 2001); Kevin Kinser, *From Main Street to Wall Street – The Transformation of For-Profit Higher Education* (Jossey-Bass 2006); David W. Breneman, Brian Pusser and Sarah E. Turner, *Earnings from Learning – The Rise of For-Profit Universities* (State University of New York 2006).

[82] Knight, *supra* n. 75, p. 219.

bonus of 7,000 crowns, one in Norwegian 1,000.[83] Thirdly, the quantitative criteria for assessing the quality or excellence of lecturers and of academic programmes for accreditation purposes and indirectly for receiving extra funding tend to be detrimental for minority language education. One of those criteria is the percentage of international students and teachers enrolled in a course; another is the number of doctoral theses that a lecturer has supervised. These types of criteria do not benefit higher education through lesser-used languages. The pressure is more acute in master courses than in graduate law courses, in which universities have less discretion, at least in continental Europe, as to the subjects offered as part of the law programmes. Academic leaders, education policymakers and politicians should take a long-term perspective on the opportunities and challenges inherent in globalisation and its consequences for the internationalisation of higher education.

3. *Europeanisation*

For European states, internationalisation facilitates regional integration and the Europeanisation of higher education, i.e. the processes in the field of higher education policies developed cooperatively by European states to develop a European Area for Higher Education.[84] It must be stressed that the founding stones of the Bologna process were laid down by states acting outside the EU institutional framework, and that even the EU's educational programmes to foster mobility and networking are based on voluntary cooperation between higher education institutions.[85] As of 2010, the deadline for implementing the so-called Bologna process, the main outputs of the Europeanisation of higher education were: the development and incorporation of a

[83] Phillipson, *supra* n. 20, p. 81.

[84] A process of convergence, mobility and accreditation between Latin-American and Iberian states was launched in Guadalajara (México) on 31 May 2010 at the Second Universia Meeting of University Chancellors, with one thousand representatives from Latin-American and Iberian states. The so-called Guadalajara Agenda aims at a convergence similar to that of the Bologna process in ten years. Therefore, Spain and Portugal could take part at the same time in two global spaces of higher education. There are fourteen million people enrolled in higher education in the Latin-American and Iberian states. This vast market for Spanish-medium higher education will be a new pressure for Catalan, Basque and Galician universities as more Spanish-medium master and doctoral courses are offered.

[85] Kurt De Wit, 'The Consequences of European Integration for Higher Education', 16 *Higher Education Policy* (2003) p. 161–178; Sacha Garben, 'The Bologna Process: from a European Law Perspective', 16 *European Law Journal* (2010) p. 186–210.

common measure unit (the European Credit Transfer Scheme, ECTS) which includes diverse forms of learning with a view to allowing for a relative comparability of higher education systems, the adoption of a common structure of higher education cycles around the Anglo-American model of bachelor, master and doctoral degrees, with a minimum of three years study within the first cycle (3+2+3 or 4+1+3) with the aim of fostering the compatibility and transportability of degrees obtained in another state, an increased mobility of students through cooperative networks between individual institutions, and the creation of national institutions for quality assurance through accreditation and audit of the different elements of national higher education systems.[86]

However, many obstacles still exist under the surface or even at the surface, due to the lack of willingness of replacing well-rooted national traditions. Legal studies are the discipline which states show most reluctance to the implementation of the bachelor-master model. Many states (Poland, Czech Republic, Hungary, Slovak Republic, Greece, and Germany) resolutely reject the application of the Bologna process to academic legal education. France has limited itself to a formal implementation without touching the essence of its system. Italy has suppressed the initial implementation and has gone back to the five years long formation.[87] Germany, which is very proud of its outstanding problem-oriented legal formation that leads to the key legal professions, finds no sense in a total reform of legal studies.[88] By contrast, Spain has not only adopted the new degree system (4+1) but also abridged the curriculum of the first cycle in comparison to the previous five years degree. With regard to the law curriculum or to access to the legal professions, however, no significant progress has been made.[89]

---

[86] Manuel Ángel Bermejo Castrillejo, '¿Realidad o ficción? El proceso de convergencia de las enseñanzas jurídicas dentro del marco del proyecto de creación de un Espacio Superior de Educación Superior', 9 *Cuadernos del Instituto Antonio de Nebrija* (2006) p. 237–296 at p. 295–296.

[87] Roberto Moscati, 'The Implementation of the Bologna Process in Italy', in A. Amaral et al. (eds.), *European Integration and the Governance of Higher Education and Research* (Springer 2009).

[88] Horst Konzen, 'Bologna-Prozess and Juristenausbildung', 5 *Juristen-Zeitung* (2010) p. 241–245.

[89] Webb, *supra* n. 25; Katarzyna Gromek-Broc, 'The Legal Profession in the European Union – A Comparative Analysis of Four Member States', 24 *Liverpool Law Review* (2002) p. 109–130.

PART I

LEGAL EDUCATION IN MULTILINGUAL STATES

CHAPTER TWO

BILINGUALISM AND LEGAL EDUCATION IN CANADA: THE CLASSICAL APPROACH

André Braën

A. Introduction

Canada has two official languages: French which is spoken mostly in Quebec and English which is the common language used in the rest of Canada. Two legal traditions also apply on its territory: civil law in Quebec[1] and common law elsewhere. There are twenty one law schools[2] delivering a law diploma across Canada and practising law is a professional activity that is controlled by a law society set up in each province.[3] Is bilingualism a characteristic taken into account in legal education provided to future lawyers in Canada and if so, to what extent? Are lawyers in Canada instructed and trained in a bilingual manner or is in any case the Canadian model influenced by the bilingual nature of the country? What can be the lesson learned from the Canadian experience to this regard? In a bilingual country one may think that bilingualism is a condition for a candidate being successful in legal studies.

Bilingualism in Canada is institutionalised and does not mean that the population (32 million people) itself is bilingual. Outside Quebec

[1] In the province of Quebec, civil law applies in matters of private law and common law applies in matters of public law. Whether or not civil law applies to a specific matter is on a legal basis a question of public law and therefore has to be settled by common law.

[2] More law schools or departments are offering a wide range of law programmes in Canada and also graduate studies and various joint programmes but 21 deliver undergraduate studies in law which is the professional degree required for practising law. Discussions are undertaken for the implementation of new law schools. See the Council of Canadian Law Deans' website: www.ccld-cdfdc.ca.

[3] E.g. the Law Society of Upper Canada regulates the practising of law in the province of Ontario (see *The Law Society Act*, R.S.O., 1990, c.L.8, website: www.lsuc.on.ca.). The *Barreau du Québec* does the same in the province of Quebec (see R.S.Q., B-1, website: www.barreau.gc.ca.).

and according to the 2006 census,[4] only 7.4 percent of Anglophones said they could carry on a conversation in French and the census shows that Anglophone population's knowledge of French is declining among young people. To the contrary, in the province of Quebec 35 percent of the Francophones declared being able to conduct a conversation in both official languages and elsewhere in Canada, 84 percent of the Francophones are bilingual.

The constitution of Canada contains a number of important language guarantees and in order to implement them a competent public service with bilingual skills is needed. Furthermore, Canada is a federation and the power to legislate is shared between the Parliament of Canada and the Legislative Assembly of each of the ten existing provinces. Who can exercise the authority over education and over professions and regulate their linguistic aspects?

In order to answer these questions, it is necessary first to highlight the elements of the Canadian constitution dealing with the distribution of power and the entrenched language guarantees. Then, I comment on the organisation of legal education and the practice of law in Canada and see what the impact is, if any, of the bilingual nature of Canada on them. I conclude with the key findings of a recent report made by the Office of Commissioner of Official Languages about second-language learning in Canadian universities.[5]

B. Distribution of Powers and Language Rights

In Canada the provinces are given the exclusive authority to make laws in relation to education.[6] Thereby making instruction at all levels, including colleges and universities, falls under the provincial jurisdiction. Regarding the organisation of a university system and its governance, university programmes, research and diploma, all are matters regulated by the province.[7] Education includes professional training

---

[4] See generally www.statcan.gc.ca. And more particularly for the linguistic portrait findings, see www12.statcan.ca/census-recensement/2006/as-sa/97-555/index-eng.cfm.

[5] Office of the Commissioner of Official Languages, *Two Languages, a World of Opportunities, Second-language Learning in Canada's Universities* (Minister of Public Works and Government Services Canada 2009). Also available on the Commissioner of Official Languages' website: www.ocol-clo.gc.ca.

[6] *Constitution Act, 1867*, sec.93 which provides that each province may exclusively make «laws in relation to education».

[7] See P.W. Hogg, *Constitutional Law of Canada*, 4th ed. loose leaf (Thomson 2002), ch 53.

and the regulation of a profession (restriction of entry, rules of conduct administered by a governing body) also comes within the jurisdiction of a province in relation to property and civil rights and matters of a merely or private nature in the province.[8]

Does it mean that the federal government does not intervene in these fields? Generally speaking the federal jurisdiction over education is exceptional and limited to what is incidental to particular heads of federal power.[9] But according to Canadian constitutional law, one level of government may spend money in areas coming under the authority of the other but in doing so it cannot attempt to control or regulate those areas of power that come under the other's jurisdiction.[10] This spending power is often used by the federal government particularly when it wishes to implement so-called national standards.[11] For example in the area of education, federal grants are made to provinces in order to sustain instruction of English and French as second official languages. Similarly, grants from the federal government contribute to the operating expenses of the universities and other post secondary institutions in each province. Thus federal agencies have been established in order to fund university research.[12] It should be noted that federal legislation which provides for the allocation of funds offered in provincial areas through transfer or grant programmes may contain conditions that provinces must comply with if they wish to receive that funding. The Supreme Court of Canada ruled that the simple withholding of funds by federal authorities when a province fails to abide by the conditions so prescribed in the federal statute does not in itself amount to regulating a provincial matter.[13]

---

[8] *Constitution Act, 1867*, sec. 92(13) and (16) which provide that each province may exclusively make laws in relation to «Property and civil rights in the Province» and «Generally all matters of a merely local or private nature in the Province». See *Beaule v. Corp. Of Master Electricians*, (1969) 10 D.L.R. (3d) 93 (QCA); *A.G. Canada v. Law Society of British-Columbia*, (1982) 2 S.C.R. 307.

[9] For example schools in Indian reserves or on military base. Note that sec.93(4) of the *Constitution Act, 1867*, gives the Parliament of Canada a remedial power in area of education but this power was never used.

[10] See H. Brun and G. Tremblay, *Droit constitutionnel*, 4th ed. (Ed. Yvon Blais Inc. 2002) pp. 430–437.

[11] See A. Braën, "Health and the Distribution of Powers in Canada", in T. McIntosh, P.-G. Gerlier Forest and G. P. Marchildon (eds.), *The Governance of Health Care in Canada* (University of Toronto Press 2004) pp. 35–37.

[12] E.g. the Social Sciences and Humanities Research Council (website: www.sshrc-crshc.gc.ca) and the National Research Council Canada (website: www.nrc-cnrc.gc.ca).

[13] *Re Canada Assistance Plan*, (1991) 2 S.C.R.525. See also *Winterhaven Stables Ltd. v. A.G. Canada*, (1988) 53 D.L.R. (4th) 413 (SCC).

As such language is not an enumerated head of power in the *Constitution Act, 1867*. The Canadian constitution allocates neither to Parliament of Canada nor to the provincial legislatures exclusive jurisdiction in relation to language. Therefore language is in Canada an area of concurrent jurisdiction and each level of government may make law in its areas of jurisdiction and regulate language matters coming with them.[14] Courts ruled that « for constitutional purposes, language is ancillary to the purpose for which it is used, and the language law is for institutional purposes a law in relation to the institutions or activities to which the law applies »[15]. Therefore a province has full authority to deal with the linguistic aspects of education and profession. But provincial legislation adopted on those matters must not contravene or conflict with the language guarantees contained in the constitution[16] or with any right or freedom protected by the *Canadian Charter of Rights and Freedoms.*[17] French and English are the official languages and have equality of status and equal rights and privileges as to their use at the federal level.[18] At the provincial level, New Brunswick is the only Canadian province that has proclaimed French and English as its official languages[19]. Quebec has proclaimed French its official language[20] and English is the language of all other provinces even if some rights have been granted to the French minority.[21]

Section 23 of the *Canadian Charter of Rights and Freedom* confers on entitled parents the right to have their children receive their primary and secondary instruction in the official minority language (English in Quebec, French in the rest of Canada). It applies everywhere in Canada but this provision does not concern education provided by postsecondary institutions. Therefore there is no right to be instructed at the university level in French or in English and a province may rule the language to be used by universities. Nevertheless, it

[14] *Jones v. New Brunswick (A.G.)*, (1975) 2 S.C.R. 182; *Blaikie v. Quebec (A.G.) (No.1)*, (1979) 2 S.C.R. 1016.

[15] *Devine v. Quebec*, (1988) 2 S.C.R.790 at 808.

[16] *Blaikie v. Quebec (A.G.), (No.1), supra* n. 14; *Arsenault-Cameron v. Prince Edward Island*, (2000) 1 S.C.R.3.

[17] *Devine v. Quebec, supra* n. 15.

[18] *Canadian Charter of Rights and Freedoms*, sec.16(1); see also the *Official Languages Act*, R.S.C. 1985, c.31 (4th Supp.) sec.2.

[19] *Ibid.*, sec.16(2).

[20] *Charter of the French Language*, R.S,Q. c.C-11.

[21] E.g. for the province of Ontario, see *The French Language Services Act*, R.S.O. 1990, c.F.32.

should be noted that throughout Canada there exists a publicly funded network of postgraduate minority-language institutions: there are a network of colleges and three universities providing instruction in English in Quebec and there are also publicly funded post-secondary institutions providing French language instruction in many other parts in Canada.

The constitution of Canada contains other important language guarantees.[22] Thus, the constitution holds the compulsory use of bilingualism (French-English) in Parliament and in legislative assemblies of Quebec, Manitoba and New Brunswick.[23] They have the obligation to keep their records and journals in French and English and they also are under the duty to print and publish their laws in both languages.[24] The Supreme Court of Canada has ruled that this obligation for statutory bilingualism applies to the printing and publishing of legislative enactment as well as their adoption processes with the latter requirement being implicit.[25] The obligation to use French and English also extends to statutory instruments adopted by the government, a minister or a group of ministers or to those regulations that need a government approval before they can be put into force.[26] Both version of a legislative enactment are equally authoritative.[27] Does it mean that knowledge of both languages is required in order to interpret efficiently and correctly a bilingual enactment? I believe so.

Concerning the language of judicial proceedings, the Canadian constitution confers on individual the right to use French or English before the courts established by the Parliament of Canada or by the Legislature of Quebec, Manitoba and New Brunswick.[28] This right does not include the right to be understood directly without translation or to be answered, orally or in writing in the language chosen.[29] Of course

---

[22] For an analysis of the constitutional language regime in Canada, see M. Bastarache (ed.), *Language Rights in Canada* (Éd. Yvon Blais Inc 2004).

[23] *Constitution Act*, 1867, sec.133, *Manitoba Act, 1870*, sec.23, *Canadian Charter of Rights and Freedoms*, sec. 16(1) and (2).

[24] *Ibid.*

[25] *Blaikie v. Quebec (A.G.), (No.1), supra*, n. 14; *Blaikie v. Quebec (A.G.), (No.2)*, (1981) 1 S.C.R.312; *Reference re Manitoba Language Rights*, (1985) 1 S.C.R.721.

[26] *Ibid.*

[27] *Reference re Manitoba Language Rights, supra*, note 25.

[28] *Constitution Act, 1867*, sec.133, *Manitoba Act, 1870*, sec.23, *Canadian Charter of Rights and Freedoms*, sec.19.

[29] *MacDonald v. Montreal (City)*, (1986) 1 S.C.R. 460; *S.A.N.B. v. Association of Parents for Fairness in Education*, (1987) 1 S.C.R. 549.

a legislature may add to this minimum. Today French and English may be used on an equal basis before federal courts. Even if criminal proceedings occur in provincial courts, Parliament of Canada has the authority to legislate with respect to criminal procedure[30] and now the *Criminal Code of Canada* allows for criminal trials to be conducted in French or in English everywhere in Canada.[31] Regarding civil proceedings, French may be used before certain provincial courts but not all.[32]

Finally, it should be noted that in matter of public services, there is a constitutional right for any member of the public in Canada to communicate with and to receive services from the federal government and from the New Brunswick government and their agencies in either French or English.[33] In some other provinces public services may upon request be provided in the language of the linguistic minority.[34] Therefore it follows that a competent public service with bilingual skills is needed in those jurisdictions in order to implement this requirement. Of course what has been said is just an overview but it demonstrates how language rights and bilingual requirements have roots in the Canadian society and more particularly in its legal, judicial and parliamentary institutions.

C. Legal Education and Languages

Despite this legal environment that favours bilingualism, one may think that instruction given by law schools and law societies in Canada takes into account this genuine characteristic and that a lawyer in Canada is generally bilingual. Is this the case? What is the Canadian experience regarding this matter? The responsibility for legal training in Canada is shared between law schools and law societies established by the provinces. Law schools are of course dedicated to the study of

---

[30] *Constitution Act, 1867*, sec. 91(27).

[31] Sec. 530 of the *Criminal Code of Canada*, R.S.C. 1985, c.C-46. In *R v. Beaulac*, (1999) 1 S.C.R. 768, para. 34, the Supreme Court of Canada held that the purpose of this section is to provide equal access to the courts to accused persons speaking one of the official languages of Canada in order to assist official language minorities in preserving their cultural identity.

[32] E.g. *The Courts of Justice Act*, R.S.O. 1990, c.C.43, sec.125–126 which provides for the use of French and English in proceedings before Ontario's courts.

[33] *Canadian Charter of Rights and Freedoms*, sec. 20(1) and (2). The scope of the right may vary according to these provisions.

[34] See *supra* n. 21.

law as an academic discipline. A law society assures that legal services are provided to the public by qualified and competent lawyers. Even if the latter is strongly interested in the academic program delivered by law schools, it remains primarily involved in the operation of bar admission courses and also continuing education program for lawyers.

Concerning the law school admission requirements, universities in Canada are established by provincial private or public acts or by letters patent issued by a province.[35] A province is free to organise the academic program according to its own choices. Even if most Canadian universities are private institutions, all receive important public funds primarily from the provinces and also, as we have seen, from the federal government through different programmes. University of Ottawa has declared itself to be an official bilingual university[36] and is by far the largest bilingual institution in Canada.[37] Therefore students may attend classes in either French or English and most, but not all programmes, in most disciplines are available in both languages. The data on language use indicates that there are some 25,000 students studying in English and approximately 11,000 studying in French at University of Ottawa. However, the number of English-speaking students taking courses in French is believed to be less than 5 percent.[38] In fact, it is a minority of students who effectively choose such a bilingual curriculum. In Canada, there are six civil law schools and fifteen common law schools.[39] Five civil law schools are located in Quebec and the sixth one is the Civil Law Section of University of Ottawa and according from the information picked up from their websites,[40] French being the language of instruction, an excellent knowledge of French by the candidate is an implied or explicit requirement to admission and to this

[35] Eg see *An Act Respecting Université d'Ottawa*, S.O. 1965, c.137; an *Act Respecting the Université du Québec*, R.S.Q. c.U-1; *University Act*, R.S.B.C. 1996, c.468.

[36] *An Act Respecting Université d'Ottawa*, *supra* n. 34. See also the University of Ottawa's website: www.uottawa.ca.

[37] With approximately 36,000 students.

[38] These figures strangely come not from University of Ottawa itself but rather from a study produced by the Office of the Commissioner of Official Languages, see *Two Languages, a World of Opportunities, Second Language Learning in Canada's Universities*, *supra* n. 5, p. 7.

[39] See *supra* n. 2.

[40] See www.droit.umontreal.ca; www.fd.ulaval.ca; www.usherbrooke.ca/droit; www.juris.uqam.ca; www.mcgill.ca/law; www.droitcivil.uottawa.ca. See also the website of the Council of Canadian Law Deans: www.ccld.cdfd.ca.

regard, tests may be imposed on candidates. Some law schools in Quebec also require from their candidates knowledge of English as a condition for the delivery of the diploma. McGill offers a joint diploma in civil and in common law and requires from its students a substantial reading ability in and oral comprehension of both French and English; it also uses both languages as languages of instruction[41]. Certain faculties of law in Quebec offer a diploma in common law and thus knowledge of English is required since courses may be offered in English. At the Civil Law Section of the University of Ottawa, French is the language of instruction but students may attend courses given in English by the Common Law Section. Pedagogical material is normally available in the same language, French or English, than the language of instruction. In fact since common law is taught in French important efforts have been made in order to use materials written in French.[42]

Regarding the common law schools with the exceptions of Université de Moncton and University of Ottawa, the language of instruction is English so knowledge of this language is an explicit or, most of the time, an implied requirement for a candidate wishing to be admitted.[43] At the *École de droit* of Université de Moncton, common law is taught in French and the Common Law Section of University of Ottawa offers a French Common Law Program and an English Common Law Program. Students from one program may choose courses offered by the other program. But only few students from the English program are attending classes in the French program.[44] With the exceptions of Moncton and the French Common Law Program in Ottawa, marks of an applicant and especially his or her results at the LSAT[45] are the main criteria considered in order to be admitted by a

---

[41] See the website of McGill, *supra* n. 40.

[42] See *infra* n. 49.

[43] See the websites of the common law schools: www.law.ubc.ca; www.law.uvic.ca; www.law.ualberta.ca; www.law.ucalgary.ca; www.usask.ca/law; www.umanitoba.ca/law; www.law.uwo.ca; www.uwindsor.ca/law; www.law.queensu.ca; www.osgoode.yorku.ca; www.law.utoronto.ca; www.commonlaw.uottawa.ca; www.umoncton.ca/umcm-droit; www.unb/fredericton/law; www.law.dal.ca. See also the Law Schools Admission Council's website: www.lsac.org.

[44] There are no official figures regarding this point. The information is provided by the persons in charge of the programmes.

[45] Law School Admission Test. It was created in 1948 in order to give common law schools a standardised procedure to judge applicants. For details regarding the test, see the LSAT website www.lsac.org.

common law school.[46] The LSAT is an examination created in order to give common law schools a way to judge applicants uniformly and the test is a critical part of the law school admission process. It measures skills that are considered essential for success in law schools. The test is administered only in English; for linguistic and cultural reasons, the two common law schools having French as the language of instruction have not implemented it. The explicit requirement of English is stated in the admission criteria of various common law school as part of their policies to ensure that the new admitted student is successful in the program as English is the language of instruction and evaluation.[47] The other common law schools have an implicit English language requirement because English is the language of instruction and evaluation. Foreign applicants are invited to pass the TOEFL[48] before being admitted by an English common law school. Therefore, proficiency in French is not a requirement for studying in a common law school except, of course, when common law is taught in this language.[49] Nevertheless it should be noted that some efforts are made in order to promote bilingualism between Canadian law students and for example, it now exists national moot courts requiring from their participants the conduct of their written and oral proceedings both in French and in English.[50]

Legal research carried on in law schools deals primarily with Canadian jurisprudence and doctrine. The decisions from federal courts including the Supreme Court of Canada are available in French

---

[46] D. A. Soberman, *Admission Requirements in the Common Law Faculties in Canada*, (1980) 1 R.G.D. 375.

[47] See the websites of the law faculties of University of Alberta, Manitoba, Victoria, Queens and also of Osgoode Hall, *supra* n. 41.

[48] Test of English as a Foreign Language. For details regarding this test, see www.ets.org/toefl.

[49] Common law is taught in French since the seventies mainly in Moncton and Ottawa. To this effect a terminology network has been set up and many tools for legal translation were produced by the *Centre de traduction et de terminologie juridiques* (www.cttj.ca) from Université de Moncton and by the Centre for translation and Legal Documentation (www.uottawa.ca/associations/ctdj) from University of Ottawa. The federal Department of Justice Canada also is involved in this area. For example, see the *Legal Dictionary of Property in Canada, Common Law- Civil Law/Dictionnaire juridique de la propriété au Canada, droit civil-common law* at www.dualjuridik.org.

[50] E.g. all Canadian law faculties are invited to participate to the Laskin Moot Court in constitutional and administrative law. A faculty sends a team consisting of 4 students and the team is assessed on the basis of the written factum and the oral arguments. A member of a moot court must use French when the language of instruction of his or her faculty is English, and vice versa.

and in English.[51] But those rendered by provincial courts are written most of the time in English except in Quebec where the contrary prevails. According to Canada's constitution, a citizen has the right to use French or English at his or her choice before certain (not all) tribunals. Nevertheless, the same choice belongs to the judge whatever is the choice made by the citizen and a decision may be written in French or in English[52]. Generally Canadian law schools host a law review.[53] Even if articles and comments may be published in French or in English, most of the time the review speaks the same language of its school and in fact doctrine written in French is published mainly by French-speaking law school journals. The readership of an English law journal often is unable to read articles written in French. To my knowledge, the contrary prevails among Francophone readers, who generally can read English. Concerning the journals and reviews edited by a national association like the Canadian Bar Association[54] or by a provincial law society both languages may be used.[55] Finally, electronic research (on the Web) may be conducted most of the time in both languages.

Concerning the provincial law societies and with the exceptions of Quebec, New Brunswick and Ontario, all other jurisdictions in Canada have either implicit or explicit English language requirements to become a practising lawyer. For example and in the case of British Columbia, English proficiency is expressly required by regulation.[56] Regarding other jurisdictions, even if the enabling legislation and rules applicable to the law society do not explicitly require an applicant to be proficient in English, the same rules require the applicant to make the

---

[51] Including those decisions available on the website of the courts. For example, see www.scc-csc.gc.ca; www.fct-cf.gc.ca.

[52] *MacDonald v. Montreal (City), supra* n. 29; *Association of Parents for Fairness in Education, supra* n. 29. But see sec.530 of the *Criminal Code of Canada, supra* n. 31.

[53] In the case of University of Ottawa, there is the Revue générale de droit published by the Civil Law Section (www.revuegeneralededroit.ca) and the Ottawa Law Review/ Revue de droit d'Ottawa (www.commonlaw.uottawa.ca).

[54] See the Canadian Bar Review at www.cba.org/CBA/canadian_bar_review/main.

[55] See the *Ontario Lawyers Gazette* published by the Law Society of Upper Canada (www.lsuc.on.ca) and the *Revue du Barreau du Québec* published by the *Barreau du Québec* (www.barreau.qc.ca/publications/revue/index.html).

[56] The rule states: «An applicant who does not satisfy the Executive Director that he or she has an adequate knowledge of the English language must complete satisfactorily the training required by the Credential Committee». See Law Society of British Columbia Rules «Transfer from another Canadian Jurisdiction», Rule 2-49(4) and available on the society's website www.lawsociety.bc.ca.

corresponding applications and procedures to be admitted to the law society in English only. In fact, the Bar courses and examinations necessary for Bar admission are to be taken in English only. In New Brunswick which is officially bilingual and in Ontario where French is recognised as an official language in the courts,[57] courses for Bar applicants are available in French and examinations may be passed in either French or English. In the province of Quebec, Bar courses are given in French but both languages may be used for examination. In the latter case it should be noted that the *Charter of the French Language* provides expressly that a professional order shall not issue permits except to those whose knowledge of French is appropriate to the practice of their profession.[58] And on a practical basis bilingualism is a long well established tradition in Quebec courts. Outside the province of Quebec and except in few regions of Ontario and New Brunswick, legal services are by the rule available only in the English language.

D. The Report of the Office of the Commissioner of Official Languages

The Office of the Commissioner of Official Languages established according to the *Official Languages Act*[59] ensures that federal public service comply with the requirement of the *Act* regarding bilingualism. Promoting bilingualism among the Canadian population, the Office also investigates complaints, makes investigations and reports to the Parliament of Canada. According to its view, a second-official-language learning is essential to Canadian identity and citizenship and for fostering a better understanding among Canadians. Language skills and openness to other cultures are also important in a world of globalisation. Finally, considering its legal duties and in terms of renewal of the public service, the government of Canada should have access to a larger pool of bilingual recruits. These considerations and others led recently the Office of Commissioner of Official Languages to undertake a major study of second-language learning in Canada's

[57] *Supra* n. 32.

[58] R.S.Q. c.C-11, sec.35 that provides: «The professional orders shall not issue permits except to persons whose knowledge of the official language is appropriate to the practice of their profession…». The *Charter* declares French the official language of Quebec.

[59] *Supra* n. 18.

universities.[60] Its conclusion is that Canadian universities need by far to improve second-language learning.

This in-depth survey of institutions in Canada found that, while many universities offer a range of second-languages learning programmes and courses, nevertheless there are serious gaps and unmet needs. Particularly, opportunities for intensive second-language study are limited: for example, to enrol in immersion programmes, to take subject-matter courses taught in the second language or to take second-language courses tailored to different academic disciplines. Moreover, collaboration among English and French-language universities in Canada in order to promote second-language learning, including exchange opportunities, is weak and university second-language policies and requirements are generally minimal or non-existent. Certainly each university works within a unique context in terms of size, mission, location, resources, majority or minority-language location, proximity to other language institutions, etc. Therefore, each university can select from a range of potential models and approaches for promoting the second-official-language learning and even choose a mix of them. The models identified in the report are:[61]

- the other-language institution model: students attend a university where the language of instruction is the other official language;
- the bilingual institution model: the university identifies itself as a bilingual institution;
- the buffet model: the university offer students the possibility of following various courses in the other official language)
- the centre model: the university offers intensive second-language learning opportunities;
- the partnership model: this involves partnership and collaboration with institutions using the other official language;
- the targeting model: the university identifies academic disciplines and career interests where second-language ability is seen relevant and applies a variety of tools to foster second-language learning within those disciplines; and
- the tailoring model: this involves teaching and learning the second official-language focusing on the content and vocabulary of different academic areas.

[60] *Supra* n. 5.
[61] *Ibid.*, at 23–25.

The study suggests a number of areas where Canada needs to do better in second-language learning at the university level. More particularly and according to the report the way forward involves:[62]

- to improve opportunities for intensive second-language learning in universities;
- to exploit potential of minority-language institutions;
- to enhance partnership, collaboration and the use of technologies;
- to expand exchanges and real life opportunities to use second language;
- to adopt stronger second-language policies and requirements; and
- to expand information, promotion and marketing efforts.

Of course and even if these recommendations are proposed to be generally applicable by universities, it is clear that a faculty of law may pick up some inspiration from them in order to take a better account of the Canadian duality.

E. Conclusion

As we have seen, many language rights in Canada are constitutionally-based and require from the government the obligation of promoting bilingualism in order to be implemented. Moreover, it can be said that since the early days of the Canadian federation, bilingualism has played an important role and has become a genuine value. Despite some efforts, it is curious to note that in Canada, universities, law schools and law societies do not play a significant role to foster this fundamental characteristic except in Quebec where bilingualism (or a certain level of) appears to be traditional. Perhaps it is because English is the dominant language in Canada and that is it up to the minority to learn and speak the language of the other and also that there is no real need neither a feeling for the majority to learn the language of the minority. Canada's universities train and instruct unilingual graduate students. This is what we call the classical approach. Like the unilingual population a university serves, it speaks the same and unique language. In Canada, the classical approach means that each official language community has developed legal studies in its language

[62] *Ibid.*, at 25–27.

without being necessarily concerned with the language of the other community. This is less true in the case of the French community. For the latter and being the minority, knowledge of the English language has always been felt necessary in order to be successful in a legal career.

A bill is now before the Parliament of Canada.[63] It proposes to modify the *Supreme Court Act*[64] in requiring that, in order to be appointed as judge at the Supreme Court of Canada, a candidate shall understand French and English without the assistance of an interpreter. This proposed amendment is now strongly debated and polls show that the majority of people in Quebec are favourable to this proposal while the majority of Canada is against.[65] Many opponents argue that for being a good candidate competence in the law discipline is the only criteria that counts and bilingualism is not an element of competence. Those in favour say that bilingualism is an essential skill of a competent candidate. A former judge of the Supreme Court of Canada (unilingual English) publicly opposes the proposal saying that during the time he was on the bench he was well served by the interpreters' work and never had he complained. Being unilingual, was this judge capable of estimating correctly the quality and the accuracy of the interpreters' services?

---

[63] *An Act to Amend the Supreme Court Act* (understanding the official languages), 1st session, 40th Parliament, 57 Elizabeth II, 2008, bill C-232.

[64] R.S.C. 1985, c. S-26.

[65] *Le Devoir*, Montreal, 26/05/2010.

CHAPTER THREE

LINGUISTIC LAW IN HIGHER EDUCATION IN BELGIUM: NEW TRENDS FOR BILINGUAL EDUCATION, BUT WHICH ONE?

Sophie Weerts

A. Introduction

The Belgian State is composed of three national language groups. Dutch is the most common language among the population, followed by French and then German. Since 1970, the Belgian territory comprises four linguistic regions: the Dutch-speaking region, the French-speaking region, the bilingual region of Brussels-Capital and the German-speaking region.[1] The decentralised unitary State has also evolved into a federal political model. The federal power has two

[1] Art. 4 of the Constitution: 'Belgium comprises four linguistic regions: the Dutch-speaking region, the French-speaking region, the bilingual region of Brussels-Capital and the German-speaking region.

Each municipality of the Kingdom forms part of one of these linguistic regions.

The boundaries of the four linguistic regions can only be changed or corrected by a law passed by a majority of the votes cast in each linguistic group in each House, on condition that a majority of the members of each group is present and provided that the total number of votes in favour that are cast in the two linguistic groups is equal to at least two thirds of the votes cast.'

We would like to stress that *Regions* and *linguistic regions* are two different legal concepts. The first is one of two kinds of federate entities while the second refers to an administrative division of the territory. Regarding federate legislative powers, the Belgian federal system has the peculiarity that territorial jurisdiction of Communities and Regions almost match without overlapping. For example, the Walloon Region's geographic scope covers the German-speaking region (also administered in this specific linguistic region by the German-speaking Community) and the French-speaking region (also administered for some matters by the French Community). On the other hand, the French Community's scope of action covers the bilingual region of Brussels-Capital (which is also the territory of the Brussels Region) as well as the French-speaking region (meaning the territory of the Walloon Region without the territory of the German-speaking Community). On the Flemish side, the Flemish Region territory corresponds to the Dutch-speaking region whilst the territory of the Flemish Community covers the Dutch-speaking region as well as the bilingual region of Brussels-Capital. Therefore both Communities are competent on the territory of the bilingual region of Brussels-Capital.

official languages - French and Dutch - and a language of official translation – German.[2] All federal institutions are organised on the basis of a division between the two main linguistic groups (Dutch and French).[3] The principle of linguistic equality between groups is applied to the Federal Government,[4] the Constitutional Court[5] all the way through to the division of the federal high civil services[6]. The Belgian federalism is thus seen as a *bipolar federalism*. In addition to the federal power, three Communities[7] –Flemish, French and German-speaking– and three Regions[8] –Brussels-Capital, Flemish and Walloon– have been created as federated entities.[9] Since constitutional revisions of 1970 and 1988, language use policy[10] and education policy[11] are allocated to Communities, under any reserves for the benefit of federal power.[12] Each Community is free to implement the educational model it wants.

---

[2] Law of May 31, 1961 concerning the use of languages in presentation, publication and entry of force of laws.

[3] German speakers are around 70,000 over 10 million inhabitants. The Constitution does not guarantee them a political representation inside the federal government.

[4] Art. 99 of the Constitution: 'The Council of Ministers is composed of no more than fifteen members.

With the possible exception of the prime minister, the Council of Ministers is composed of an equal number of Dutch-speaking members and French-speaking members.'

[5] Special Law of Jan. 6, 1989 on the Constitutional Court, Art. 31: 'The Constitutional Court shall be composed of twelve judges: six Dutch-speaking judges, who form the Dutch language group of the Court, and six French-speaking judges, who form the French language group of the Court. The title of Dutch-speaking judge or of French-speaking judge of the Constitutional Court shall, for the judges referred to in Article 34 (1) (1) be determined by the language of their degree, and for the judges referred to in Article 34 (1) (2) by the parliamentary language group to which they last belonged.'

[6] S. Weerts, 'L'emploi des langues à la lumière de la réforme Copernic', 3–4 *Administration publique* (2005) p. 339 at p. 349; F. Delpérée, 'L'équilibre du recrutement dans la fonction publique belge', 118 *Revue française d'administration publique* (2006) p. 307 at p. 319.

[7] Art. 2 of the Constitution: 'Belgium comprises three Communities: the Flemish Community, the French Community and the German-speaking Community.'

[8] Art. 3 of the Constitution: 'Belgium comprises three Regions: the Flemish Region, the Walloon Region and the Brussels Region.'

[9] About the Belgian Constitution, explained article by article, see M. Verdussen (ed.), *La Constitution belge. Lignes et Entrelignes* (Le Cri 2004). About the Belgian Federalism, see M. Uyttendaele, *Précis de droit constitutionnel belge. Regard sur un système institutionnel paradoxal* (Bruylant 2005); F. Delpérée, *Le droit constitutionnel de la Belgique* (Bruylant/LGDJ 2001).

[10] Art. 129 of the Constitution.

[11] Art. 127 of the Constitution.

[12] Art. 30 of the Constitution.

No constitutional provision restricts the exercise of this power, except the respect of individual liberties enshrined in the Constitution.

Considering that at the federal level, institutions are mainly based on a linguistic duality and considering that each linguistic group has a relatively homogeneous linguistic territory, except for the constitutional bilingual territory of the region of the Brussels-Capital, it is not surprising that the Communities –which have the power to regulate education and language use within the region of their language and the bilingual region of Brussels-Capital– have opted for a monolingual system of education, especially for higher education such as in universities. At a time when the 'bipolarity' of Belgian federalism is more than ever questionable,[13] the development of a bilingual education system to create social and political cohesion can be imagined as a –late– tool to counter the lack of common vision that endangers the political stability of the federal State. The aim of this paper is to analyse whether a legal basis for the creation of a bilingual education in universities within Community education law adopted by the French and Flemish Communities exists or is at least constitutionally or legally possible. The underlying assumption will be the decisive social influence of bilingual or multilingual education to allow individuals to move beyond exclusive identifiers and frequent minority issues. Independently of the status of a linguistic group in the State, the social cohesion created through bilingual education can also be applied to sustain the reinforcement – or even creation – of a federal citizenship in a multilingual context.

In order to understand the Belgian context well, the first section of the paper is devoted to the origins of this monolingual system of education in a multilingual state. The focus is put on the underlying function of the language in higher education. The second section offers, from a constitutional point of view, a presentation of the share of competences in education and language use in Belgium as a legal basis for

[13] Hugues Dumont explained that Belgian law was mobilised by specific political projects that endanger the Belgian federal system. See H. Dumont, 'La mobilisation du droit comme instrument de changement du cadre national en Belgique', in P. Noreau and J. Woehrling (eds.), *Appartenances, institutions et citoyenneté* (Wilson & Lafleur 2005) p. 87 at p. 107 ; H. Dumont, 'Saint-Polycarpe ou l'impossible cohérence du fédéralisme belge' ([The] Saint Polycarpe [agreements] or the impossible coherence of Belgian federalism), 2-3-4 *Administration publique* (2002) p. 314 at p. 319. Also H. Dumont and S. van Drooghenbroeck, 'The status of Brussels in the hypothesis of confederalism', 10 *Brussels Studies.be* (Oct. 1, 2007).

monolingual higher education. The third section discusses the reception of the Europeanisation of education as a factor of change of the rules of language use in universities. The fourth and last section concludes by highlighting the options for creating a bilingual higher education.

B. Origins, Reasons and Purpose of the Share of Powers on Education and Languages

1. *Origins: The Difference of Status between French and Dutch in the 19th Century*

It is generally accepted in Belgian constitutional history that issues of education and languages are those that crystallised the strongest political tensions.[14] The first resulted in *Le pacte scolaire* (school pact) of 1959. The second led to the country's division into linguistic regions in 1962.[15] Both have very old historical roots and are considered to have polarised Belgian society. Indeed, education was initially the preserve of the Church. Since the French (1795–1815) and Dutch (1815–1830) occupations, the political power invested in the creation of official schools. At the university level, the Catholic University of Louvain was established in 1495 – on what would become Belgium territory. William of Orange, King of the Netherlands who reigned over the Belgian provinces from 1815 to 1830, founded in 1816 the first state university with the University of Ghent and modernised the University of Liège in 1817. After the Belgian revolution of 1830, the National Congress adopted the Constitution in February 1831. Article 17 of the Constitution stipulates that:

> Education is free; any preventative measure is forbidden; the repression of offences is only governed by law or decree….

With the adoption of this constitutional article, the question of the organisation of education generated differing visions between the upholders of a state intervention in education and the partisans of the liberal logic. These visions reflected fundamental ideological

[14] V. Mallinson, 'Education in Belgium', 3 *Comparative Education Review* (1967) p. 285 at p. 287.

[15] The linguistic regions are mentioned in Art. 4 of the Constitution.

differences, which also embodied a political division between the Catholics and Liberals, and later between Catholics and Socialists.[16] While the Belgian State already had catholic universities and official universities, the constitutional academic freedom allowed for a new type of university, outside the pale of the church or the State. In this particular case, Liberals established the *Université libre de Bruxelles* (ULB) in 1834. Thus, two main categories of academic institutions stood in the landscape of higher education in 19th century Belgium: state universities (as those in Ghent and Liège) and private higher education institutions called the *réseau libre* (free universities or non-state-controlled universities). Within these free universities, two subcategories emerged: on the one hand, denominational universities (the main one being the *Université catholique de Louvain*) and on the other hand, non-denominational universities (as the Free University of Brussels, *Université libre de Bruxelles*). Development and democratisation of higher education throughout the 20th century then led each of these networks to be joined by other institutions.

In terms of languages, the Belgian revolutionaries of 1830 repelled the Dutch out of the nine southern provinces. The Netherlands recognised the Belgian State and its borders under the Treaty of London of April 19, 1839. Thus, during the early years of the Belgian state, the need to single out the Dutch regime was important. Although a large majority of the population spoke Dutch[17] (or Flemish dialects) the Belgian authorities made a clear choice for the French language. French was declared the official language of the Belgian State through the rules on disclosure of official acts.[18] The legislator also outlawed the use of Dutch in education.[19] Universities that were still operating in Latin were requested to use French. Indeed, political leadership being in the hands of the French-speaking bourgeoisie was all the more reason for choosing French. Other languages were identified with underprivileged and less educated social classes. Flamingo, Walloon, Picard, or

---

[16] About the education policy in Belgium, see H. Dumont, *Le pluralisme idéologique et l'autonomie culturelle en droit public belge, vol. 1: de 1830 à 1970* (Bruylant 1996) p. 97 at p.11; J. Fitzmaurice, *The politics of Belgium: unique federalism* (Hurst 1996) p. 29.

[17] K.D. McRae, *Conflict and compromise in multilingual societies: Belgium* (Wilfrid Laurier University Press 1986) p. 64.

[18] Pandectes belges, V° *langue flamande* (Larcier 1897) p. 787.

[19] For a chronological analysis, see N. Bonbled and S. Weerts, 'La liberté linguistique', in M. Verdussen and N. Bonbled (eds.), *Les droits constitutionnels en Belgique* (Bruylant 2011) p. 1085.

Low German were thus relegated as accessory local dialects despite being the communication tools of the majority population.[20] The language cleavage between the official language and dialects had a strong social footprint. The territorial division was marked between the roots of different dialects, some close to the French and others of Germanic origin such as Flemish. Whilst the authorities adopted French, they wrote in the Constitution of 1831 an article devoted to the free use of national languages.

> The use of languages current in Belgium is optional; only the law can rule on this matter, and only for acts of the public authorities and for legal matters.

Thus, in the early years of its existence, the Belgian State generated a perfectly legal contradiction: on the one hand, the desire to guarantee citizens the freedom of language and, on the other hand, public authorities choosing to speak only French without any obligation for persons in public service to learn Dutch. However, the idea of limiting the constitutional freedom was enshrined in Article 30. These limitations, however, specifically address acts of the public authorities and judicial matters.

The limitation was not due to the law but to the facts. It created an implicit limitation of linguistic freedom for people who did not speak French and this limitation was rapidly perceived as unfair. In addition, State officials and judges, solely educated in French, invoked also the benefit of linguistic freedom to choose their language when confronted with Dutch-speaking citizen's demand for the use of their own language in their dealings with authorities. French was less widespread in Belgian society than Flemish dialects. Thus, limiting the freedom of language was clearly in contradiction with the principle of equality among citizens. In this context, the Flemish organised a social and political movement, the 'Flemish movement' (*Vlaamse Beweging*).[21] Its initial goal was that of recognising its language as an official language of the State followed by the necessity to create an adequate linguistic organisation of the State. The standardisation of Flemish into a standard Dutch language and development of cultural material were therefore essential and fundamental for Flemish

---

[20] McRae, *supra* n. 17, p. 64.

[21] See E. Witte, E. Gubin and J.-P. Nandrin, G. Deneckere, *La nouvelle Histoire de Belgique, vol.1: 1830–1905* (Complexe 2005) pp. 149–165.

speakers. In this case, a broad recognition of the Dutch culture started in 1856 with an official commission on Flemish grievances.[22] From a legal standpoint the first language legislation dating from the 1880s primarily concerned the right to use both languages in administration and in justice.[23] It was certainly not intended to limit the freedom of language, as permitted under Article 30 of the Constitution, but rather to ensure that every citizen could use both French and Dutch with public services and, in any event, within administrations and courts located in the northern provinces of the country.[24] These laws, however, did not achieve the desired goal, that is, to ensure the effectiveness of constitutional liberty in the use of languages. No obligation of linguistic knowledge was imposed on the civil servants and magistrates who were educated in French. Despite the adoption of the Law on the publication of legislation – called Law on linguistic equality[25] – prescribing that all the laws must be adopted and published in French and in Dutch,[26] the implementation of this linguistic equality remained weak due to the lack of provision requiring the knowledge of Dutch for judges and officials and, above all, due to the lack of offer of higher education in Dutch. Few legal matters – as criminal law and criminal law procedure – were indeed taught in Dutch at the University of Ghent.[27]

In brief, the idea of a bilingual society was finally admitted but actual linguistic implications for French-speaking authorities remained non-existent. The lack of university legal education in Dutch has been one of the obstacles to the development of official use of Dutch, especially on the part of persons entitled to hold public office. Thus, two

---

[22] McRae, *supra* n. 17, pp. 24 and 56.

[23] Law of 17.08.1873 concerning the use of Flemish language in criminal matters, Law of 22.05.1878 concerning the use of Flemish language in administration, Law of 15.06.1883 concerning the use of Flemish in schools. See P. Maroy, 'L' évolution de la législation linguistique belge', *Revue de Droit Public* (1966).

[24] This positive approach is considered by historians as a new break in the liberal philosophy of the State (see Witte et al., *supra* n. 21, p. 149. From a constitutional point of view, it indicates also a certain conception – quiet unusual at that time – of the linguistic freedom as a positive right, which needs to be implemented through the intervention of the legislator. More than that, it also shows that the linguistic freedom was not interpreted as a freedom of the private sphere, but as an individual right in the public sphere.

[25] J. Clement, *De taalvrijheid. Bestuurstaal en Minderheidsrechten. Het Belgisch Model* [The linguistic freedom. Administrative language and minority rights. The Belgian Model] (Intersentia 2003) pp. 206–217.

[26] Law of Apr. 18, 1898 concerning the use of the Flemish language in official publication, *Moniteur belge* (Official Journal) May 15, 1898.

[27] Maroy, *supra* n. 23, p. 459

options were possible: the development of bilingual educational institutions or the establishment of independent institutions, each monolingual.

2. *Reasons and Purpose for Developing Flemish Unilingual Universities*

New language laws were adopted around 1930.[28] Their purpose was no longer to say that people could exercise their freedom in choosing a particular national language, but to define the languages of public services according to their location and territorial coverage. The results of the decennial census carried out in Belgium were then used as the basis for identifying language areas and languages to be applied accordingly. The majority language used in each *commune* (municipality) became the principal rule to define language use, but minority languages could also be used in relationships with public authorities if a certain percentage of minority language speakers were available. This link with the linguistic definition of the territory was also applied to official educational institutions with the Law of July 14, 1932, thus organising the use of languages in lower and middle education. Ghent University, a state university, established in one of the provinces of Flanders, also adopted Dutch as both the administrative and teaching language. It was the same for the University of Liège, established in the French-speaking province of Liège. The free universities –the *Université catholique de Louvain* and the *Université libre de Bruxelles*– adopted a system of bilingual education in some faculties on the basis of a halving of their sections. In 1935 the first Flemish students began a complete program of legal studies in Dutch at the Free University of Brussels.[29]

The development of a range of higher education programmes in Dutch was aimed at providing officers of the Belgian civil service as well as judges and lawyers with the knowledge of Dutch. This would

---

[28] The legislator adopted many laws concerning the use of languages in public services: the Law of July 31, 1928, which was replaced by the Law of June 28, 1932 (about those laws: J. Clement, *supra* n. 25, p. 398 at p. 406). The Law of June 15, 1935, still in force, concerns the use of language in judicial matters (see L. Lindemans, *Taalgebruik in gerechtszaken* [The use of languages in judicial matters] (story-Scientia 1973). The Army had their own law concerning the use of languages (Law of July 30, 1938 concerning the usage of languages in the Army). Concerning education the Law concerned only primary and secondary school: Law of July 14, 1932 organising the use of languages in primary and secondary school.

[29] www.vub.ac.be/home/historiek.html

guarantee the effectiveness of the principle of linguistic freedom. However, the provision of education did not guarantee that people would effectively study in Dutch or use it in administrative and judicial life. In addition, the process of determining the language of administrative services, including municipal, which was based on the language census, generated many doubts. Significant variations in results were recorded between censuses resulting in changes to the language rules of the municipal authorities every time. It also appears that despite the measures taken by the legislature, French continued to enjoy a dominant social status.[30] The use of censuses as an objective criterion for defining the language proportions of the Belgian population understandably ended up being rejected by the Flemish.[31] They argued for a definitive territorial organisation that would prohibit any change of languages in public services. They also claimed direct management of the territorial space in terms of language, their education and their administrations.

After a lengthy parliamentary work (1957–1962), the first political compromise was reached on the linguistic territorial organisation of public services: the legal recognition of linguistic regions.[32] In the new geographical framework, utilities had to operate in the official language of the locality in which they were established.[33] Private educational institutions such as the *Université catholique de Louvain* were initially still free – in accordance with the constitutional freedom – to function in French, even if established in a locality in which the administrative language was now Dutch. Such a practice would however be

---

[30] M. Dumoulin, E. Gerard, M. Van den Wijngaert and V. Dujardin, *Nouvelle Histoire de Belgique, vol. 2: 1905–1950* (Complexe 2006) p. 144 at p. 145.

[31] E. Witte and H. Van Velthoven, *Langue et politique: la situation en Belgique dans une perspective historique* (VUBpress 1999).

[32] Law of Nov. 8, 1962 (modifiant les limites des provinces, arrondissements et communes et modifiant la loi du 28 juin 1932 sur l' emploi des langues en matière administrative et la loi du 14 juillet 1932 concernant le régime linguistique de l'enseignement primaire et de l'enseignement moyen), Moniteur belge 22.11.1962. In 1970, the notion of linguistic region was then placed in Article 4 of the Constitution: "Belgium has four linguistic regions: The French-speaking region, the Dutch-speaking region, the bilingual region of Brussels Capital and the German-speaking region. Each «commune» (county borough) of the Kingdom is part of one of these linguistic regions. The limits of the four linguistic regions can only be changed or modified by a law adopted by majority vote in each linguistic group in each Chamber, on the condition that the majority of the members of each group are gathered together and from the moment that the total of affirmative votes given by the two linguistic groups is equal to at least two-thirds of the votes expressed."

[33] New linguistic laws were collected as the Coordinated Laws of July 18, 1966 concerning the use of languages in administrative matters.

quickly denounced by the Flemish. The direction of the university chose to duplicate all courses in each language and implemented bilingualism in its administration. Hence, the *Université catholique de Louvain*'s experience was that of fully bilingual university in Belgium. This experience was however short-lived.[34] Events were organised in Leuven to seek the expulsion of the French-speaking people from the city. This resulted in a major political crisis leading to the collapse of the government and a deep rift within the Catholic Church and national political parties split by language. In 1968, the Catholic Church finally accepted the idea of dividing the Catholic University of Louvain into two universities, one Dutch (*Katholieke Universiteit van Leuven*, KUL) remained in the city of Leuven, the other francophone (*Université catholique de Louvain*, UCL) that moved to a French-speaking region and built a new city, Louvain-la-Neuve. The strong shock of this crisis in the largest university of the country had a ripple effect, splitting the Free University of Brussels into two separate entities, one Francophone (ULB), the other Dutch-speaking (VUB), both located on the territory of the bilingual region of Brussels-Capital.

Thus, both official and free universities, higher education in general, in the late 1960s, became unilingual and the responsibility of unilingual institutions. This split between Dutch and French was deep and reinforced the desire for autonomy of each language group. A constitutional reform on the institutional level became inevitable.

C. Federate Entity, Powers in Matters of Language and Education: Constitutional Basis for Unilingual Higher Educational Institutions

Since the constitutional revision of 1970, the Regions have the legislative power in areas related to economic, environmental or urban planning, while Communities have the legislative power for culture and language use. In 1988, education was added to their legislative power.[35] The territorial jurisdiction of these entities is also distinct. The Regions are based on a provincial division, except for the Brussels-Capital Region

[34] Coordinated Laws of July 18, 1966 concerning the use of languages in administrative matters extended the scope of entities that are obliged by linguistic rules. Private companies and schools must then use the language of their geographical region. Up to then, a special regime was fixed for the Catholic University of Louvain (Art. 51 of the coordinated laws), *Moniteur belge* Aug. 2, 1966.

[35] Delpérée, *supra* n. 9, p. 232.

which is limited to nineteen municipalities, whilst the territorial jurisdiction of Communities is based on the linguistic regions and in the case of the bilingual region of Brussels-Capital, the Flemish and French are both competent, providing public services in their respective language. The sharing of powers between federal power, Communities and Regions is exclusive.[36] Hence, in matters of education, Article 127 of the Constitution explicitly assigns the power to regulate to the Flemish and French Communities:

> § 1. The Parliaments of the Flemish and French Communities, each one in so far as it is concerned, regulate by federate law:
> 1) cultural matters;
> 2) education, with the exception of:
> a) the setting of the beginning and of the end of compulsory education;
> b) minimum standards for the granting of diplomas;
> c) the pension scheme;
> 3) cooperation between the Communities, as well as international cooperation, including the concluding of treaties for those matters referred to in 1) and 2).
> A law adopted by a majority as described in Article 4, last paragraph designates the cultural matters referred to in 1) and determines the forms of cooperation referred to in 3), as well as the specific arrangements for the concluding of treaties referred to in 3).
> § 2. These federate laws have the force of law in the Dutch-speaking and French-speaking regions respectively, as well as in those institutions established in the bilingual region of Brussels-Capital which, because of their activities, must be considered as belonging exclusively to one Community or the other.

Therefore, the two most important Communities legislate on education for the respective linguistic region as well as on the territory of the Region of Brussels-Capital for the institutions that belong, due to their activity, to one or the other.[37] Concerning the use of languages, Article 129 states that:

---

[36] See A. Alen, *Belgium: Bipolar and centrifugal federalism, Text and documents* (Ministry of Foreign Affairs, External trade and Cooperation for Development 1990); Delpérée, *supra* n. 9, p. 603.

[37] The German-speaking Community - grouping together a population of 70,000 inhabitants - has, by virtue of Art. 130 (1) of the Constitution, a less vast competence:

> The Parliament of the German-speaking Community regulates by federate law:
> 1° cultural matters;
> 2° person-related matters;

> § 1. The Parliaments of the Flemish and French Communities, to the exclusion of the federal legislator, regulate by federate law, each one as far as it is concerned, the use of languages for:
> 1° administrative matters;
> 2° education in the establishments created, subsidised or recognised by the public authorities;
> 3° social relations between employers and their personnel, as well as company acts and documents required by the law and by regulations.
> § 2. These federate laws have the force of law in the Dutch-speaking and French-speaking regions respectively, except as concerns:
> • municipalities or groups of municipalities adjacent to another linguistic Regions and in which the law prescribes or permits the use of another language than that of the Region in which they are located. For these municipalities, a change to the rules governing the use of languages in the matters as described in § 1 may be made only by a law adopted by a majority as described in Article 4, last paragraph;
> • services whose activities extend beyond the linguistic region within which they are located;
> • federal and international institutions designated by the law whose activities are common to more than one Community.

Once again the French and Flemish Communities are competent to determine the rules of language use in a large part of their administrative services including educational institutions created, subsidised or recognised by the public authorities. Some educational institutions are nevertheless beyond the competence of Communities in terms of education. The linguistic status of the Royal Military Academy, part of the organisation of the Army, which is a federal institution based on the bilingual region of Brussels-Capital, is bilingual as part of the federal power but divided in two teaching sections

---

> 3° education, within the limits established by Article 127, § 1, first paragraph, 2°;
> 4° cooperation between the Communities, as well as international cooperation, including the conclusion of treaties, for matters referred to in 1°, 2° and 3°;
> 5° the use of languages for education in establishments created, subsidised or recognised by the public authorities.

The German-speaking Community has only one higher education institution, the *Autonome Hochschule in der Deutschsprachigen Gemeinschaft*. This institution offers a program of formation in health care. The German-speaking Community has no specific linguistic law concerning higher education. But there is a decree that governs language use in the other levels of education (Decree of Apr. 19, 2004 concerning the transmission of linguistic knowledge and the use of languages – *Dekret über die Vermittlung und den Gebrauch der Sprachen im Unterrichtswesen* (*Moniteur belge* of Nov. 9, 2004).

each monolingual.[38] Private educational institutions that do not receive financial support from Communities are also theoretically free to choose the language of their educational program.

There is a fundamental difference between Articles 127 and 129 of the Constitution in terms of territorial jurisdiction. Article 127 stipulates that Communities legislate on education in their language region and on the territory of Brussels-Capital for the institutions that affect them. However, in terms of use of languages, Communities are only competent to regulate the use of languages in their respective regions and under certain internal limits. The Constitution remains silent as to the Brussels-Capital Region where several academic institutions are established. This means that on the territory of the Brussels-Capital Region, the organisation of education is shared between the two Communities. However, regarding their power to adopt rules on language use, the two Communities are not competent on the territory of the Brussels-Capital Region. In the absence of special attribution to the Communities, the legislative power on language use in the bilingual Region of Brussels-Capital is a residual power of the federal authority.[39] Therefore, what happens for the use of languages in education on the territory of the Brussels-Capital region? This issue was clearly raised by the Dutch associations of teachers who questioned more generally the implementation of the reform of higher education in the Flemish Community. The Constitutional Court held that in light of the provisions challenged, it was necessary to distinguish the concept of 'language of education' and the 'administrative language' in the field of organisation of education:

> B.12.1. Contrary to the decrees that regulate the use of languages in education, decrees that regulate the teaching have legal force under Article 127 (2) of the Constitution, respectively in the French-speaking region and in the Dutch-speaking region, and the institutions established in the bilingual region of Brussels-Capital which, because of their activities, must be regarded as belonging exclusively to one or the other community.

[38] Law of July 30, 1938 concerning the usage of languages in the Army.

[39] Art. 35 of the Constitution implies that federal power is only competent for matters expressly attributed by the Law. The Communities and the Regions are competent for the others matters. The law attributing those matters to the federal power has not been so far adopted and institutional laws have attributed matters to the Communities and the Regions.

> B.12.2. Communities may, by order, establish criteria, particularly in the areas of language, showing that, in their view, a school of Brussels-Capital belongs to one or the other Community.
>
> In what they express that the administrative language and the language of education of the establishments of higher education is Dutch, the contested norms must, as regards the institutions of education established in the bilingual region of Brussels-capital, be considered not as establishing a regulation of the use of the languages for the education, in the sense of the Article 129 (1) (2) of the Constitution, but as determining, by application of the Article 127 (2) of the Constitution, the criteria on the basis of which higher education institutions established in the bilingual region of Brussels-capital must, because of their activities, 'be considered as belonging exclusively to' the Flemish Community.
>
> B.12.3. The criticised norms derive then from the competence of the decretal legislator. They do not violate the competence of the federal legislator in use of the languages in the bilingual region of Brussels-capital or at the federal linguistic legislation.[40]

For the Constitutional Court, the regulation of language in education or in educational institutions has been interpreted as an extension of the power of Community to regulate education. This interpretation

[40] Constitutional Court no. 44/2005 of Feb. 23, 2005, B.12.1 to B.12.3 :

> B.12.1. Contrairement aux décrets qui règlent l'emploi des langues dans l'enseignement, les décrets qui règlent l'enseignement ont force de loi, en vertu de l'article 127, § 2, de la Constitution, respectivement dans la région de langue française et dans la région de langue néerlandaise, ainsi qu'à l'égard des institutions établies dans la région bilingue de Bruxelles-Capitale qui, en raison de leurs activités, doivent être considérées comme appartenant exclusivement à l'une ou à l'autre communauté.
> B.12.2. Les communautés peuvent, par voie de décret, fixer des critères, notamment dans le domaine de la langue, faisant apparaître, à leur estime, qu'un établissement d'enseignement de Bruxelles-Capitale appartient à l'une ou à l'autre communauté.
> En ce qu'elles énoncent que la langue administrative et la langue d'enseignement des établissements de l'enseignement supérieur est le néerlandais, les dispositions attaquées doivent, en ce qui concerne les institutions d'enseignement établies dans la région bilingue de Bruxelles-Capitale, être considérées non pas comme constituant une réglementation de l'emploi des langues pour l'enseignement, au sens de l'article 129, §1er, 2°, de la Constitution, mais comme déterminant, par application de l'article 127, § 2, de la Constitution, les critères sur la base desquels les institutions d'enseignement supérieur établies dans la région bilingue de Bruxelles-Capitale doivent, en raison de leurs activités, 'être considérées comme appartenant exclusivement à la Communauté flamande.
> B.12.3. Les dispositions critiquées relèvent dès lors de la compétence du législateur décrétal. Elles ne portent pas atteinte à la compétence du législateur fédéral en matière d'emploi des langues dans la région bilingue de Bruxelles-Capitale ni à la législation linguistique fédérale.

has the merit of allowing a degree of consistency in language education policy. It is also part of a broader process of redefinition of the judicial power to regulate the use of languages in the federal legislature.[41] In this sense, the question of language use in education on the bilingual territory of Brussels-Capital or in the unilingual regions will anyway require the intervention of the Communities.

Finally, the constitutional share of powers and its judicial interpretation gives a large autonomy to the Communities to organise their education on their linguistic territory and on the territory of the bilingual region of Brussels-Capital. The creation of a bilingual higher education institution has to be decided by each Community, except in the case of educational institutions linked to federal power. Considering the linguistic character of Communities, such an option could seem very hypothetical. However, and despite that the Communities have been created to protect the language and their culture, limited bilingual education programmes within the network of free higher education institutions have been proposed since 1992 in the bilingual region of Brussels-Capital.[42] Other than this limited and very progressive experience, the linguistic question remains sensitive between the two groups who view each other warily. Nevertheless, the legal framework is evolving towards more for openness to bilingual higher education in the light of new legal rules on the organisation of higher education under the influence of the Bologna process.

D. The Evolution of the Linguistic Law of Higher Education As a Means to Participate in a Multilingual International Order

Following the adoption of the Bologna declaration, each Community launched a legislative process of revision.[43] Two decrees were

---

[41] For an analysis of the jurisprudential redefinition of competences of language use, see N. Bonbled and S. Weerts, 'La liberté linguistique', in M. Verdussen and N. Bonbled (eds.), *Les droits constitutionnels en Belgique* (Bruylant 2011) p. 1069 at p. 1119.

[42] The *Facultés Universitaires Saint-Louis* (FUSL) and the *Katholieke Universiteit van Brussel* (KUB) created a bilingual program for the first two years of the study of Law (*candidatures en droit*).

[43] About universities in the French Community, see M. Molitor, *La transformation du paysage universitaire en Communauté française* (7/8 CRISP 2010) n° 2052–2053. Due to the fact that, as mentioned below, the German-speaking Community has not adopted a specific linguistic law concerning its only higher educational institution, we will focus on the two main Communities. Nevertheless, the German-speaking

respectively adopted: the decree of April 4, 2003 of the Flemish Community concerning the restructuring of higher education in Flanders[44] (the decree of April 4, 2003) and the decree of March 31, 2004 of the French Community defining Higher Education, facilitating its integration in the European Space of Higher Education and re-financing universities[45] (the decree of March 31, 2004). With the adoption of those decrees, the Communities wanted to create the legal background to participate in the Europeanisation of higher education, which included the question of mobility of students. Although the process of Bologna dealt very little with the language question – only with regards to diplomas –, it is certainly one of the most important questions to resolve at the national level if public authorities want to create the legal basis for universities to welcome those students who will only come to study a few terms in Belgium. In this context of European mobility, English appears as the preferred language to create a 'friendly linguistic environment'. From a national point of view, however, the use of English can be seen as a dangerous risk of impoverishment of a less expanded language in the medium-and long-term, especially if all research, books, lectures and talks are in English. Furthermore, it can also be seen as dangerous in a multilingual State if citizens preferred to firstly study an international language instead of the other national languages of the country. In this case, the political dilemma between the will to succeed in the Europeanisation of higher education and the importance of language in education as a tool to strengthen the status of language has been put forward to both Community legislators. The Flemish and the French-speaking legislator responded by elaborating specific rules for the use of languages (1.). The Flemish Parliament,

---

Community adopted two decrees regarding the European reform of higher education: the special Decree of Feb. 21, 2005 and the Decree of June 27, 2005, both were creating a higher educational institution.

[44] *Moniteur belge*, Aug. 14, 2003

[45] *Moniteur belge*, June 18, 2004. In the case of the French Community, it must also be mentioned that other decrees have been modified or adopted to regulate higher education in the context of Bologna: Decree of June 16, 2006 about cooperation agreements concerning joint programmes between Universities (*Décret du 16 juin 2006 relatif aux conventions de coopération pour l'organisation d'études entre institutions universitaires et portant diverses dispositions en matière d'enseignement supérieur)*, Decree of Aug. 5, 1995 fixing the general organisation of Higher Education in the Hautes Ecoles (*Décret du 5 août 1995 fixant l'organisation générale de l'enseignement supérieur en hautes écoles*), Decree of May 17, 1977 concerning Artistic Higher Education (*Décret du 17 mai 1999 relatif à l'enseignement supérieur artistique: article 29*) and Law of Feb. 18, 1977 concerning Architecture Higher Education (*Loi du 18 février 1977 relative à l'organisation de l'architecture: Art. 2*).

which is even more sensitive to the issue of the protection of its language, completed its legal arsenal, nevertheless, with several provisions to protect the use of Dutch (2.).

1. *Official Language of the Communities and Legal Rules to Admit the Use of Another Language*

As mentioned, both decrees contain several measures regarding the question of language. Indeed, they concern two aspects: the administrative language and the language of education of universities.

First of all, the Community legislators took care of determining the administrative language of their university establishments.[46] Remaining completely in line with the linguistic policy based on the territorial linguistic distribution, every institution has the obligation to use the official language of the Community to which it belongs. In addition, the institutions in each Community can establish cooperation agreements with other institutions outside the French or Flemish Communities. In other words, they can cooperate with other universities – using another language – but they remain nevertheless linked to their official language. The Flemish Community and the French Community assert that their 'official' language is not only the language of education, but also the 'language of evaluation' of this education. Without doubt, for the administrative language or for the language of education/evaluation, the rule is thus, the unilingualism of Community language. In addition, the students must explicitly or implicitly prove their knowledge of the language of education.[47] This suggests that despite the language policy as defined by Community legislators, it should not be allowed for Belgian universities to drift towards an all-in-English education driven by the logic of the smallest linguistic common denominator in the Europeanisation of higher education. However, both Communities have added a series of exceptions, which vary from Community to Community.

In the Flemish case, the decree presents a mechanism to preserve the vitality of the 'official' language. Indeed, for the universities of the *Flemish Community*, the legislator regulates three situations. In principle,

[46] Art. 21 of the Decree of the French Community stipulates: "§ 1er. La langue administrative des établissements d'enseignement supérieur est le français." Art. 90 of the Flemish Decree reads: "La langue administrative dans les instituts supérieurs et les universités est le néerlandais".

[47] Art. 49 of the Decree of the French Community.

the first relates to bachelor's and master's degrees. In line with the general rule concerning language use, it requires university programmes at these two levels to be organised in Dutch. But courses can also be organised in another language: at the bachelor's level, these cannot exceed 10 percent of the ECTS credits. At the master's level there is no explicit limit or quota, which leads to believe that other languages could be largely employed, although not in all the courses of the program. To this the Flemish legislator adds another series of exceptions:[48] firstly, he allows the organisation of tuition in another language if the subject studied concerns that very language – for example a degree in Spanish –; secondly, another language can be used if some subdivisions of the tuition are taught by foreign language speaking professors – in the case of the mobility of academics – and the same in the case of the mobility of students (this exception could alter significantly the application of the linguistic law); and thirdly, another language can be used if the program is offered in cooperation with other universities that are not part of the Flemish Community (i.e., universities of the French Community or foreign universities).[49] If the first exception is obvious, the following two –foreign language speaking guest professors and joint programmes with other universities– demonstrate a linguistic policy of genuine openness towards offering a bilingual education.

The decree of 2003 adds yet a fourth exception, which could turn out as much more vague. It is based on the hypothesis that there are 'serious indications that the tuition in another language than Dutch would provide a 'capital gain (increase in value)' or would add a 'particular' feature'.[50] In this case, the legislator requires the following two conditions: one, that the university will need to communicate an act of motivation to the Minister of Education and two, that the Board of the institution must maintain the dominant part of the training program in Dutch. It remains that the appreciation of the 'capital gain' or the 'feature' of the measure confers a real power to university institutions to set up not only a bilingual education, but also a complete training program in another language.[51] Despite the principle of education in

[48] Art. 91 (1) (2) of Decree of Apr. 4, 2003.
[49] Art. 91 (1) (2) of Decree of Apr. 4, 2003
[50] Art. 91 (1) (3) of Decree of Apr. 4, 2003.
[51] In this case, this opportunity is well used by Flemish universities as it can be see on the website: Study in Flanders (www.studyinflanders.be/en/study-programmes) presenting 225 university programmes from bachelor to advanced master (12 law programmes) taught in an another language then Dutch.

Dutch, with these exceptions, the Flemish legislator provides so many dispensations that universities end-up with the right to offer a full educational program in another language than Dutch. This freedom is given to institutions for the tuition of bachelor's or master's degrees open to foreign students. One very important prerequisite must be met in order to benefit from this allowance: a non-Dutch program can be implemented only as far as an equivalent program is also offered in Dutch within the territory of the Flemish Community.[52] Summing up, the decree of April 4, 2003 consents to two types of linguistic policy: the obligatory use of Dutch while tolerating certain dispensations (when the programm includes foreign teachers, or it concerns the study of foreign languages, or the use of another language does not exceed a certain number of ECTS); and the complete use of another language but under certain conditions (when it is a joint venture programm, or the same programm is already offered in Dutch, or the programm is open to bachelor or master students). One could already say that this legal framework constitutes a real change of paradigm in the organisation of education, which had been dominated at every level by the principle of the exclusive use of Dutch. These rules do not oblige universities to build bilingual programmes but rather demonstrate that bilingual education is feasible in the Flemish Community. In this sense, it is a complete change of attitude from the perspective of the Flemish legislator whereas a strict unilingual model was secured as it was claimed in the past.

In the French Community, the decree does not show the same level of audacity and not the same amount of detail as its Dutch-speaking counterpart. The linguistic organisation of education and evaluation varies only according to the level of university education. At the bachelor's level, the program can contain, from the second year on, one-fifth of the ECTS credits in another language.[53] At the master's degree level, half of the ECTS credits can be taught in another language.[54] As for advanced master's degrees and doctorates, they can be organised entirely in another language. Bilingualism is thus gradually permitted throughout university education. Increasing the foreign language proportion per level of education could even end up with a complete program in a foreign language at the highest level. With this logic of a university

[52] Art. 91 (2) and (3) of Decree of Apr. 4, 2003. The requirement for an equivalent education given in Dutch is not required when a program of courses is offered to foreign students as part of the International Program for Development Cooperation.
[53] Art. 21 (2) (1) of Decree of Mar. 31, 2004.
[54] Art. 21 (2) (2) of Decree of Mar. 31, 2004.

education that can gradually pass from French to another language (English), the legislator of the French Community added a dispensation at the master's level.[55] Thus, the government can grant the authorisation to organise a program in another language when the subject studied has an 'international character deriving from the excellence of the scientific field or from its particular nature'.[56] Just as with the Flemish Decree, this sort of exception makes it possible for universities to teach in another language than the official language of the Community.

It already emerges from this presentation that both the Flemish and the French Community have to fix the frame of the linguistic regime of their educational system. In this case, there is a sequencing of the linguistic law of education according to the level of studies which lays the foundations for the development of a much more complex linguistic policy for higher education – and much broader than the one that we have known since the 1970s. Indeed, in both Communities, the introduction of an education in another language varies according to the level of the diploma. Their respective point of departure is to enable a gradual inclusion of students in a bilingual education scheme and in both cases legislation allows for a monolingual education in a non-official language. For both Communities, this whole process fosters the international development of a new *lingua franca*, English. Since 2001, when the Flemish Parliament was seized by the proposal of the decree to modify the linguistic regime of these universities,[57] it was faced with a dilemma:

> (…) attracting international students through the provision of (mostly postgraduate) programmes taught in widely spoken languages and the recruitment of international staff who teach in another language. At the same time it preserves the status of Dutch as a language for academic and scientific work.[58]

The need to find a *modus vivendi* between openness to other languages and linguistic protection has been underlined by the Belgian Constitutional Court:

> B.13.1. The undertaken measures fix the conditions upon which education is authorised in another language than Dutch: on the one hand, the

[55] French Decree of July 20, 2005, *Moniteur belge* of Sept. 1, 2005.
[56] Art. 21 (2) (3) Decree of Mar. 31, 2004.
[57] Documents, Flemish Parliament, session 2000–2001, no. 530/1 to 3.
[58] Follow-up of the Action Plan on Languages Learning and linguistic diversity, National report Template, Belgium (Flemish Community), p. 5, http://ec.europa.eu/education/languages/archive/policy/report/benl_en.pdf.

> use of another language is authorised for subdivisions of programmes whose object is a foreign language and which are taught in this language; on the other hand, the use of another language is authorised only on condition that the programmes subdivisions are taught by foreign speaking professors, are organised for the needs of foreign students or for some particular programmes.
>
> B.13.2. These measures belong to the education legislator's competence since some exist for settling education while others are connected to other measures of the decree which establish a new structure in higher education, which are being integrated into a wider European context. It emerges from the elaboration of the proposed measures that linguistic regulations are dictated by the (Flemish) legislator's concern to guarantee the full participation of the Flemish Community in international exchanges in research and teaching in an European and worldwide context (Doc., Flemish Parliament, on 2002–2003, n°1571/1, p. 30).[59]

For the Court, the organisation of linguistic education belongs to the competence of the Communities, which are supposed to advocate the use of their language. In today's context of higher education, the Court considers it legitimate for certain measures to be taken by the legislature in order to allow universities to participate in the new European Area of Higher Education, which implies the adoption of a certain policy of bilingualism. Finally, the Court identifies no specific obligations for the Communities to 'defend' their linguistic identity at the level of higher education though it has been argued in other areas of language use and even at other levels of education. As mentioned, this change could nevertheless turn out to be dangerous for the preservation of less widely spoken European languages. Thus, the Flemish Community has provided a series of important institutional and individual guarantees to face the expansion of a language other than the official language in Education.

2. *Mechanisms of Guarantee within the Framework of Teaching in Another Language*

Keen to supervise its openness to the *lingua franca*, the Flemish legislator has elaborated a series of mechanisms of guarantee, the efficiency of which is still too early to estimate in terms of linguistic policy. These mechanisms are of two types: institutional mechanisms and individual mechanisms.

---

[59] Constitutional Court no. 44/2005 of Feb. 23, 2005.

At the institutional level, the organisation of a complete program in another language than Dutch is subjected to various controls. First of all, universities have to announce to the government the programmes that they organise and indicate the language that will be used.[60] This allows the government to exercise control over the linguistic policy of all universities whether public or private. In addition, every university is required to send an annual report on the usage of another language other than Dutch to the government and to the Flemish Parliament.[61] This report must outline the objectives of its policy of education in another language, as well as the results obtained based on quantitative data and the implemented legal data. Finally, the decree requires universities to establish a code of ethics on the use of languages, to be inserted into the statutes of studies and examinations.[62]

At the individual's level, Dutch-speaking students are guaranteed within the Dutch-speaking territory the right to study at university level in their own language. Thus, an education in another language than Dutch is only allowed if the same curriculum is taught in Dutch in its geographical proximity. On the other hand, depending on the level of education, a student always has the right to take examinations in Dutch, except when the subject studied is a particular language or when teaching in another language has been demonstrated to generate a capital gain.[63]

Without consulting each other, the Flemish and French Communities have emphasised their official language in the sphere of education. They have also tried to manage the question of students and academics' mobility by providing legal measures in which education can be provided in another language. In this respect, the measures of the Flemish Community by far exceed those of the French Community.

---

[60] Art. 123 and 125, Flemish Decree of Apr. 4, 2003 provide that higher education institutions must present their program offer including the language in which they are given to their government. For the first time, this information has been published as part of the Flemish Government Order of Febr. 13, 2004 establishing the list of courses of Bachelor and Master Degrees in higher education (*Moniteur belge* of Aug. 31, 2004). According to that list, about 15 percent of university and college programmes are proposed in English.

[61] Art. 91 (6) of Flemish Decree of Apr. 4, 2003.

[62] Art. 91 (5) of Flemish Decree of Apr. 4, 2003. Some of these information are available on the website of universities: Catholic University of Leuven (KUL): http://kuleuvent.be/onderwijs/aanbod2009/info/algemeen/e/060403.htm# 44; University of Antwerp (UA):

[63] Art. 91 (2) (6) of Flemish Decree of Apr. 4, 2003.

From a legal point of view, those measures could really create a policy of bilingualism[64] in higher education, in which case the linguistic dilemma in education will be to find a mechanism whereby English -or another language- can be used without endangering the official language of each Community. Having seen the context of Belgian sensitivity over languages in education, the speed at which language options were taken by the two legislators in the Bologna process, without further discussion, is frankly baffling. Furthermore, the language question in the reform of higher education in Belgium was not aiming at strengthening the bilingualism of the Belgian State. It did not concern relations between French and Dutch peoples but rather, to ponder the best way for a less extended European language to maintain its social status within its own community and, at the same time, attract foreign students at higher levels of education. Nevertheless, spurred by the Europeanisation of higher education, those new rules are not only reserved to English. An introduction of bilingual teaching in French / Dutch is made possible to a much wider extent. As before, however, nothing requires universities to take this route (French/Dutch bilingual programmes), especially where international attraction has become an internal educational issue.

E. Conclusions: Is There Still a Way to Create a Bilingual Higher Education in Belgium and Which One?

At the beginning of this chapter, we recalled that education policy and language use policy are both the competence of the Flemish and French Communities, but for very few exceptions. Organised as unilingual powers, these authorities adopt unilingual programmes of education. In this way, a paper on bilingual education in higher education in Belgium could be seen as an outdated subject in today's Belgian legal context. The linguistic-political tensions in Belgium show nonetheless that the issue of languages is still not resolve or poorly resolved. We also have assumed the hypothesis that bilingual education can help to resolve this question. From a legal point of view, the question was then

[64] Nevertheless, it appears that those measures are seen as too restrictive by higher educational institutions to response to their policy of internationalisation. See the report of M. Kirsch and Y. Beernaert, *La diplomation double, multiple et conjointe en Belgique. Un défi Intercommunautaire* (Fonds Prince Philippe 2009) p. 28 (available at www.kbs-frb.be).

to evaluate if a legal framework exists to create this bilingual higher education.

We underlined firstly the purpose of the linguistic educational policy in Belgium: creating an effective equality between Dutch and French through the law. A monolingual education and the strict division of the national territory have been considered as the only way to create this equality between languages and speakers. Due to the historical background and the share of competences in education between Communities, which is considered as the heart of their autonomy, the option to create bilingual programmes has been chosen by free universities which have tested together a bilingual joint program. This experience took place in the bilingual region of Brussels-Capital, and was strictly limited to two free universities.

Secondly, against all expectations, the Bologna process has focused the attention of Community legislators on the question of languages in higher education in Belgium. Fortunately, this revival has not made the French / Dutch issue a new phoenix. The question of languages has moved to another plan: the relation between national languages and English in higher education. The process has led both legislators to think about their linguistic policy in higher education and has created a new point of convergence between the two educational systems due to the fact that both want to keep their universities in the run of competition. In this way, both have changed their legislation to allow the creation of bilingual programmes. This change is first and foremost to help provide education in English. From a legal perspective it has nonetheless created the legal conditions to develop any kind of bilingual programmes in Belgium. However, this implies that stakeholders still find interest in developing a policy of French/Dutch bilingualism in Belgium. In this way, we must underline the private initiative of 'Prince Philippe Fund' set up in 2004 to expressly strengthen the links between Communities, with a student exchange program modelled on the European exchange program Erasmus, for increasing student mobility within Belgium: *Erasmus Belgica*. This – small – program is now even subsidised by the Flemish and French Communities.[65] Having come a long way, we can thus say that today in Belgium

[65] In 2005–2006, 242 students from the French Community have partly studied in a higher educational institution of the Flemish Community and 120 students from the Flemish Community came to study in the French Community (Parlement de la Communauté française de Belgique, Commission de l'Enseignement supérieur et de la

educational language law in both Communities provides the legal framework to create a bilingual policy in higher education. The question is no longer whether a bilingual higher education in Belgium is legally possible but rather whether it is still politically desired. Public subsidies from the Communities in *Erasmus Belgica* lead to believe that this option - though hardly audible in a climate of politico-linguistic tensions - could be discreetly moving on…

---

recherche scientifique, compte-rendu integral, Session 2006–2007, no. 50, p. 3). The annual average of students from the French Community going in the Flemish Community turns around 260 students (Parlement de la Communauté française, Commission de l'Enseignement supérieur et de la recherché scientifique, compte-rendu integral, session 2010–2011, no. 47, p. 3).

CHAPTER FOUR

THE SWISS PARADOX: MONOLINGUAL HIGHER EDUCATION IN A MULTICULTURAL ENVIRONMENT

Nicolas Schmitt

A. Introduction

Two specificities of the Swiss system could be of interest for readers from other countries: its federalism and its multiculturalism. These two elements of the political thinking represent the cornerstone of the Swiss identity. But how do they articulate within the frame of (bilingual) higher education?

This chapter tries to answer the question. But in doing this we shall discover a paradox: if Switzerland is a multicultural and multilingual *state*, federalism transfers the linguistic question to the *cantons*. And at the cantonal level, the principle of territoriality (see 3.3.) means that most of the cantons are monolingual. As education is a competence that belongs to the cantons, due to the constitutional allocation of powers between Confederation and cantons, the result is that higher education in Switzerland remains almost purely monolingual, despite the so-called multilingual frame of the country.

Among the four official languages of Switzerland (German, French, Italian and Romansh), two can be considered as more endangered than others: Italian and Romansh. Both these are an issue for concern with the European Charter for Regional or Minority Languages. A brand new federal law foresees some means to protect these two idioms. Moreover, the newly opened University of Lugano is the only university working with an "endangered language", Italian, but it remains primarily monolingual.

Examples of *bilingual* higher education are therefore very seldom, and depend upon the goodwill of some cantonal authorities. The only example is to be found at the Law Faculty of the University of Fribourg, because political authorities, followed by academic authorities, have considered that bilingualism had to be supported in the canton at any price.

The conclusion of this study is that in Switzerland as elsewhere, the promotion of multilingualism and the defence of endangered languages requires a strong political will.

B. Federalism

1. *Federalism in General (a Reminder)*

As a matter of fact, the definition of a federal state is not so easy. For instance, Spain is considered by all experts as a fully fledged federation, although its constitution does not mention the word *expressis verbis.*

But despite many differences, a few common characteristics distinguish federal systems from other kinds of government. The most important is the existence of *at least two orders of government*, one for the whole country and the other for the regions (states, *Länder*, autonomous communities, cantons etc.).

Moreover, in a Federal system, a written constitution formally allocates legislative, including fiscal, powers to the two orders of government ensuring *some genuine autonomy for each order.* However, federations differ greatly in the way and extent to which they define distinct powers for the two orders. Traditionally, if foreign relations and defence are given to the national level, health and *education* belong to the topics which are dealt with at the regional level, as they are supposed to have stronger links with local communities.

As a result, if there is an essence of federalism, it is that there are two constitutionally established orders of government with some genuine autonomy from each other, and the governments at each level are primarily accountable to their respective electorates.[1] This feature creates quite complicated systems. Denis de Rougemont characterised federalism as a "love of complexity, in comparison with the rough simplicity of totalitarian regimes".[2]

2. *Federalism is Switzerland*

Switzerland, covering an area 41,285 square kilometres and located in the heart of Europe, is home to 7.785,800 people (2009)[3].

[1] G. Anderson, *Federalism: An introduction* (Forum of Federations 2008).

[2] He said that during the inaugural conference of the first Congress of the European Union of federalists in Montreux on Aug. 27, 1947; see D. de Rougemont, 'L'Europe et la crise du XXe siècle', 3 *L'Europe en formation* (2006) p. 33.

[3] <www.ofs150ans.ch>

Its distinguishing feature is the diversity: there are two main religions, three main geographical areas, four national languages, 26 cantons, ca. 2,600 municipalities (the number varies constantly because of the tendency to merge municipalities), and a kaleidoscope of local cultures and specificities. Switzerland is not a nation in the traditional sense of the term but a *Willensnation* forged by the desire of its citizens to renew constantly the links that unite them: "Together, we defend the right to remain different."[4] It is this very unity in diversity that makes Switzerland a paradigm of political integration. The Preamble to the Swiss Constitution expresses the determination of the cantons "to live together with our diversities, with respect for one another and in equity." The defence and promotion of cultural and linguistic diversity of the country can be considered as a constitutive or even ontological element of the theory of the Swiss state and cultural policy[5].

The 26 cantons composing Switzerland are enumerated in Art. 1 of the Constitution and the local autonomy is guaranteed in Art. 50 (1). It means that there is a large allocation of powers between the centre and the periphery; and an important part of the Swiss Constitution (henceforth, SC) organises this allocation of powers. Switzerland is the most decentralised federation in the world (with Canada second), and as such cantons enjoy a wide range of tasks and duties.[6]

This very strong diffusion of power among several authorities can be considered as the very essence of the Swiss system. This characteristic has a strong influence on the topic we are dealing with, because only federalism can offer so easily a room to manoeuvre to regional communities.

C. The Swiss Linguistic Constitution

1. *Historically: The Birth of the Constitutional Provisions*

If multilingualism can be currently considered as a constituent element of Switzerland, this has not always been the case. The old Confederation of XIII Cantons (1513) was almost exclusively German-speaking, with

[4] D. de Rougemont, *La Suisse ou l'histoire d'un peuple heureux* (L'Age d'Homme 1990) p. 18.

[5] A. Previtali, 'Le plurilinguisme suisse entre droit et réalité', 2 *Gesetzgebungsbulletin/Bulletin de législation* (2005) p. 19 at p. 22.

[6] R. Watts, *Comparing Federal Systems*, 3rd ed. (Montreal 2008).

the exception of Fribourg. There were some "Roman" languages, but not in the "fully fledged" cantons, only in some subordinated territories. After Napoleon's invasion in 1798, and the introduction of the equality of citizens before the law, the country started considering its multiculturalism. During the "Helvetian Republic" (1798–1803) laws were written in the three languages. But this equality between languages was abandoned with the end of the Helvetian Republic, and after Napoleon's collapse in 1815 German became again the unique language. But the idea of equality of languages remained in the minds and was institutionalised in the 1848 federal system.

The 1848 and 1874 Constitutions contained a provision enshrining the equality between the three national languages. In 1938, in order to strengthen the national unity in a troubled period, Switzerland recognised also Romansh as the fourth national language[7]. This process (insisting on diversity in order to reinforce unity) is the best proof that preservation and promotion of cultural and linguistic diversities were the basis of the national cohesion. But the 1938 amendment created a distinction: for technical reasons which are quite easily understandable, Romansh was recognised as national language, but not as official language.

Another amendment of the linguistic constitution took place in the 1990s. Its aim was to enshrine the possibility to take measures in order to facilitate understanding and exchanges between communities, but also to safeguard Romansh and Italian. After the redrafting of the Federal Constitution in 1999, the provision concerning the four national languages became a provision *per se* at the beginning of the text (Art. 4), and the provisions devoted to the protection of linguistic diversity also became an article *per se* (Art. 70)[8].

Switzerland's four national languages are German (spoken by 63.7 percent of Swiss), French (20.4 percent), Italian (6.5 percent), and Romansh (0.5 percent) – each of which is of equal importance.[9] If the

---

[7] Romansh is spoken only in the Canton of Graubünden, the only trilingual canton in Switzerland, where it is the official language alongside German and Italian. Romansh is not so much a single language as it is a collection of five dialects. Migration and economic development have increased the number of German speakers in the canton, to the extent that Romansh is gradually disappearing, exacerbated by the fact that it does not benefit from sharing the linguistic culture of a large neighboring country.

[8] For more details see D. Thürer and T. Burri, 'Zum Sprachenrecht der Schweiz', in Christoph Pan and Beate Sibyle Pfeil (eds.), *Zur Entstehung des modernen Minderheitenschutzes in Europa* (Springer 2006) at p. 242.

[9] The remaining 8.9 percent (mostly immigrants) speak several other languages.

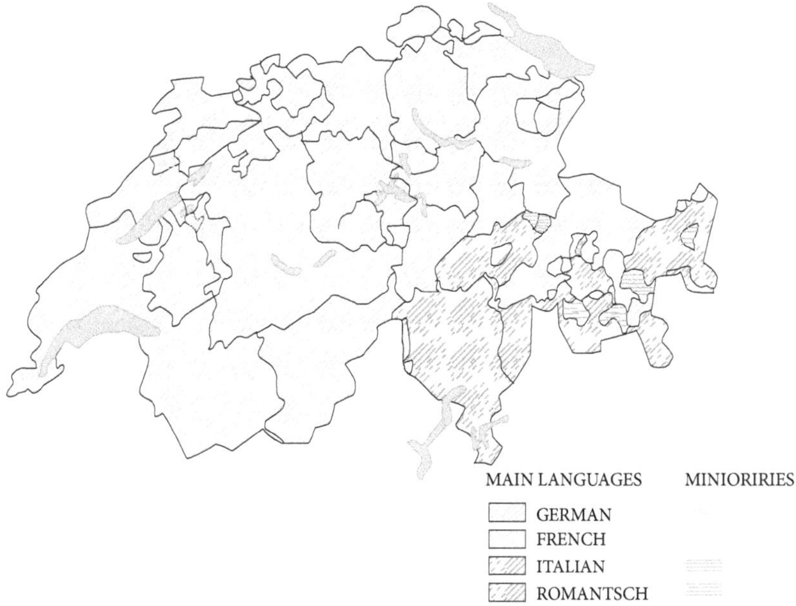

Figure 1: The four linguistic zones in Switzerland.

three official-language versions of a federal law differ, it falls to a judge to choose the one that best conveys the will of the legislator because no language has precedence over the others. Romansh speakers may use Romansh in their official dealings with the federal administration; thus in federal-government matters, Romansh is a semi-official language. As the Confederation wishes to preserve and promote linguistic diversity, according to Article 70 (3) it is obliged to provide financial support to the four multilingual cantons in order to help cover the costs of working in multiple languages (e.g., bilingual schools, translation services, and publication of laws in several languages).[10]

But it would be wrong to conceive the country as a "mosaic" of languages.[11] In fact, languages are allocated according the so-called principle of territoriality (see 3.3.). As it is possible to see on the map above, Switzerland is divided into three main linguistic zones: a German one

---

[10] A. Previtali, 'L'encouragement du plurilinguisme en Suisse, l'exemple du domaine scolaire', 4 *Aktuelle Juristische Praxis / Pratique juridique actuelle (AJP/PJA)* (2000) p. 379.

[11] University of Montreal (ed.), *La mosaïque suisse: les représentations de la territorialité et du plurilinguisme dans les cantons bilingues*, <www.cerium.ca/La-mosaique-suisse-les>, visited July 26, 2011.

at the border with Germany, a French one at the border with France and an Italian one at the border with Italy. Romansh is scarcely secluded in one canton.

Multilingualism in Switzerland does not mean that people communicate in several languages and take an interest in several cultures. Switzerland knows rather a certain "social multilingualism".[12] It is composed of four quite homogenous linguistic communities, which communicate with difficulty with one and another and have little interest for the culture of their neighbour. This reality is quite away from the beautiful principle enshrined in the constitution. It represents even a corruption of the constitutional ideal.[13]

Therefore, the question of bilingualism in the higher education could not be discussed in another canton than a bilingual one. There are no universities in Valais and Graubünden, a mostly German-speaking one in Bern, and therefore Fribourg is the only one suitable for this study (see section F below).

2. *Legally: The Swiss Linguistic Territoriality*

The Swiss linguistic constitution is based upon four principles which are (1) equality of languages, (2) freedom of citizens concerning the language, (3) territoriality of languages, and (4) protection of minority languages.

Following the principle of *equality*, the four national languages at the federal level have the same legal status and are legally equal. According to the principle of *freedom*, all Swiss citizens have the right to use the language they prefer, but in reality the jurisprudence of the Federal court has always given priority to the principle of *territoriality* to the expense of freedom of language. Therefore this third principle, the territoriality of languages, represents the cornerstone of Swiss linguistic law. The four linguistic zones remain almost exclusively monolingual. Even in a city crossed by the linguistic border (e.g. Biel/Bienne or Fribourg/Freiburg), territories remain monolingual and respect this border the Swiss call "Röstigraben".

It also means that federal and cantonal authorities should never try to modify current linguistic borders. As such, these borders have not been moved for more than 1000 years. In Switzerland, the practice

[12] M. Borghi, 'Langues nationales et langues officielles', in D. Thürer, Müller and Aubert, *Droit constitutionnel suisse* (Schulthess 2001) p. 593 at p. 596.

[13] See Previtali, *supra* n. 5, p. 24.

establishes the supremacy of territorial separation of languages upon any other consideration. The federal government does not define the linguistic borders but cantons do, and they can transfer this power to local authorities (as in Graubünden). Finally, the fourth principle means that, according to Swiss law, the Constitution guarantees the preservation of the four national languages and forces special measures to be taken in order to protect Italian and Romansh.

3. *The Principle of Territoriality*

a. *The Principle of Territoriality in the Federal Court's Case-Law*

The principle of territoriality, which plays such an important role in Switzerland, is based upon the fact that every language is historically linked to a certain territory. The preservation of the linguistic composition of a territory should avoid the fact that an indigenous language disappears in favour of a foreign language.[14]

According to the court's jurisprudence, the principle of territoriality implicitly derives of Art. 116 of the old (1874) Federal Constitution (henceforth, SC 1874), which recognises the existence of four national languages as well as their traditional geographical allocation.[15] As cantons have the power to legislate on all fields which have not been transferred to the Confederation (Art. 3 SC), they have the right to legislate on linguistic topics and to establish norms concerning the use of language in the relations between state and citizens. The Federal court states, cantons can base themselves on the principle of territoriality in order to take measures aiming at the upholding of the traditional borders of linguistics regions and the preservation of their homogeneity.[16] For that purpose, they have the right to restrict the freedom of any person to use its mother tongue, but these measures have to be proportionate and they should respect as much as possible the freedom and the dignity of citizens. But the Federal Court states also of the fact that Art. 116 (1) SC 1874 forbids cantons to oppress and endanger groups speaking a national language and forming a minority in a canton.[17] Moreover, cantons should not do anything in order to change the linguistic borders.[18]

---

[14] C. Marti-Rollin, *La liberté de la langue en droit suisse* (Zurich 1978) p. 36.
[15] See among others BGE/ATF 106 Ia 303.
[16] See BGE/ATF 106 Ia 303 [305].
[17] *Ibid.*, p. 302.
[18] See BGE/ATF 100, Ia 462 [466].

b. *Critics Addressed to the Principle of Territoriality*

In the doctrine, this principle is often questioned,[19] not as such but in the way it has been applied by the jurisprudence.[20] As the principle is too openly focusing on the preservation of traditional linguistic borders, it can drive a result which is exactly the contrary of its goal, which is the protection of minorities. The limitations of the freedom of language should rather be considered as a restriction (according to Art. 36 of the Constitution) rather than limitations of its object *a priori*, and as such submitted to the three conditions of legal base, public interest and proportionality.[21]

As a result, what has been primarily conceived as a principle aiming at the protection of minorities proved in practice to be an obstacle for these minorities. For instance, authorities of the canton of Zurich obliged French-speaking children in Zurich to go to a German-speaking school after two-years in a private French-speaking school.[22] Similarly, the small municipality of Graubünden, St. Martin, whose population is about 80 per-cent German-speaking, has not been obliged to create classes in which teaching takes place in Romansh. The Federal Court has decided that this municipality was also not obliged to pay the scholarships for the children visiting a neighbouring Romansh school.[23] Finally, it is also because this principle of territoriality that the German-speaking minority living in the small mountain municipality of Bosco-Gurin in the Italian-speaking Ticino does not deserve any mention in the cantonal constitution. This small municipality is yet the

[19] See A. Auer, 'D'une liberté écrite qui n'aurait pas dû l'être: la «liberté de la langue»', *Aktuelle Juristische Praxis / Pratique juridique actuelle* (1992) p. 955.

[20] See among others A. Papaux, 'Droit scolaire et territorialité des langues: bilan critique de la jurisprudence récente du tribunal fédéral', 40 *Revista de Llengua i Dret* (2003) p. 149.

[21] J.-F. Aubert and P. Mahon, *Petit commentaire de la Constitution fédérale de la Confédération suisse du 18 avril 1999* (Schulthess 2003) p. 562.

[22] BGE/ATF 91 I 480, case *Association de l'Ecole française*. In this famous case, the Federal Court had to decide on the use of French as teaching language in a private school in the German-speaking city of Zurich. In doing this, the Court insisted – what has been widely discussed – on the preservation of the German language in Zurich to the detriment of French. Therefore, it is surprising to see how many French-speakers insist on the principle of territoriality for the protection of minority languages, taking into account that this principle has been used to avoid the use of French in a German-speaking canton.

[23] BGE/ATF 100 Ia 462, *Derungs*. See also M. Borghi and A. Previtali, 'L'insegnamento in romancio e della lingua romancia nelle regioni di diffusione tradizionale di tale idioma', in 3 *Zeitschrift für Gesetzgebung und Rechtsprechung in Graubünden* (2003) p. 101.

only one where German is spoken in Ticino; the population speaks a so-called Walser-dialect. The second Report of the Expert Committee concerning the implementation of the Language-Charter of September 22, 2004, says about this topic: "It does not appear that any other measures exist to preserve German Walser in the municipality in question. […] The Committee of Experts considers that the above-mentioned development clearly shows that German (Walser) in the municipality of Bosco-Gurin is dying out: "The Committee of Experts encourages the competent Swiss authorities to take urgent measures to support German (Walser) in the municipality of Bosco-Gurin".

D. Monolingual and Bilingual Cantons

Because of the territoriality, if Switzerland is a multilingual *country*, in fact it is made of monolingual *cantons*. Twenty-two of them are monolingual, three are bilingual and one is trilingual.[24]

1. *Three Bilingual Cantons …*

Cantons of Fribourg, Valais and Bern are the *only* officially bilingual cantons of the Confederation. Official languages of the three cantons are German and French. But once again the principle of territoriality prevails: languages do not mix on the cantonal territory. No bilingual canton recognises German *and* French everywhere on its territory, even in a district.

In the cantonal parliament, MPs express themselves in the language of their choice: German, Swiss-German or French. Traditionally, laws are discussed in German in Bern and in French in Fribourg and Valais; they are then translated and promulgated in both French and German. Bilingual legal writing remains quite seldom (it has been the case for the new Constitution of Bern). In all other fields (justice, education, administration etc.), the language of the district prevails. Only one exception prevails in the cantonal administration based in the three cantonal capitals (Bern/Berne, Fribourg/Freiburg and Sion/Sitten) which answers in the language (French or German) of the citizen. It is the same principle at the federal level: centrally bilingual and locally monolingual.

[24] Domaine Public (ed.), *Pourquoi une crise linguistique "à la belge" n'est pas possible en Suisse*, <www.domainepublic.ch/articles/9717>, visited July 26, July 2011.

2. … *and One Trilingual Canton*

a. *Presentation of the Canton*

German, Italian and Romansh are the three official languages of the canton of Graubünden/Grigioni/Grishun. It encompasses 212 municipalities, which are officially German-speaking (about 60 percent), Romansh-speaking, Italian-speaking or mixed (about 30 municipalities). Bivio is even trilingual. German monolingualism has imposed itself quite easily in the German-speaking municipalities, but Italian monolingualism applies less easily in the Italian and Romansh municipalities. The Romansh monolingualism has been replaced by a Romansh and German bilingualism.

In the cantonal parliament, the three languages are authorised, but German dominates with more than 80 percent of parliamentary interventions taking place in German. The debates are held in German, and discussions made in Italian or Romansh are extremely seldom. Minutes are written in German only. Laws are usually written in German and then translated into Italian and sometimes Romansh, but the new law on languages obliges the canton to provide "equally binding" versions of laws. Usually, the cantonal administration, as well as courts, speak German, but it also answers to the citizens in the language of their choice, providing it is one of the three official languages of the canton. There are German, Italian and Romansh schools. The teaching of a second language is compulsory. Italian in the German schools, German in the Italian and Romansh schools and Romansh in the mixed municipalities. The latter define the teaching language. German-speakers living in a Romansh municipality follow lessons in German, but they have to learn Romansh as a second language; Romansh-speakers have to learn German as a second language.

b. *A New Law on Languages in the Canton of Graubünden*

On January 1, 2004, the new Graubünden Constitution entered into force. It contains an important provision devoted to languages, Article 3. This provision means that municipalities are no longer fully autonomous – as they were previously – to define their languages. They should take care of the established minorities and discuss with the canton. This should/could have a positive impact on municipalities where there is a weak Romansh community. In order to apply this constitutional provision, a "law on languages" has been adopted on October 19, 2006.[25]

Previously, the linguistic law of the canton was marked by a strong local autonomy: municipalities were free to choose one official language among the three official languages of the canton. Fundamentally, the new linguistic law of the canton will not change the system, but it foresees the division of the canton in one or two languages municipalities. In order to implement in a dynamic way the principle of territoriality at the cantonal level, it will be based on the last census. Monolingual are the municipalities where the minorities represent less than 10 percent of the population, and bilingual those where this proportion is between 10 and 50 percent. Municipalities are obliged to define their language in the so-called "local constitution" (*Gemeindeordnung*).

3. *The Principle of Territoriality during the Drafting of the New Constitution of Fribourg*

The situation in the bilingual canton of Fribourg is quite peculiar, as the French-speaking population (a minority at the federal level), represents on the contrary the majority at the cantonal level. 63.2 percent of the population speaks French and 29.2 percent German. From that point of view, the canton is a "reversed Switzerland". In the centre of the canton, along the linguistic border, there are two bilingual districts: Sarine/Saane (but here only the capital Fribourg is supposed to be bilingual although it is officially unilingual French-speaking with a certain tolerance for the German-speaking minority) and Lac/See.

Because of this special situation within the Swiss context, the French-speaking population is oversensitive. Many fear a "creeping germanisation" of the bilingual municipalities located on the linguistic border by an influx of German-speaking inhabitants. Therefore, they ask for a strict application of the principle of territoriality, which means that all newcomers have to adapt themselves to the traditional language of the community. But the reality described by the last census in 2000 shows that there is a slight homogenisation. In the Sarine district, where French predominates, French tends to increase slightly and it is

[25] Systematic collection of cantonal laws of Graubünden (BR) 492.100; it was the third attempt to adopt such a law, after unsuccessful trials in 1981 and 1985.

the same for German in the predominantly German-speaking district of See/Lac.

During the drafting of the new 2004 cantonal Constitution, the Constitutional Assembly faced a difficult question: should it enshrine *expressis verbis* the principle of territoriality? The French-speaking majority expressed itself in favour of such a guarantee, and after long and passionate debates it could impose its point of view. As such, the Constitution of Fribourg is the only one in Switzerland enshrining explicitly this principle. But one could doubt that this provision will change something in the reality. It has mainly psychological reasons and is due to the tensions between communities along the linguistic border. One has to remember the fact that a committee in charge of applying the principle of territoriality when it was first enshrined in the former cantonal constitution on September 23, 1990, abandoned its work after 10 years of unsuccessful debates.[26]

E. The Need for Political Will

As we have seen, Switzerland is supposed to be a multilingual state, but in fact it is rather a collection of unilingual cantons. Therefore, every attempt to strengthen bi- or multilingualism requires a strong political will.

1. *An International Incentive: The European Charter for Regional or Minority Languages*

Although Switzerland is not a member of the EU, it has been a member of the Council of Europe since 1963. On October 8, 1993, the Federal Council signed the European Charter for Regional or Minority Languages, a treaty whose aim is to promote the use of regional or minority languages where the public live and among others education, justice, administration, public services, medias, culture, economic and social life, as well as cross-border co-operation. The Charter was ratified on December 23, 1997 and entered into force for Switzerland on April 1, 1998. In the declaration contained in the instrument of ratification, the government declared, in accordance with Article 3 (1) of the Charter,

[26] B. Altermatt, *La politique du bilinguisme dans le canton de Fribourg/Freiburg (1945–2000)* (Fribourg 2003) p. 180.

that in Switzerland Romansh and Italian are the less widely used official languages to which a certain number of paragraphs (first of all, Art. 8 to 14) chosen in accordance with Article 2 (2) of the Charter, shall apply.[27]

The Charter entered into force on April 1, 1998, but it does not create new obligations for the Confederation or the cantons. According to the federal department of Interior,[28] it was judicious for Switzerland to join this Charter because the country "could face its international responsibilities and express in a concrete way its solidarity with other European states". But above all the ratification of the Charter allows Switzerland to "express its commitment to the problems concerning protection of minorities in Europe", which is in accordance with the new Constitution in force since January 1, 2000.

2. *A National Incentive: The New Law on Languages*

Taking into account the new 1999 constitutional frame (Art. 70(5) SC), the federal administration elaborated a law in order to implement the linguistic policy. Nevertheless, on April 28, 2004, the Federal Council decided not to submit this draft to the parliament. The government explained that this decision was due to the necessity to save money. But based upon a parliamentary initiative,[29] the Parliament decided to prepare its own draft. Once again, the Government expressed its opposition for reasons due to federalism (linguistic protection belonging exclusively to the cantons and the federal state should not interfere) and budgetary restrictions. But despite its opposition, the "Loi sur les langues, LLC" (Federal law on national languages and understanding between linguistic communities) has been passed by the parliament on October 5, 2007. It took then about three years to adopt the implementation regulations, and therefore the law entered into force on January 1, 2010 and the ordinance on languages on July 1, 2010.[30]

The ordinance rules four fields: (1) use of Confederation's official languages and the fostering of multilingualism in the public service; (2) measures to promote understanding and exchanges; (3) support for

[27] For all information: http://conventions.coe.int (consulted July 26, 2011).

[28] <www.admin.ch/cp/f/329B7AAC.7A1C@gs-edi.admin.ch.html>, visited July 26, 2011.

[29] Levrat 04.429, Loi fédérale sur les langues nationales.

[30] Systematic collection of federal laws (RS) 441.1; see A. Previtali, 'Della presunta inutilità della nuova legge federale sulle lingue nazionali', in 2 *LeGes* (2004) p. 177.

multilingual cantons; and (4) safeguard and promotion of Italian and Romansh languages and cultures.

3. *At the Cantonal Level: The Example of the University of Lugano*[31]

The two most endangered languages of Switzerland are Italian and Romansh. In order to strengthen "italianity", some personalities of the canton of Ticino have recently decided to create a university, because there was no Italian university so far. Nevertheless, according to the principle of territoriality, teaching in Lugano is basically in Italian, although the University tries to improve multilingualism, especially using English.

The University of Lugano (USI)[32] was founded in 1996, but the idea of a university had a much longer history. It was at the beginning of the nineteenth century that the first proposal for an institution of higher education was designed, addressing the aspirations of the Italian-speaking culture of Switzerland. In 1803, Ticino acquired sovereign status as a Canton of the Swiss Confederation. The realisation of the university project, however, required stronger demographic and economic resources than the Italian-speaking region of Switzerland could afford at that time.

USI was established by a law passed by cantonal parliament on October 3, 1995.[33] The first academic year opened on October 21, 1996 with some 300 full-time undergraduate students in three faculties. Besides Ticino residents, the initial student body included a number of students from the rest of Switzerland, Italy, and other countries.

USI, as the only Italian-speaking university outside Italy, promotes and preserves the culture of Italian Switzerland in the Swiss academia, and serves as a cultural bridge to Italy, especially thanks to its tight collaborations with the main universities of Lombardy (Northern Italy). While the official language at USI is Italian, some courses and entire Master programmes are taught in English. Knowledge of French and German is also encouraged. Basic and advanced courses in these four European languages prepare students for international careers. This again shows that bilingualism in the Swiss universities could foster English to the detriment of national languages.

---

[31] <www.usi.ch>, visited July 26, 2011.

[32] University of the Italian-speaking Switzerland (USI in Italian).

[33] Systematic collection of cantonal laws of Ticino (RL) 5.3.1.1.

At present the USI comprises the four following faculties: (1) Academy of Architecture in Mendrisio; (2) Faculty of Communication Sciences in Lugano; (3) Faculty of Economics in Lugano and; (4) Faculty of Informatics in Lugano. It means that there is no Law School in USI, in other words no legal education in Italian in Switzerland. It explains why many students from Ticino study law in Fribourg.

4. *At the Cantonal Level: Example of Fribourg*

Among the four bi- or multilingual cantons, Fribourg seems to be the only one trying to promote its bilingualism and to take advantage of. Examples of this are the bilingual University (see section G below), or the creation, on November 15, 2007, of the "Foundation for Research and Development of Multilingualism" and the "Institute for Research in Multilingualism and Multilingual Education", supported by the University and the Pedagogical High School. These efforts have been distinguished by the 2009 Swiss periodical report concerning the application of the European Charter for Regional or Minority Languages.[34]

F. The Question of Higher Education

1. *Higher Education and Languages*

As cantons play a major role in the implementation of the linguistic Constitution, they also play a major role in drafting the educational landscape. As a logical consequence of the principle of territoriality, education also takes place in a mostly monolingual frame. Therefore, the two most endangered languages, Italian and above all Romansh, are not so much concerned with higher education. There is no university in Romansh, and only a rather small one in Italian, which is also monolingual. That is another paradox: the two languages being most supported for their survival are not concerned with higher education.

If we consider that French is also a minority language, the topic of higher education in minority languages concerns only French, as there are French-speaking universities besides the German-speaking ones, although they are all monolingual. Fribourg remains the only bilingual

---

[34] <www.bak.admin.ch/themen/sprachen_und_kulturelle_minderheiten/00506/00509/index.html?lang=fr>, visited July 26, 2011.

university and the topic of bilingualism in the legal education concerns only Fribourg.

2. *Management of Universities*

According to Article 63 SC, the management of universities belongs to the cantons. Even if in the practice there is a close and intricate co-operation between cantons and the Confederation, the ground regulation belongs exclusively to the cantons. There is no federal law on universities, but only cantonal laws.

This means that cantons are free to organise their universities as they want. Currently, there are eight main universities (Zurich, Bern, Basel, St. Gallen, Fribourg, Neuchâtel, Lausanne and Geneva), some smaller universities (Lucerne, Lugano) and two federally managed high technical schools (Zurich and Lausanne).

Cantons negotiate and sign agreements (called *concordates* in Switzerland) on matters requiring interdependence, and they institutionalise their cooperation, often with the help of the Confederation. The Constitution is accommodating in this area, particularly through Art. 48, which authorises largely intercantonal treaties to such an extent that the reorganisation of financial equalisation and allocation of powers (RPT) gives the possibility of granting these treaties general binding force in certain circumstances. An interesting example concerns university policy. A "triangular" structure has been adopted. The aim was to give the Confederation, the university cantons, and the universities a joint body vested with real decision-making powers in this area of shared responsibility. The new 1999 federal law on assisting universities[35] has therefore delegated powers to the Swiss Universities' Conference. The university cantons had to conclude a *concordate* containing a parallel delegation rule, and an administrative convention organises the joint body and governs the details of its activities.

G. The University of Fribourg and Its Law Faculty

Located in the medieval town of Fribourg, just at the border between German and French communities, the University founded in 1889 is

[35] Loi fédérale du 8 octobre 1999 sur l'aide aux universités et la coopération dans le domaine des hautes écoles (Loi sur l'aide aux universités, LAU), RS 414.20.

currently ruled by a Law of November 19, 1997.[36] Article 6 (3) of that Law stipulates that "the University facilitates and develops the understanding between the persons of different languages and cultures; *it encourages in particular the bilingual studies in French and in German*" (emphasis added). Within the University, faculties also feel free to organise themselves and to promote the kind of program and specificities they want to emphasise on. Interestingly, in its draft dated April 2, 1996 concerning the law on University,[37] the cantonal government wrote:

> One of the characteristics and the forces of our University is its *bilingualism*. Art. 6 tends to underline this aspect, whilst prescribing the university to favour the understanding between persons of different languages and cultures. [...] The bilingual character of the University is a great advantage. [...] The University of Fribourg is one of the few in Europe where students can make all their *cursus* both in French and in German. *Even if it makes sometimes the organisation of lessons complicated and if it requires substantial means*, this possibility has to be favoured at the service of a better understanding between two of the main linguistic communities at the national but also European level. It is one of the assets, but also one of the responsibilities of the High School and the canton.

The University of Fribourg is therefore characterised by its bilingualism, not to mention its international character as well as its numerous specialisations in research and teaching. The Law Faculty has an excellent reputation, and based on the number of students is the third largest in Switzerland. The Faculty is very active in research and has many widely recognised publications and legal journals to its name. It contributes to legal practice through the many conferences held at the University, such as those on construction law, traffic law, civil liability law, family law, criminal law, and European law.[38]

The Faculty – as *the only fully bilingual Faculty in Switzerland and Europe* – offers students the possibility to complete their studies exclusively in German or in French or in German *and* French (bilingual studies) and in addition, couple this with a comprehensive introduction into the other language and culture («bilingue *plus*» see 8.2).

[36] Systematic collection of cantonal laws of Fribourg (RSF/SGF) 430.1.
[37] Projet de loi sur l'Université: 1996.318, p. 13–14 (own transl. and emphasis).
[38] For further information: Studies Guide - Law in Fribourg: <www.unifr.ch/droit/files/pdf/Guide-09-web.pdf>, visited July 26, 2011.

All courses are offered in French and German, and it is possible to study law in *one* language or in *both* languages.

H. Bilingual Mention and Formation "Bilingue *Plus*" at the Law Faculty

There are two ways of enjoying a bilingual formation in Fribourg: a special *mention* or even a special *formation.*

1. *The Special Mention "Bilingual"*

a. *At the Bachelor Level*
For those who wish to work as a lawyer in Switzerland it is necessary to have good skills in German as well as in French. For this reason the Law Faculty offers its students the possibility to complete their courses in French and/or German and in this way to earn the special mention «Bilingual».

The bilingual Bachelor can be earned in two ways:

(1) All the three blocks of exams are successfully taken in the *second study language.* In addition, one seminar is written in the second study language.
(2) At least 40 percent of the ECTS-credit points are earned in the *second study language.* In addition, one seminar is written in the second study language.

The *first study language* is the language in which the candidate takes most of his exams. The seminar can be replaced by a written report on legal practical training (done in the second language of study) lasting at least two months. The student who aims for the special mention «Bilingual» is recommended to enrol in the elective «Introduction to French legal terminology» or «Introduction to German legal terminology». The special mention «Bilingual» can be combined with the special mention «European Law» or «Religious Law»; it is required for participation in the formation «bilingue *plus*».

b. *At the Master Level*
The Law Faculty also offers students the possibility to complete certain courses in the second language, and in this way earn the special mention «Bilingual».

The special mention «Bilingual Master of Law» can be earned in two different ways:

(1) With the bilingual Bachelor of Law: at least 40 percent of the credit points in the Master degree have to be earned in the *second language*.
(2) Without the bilingual Bachelor of Law: at least 40 percent of the credit points in the Master degree have to be earned in the *second language*. A thesis must be written in the second language – a Master thesis or another written assignment, which must be accepted by a professor.

2. *The Formation "Bilingue Plus"*

The goals of this sophisticated formation «bilingue *plus*», which has been introduced in Fribourg in 2004/2005, could be summarised as follows: bilingualism *and* intercultural competence. The formation takes place on both a practical and a theoretical level.[39] It is enshrined into a University regulation.[40]

More precisely, the goals could be described as follows:

(1) Students communicate easily in the partner language, both on a specialised and a professional plan. They handle written and oral documents of the partner language, professionally or for private purpose. In particular, they are capable of drafting in an independent way a text which is clear and correct for a person of partner mother tongue.
(2) They can express themselves successfully to the paper and orally, in intercultural situations of the everyday life, in the professional life, and in situations appealing to a specialist language, to a level C1 according to the Common European Framework of Reference for Languages (CEFR).
(3) They are prepared for the situations of multilingual communication which they can analyse, and they are capable of operating the tools of decoding of the situations of interculturality to act by using the adequate strategies as mediator.

---

[39] For further information: <www.unifr.ch/bilingueplus>, visited July 26, 2011.
[40] *Règlement du 7 juillet 2008 sur les formations «Bilingue Plus»*: <www.unifr.ch/bilingueplus/assets/files/2008%2007%2007%20Rglt.pdf>, visited July 26, 2011.

(4) They adopt a constructive attitude towards persons stemming from the other cultures thanks to the knowledge and in acquired experiences in the field of the interculturality.
(5) They possess a deep knowledge on political, cultural and "civilisational" themes of current events in Switzerland, in Europe and in the world which make them sensitive to the political, historical and social aspects of the multiculturalism in Switzerland and in Europe. This raising awareness should help them to react to the situations of intercultural communication in the everyday life as in the professional environment.

This formation is unique in Switzerland. The bilingualism that is already deeply anchored in the Law Faculty is supplemented. To this end, students complete an additional study and career oriented training in their second language of study.

Further, students are sensitised on the questions of multiculturalism and multilingualism. They will gain practical and theoretical knowledge on the relationships between multicultural communities, in which historic, cultural, political and social aspects are taken into consideration. The goal is that the students who complete this training are able to speak and write effortlessly in their second language of study while working in administration or in business. In order to be admitted to the training, a language test is required as well as a personal consultation.

a. *At the Bachelor Level*[41]

The formation "bilingue *plus*" is distributed on four semesters. It consists of the program "Language and inter-cultural communication" in German or French, dispensed by the University Centre for Languages. It is enriched by the follow-up of a course of cultural deepening with choice among the offer of so-called CTC/soft skills courses (additional transverse skills) of the University.

The program "Language and intercultural communication" includes four hours a week over two years. In specific cases determined by the reader, the hourly distribution can be organised in the form of blocks-seminaries or in other forms. It consists of one module by semester, over two years that makes four modules. It is centred on the learning

[41] For all details, see <www.unifr.ch/bilingueplus/assets/files/planetudes_certificat(1).pdf>, visited July 26, 2011.

and the development of the necessary skills at the same time in the university and professional context in a frame of multilingual and inter-cultural communication. The students having carried out the program are all capable of reading and writing specialised texts, of leading a conversation or debate by considering the intercultural constituents of a negotiation. The current themes in the cultural and civilisational domains in Switzerland, Europe and the World, as well as themes related to the university education and the profession, constitute the foundations of the program in connection with the elements of interculturality. The objectives of the training rely largely on the CEFR, which allows the students to estimate their levels of linguistic skills through an international comparison. The lessons take place in small groups, generally limited to 15 persons, which allow for a wide measure of interactivity and an extensive individual coaching of the students.

b. *The Master Course*[42]

The master course is first of all composed of the module "Language, intercultural communication and multiculturalism." Lessons are also organised in small groups limited to 15 persons, which allows for a wide interactivity and an intensive coaching of the student.

Multilingualism and multiculturalism constitute the fundamental orientation of the module. Concrete projects put in relation themes and contents of the courses with the professional context. A particular importance is given to the deepening of the linguistic and intercultural skills of communication through readings, written and oral redrafting stemming from the specialised literature and from the collaborative projects, all done in multilingual groups. Intensification of language skills (presentations, oral and written dialogues, production of discursive kinds), applied by the diverse forms of "autoapprenticeship", mediation, as well as the collaborative work in tandem or workshops in a multilingual and multicultural context are nothing but few examples of the practical work offered to the students.

In the first semester, the course is concentrated on "Language in multilingual studies", and in the second "Multilingualism in the everyday life".

[42] For all details, see <www.unifr.ch/bilingueplus/assets/files/planetudes_diplome.pdf>, visited July 26, 2011).

3. *Remarks about the Program*

The goal of these programmes is to enjoy everyday life in a bilingual environment. Fribourg is a bilingual city, and therefore it allows for a real "immersion" in the "other" language. It is not necessary to follow a special *cursus* to enjoy the possibility to benefit from an immersion into a bilingual environment. The idea is not to offer this formation to students who are already bilingual, but to allow for the possibility of purely monolingual students to become real multicultural citizens. Therefore it starts with a special course called "Introduction in the French/German legal terminology."

The formation "bilingue *plus*" could be qualified as quite "elitist", because it is made with groups up to 15 persons, and it also costs CHF 500.- per semester. Every student is guided by a personal coach who supports their personal development. The goal is really to make these students sensitive even to the subtleties of the other language. A very simple example: in French it is common to write in a text "*We* are about to...", but this "*We*" is completely different in German where the *Pluralis Majestatis* is not used. Every year, about 25 per cent of the students start a bilingual formation, and at the end ca. 15 per cent of them arrive at the end. This means that almost half on the students cannot complete their studies with this additional mention.

Nevertheless, this bilingual education in Fribourg is a luxury, as it means that all lessons, courses, seminars, exams etc. have to be doubled in order to be given in French *and* in German. But it is not necessary to follow a special formation to have the opportunity to enjoy a special bilingual atmosphere in Fribourg, and sometimes the everyday life can prove to be as important as the lessons.

I. Conclusion

To guarantee the survival of endangered languages, it is necessary to rely on political will and affirmative action. Considering the example of Switzerland, the full constitutional recognition of four national languages in such a small country (and all legal and political implementation means which have followed, among others the permanent representation of minority languages in the government) has contributed to the peaceful *co-existence* of the diverse linguistic communities. It was not enough neither to protect the most minority languages (Italian and above all Romansh), nor to create a living multilingualism in the population. From that point of view, legal studies reflect this paradox: they are fully monolingual except in one canton which has taken great care to insist on its bilingualism to foster German and French studies at the university, in all other cantons, legal studies remain monolingual.

Federalism, openness of cantonal authorities, wisdom of the University of Fribourg and its Law Faculty, and dedication of all people who are engaged in these programmes which are not so easy to organise, make it possible for students to experience something that is unique in Europe and to improve dramatically their linguistic and legal skills. Language regulation in Fribourg represents an epitome of paradox: this canton is the only one to enshrine *expressis verbis* the principle of territoriality in its constitution, and at the same time it is also the only one to do the contrary, e.g. to allow for a fully bilingual legal education.

CHAPTER FIVE

IMPLEMENTING LINGUISTIC RIGHTS IN FINLAND THROUGH LEGAL EDUCATION IN FINNISH AND SWEDISH[1]

Markku Suksi

A. Introduction

Education in the field of law has a direct connection with the Finnish system of linguistic rights and their realisation.[2] Section 17, sub-section 2, of the Constitution of Finland gives the right to speakers of both Finnish and Swedish to use their language in dealings with courts and administrative agencies. These linguistic rights must be guaranteed on equitable grounds for both linguistic groups in social life as established in law, that is, in Acts of Parliament. In addition, section 122, sub-section 1, requires that in the organisation of administration, the objective shall be suitable territorial divisions, so that the Finnish-speaking and Swedish-speaking populations have an opportunity to receive services in their own language on equal terms.

At the same time, under section 79 of the Constitution, the Parliament of Finland enacts all legislation in both Finnish and Swedish,[3] and the Government issues its decrees in both national languages as well. These acts and decrees are published in both Finnish and Swedish in separate series of the Statutes of Finland. The norms

[1] I wish to thank dr. Kristian Myntti and dr. Johan Boucht for comments to a draft of this article and professors Johanna Niemi, Niklas Bruun and Dan Frände of the University of Helsinki for information concerning law studies at Helsinki and concerning legal literature published in Swedish in Finland as well as Mr. Henno Erikson Parks for the linguistic check-up. I am obviously alone responsible for the text.

[2] While the total number of inhabitants in Finland is 5.2 million persons, the Swedish-speakers are only 290,000, that is, around 5 percent of the population.

[3] As established in Section 51 of the Constitution of Finland with regard to the languages used in parliamentary work, "[t]he Finnish or Swedish languages are used in parliamentary work. The Government and the other authorities shall submit the documents necessary for a matter to be taken up for consideration in the Parliament both in Finnish and Swedish. Likewise, the parliamentary replies and communications, the reports and statements of the Committees, as well as the written proposals of the Speaker's Council, shall be written in Finnish and Swedish".

are equally authoritative in both languages. Government bills and reports and statements by the Committees of the Parliament also emerge in the two languages (although the Swedish version is, in most cases, a translation).[4] In fact, Finnish and Swedish are identified as the national languages of Finland in section 17, sub-section 1, of the Constitution, a characterisation that results in different types of linguistic arrangements, some of which are based on a combination of the personal principle[5] and territorial principle,[6] and some on a functional autonomy of some sort in a manner that may result in organising, for instance, education along a notion of "separate but equal". The legislation passed and published in Finnish and Swedish is hence also implemented in one of the two languages, depending on the language of the party.[7]

Several pieces of law exist that implement the constitutional requirement in section 17 of the Constitution. This legislation contains the Language Act (423/2003) and the Act on the Knowledge of Languages Required of Personnel in Public Bodies (424/2003), as well as a great number of substantive pieces of law, such as the Basic Education Act (628/1998), the Conscription Act (1438/2007), the Act on Courts of

---

[4] However, court cases are not issued in two languages, but in the language in which the case was initiated. Hence decisions of the Supreme Court or Supreme Administrative Court are mainly in the Finnish language, and only a small minority of them are in Swedish, probably even less than the share of the Swedish-speakers in the country would warrant, because for various reasons, Swedish-speakers or their legal counsel (which may be Finnish-speaking) may choose to use the Finnish language in the proceedings or because the courts are not always catering for the linguistic rights of the parties and carry out the trial in the language of the party in the case that the language would be Swedish. See *Report of the Government on the application of language legislation 2009*, pp. 53–59, at www.om.fi/en/Etusivu/1236880953561 visited May 18, 2010. Although a case is not handed down in two languages in its entirety, the two Supreme Court instances publish their case summaries in both Finnish and Swedish.

[5] The personal principle means that an individual has a subjective right to use his or her language in dealings with authorities.

[6] The territorial principle means that the country is divided into unilingually Finnish-speaking and unilingually Swedish-speaking municipalities and into municipalities that are bilingual with either Finnish or Swedish as the language of the majority of the population.

[7] In principle, the language of the party can be determined on the basis of the mother tongue and contact language that is registered on the basis of Section 13(1), number 20, of the Act on the Population Data System and the Certificate Services of the Centre of the Population Registry (661/2009). While this works well in some areas, such as tax administration (the taxation forms of are always mailed to the person in his or her mother tongue, Finnish or Swedish, wherever in Finland he or she is living), some other authorities, such as the police, the prosecution and courts are using the population registry much less frequently.

First Instance (581/1993) and the Local Government Act (365/1995).[8] The constitutional provision is also implemented by means of the Universities Act (558/2009), which establishes the universities as unilingual, either Finnish-speaking or Swedish-speaking, or bilingual.[9] It is important to notice that the Language Act, which sets up a general scheme for the application of the regime with two national languages, does not, according to section 3, sub-section 2, para. 1, of the same, apply to the universities, perhaps because they are not administered on the basis of territorial jurisdictions, but rather operate without any territorial jurisdiction. Instead, the Universities Act creates a linguistic determination of its own.

The origin of the Finnish linguistic regime is an oddity in comparison with a number of other European countries, if the historical context in which it was created is considered. The roots of the constitutional regulation of two national languages goes back to the Finnish independence in 1917 and to the subsequent adoption in 1919 of the Form of Government (Constitution) Act, which outlined the application of the national languages, Finnish and Swedish, much in the same way as the current Constitution. In the aftermath of the First World War, the normal constitution adopted elsewhere in Europe would have been created along the lines of "one people – one state – one language". The Finnish Form of Government (Constitution) Act did not apply this organisational principle of the nation state in its pure form. Instead, the constitutional document was adopted along the principle of "one people – one state – two languages".[10] By doing this, Finland was

---

[8] A search in the Finlex database for the combined occurrence of the terms "Finnish" and "Swedish" yields a result of 190 different norms, which indicates that the provision of services in the two national languages is regulated in great quantities also outside of the scope of the Constitution and the Language Act. A good number of Finnish norms have been translated to other languages, mainly into English, but also into French and German. The translations can be found through http://www.finlex.fi/en.

[9] The bilingual university is an exception of some sort in the Finnish educational system, because the schools are, as a rule, unilingual, either Finnish-speaking or Swedish-speaking.

[10] Many of the states created as nation states after the First World War took a turn towards authoritarianism and they often applied policies that in one way or the other stigmatised the so-called national minorities. This mentality of the nation state still prevails in some European states, and even in Finland, there are certain calls from nationalist circles that Finland should be declared a state where only the Finnish language is an official language.

actually placed in the category of countries which take a liberal position on languages[11] and where the concept of a nation state is not embraced in its pure form. The bilingual set-up was challenged in the 1930s, in particular by nationalists and the extreme right, but the arrangement survived the attacks intact, the only result of it being that the University of Helsinki, which had been dominated by Swedish-speaking staff, especially at the professorial level, underwent a linguistic change. As a consequence of this "Fennomanisation" of the University of Helsinki, a number of chairs and other positions were, in 1937, statutorily defined as Swedish-speaking,[12] four of which are currently placed at the Faculty of Law of the University of Helsinki, and special admissions quotas were introduced for the Swedish-speakers. At the same time, Finnish was established as the language of instruction and administration of the University of Helsinki, although it was still possible to give academic instruction also in the Swedish language.[13]

[11] Switzerland and Canada would be examples of states that preceded Finland in this respect. In addition to the national languages, Section 17, sub-section 3, of the Constitution of Finland recognises the Sami languages, the Roma language and the sign language and indicates the possibility of recognising also other language-based groups of persons. Although the Sami languages are not national languages, they nonetheless are official languages in the northernmost part of Finland under the Sami Language Act (1086/2003) and may be used in that area ways akin to the national languages in contacts with courts and public authorities. In addition, although the Acts of Parliament are not enacted in Sami, it is possible to publish such translations of Acts in the Statutes of Finland which are of direct concern for the Sami. By way of a special quota, the Faculty of Law of the University of Lapland has reserved maximum three admission positions out of a total of 140 for speakers of Sami. However, that quota is not used every year. There seems to be no regular instruction in Sami at the Faculty of Law of the University of Lapland, which is understandable with a view to the small number of Sami, less than 10,000. This means that a Sami law student would take his degree in Finnish.

[12] The "Fennomanisation" of the University of Helsinki actually involved two pieces of law, the Act on the Amendment of the Act concerning the Basis for the Organisation of the University of Helsinki (271/1937) and the Act on the Implementation of the Act concerning the Basis for the Organisation of the University of Helsinki (272/1937). Currently, under Section 74 of the Universities Act, the University of Helsinki shall have a minimum of 28 professorships for Swedish-speaking instruction in disciplines determined in the university regulations. Currently, there are four "Swedish" chairs in law at the Faculty of Law of the University of Helsinki, which are civil and business law, public law, private law, and criminal and procedural law.

[13] Currently, legal degrees are awarded in Finland by four educational establishments, the faculties of law of the University of Helsinki, the University of Turku and the University of Lapland as well as by the Department of Law of Åbo Akademi University.

B. Two Institutional Strands of Legal Education in the Two National Languages

Because the universities are enumerated in the Universities Act, the power to establish universities is in principle with the state, although private foundations may feature as platforms for universities, too. Also the language of instruction is determined in the Universities Act. All this would indicate that the legislative competence in the area of academic education is held by the Parliament of Finland, but this is actually not the entire picture. As stipulated in the Act of Self-Government of the Åland Islands (1144/1991), section 18, para. 14, the Legislative Assembly of the Åland Islands is vested with the legislative competence as concerns education for the purposes of the territory of the Åland Islands. Hence, the legislative competence in the area of education is divided, but the Legislative Assembly of the Åland Islands has not enacted any legislation concerning education at the university level.[14] Therefore, legal education is provided under the Universities Act, which applies only in mainland Finland, not in the Åland Islands.

Section 1 of the Universities Act enumerates altogether 16 universities, 14 of which are incorporated as legal persons of public law, while two universities function on a platform of private foundations under the Foundations Act (109/1930). Section 12 of the Universities Act provides for the education of persons proficient in Swedish. For that purpose, Åbo Akademi University, the Swedish School of Economics and Business Administration, the University of Helsinki, the University of Art and Design, Sibelius Academy, the Theatre Academy and Aalto

[14] The legislative competence is divided so that the Parliament of Finland enacts legislation in that substantive area for mainland Finland, while the Legislative Assembly of the Åland Islands enacts legislation in that substantive area for the Åland Islands. The Legislative Assembly of the Åland Islands has, however, not enacted any legislation concerning education at the university level, but has, at least so far, only covered the level of polytechnic education through the Ålandic Act on the Åland University of Applied Sciences (81/2002). Because the Åland Islands are, under the Self-Government Act, unilingually Swedish-speaking and an area where the general linguistic regime of Finland is not applied, the instruction is in Swedish only. However, because the institution is not a university but a polytechnic, it is not possible to study law there. Instead, students from the Åland Islands study law in mainland Finland or in Sweden. It may be regarded a problem that generally speaking, around 70 percent of Ålandic students choose to study in Sweden, not only because students often establish professional lives close to such main hubs where universities are situated and stay there without moving back to the Åland Islands, but, more specifically for the legal field, because the law in Sweden, in particular in the sphere of public law, is different from that of the Åland Islands and Finland.

University shall be responsible for educating a sufficient number of persons proficient in Swedish for the needs of the country. In addition, under section 76, sub-section 1, of the Universities Act, a special mission is identified for Åbo Akademi University, to specifically satisfy the educational and research needs of the Swedish-speaking population and to take into account the bilingualism of the country in its activities (see below).

As a consequence of these provisions, universities have different linguistic determinations under the Universities Act. Section 11, sub-section 1, of the Universities Act stipulates that both Finnish and Swedish are the languages of instruction and examination in the University of Helsinki, the Academy of Fine Arts, Sibelius Academy and the Theatre Academy, as well as some parts of Aalto University. Of these, formal law degrees are awarded only at the University of Helsinki (see below in chapter 5).[15] Swedish is the language of instruction and examination of Åbo Akademi University, the Swedish School of Economics and Business Administration, and the Swedish School of Social Science of the University of Helsinki. Of these institutions, law is taught as a degree subject at the Department of Law of Åbo Akademi University (see below in chapter 5) and at the Swedish School of Economics and Business Administration. The language of instruction at other universities is Finnish. In spite of possible bilingualism in instruction, the language of internal administration of universities is determined in a different manner than the language of instruction. According to section 35(2) of the Universities Act, the language of administration in a university is Finnish. However, the language of administration of Åbo Akademi University and the Swedish School of Economics, and the Swedish School of Social Science at the University of Helsinki is Swedish. Therefore, there are only three universities or parts thereof where the internal language of administration is Swedish.[16]

---

[15] A part of Aalto University, the School of Economics and Business administration, is unilingually Finnish-speaking, and there, law is taught as a major within the BA and MBA degrees.

[16] In Section 35, sub-section 3, of the Universities Act, it is provided that everyone shall have the right to use Finnish or Swedish in matters concerning them and to obtain a document in the language he or she uses. This is a curious provision, the application of which probably could be limited to the activities outside of instruction and examination. However, analogously with Section 2, sub-section 3 of the Language Act, it could be said that the provision in the Universities Act would make it possible

The university system in Finland is thus a mixed one, with two strands: one dual strand that results in unilingual universities that operate either in Finnish or in Swedish, and another bilingual, where the faculties are actually bilingual, granting their degrees either in Finnish or in Swedish, depending on the language of the student. The universities themselves cannot influence the choice of the language very much at all, but are instead dependent on the Act, on the one hand, and on the language of the student, on the other.

The system is designed so as to provide for legal education in both Finnish and Swedish. Whether that is a full legal education through all levels of degrees or to a partial education is not in the hands of the universities, but is, under section 3 of the Act on the Implementation of the Universities Act (559/2009) determined by the Appendix of the Government Decree on University Degrees (794/2004), which details the areas of education at different universities. Law is established as an area of education for the University of Helsinki, the University of Lapland, Åbo Akademi University and the University of Turku. At the same time, it is established for universities other than Åbo Akademi University that they can give degrees at four different levels, LL.B., LL.M., LL.Lic. and LL.D., while Åbo Akademi University is noted only for the LL.B. degree. From the point of view of linguistic proficiency and substance in the area of law, this does not constitute a problem because the core areas of study required for the legal profession as a judge or other position for which a law degree is a qualification requirement are given during the first three years of study, that is, within the LL.B. degree, while the latter two, up to the LL.M., are reserved for specialisation, optional courses, exchange studies, thesis work, etc. However, for positions as a judge, prosecutor or some other civil service office where a degree in the area of law is the requirement, the expectation would normally be the LL.M. Therefore, as a practical matter, the law students of Åbo Akademi University tend to continue their studies during the final two years for the LL.M. degree at the University of Turku, where the Faculty of Law admitted in 2010 up to 20 LL.B. graduates of Åbo Akademi University, or at the University of Helsinki, where the Faculty of Law admitted in 2010 up to 10 LL.B. graduates of Åbo Akademi University. Because the annual output from the LL.B. programme of the Department of Law of Åbo Akademi University is approximately 20 persons, there should be ample opportunities for them to continue their legal studies towards the LL.M. degree.

The Act on the Knowledge of Languages Required of Personnel in Public Bodies and, in particular, sections 15 and 19 of the Government Decree on Assessing the Proficiency in Finnish and Swedish within State Administration (481/2003), places the certification of language proficiency at the level of the Bachelor's degree. It is therefore possible to say that the law students graduate with excellent linguistic proficiency in Swedish already with their LL.B. degrees, that is, from the University of Helsinki or Åbo Akademi University, although the students would, almost without exception, continue on to the LL.M. in order to acquire the higher university degree, which is required for positions in the civil service and courts of law. As concerns the legal profession, it deserves to be noted that there is no absolute requirement of membership in the Bar or an LL.M. degree for representing parties before the courts, and in some situations, as outlined in Chapter 15, section 2, of the Act on Procedure (4/1734), a wider circle of persons, or at least immediate family members, could act as legal counsel on behalf of another person. However, only members of the Bar Association are allowed to designate themselves with the term "advocate", and as established in section 3, sub-section 1, para 2, of the Act on Advocates (496/1958), one requirement of membership in the Bar Association is the LL.M. degree.

If education in the field of law is considered in a wider sense, outside of the formal law school, the spectrum broadens to faculties of political and social sciences and to schools of business administration. In this respect, it is possible to say that law is taught as a major for an MA and also a PhD level degree at the Department of Law of Åbo Akademi University (private law, business law, public international law and public law)[17] and the Swedish School of Economics and Business Administration (business law), while the Swedish School of Social Science at the University of Helsinki has some instruction in the field of law within its BA programme.

---

for a university to provide better linguistic services than what is required in the Universities Act.

[17] See Appendix V (Degrees in Social Sciences: List of Areas and Some Subjects where Universities Arrange Specialisations as Major Subjects within the Field of Social Sciences) of the Decree of the Ministry of Education on the Specification of the Educational Responsibilities of Universities, on Study Programmes of Universities, and on Specialisation Instruction (568/2005) that remains in force under Section 3 of the Act on the Implementation of the Universities Act.

C. Graduation in the Mother Tongue, and Proficiency in the Other National Language

The university structure with the two languages therefore supports legal education in the two languages concerning norms that have been enacted in the two languages: the law students are taught law either in Finnish or Swedish on the basis of the legislation adopted by the Parliament of Finland simultaneously in Finnish and Swedish, and the law students graduate with either Finnish or Swedish as their language of excellent proficiency.[18] They would fill positions in the judiciary or public administration, for which excellent command of one of the two languages is a formal requirement.

The admission of Swedish-speaking students to the University of Helsinki is administered within the framework of quotas, established by the Faculty Board. In 2010, the Faculty of Law of the University of Helsinki admitted altogether 240 new law students. Of these, 24 students were admitted for law studies at the branch in Vaasa, 12 Finnish-speaking applicants and 12 Swedish-speaking applicants, within a special quota established for that branch by the University of Helsinki. Of the remaining 216 students admitted, 198 were students with proficiency in the Finnish language and 18 were students with proficiency in the Swedish language. Those admitted in the quota of Swedish-speaking students were, as a rule, students who passed the matriculation examination in Swedish. The Faculty of Law of the University of Helsinki teaches law in Swedish, not only in Helsinki, but has a branch in the city of Vaasa/Vasa, where the education takes place until the LL.B. level, after which the students move to Helsinki for their two years of LL.M. study.[19] The education in the Swedish language in Helsinki is given within the framework of the Swedish-language chairs,

---

[18] There are a number of students, those who have received their high-school education in another than their degree language at the university, who in principle do not graduate with an excellent proficiency in either of the languages. Such students can receive a certificate of excellent proficiency if passed in an official language examination, organised monthly on the basis of Section 10 of the Act on the Knowledge of Languages Required of Personnel in Public Bodies and the Government Decree on Act on the Assessment of Knowledge of Finnish and Swedish within the State Administration (481/2003) by two language examination boards, one for the Finnish language and the other for the Swedish language, both appointed by the National Board of Education.

[19] It is possible from 2010 on to also study the two years leading up to the LL.M. degree at the branch in Vaasa/Vasa.

which leaves relatively large portions of the LL.B. and LL.M. degree instruction to be given in the Finnish language without much space for the Swedish instruction.[20] The situation at the branch in Vaasa/Vasa is better, because the instruction is bilingual. There, the Finnish-speaking and Swedish-speaking students have joint instruction and for them, the share of instruction in each language is more or less the same.[21] In practice, a course is taught in one of the national languages, and the students write their answers in exams in their mother tongue.[22]

In the former Universities Act (645/1997), there was a provision in section 26 concerning the education of persons who are proficient in the Swedish language, which stipulated that "[i]n the admission of students to disciplines which are taught in the Swedish language only at the University of Helsinki, care must be taken to ensure that a sufficient number of Swedish-speaking people can be educated to meet the national need. The University may reserve a quota in the intake for applicants proficient in Swedish."[23] The provision is not featured anymore in the current Universities Act of 2009, but there is, instead, the general clause in section 12, placing the general responsibility on, *inter alia*, Åbo Akademi University and the University of Helsinki (see above). In spite of the fact that the explicit provision concerning the

---

[20] These courses are The Foundations of Legal Thinking (which has a particular Swedish-language content), Introduction to Private Law, General Law of Obligations, Contract Law, Accounting, Family and Inheritance Law, Law of Taxes and Finance, Continuation Course in Accounting, Administrative Law, Business Law, Law of Procedure, Law of Property, Criminal Law, Preparatory Seminars, Business Acquisitions, LL.B. Thesis, and languages and communication. This means that around two-thirds of instruction for the LL.B. degree at the Faculty of Law of the University of Helsinki is offered in the Swedish language, while one third of the instruction is offered only in Finnish.

[21] Half of the courses are in Finnish and the other half in Swedish.

[22] When the course is taught in one language, there may be questions from students in the other language which the teacher would normally be able to answer in the language of the person who asked the question. In addition, the trainers often provide the students with lists of concepts and terminology on both national languages.

[23] The quota issue was dealt with by the Constitutional Committee of the Parliament of Finland during the adoption of the previous law. The Constitutional Committee held in its Opinion 3/1997 that the Bill with the quota regime for the University of Helsinki implements the constitutional mandate of what is now Section 17, sub-section 2, of the Constitution of Finland and that the arrangement was laid on the acceptable basis which, in what today is the non-discrimination rule in Section 6, sub-section 2, of the Constitution, permits special treatment on the basis of language. The Committee, however, pointed out that the quota should not become so large and the admission criteria for different groups should not display so great divergence that the departure from the formal equality cannot anymore be viewed as acceptable.

quota is not anymore included in the Universities Act, the existence of such a quota is defendable under section 17, sub-section 2, and section 6, sub-section 2, of the Constitution as a special measure. In 2010, the quota was set at 18 Swedish-language students, while the admission of Finnish-language students was set at 198. In addition, the bilingual legal programme at the branch of Vaasa/Vasa of the Faculty of Law of the University of Helsinki, admitted 12 Finnish-speaking and 12 Swedish-speaking students.

At Åbo Akademi University, the admission in 2010 was 25 students for the LL.B. degree. The persons seeking admission at Åbo Akademi University would in most cases be Swedish-speakers, but the university also admits in the order of 20 percent of students from a Finnish-speaking educational background, but with knowledge of Swedish, as a part of its special mission under section 76 to take into account the bilingual character of the country. For this purpose, Åbo Akademi University has set up mechanisms to assess the proficiency in the Swedish language of such applicants who have received their upper secondary school/high school education in Finnish. This is reflected also in the admissions to the LL.B. degree, where a small number of Finnish-speaking students are featured amongst the Swedish-speaking students. After completion of their LL.B. degrees, students are entitled to seek admission to the two-year LL.M. studies, which they would do at the Finnish-speaking Faculty of Law of the University of Turku or at the Faculty of Law of the University of Helsinki. The University of Turku has reserved annually a separate admissions quota by the decision of the Faculty Board for admission of LL.B. students from Åbo Akademi University, without imposing any entrance examination upon them,[24] and a similar practice is followed by the Faculty of Law of the University of Helsinki.

[24] This arrangement was approved of by the Parliamentary Ombudsman (cases 247/4/00 and 946/4/00, both decided on Dec. 12, 2001) as a consequence of a complaint filed by two students who had graduated with an LL.B. of an old kind, *inter alia*, under the motivation that the arrangement involving special treatment concerned only LL.B. graduates from a Swedish-speaking university (with degrees as specified by new degree rules), the purpose of which was to secure that a sufficient number of LL.M. graduates proficient in the Swedish language is produced. The Ombudsman opined that the fulfilment of the duty in Section 17, sub-section 2, may in some situations require that Swedish-speakers are granted special measures, for instance, by using quotas for further studies. Because passing of an entrance examination is a general precondition of admission to law studies at the University of Turku, set up as a combined LL.B. and LL.M. programme (3+2 years), admissions to the LL.B. studies at

At the Faculty of Law of the University of Helsinki, the curriculum of the legal studies of the Finnish-speaking students include courses in the Swedish language, in particular, legal Swedish, while the Swedish-speaking students will attend classes in the Finnish language, in particular legal Finnish. At the Department of Law of Åbo Akademi University, the students who are admitted as Swedish-speakers would attend classes in the Finnish language. In principle, the purpose of the language training in the other national language would be to prepare the student also for situations in which he or she would have to provide public services in the other national language. Because there seems to exist a shortage of Swedish-speaking applicants to positions in public administration and the administration of justice, it seems likely that most of the Swedish-speaking law students find employment in other fields, such as private practice or business, which may be explained by the better salary levels in combination with the need of linguistically versatile employees.

D. Teaching Law Either in Finnish or in Swedish, but Not in Two Languages at the Same Time

During the past 25 years, all Finnish universities have been state universities, that is, parts of the state as a legal person, funded over the state budget (but securing an increasing share of their resources from external sources). As state universities, the Finnish universities were, until January 1, 2010, state agencies whose employees were, as a rule, civil servants, although a smaller portion of the staff was employed on regular employment contracts under private law. As of 1 January 2010, at which point the new university legislation entered into force and a reform of the legal status of the universities went into effect, the situation is legally speaking quite different. The Finnish universities are not anymore formally attached to the state as state agencies, but continue their existence as independent legal persons, organised either as

the Department of Law of Åbo Akademi University have been arranged so that one representative of the Faculty of Law of the University of Turku is designated as member of the admissions committee of the Department of Law of Åbo Akademi University. The arrangement was created prior to the Bologna reform, when the legal degree in Finland was, in principle, a more coherent five year degree, but the arrangement has not been re-visited after the Bologna reform, although it should, in principle, be possible to move over from one university to another after obtaining a Bachelor's degree.

incorporated entities of public law (corresponding in the German doctrine to the concept of *Anstalt des öffentlichen Rechts*) or as foundations of private law under the Foundations Act. As a consequence of the reform, the number of employees that the state had until the end of 2009, around 121,000 persons, was reduced overnight to around 31,000 employees, when they became employees of the 16 universities on January 1, 2010.

The qualification requirements for appointment at universities include linguistic ones as well, but they are determined at different normative levels. As laid down in section 35 of the Universities Act, provisions concerning the proficiency of teaching and research personnel and other personnel in the Finnish and Swedish languages shall be enacted by Government Decree, except as concerns Åbo Akademi University, for which section 78 of the Act provides that a requirement for a teaching post at Åbo Akademi University shall be excellent proficiency in the Swedish language and an ability to understand the Finnish language. The decision on the proficiency in Swedish and Finnish required of a foreigner or a non-native Finnish citizen shall rest with Åbo Akademi. Under the same provision, Åbo Akademi has a language board in front of which the proficiency in Swedish can be demonstrated.

According to section 1 of the Government Decree about Universities (770/2009), it is required by persons carrying out functions related to instruction or research at a unilingual university other than Åbo Akademi University that they are proficient in the language in which they have to give instruction. The proficiency may be demonstrated in a way determined in a regulation of the university. However, at bilingual universities, that is, such universities where a degree can be conferred both in Finnish and in Swedish, a person involved in instruction or research is, in addition, required to have at least satisfactory oral and written proficiency in Finnish and Swedish. Within the area of legal studies, this requirement is relevant only in respect to the University of Helsinki. The university may grant an exception from these linguistic requirements in manners established in a university regulation. In principle, the required level of language proficiency is showed *ex ante* of hiring and not controlled *ex post*.

Particular employment provisions are laid down for professors in section 33, sub-section 2, of the Universities Act. The post of professor must be publicly announced vacant when a person is hired into an employment relation in force until further notice. The post of professor may be filled by invitation without public notice of vacancy when a professionally distinguished person may be invited to the post or a person is appointed for a fixed period to the post. Only a person who indisputably fulfils the qualification requirements may be appointed to the post by invitation.[25]

The teaching staff would not normally teach in both Finnish and Swedish, but in the language for which they have been employed. Hence, the Finnish-speaking professors and teachers of law at the University of Helsinki would teach law in Finnish and the Swedish-speaking professors and teachers of law would do so in the Swedish language. Therefore, at the University of Helsinki, it is to some extent possible to speak about two linguistically delineated teaching sections, a Finnish-speaking one and a Swedish-speaking one. At Åbo Akademi University, the professors and teachers give their instruction in the Swedish language. Normally, the teaching staff is not obliged to teach in more than one of the national languages.[26]

Except for the branch in Vaasa/Vasa of the Faculty of Law of the University of Helsinki, the lawyers trained in Finland are not trained bilingually to become bilingual in practice. They are trained, at least in principle, in one of the two languages. As a practical matter, courses offered in legal education are taught either in Finnish or in Swedish, but not in both languages simultaneously. This should ensure that the students have, already at graduation with their LL.B. degrees, excellent proficiency in one of the national languages and satisfactory proficiency in the other national language. This should also, at least in principle, satisfy the requirements of the Language Act as concerns the provision of public services on the basis of the personal principle, as conditioned by the territorial principle as well as the Act on the Knowledge of Languages Required of Personnel in Public Bodies and

[25] According to sub-section 3 of the provision, statements concerning the qualifications and merits of persons applying for and invited to the post must be requested from a minimum of two experts where a person is appointed to a position in effect until further notice or for a fixed period of at least two years. The disqualification of the expert is governed by the provisions of Sections 27 - 29 of the Administrative Procedure Act. Provisions concerning the selection, activities and remit of the experts shall be enacted in the university regulations, where needed.

[26] It should be noted in this context that the increasing internationalisation has resulted in an increasing share of the instruction to be given in the English language, not so much for the LL.B. students, but for those doing the last two years for the LL.M. degree.

the Act on Judicial Appointments (205/2000). Those with excellent proficiency in Finnish would be appointed to positions at such courts and other authorities where the territorial determination is unilingually Finnish-speaking or bilingual with Finnish as the language of the majority, while those with excellent proficiency in Swedish would be appointed to positions at similar institutions where the territorial determination is unilingually Swedish-speaking or bilingual with Swedish as the language of the majority. However, in particular in bilingual jurisdictions, be they courts or administrative authorities, the requirement to provide services in the language of the minority are accentuated. Therefore, in bilingual jurisdictions, it is not enough to be satisfactorily competent in the other national language so that the judge or the civil servant can understand and use orally the other national language, which is the requirement in unilingual jurisdictions, but the appointee has to have a satisfactory proficiency to use orally and in writing the other national language, as laid down in section 12, sub-section 1, of the Act on Judicial Appointments and section 6, sub-section 1, of the Language Competence Act.

Although lawyers are not, during their legal studies, trained to become bilingual *per se* (except at the branch in Vaasa/Vasa of the Faculty of Law of the University of Helsinki),[27] it seems that many Swedish-speaking law students actually are bilingual and will be fluent in both Swedish and Finnish. This is tangible, in particular, in private practice and business law, where linguistic skills are appreciated and where there may be a somewhat greater demand for Swedish-speakers than Finnish-speakers. Bilingualism for Swedish-speakers may actually be a consequence of the fact that not all of the courses in the LL.B. curriculum of the Faculty of Law of Helsinki are offered in the Swedish language, but slightly more than two-thirds of the courses, while the students are expected to study the rest of the courses in the Finnish language. At the branch of Vaasa/Vasa of the Faculty of Law of the University of Helsinki, even less of the LL.B. curriculum is offered in Swedish, because the intention within this special bilingual education is to offer 50 percent of the courses in Finnish and 50 percent in Swedish.

[27] In the Fall of 2010, an experiment started at the branch in Vaasa/Vasa that is aimed at strengthening the skills of the speakers of one of the national language in the other national language by way of offering a package of 60 ECTS in the other language.

A somewhat similar situation exists at the Department of Law of Åbo Akademi University, where the LL.B. degree is produced in cooperation with the Faculty of Law of the University of Turku: around three-fourths of the LL.B. curriculum at Åbo is offered in Swedish,[28] but a number of courses, amounting to around one-quarter of the LL.B. curriculum, are offered in Finnish at the Finnish-speaking Faculty of Law of the University of Turku.[29] In the event that Åbo graduates with an LL.B. degree are admitted to the Faculty of Law of the University of Helsinki for the two-year "domestic" LL.M. degree, they probably will find at least some courses in Swedish, they will be entitled to take their exams in the Swedish language and they will be entitled to write their Master's Thesis in the Swedish language. Most of the Åbo LL.B. graduates tend to continue towards their "domestic" LL.M. degrees at the Faculty of Law of the Finnish-speaking University of Turku,[30] where none of the courses are offered in the Swedish language. However, they have been granted the possibility to write their exams in Swedish and to author their Master's Thesis in the Swedish language.

E. Scarcity of Teaching Materials in Swedish

It is recalled in this context that the linguistic proficiency of a law student is assessed at the point when they are about to graduate with the LL.B. degree. This means that a Swedish-speaking LL.M. graduate is, in effect and *de facto*, relatively bilingual, while their Finnish-speaking colleague would, almost without exception, be unilingual. In fact, it is possible for Finnish-speaking law-students to graduate without ever having read an Act of Parliament or a textbook in Swedish as a part of

---

[28] These courses are Basic Course in Law, Constitutional Law, Jurisprudence, Tax Law, Companies Law, Competition and Intellectual Property Law, Family and Inheritance Law, Law of Obligations, Law of Damages, Administrative Law, Introduction to Public International Law, The Relationship between International Law and Domestic Law, Accounting, Optional Courses, Literature Review and Essay, and the LL.B. Thesis as well as language and communication studies.

[29] These courses are Legal History, Legal Sociology, Law of Property, Labour Law, Environmental Law, Criminal Law, and Law of Procedure.

[30] The natural reason for this is probably the fact that Åbo Akademi University and the University of Turku are situated in the same city, the name of which is Turku in Finnish and Åbo in Swedish. Under the Language Act, Turku/Åbo is classified as a bilingual municipality with Finnish as the language of the majority, which is also the case for Helsinki/Helsingfors as well as for Vaasa/Vasa, where the Faculty of Law of the University of Helsinki has a branch.

their general curriculum, except in the language classes in which Swedish is taught to the Finnish-speakers. The effect of this is that a Swedish-speaking graduate in law would generally speaking be better equipped to serve as a judge or a civil servant in a bilingual jurisdiction and would probably have a certain linguistic advantage. However, *de jure*, a Swedish-speaking graduate in law would normally have excellent proficiency in the Swedish language and satisfactory proficiency in the Finnish language. This is mirrored in the reverse order by the *de jure* linguistic proficiency of the Finnish-speaking graduate.

While Finnish is only spoken in Finland, Swedish is, of course, also spoken in Sweden, which at least in principle could be an important feature in the support of Swedish as a legal language in Finland. In the area of legal education, the impact of the proximity to Sweden is, however, smaller than an outside observer might expect. However, the Nordic space (Denmark, Finland, Iceland, Norway, Sweden) is important since the 1950s in the harmonisation of legislation, especially in the area of so-called private law and as an area of free movement of workers. This means that Swedish-speaking lawyers from Finland have a relatively great opportunity to involve themselves also in activities in the Nordic countries, mainly in the area of business law, but also in other areas.

Both Finnish and Swedish are official languages of the European Union, a legal fact that contributes to the possibilities to continue operating in the Swedish language in Finland. For instance, some Finnish requests for preliminary rulings from the European Court of Justice have been filed in Swedish, because the cases have originated in Swedish.[31] Also, the normative materials of the European Union are published in the two national languages of Finland. Hence as such, the bilingualism of the country is matched by the Europeanised legal environment.[32] At the same time, law is becoming internationalised beyond

[31] For instance, Supreme Administrative Court (SAC) 2003:78 in case C-113/01 *Paranova Oy* and the Administrative Court of the Åland Islands in the case *Diana Elisabeth Lindman* C-42/02, [2003] ECR.

[32] However, legal Swedish is terminologically not always exactly the same in Finland and Sweden, and this is reflected in the EU-Swedish, which follows the terminology used in Sweden. See H. Bruun et al., *Svenskt lagspråk i Finland* (Statsrådets svenska språknämnd) (Schildts 2004) p. 53. See also new version of *Svenskt lagspråk i Finland - Ruotsinkielinen lakikieli*, Föreskrifter, anvisningar och rekommendationer från statsrådets kansli - Valtioneuvoston kanslian määräykset, ohjeet ja suositukset 1/2010, at <www.finlex.fi/sv/viranomaiset/normi/125002/35799> visited May 31, 2010, pp. 47–53.

the European space. Graduates in the field of law have already during their school education learned English in addition to Finnish and Swedish, because English is a compulsory foreign language in the curriculum of Finnish schools from the elementary onwards. During their law studies, English is supported by way of compulsory courses. It is also possible to find some texts in English in the reading materials of law students.

Already in secondary school, but at the latest in high school, most students would have learned at least one additional language, probably two, German and French being the most likely ones, although other languages, such as Spanish, Italian and Russian are available too, at least to some extent. As a part of legal education, these languages can be included as optional topics or electives in the degrees. To some extent, the courses in these languages may also be set up as field-specific from the point of view of law.

One vehicle of instruction of law for the globalised world is comparative law. Work is done in this direction at all universities with legal programmes, such as the Faculty of Law of the University of Helsinki, which maintains a one-year LL.M. programme that operates in English. The situation is similar at the Department of Law of Åbo Akademi University, which maintains, together with the Finnish-speaking Faculty of Law of the University of Turku, the so-called Turku Law School, which is a framework for the provision of legal education in foreign languages, mainly in English, for foreign exchange students and for domestic students.[33] The activities of the LL.M. in Helsinki and the Turku Law School are, of course, not only in the area of comparative law, but in legal instruction in a variety of fields, such as competition law, public international law, intellectual property law, etc. In addition, it should be mentioned that there is a specialisation in Legal Linguistics at both the University of Helsinki and the University of Lapland, which is in no way irrelevant from the point of view of bilingual legal education in the national context or from the point of view of globalisation.

[33] It should also be mentioned that the Department of Law of Åbo Akademi University offers a two-year Master's Degree in Human Rights Law on the basis of Section 11, para. 5, of the Decree of the Ministry of Education on the Master's Programmes of the Universities (1665/2009). That Master's degree is formally speaking not a degree in the field of law, but is categorised in the Finnish degree system as an MA in political science.

In spite of the Europeanisation and internationalisation of the legal sphere, the main focus of legal instruction is, however, domestic law. Because all norms in mainland Finland are enacted or issued in both Finnish and Swedish,[34] and because the EU legislation uses Finnish and Swedish as official languages, the starting point for normative studies, the law itself and the primary sources of law, are available in both Finnish and Swedish. On the basis of these primary sources, court judgments and administrative decisions are made in both national languages (although each judgment or decision is not issued in two languages, but only in one, depending in principle on the language of the party; practice may be different with respect to Swedish-speaking parties).

Of the secondary sources of law, the *travaux préparatoires* with regard to acts of parliament are available in both Finnish and Swedish, and because government bills and statements and opinions of the committees of the parliament have a relatively strong impact on the interpretation of the primary sources of law, and for this reason it is important that they are available also in the Swedish language.[35] Of equal importance as secondary sources of law are court decisions, in particular decisions of the Supreme Court and the Supreme Administrative Court.[36] However, the decisions of the highest court instances are not translated *in extenso* into the other language, but published only in the language in which the case originated. Because most cases originate in and are decided in Finnish, there is a certain burden on the Swedish-speakers as concerns their ability to find legal information in the case law, but this burden is to some extent eased by the fact that the highest court instances publish short case summaries in both languages.

---

[34] In the autonomous Åland Islands, the Ålandic Acts and Decrees are issued in Swedish only within the framework of the legislative competence of the Åland Islands, which is in the area of public law in a broad sense, although with certain exceptions for some laws of private law. In so far as the Parliament of Finland is competent to enact laws that apply in the territory of the Åland Islands (which would mainly be in the area of private law), the legal life on the Åland Islands is, of course, facilitated very much by the fact that the laws of Finland are enacted also in the Swedish language.

[35] However, Governmental Committees normally work in the Finnish language and produce their reports in Finnish, although a Committee Report would, as a rule, contain a summary in Swedish.

[36] It should be noted that Finland has no Constitutional Court, and the judicial review of legislation that is accorded to courts of Finland in a decentralised way under section 106 of the Constitution of Finland is a relatively weak form of judicial review in comparison to most other jurisdictions.

Tertiary sources of law, such as publications authored by academics and other persons in the area of law, are heavily dominated by the Finnish language, because the commercial market is mainly Finnish-speaking. While the publication quantities of individual pieces in the Finnish language are (or at least may be) commercially sustainable, the situation is completely different for publications in the Swedish language. Some original works, such as textbooks, commentaries and treatises, are published in the Swedish language,[37] and there are also some translations of legal texts from Finnish to Swedish,[38] but most legal materials in this category would be published in Finnish. There is one legal journal published in the Swedish language in Finland, featuring original articles in Swedish, but also translations from Finnish into Swedish of articles that perhaps have been previously published in Finnish.[39]

Although the legal orders of Finland and Sweden are close to each other in terms of language, terminology and concepts, and style, books written in Sweden about the Swedish legal order are not used to any greater extent, because the references and cases are, nonetheless, different. There are certain fields of law that are of a common character, such as public international law and EU law, where textbooks and commentaries are available in Swedish in Sweden. In such cases, they are used in Finland, at least to some extent. Nonetheless, the readings for courses might not be entirely in the Swedish language, but would also relatively frequently feature textbooks and other materials in the Finnish language. Because the government bills are often a basis for commentaries written in the Finnish language, a Swedish-language government bill and parliamentary papers from committees of the parliament might be used to fill the void, but because this is not always feasible, courses could also be based on readings in Finnish, as is mostly the case at the Faculty of Law of the University of Helsinki, where 11.2 percent of the titles of readings are in Swedish (both LL.B.

---

[37] During the past decade, at least 18 monographs (excluding doctoral dissertations) within the area of law were published in Swedish in Finland.

[38] During the past decade, at least seven monographs within the area of law were translated from Finnish to Swedish. However, it also happens that monographs originally authored in Swedish are translated into Finnish.

[39] The journal *Tidskrift, utgiven av Juridiska Föreningen i Finland* (abbr.: JFT), published since 1865, is refereed and relatively well read also in Sweden. See <jff.fi/index.asp?page=5>. The JFT is also available in the electronic form through <www.edilex.fi>.

and LL.M. studies, including optional courses).[40] At the Department of Law of Åbo Akademi University, the readings are to a greater extent in the Swedish language, although a number of books in the Finnish language are featured in the readings as well, as are also texts in English: 54 percent of the titles in the readings for the LL.B. degree at Åbo Akademi University are in Swedish in 2010–2011.[41]

F. Academic Research in Swedish In Finland

The legal research tradition in Finland has been a "heavy" one as concerns doctoral dissertations: the expectation has been the production of a monograph comparable to a *Habilitation* in the German tradition. Therefore, doctoral dissertations are probably less frequent in the field of law than in other areas, although the situation is changing as a consequence of the recent emphasis on a quicker progress towards a degree. Dissertations written in the Swedish language in the field of law are probably even less frequent. The impact of English has been constantly increasing as the language of dissertations. As a consequence, out of 126 doctoral dissertations defended at the Faculty of Law of the University of Helsinki between 1999 and 2010,[42] 11 were published in the Swedish language (26 of them were in English).

It seems, however, that this is not a consequence of funding decisions per se, because the Academy of Finland, which is a major funder of academic research, receives applications in Swedish too. Instead, the low number of doctoral dissertations in the Swedish language is probably due to the linguistic choices made by authors and doctoral candidates: because English is the medium of communication in academia, in particular within some particular fields of law of a more international nature, and because publications on international forums are

[40] At the University of Helsinki, there are some limited options in individual courses to change replace a Finnish course book with a Swedish-language one and some options to replace a Finnish course book with a Swedish-language series of lectures. Some case rehearsals are also organised in Swedish.

[41] Amongst the courses offered at the Faculty of Law of the University of Turku for law students of Åbo Akademi University, one course, Legal History, contains one book in the Swedish language.

[42] For a list of dissertations, see <www.helsinki.fi/oikeustiede/tutkimus_ja_julkaisut/vaitoskirja_ja_lisensiaatin_tutkimukset.htm> visited June 18, 2010.

encouraged, the obvious language of publication is English.[43] At the same time, the internationalisation of doctoral training and research in general drives the choice of dissertation topics towards internationally interesting topics, draining the area of researchers in more national topics.

This development is universal, at least to some extent, but for a small jurisdiction like Finland, not to speak of the position of Swedish in the academic world as the non-dominant language in Finland, the consequences could be dramatic and might prevent the development of concepts and terminology in the Swedish language as it is used in the jurisdiction of Finland. The LL.B. theses are, as a rule, written in the language of the university, which means that at the Faculty of Law of the University of Helsinki and the Department of Law of Åbo Akademi University, there will be texts produced in Swedish, but already at the LL.M. level the situation starts to change. While the Swedish-language students would still seem, in most cases, to write their Master's Theses in Swedish, even those who have, after obtaining their LL.B. degree, crossed over from Åbo Akademi University to the University of Turku, there is an increasing tendency to use English in the LL.M. thesis.

G. Cooperation with Sweden

Above, the point was made that reading materials from Sweden are used less than one might expect in the courses that the law students take in Swedish at Finnish universities. That alone indicates that the contacts between the two countries are at a lower level than the fact of a Swedish-speaking minority in the adjacent country would indicate. While there have been a few Finnish professors and other researchers appointed to positions in law schools in Sweden, that domain has by no means been reserved for the Swedish-speaking academics in Finland, but has also featured Finnish-speaking persons. This in itself testifies to the fact that there is not only a Swedish-Finnish or – more broadly speaking – a Nordic basis for law in the two countries, but an active interest in relation to Sweden.

Although that interest towards the Nordic countries and thus also Sweden has been in the decline, perhaps partly due to the strong

[43] A pragmatic reason might perhaps be found in the fact that relatively few Swedish-speakers lawyers choose the academic career, because of the good availability of work elsewhere.

impact of the European integration, at least during the first few decades into the EU membership, it has strong historical roots: until 1809, the territories that we now know as Finland and Sweden were one state, the Kingdom of Sweden, and even after 1809 until 1917, when Finland was an autonomous Grand Duchy of the Russian Empire, Finland was maintained as a separate jurisdiction with the old Swedish legislation in force. At the same time, by tradition, Sweden has not, as a state, shown much interest in the Swedish-speakers in Finland and does not, for instance, support higher learning in Finland over its budget. Hence, Sweden is not really a kin-state of the Swedish-speaking Finns in the political sense, although in some ways it is much more so: the legal orders of Sweden and Finland have the same root. Probably because of this, the Swedish-speaking academic community in the area of law has been particularly active in academic exchange with Swedish counterparts, and as a reflection of the same fact, Swedish academics have reciprocated the interest. As an example of this, it could be mentioned that it is relatively common to use professors from the other country as opponents to doctoral dissertations. However, the common root of the legal orders of Finland and Sweden gives also an additional justification for upholding a competence in the Swedish language in Finland.

The mobility of academic staff from Sweden to Finland has been less frequent in the legal field, perhaps because of linguistic reasons. However, there is the flexible institution of the docent or adjunct professor, established under section 89 of the Universities Act, which can be used to create and maintain links at a personal level between the two countries. Under the provision, a university may award the title of docent (adjunct professor) to a person who has comprehensive knowledge of his or her own field, a capacity for independent research or artistic work demonstrated through publication or some other manner, and good teaching skills. This mechanism has been used by Finnish universities to incorporate Swedish professors as resource persons and by Swedish universities to incorporate Finnish professors as resource persons.

As concerns persons admitted to legal studies in the two countries, it seems that there are currently no joint study programmes in the field of law in the form of, for instance, joint degree programmes or double-degree programmes. However, there is the particular exchange programme of NordPlus, which operates in a similar way as the European exchange programmes. NordPlus is used to some extent by both

Finnish-speaking and Swedish-speaking law students for study in Sweden, but the incoming students from Sweden to Finland are fewer.

In the area of research, academics in the field of law would quite often find partners in Sweden and team up with them in research projects. In the Nordic Council, a specific branch has been set up with the research funding programme NordForsk, through which funds have been channelled also to research projects around legal topics relevant for Finland and Sweden.

H. The Impact of European Integration on Legal Education

As concerns legal studies, the perception amongst high school students seems to be that it is comparatively speaking easier to win admission at a law school in Sweden than in Finland. Therefore, a number of both Finnish-speaking and Swedish-speaking Finns would, at any given time, study at law schools in Sweden. After graduation at the LL.M. level, a number of them would seek recognition of their degrees in Finland. In addition, such upper secondary school/high school students from the Åland Islands who are interested in legal studies would more often than not choose law schools at universities in Sweden as their places of study. After the completion of their degrees in Sweden, they might wish to return to Finland, including the Åland Islands, which means that for full opportunities to practice law or to be able to apply for certain positions, they, too, would have to seek recognition of their degrees in Finland. This is done on the basis of the Act on the Competence for Civil Service Positions that University Studies Abroad Constitute (531/1986). According to section 8 of the Act, an applicant who has a foreign university degree may apply for an equivalence decision at the National Board of Education, which can grant equivalence if the degree in an academic area is at the same corresponding level as a Finnish degree that is required for a public post, or in practice at the Master's level. The Board can also issue a decision according to which the applicant must complement the foreign degree by studies in Finland in order to reach the equivalence level with a Finnish degree.[44] After the completion of the studies at a Finnish university, the

[44] According to Section 2 of the Government Decree concerning Studies that Complement University Studies that have been Carried out Abroad (1206/2007), those additional studies may, for the Master's level in Finland involve a maximum of 60 ECTS and for the Bachelor's level in Finland a maximum of 45 ECTS.

university in question issues a decision certifying that the applicant has passed the studies that were required by the Board. In addition, the Act on the Recognition of Professional Competence (1093/2007) mandates the National Board of Education to issue recognition decisions for such professional qualifications that have been obtained abroad.[45]

Recognition of degrees awarded abroad, including Sweden, has not been without problems, although more recent amendments to the legislation seem to have "regularised" the situation. In a case of an Italian person who had, in 2001, been awarded the Italian degree of *Laurea di dottore in Giurisprudenza* at La Sapienza in Rome, and thereafter an MA and a Licentiate degree in social sciences at Åbo Akademi University, and who had commenced his doctoral studies at the Faculty of Law of the University of Turku, the Supreme Administrative Court returned the matter for a new consideration at the National Board of Education because of insufficient motivation of a conditional equivalence decision.[46] The Board had based its decision on an unmotivated statement by the Dean of the Faculty of Law of the University of Helsinki. The procedure of comparison of the studies of the applicant in Italy and Finland did not fulfil the requirements that the case C-145/99 *Commission* v *Italy* of 7 March 2002, established with a view to Directive 89/48/EC art. 1, para. g. What the subsequent developments in the matter were are not known.

In another case,[47] involving a person whose law degree was awarded by a Swedish university, the National Board of Education had first made a conditional equivalence decision, stating that the certificate over the degree gives him qualifications for a public position or a function for which a Master's degree is required and that the certificate gives him qualifications for such position or function for which an LL.M. degree is required after he has passed a competence test about the structure and sources of the Finnish legal system, organised by the

---

[45] On the basis of Section 4 of the Government Decree concerning a Harmonisation Period and Suitability Attestation in relation to Professional Qualifications (1207/2007) dealing with compulsory suitability tests for positions where the requirement is a certain legal degree, such suitability tests are organised by that faculty of a university at which legal degrees may be awarded.

[46] SAC, decision 4.11.2004/2799. The Board had required that the applicant passes a test organised by the Faculty of Law of the University of Helsinki that would cover the following areas: the structure and sources of the Finnish legal system, civil law, law of property, family and inheritance law, criminal law, law of procedure, constitutional law and administrative law.

[47] SAC 2006:103.

Faculty of Law of the University of Helsinki. According to the decision of the Board, the Faculty of Law of the University of Helsinki would determine the precise contents of the exam. The person in question filed an application against this decision with the Administrative Court of the Åland Islands. Pending a decision by the court, the National Board of Education corrected its decision some three months later by issuing a new decision replacing the first decision. In the new decision, the Board concluded that the certificate concerning an LL.M. degree awarded by the University of Uppsala in Sweden gave the person not only competence for a public office or a task for which a Master's degree is required, but also for a public office or function for which an LL.M. degree is required. The decision was this time unconditional and without requirement of additional exams at the Faculty of Law of the University of Helsinki. In the material dispute in the case, doubts had been expressed in the Administrative Court of the Åland Islands by one judge about the competence of the person to act as legal counsel in a situation where the requirement was, *inter alia*, an LL.M. degree and another judge had decided that the person could not appear as counsel before the court. According to the Supreme Administrative Court, the two judges were, however, not rendered incompetent to sit a case involving the person as an applicant.

I. Delivery of Public Services through Legal Professions: Some Problems and Recent Developments

Generally, the territorial principle will indicate in which language, Finnish or Swedish, a court jurisdiction and an administrative authority's jurisdiction should address itself to a party and to the general public. As explained above, when unilingually Finnish speaking jurisdictions require, by way of recruitment conditions, a Master's degree, this also means that the applicant must have excellent proficiency in the Finnish language and satisfactory proficiency in the Swedish language, while the reverse is true for a unilingually Swedish-speaking jurisdiction. In bilingual jurisdictions where Finnish is the language of the majority, the civil service positions, including positions as a judge, that require a Master's degree also require excellent proficiency in the language of the majority of the jurisdiction and at least satisfactory oral and written proficiency in the language of the minority, because it is likely that the judge or civil servant will have to make decisions in the language of the minority in the jurisdiction.[48] Again, the reverse is true for bilingual jurisdictions where Swedish is the language of the majority.

This basic pattern has recently been complemented with two other arrangements. On the basis of section 1 b of the Act on the Courts of First Instance (581/1993), it has been made possible, for the purpose of guaranteeing the linguistic rights, to identify so-called minority judges for bilingual court jurisdictions, that is, persons who have excellent proficiency in the language of the minority in the jurisdiction. According to the provision, there shall be at least one such judge in each bilingual jurisdiction. The Government has, through section 2a of the Government Decree on the Appointment of Judges (42/72000), determined the number of such minority judges in each jurisdiction affected, which are altogether eight courts of first instance.[49] The linguistic requirements for these positions are excellent oral and written proficiency in the language of the minority population within the jurisdiction and satisfactory oral and written proficiency in the language of the majority. In effect, this means that there is a duality established for the positions as a judge in the bilingual jurisdictions at the same time that there is an assurance concerning the availability of judges in the minority language.

In addition, the same Act on Courts of First Instance makes it possible in section 18 a, sub-section 2, to create, by way of individual decisions of the Ministry of Justice, so called language sections at courts of first instance. By the Decision of the Ministry of Justice of 1 December 2009 (Nr 18/31/2009OM), it was decided that a language section would be established at the Court of First Instance of the Turku Area. The modalities of such a section and how cases are dealt with there are determined in the rules of procedure of the court itself, as adopted by the chief judge of the court. It seems that the Turku version of a

---

[48] In addition, because persons who wish to be appointed for judicial posts are required to possess practical insights in such functions, they should carry out a judicial internship at a Court of First Instance. Such internships should, of course, be available in both Finnish and Swedish.

[49] The numbers at the courts of first instance are as follows: Egentliga Finland: 4; Esbo: 2; Helsingfors: 3; Mellersta Österbotten: 4; Vanda: 1; Västra Nyland: 3; Österbotten: 8; Östra Nyland: 2. The minority judges are Finnish-speakers in only one of these bilingual court jurisdictions, Österbotten, while they are Swedish-speakers in the other jurisdictions. At the court of first instance of Åland, all judges are Swedish-speakers because the jurisdiction is identified as a Swedish-speaking one in the Act on the Self-Government of the Åland Islands.

language section is less than a physical collection of Swedish-speaking judges, clerks and other staff members in the form of a separate section of the court. Instead, the identification as a language section seems to be a recognition of the fact that at the regular sections, there are Swedish-speaking judges, clerks and other staff members who, when a case has to be dealt with in the Swedish language, may be called together to deal with the case. In other respects, the members of this so-called language section are dispersed amongst the other persons employed by the court.

As explained above, university degrees obtained so that the LL.B. degree and the school education are in the same language will automatically, under the Act on Judicial Appointments, render the person with an LL.M. degree qualified for a position as a judge. Hence, if the language of the school education and the LL.B. is Finnish, the person is deemed to have excellent proficiency in the Finnish language, and if the language of the school education and the LL.B. is Swedish, the person is deemed to have excellent proficiency in the Swedish language. In addition, language courses in the other national language during legal studies will render the person qualified at the level of satisfactory oral and written proficiency in the other national language, which information is recorded on the LL.B. degree certificate by the university that issues the degree.

Although the language regime in the legal field is quite comprehensive and systematic, Finland has not been spared from criticism by international treaty bodies overseeing the realisation of the two conventions of the Council of Europe,[50] namely the Framework Convention for National Minorities (FCNM) that creates the Advisory Committee, and the Language Charter[51] that creates the Committee of Experts. Neither of the two committees is entitled to receive individual complaints, but they analyse periodic state reports and issue opinions on the basis of them.

For instance, the Advisory Committee was, in its first report in 2000, of the opinion that art. 10 of the FCNM was a source of concern. It recognised the fact that Swedish, as a national language of Finland,

---

[50] See also A. Stark, *Nationella språkliga minoriteters rätt till offentlig service på sitt eget modersmål, med exempel från den svenskspråkiga minoriteten i Finland* (unpublished Master's Thesis in Public International Law, Department of Law, Åbo Akademi University, 2010) pp. 125–126.

[51] As concerns the Language Charter, Finland has opted for a very high level of commitments in areas that are relevant for the provision of legal services.

enjoys extensive normative protection, but expressed that it had been informed about cases where the relevant norms have not been fully implemented in practice: "Implementation difficulties appear, for example, in criminal proceedings, where, according to an investigation conducted by the Parliamentary Ombudsman in 1998, the right to use Swedish is not fully guaranteed in practice, due, *inter alia*, to the limited language skills of judges."[52] In a similar vein, the Expert Committee has criticised Finland for too few judges and other staff members proficient in the Swedish language and concluded that there exist many problems concerning the practical implementation of the Language Act, although the Act guarantees everyone the right to use Swedish in court proceedings.[53] In 2001, the Expert Committee was of the opinion that the Swedish-speakers do not have the courage to claim their right to use Swedish in court proceedings, the reason for this being that the low linguistic proficiency of the judges may result in that the Swedish-speaking parties are not understood or that they are perceived as "trouble-makers".[54] The Expert Committee concluded that, according to the information at its disposal, "there is a lack of staff with a sufficient command of Swedish among the judicial authorities responsible for civil proceedings in bilingual judicial districts. *De facto*, this situation obliges the Swedish-speakers to forego their right to request the proceedings to be conducted in Swedish".[55] Therefore, in relation to the Language Charter, the commitments were deemed to be formally fulfilled, but in practice, the undertakings were not completely fulfilled.

In its comments in 2004 to the second state report of Finland, the Advisory Committee reiterated the problems from the year 2000 with the implementation of the language legislation in, for instance, criminal proceedings.[56] The Advisory Committee also stated that "the

---

[52] Advisory Committee on the Framework Convention for the Protection of National Minorities - Opinion on Finland, adopted on 22 September 2000, ACFC/INF/OP/I(2001)002, para. 33, at <www.coe.int/t/dghl/monitoring/minorities/3_FCNMdocs/PDF_1st_OP_Finland_en.pdf> visited May 18, 2010.

[53] Report of the Committee of Experts on the application of the Charter in Finland, ECRML (2001)3, para. 76, at <www.coe.int/t/dg4/education/minlang> visited May 18, 2010.

[54] Expert Committee 2001, para. 78.

[55] Expert Committee 2001, para. 83.

[56] Advisory Committee on the Framework Convention for the Protection of National Minorities - Second Opinion on Finland, adopted on 2 March 2006, ACFC/OP/II(2006)003, para. 102, at <www.coe.int/t/dghl/monitoring/minorities/3_FCNMdocs/PDF_2nd_OP_Finland_en.pdf> visited May 18, 2010). The third cycle of opinions on Finland is due in April 2011.

far-reaching legal protection of the Swedish language has proved challenging to implement in certain areas and a number of shortcomings have been reported in practice. For example, the Swedish language capacity within the judiciary continues to be a problem in a number of courts, and the reports received by the Advisory Committee suggest that the use of the Swedish language in court proceedings has often resulted in average delays that are significantly longer than those experienced in the corresponding Finnish proceedings".[57] The Advisory Committee recommended that the "authorities ensure that there is adequate Swedish language capacity in the local, regional and central bodies concerned in order to ensure full implementation of the Language Act, including by ensuring that the proficiency requirements are adequately implemented, that in-service language training is readily available and that the teaching of the Swedish language in the educational system remains comprehensive".[58] The Advisory Committee also noted that problems exist in the linguistic services that the central government should offer in relation to the Åland Islands and stressed the "need to ensure availability of Swedish language documentation, which requires particular attention in the EU context, bearing in mind the specific status of Åland".[59] In the 2004 comments to the second state report of Finland, the Expert Committee reiterates its findings of 2001 and indicates that the state has recognised the problem, but that the practical implementation is still not in harmony with the undertaking, although the language legislation had been reformed in 2003.[60]

In its comments to the third state report of Finland, the Expert Committee explains that "the proceedings in Swedish are much longer than when Finnish is used", which in practice discourages the Swedish-speakers from using Swedish and makes them switch over to Finnish. "The authorities admit that the first reason is that at present the number of judges and other personnel with the command of Swedish is not sufficient".[61] The Committee was of the opinion that Article 9 of the

[57] Advisory Committee 2006, para. 106.
[58] Advisory Committee 2006, para. 108.
[59] Advisory Committee 2006, para. 108.
[60] Report of the Committee of Experts on the application of the Charter in Finland, ECRLM (2004) 7, para. 79, at <www.coe.int/t/dg4/education/minlang> visited May 18, 2010.
[61] Report of the Committee of Experts on the application of the Charter in Finland, ECRLM (2007) 7, para. 121, at <www.coe.int/t/dg4/education/minlang> visited May 18, 2010.

Language Charter concerning the use of a minority language in legal proceedings still is implemented only in the formal sense. Therefore, the Committee asked that Finland would undertake measures to ensure that the linguistic rights of the Swedish-speakers are fully implemented in the legal proceedings in Finland.[62] The periodic evaluation of the linguistic rights of minorities carried out by the Government indicates similar *lacunae* in 2009.[63] The problems with the implementation of linguistic rights in courts can probably be located in such bilingual court jurisdictions where Finnish would be the language of the majority and where, consequently, it would be enough for the judges to know Swedish at a sufficient level of oral and written proficiency.

The opinions of the two treaty monitoring bodies indicate a serious failure of the language regime practiced in Finland, at least as concerns courts and the availability of well-trained lawyers for the purpose. The introduction of so-called "minority judges" at a number of courts of first instance might remedy the problems, at least to some extent (see above). However, as stated by the Advisory Committee in 2004, the educational system should cater to training in the Swedish language in a comprehensive way. While universities are not directly implicated, it is not altogether wrong to understand the reference to the educational system in broad terms so as to cover the universities too. After all, it is at the university level that those persons are trained in the field of law who later on should be providing the linguistic services, not only at courts, but also in the public administration of the state and the municipalities.[64]

J. Concluding Reflections

In spite of a very good level of recognition of two national languages and a sophisticated system *de jure* for implementing the regime of two

[62] Expert Committee 2007, para. 124.

[63] *Report of the Government on the application of language legislation 2009*, pp. 53–59.

[64] Because Åbo Akademi University has, under section 76, sub-section 1, of the Universities Act, the special mission to satisfy the educational and research needs of the Swedish-speaking population and take account of the bilingualism of the country in its activities, such measures that the State should undertake could include the extension of the degree conferring power of Åbo Akademi University in the field of law from the current LL.B. degree to the LL.M. degree and the LL.D. degree.

national languages, practical implementation is lacking as concerns the *de facto* realisation of the linguistic rights of, in particular, the Swedish-speakers in the legal system of Finland. One possible remedy to the unsatisfactory situation would be to increase the number of Swedish-speaking students annually admitted for legal studies in the Swedish language in Finland. This should not be too difficult, because the necessary educational structures already exist, but would probably require that more resources be placed at the relevant educational institutions.

In principle, each law student is trained in their language to acquire an excellent level of proficiency, although at the same time the other national language is taught, so that the person would, in the professional life after studies, be able to function also in the other national language. This may not always succeed as concerns the Finnish-speaking lawyers, at least those employed by courts of law, while the Swedish-speaking law students probably emerge from their university studies as bilingual persons *de facto*, although they are unilingual *de jure*, at least until they have proven excellent proficiency in the other national language before the language examination board. Through the legal education in the two national languages, the universities involved are actually directly linked into the process of the fulfilment of the constitutional right of everyone to use their own language. In the same vein, they should be viewed as parts of the domestic mechanisms that work towards the fulfilment of linguistic commitments at the level of international law.

Complications that Swedish-speaking instruction in the field of law meets are, in particular, the low level of textbook production, commentaries and treatises. While this may be a negative thing *per se*, forcing the Swedish-speakers to accept at least some readings that contain literature in the Finnish language, the practical end-result is that the bilingualism of the students is promoted. That quality is probably a competitive edge that, at least to some extent, works to the advantage of the Swedish-speaking lawyers later on in their careers. The same effects, both negative and positive (depending on the viewpoint) can probably be attached to the fact that not all courses within the curriculum of legal education are necessarily given in the Swedish language. The situation in the labour market is speaking its own language, indicating that there is a great demand, actually a shortage, of lawyers who are competent in using both national languages, that is Finnish and Swedish.

PART II

LEGAL EDUCATION THROUGH MINORITY LANGUAGES

CHAPTER SIX

BASQUE-MEDIUM LEGAL EDUCATION IN THE BASQUE COUNTRY

Xabier Arzoz

A. Introduction

In an area of 20,742 km^2 and with a population of approximately three million, the Basque-speaking territories of Spain and France possess a high density of law schools. Legal education is offered in the Basque-speaking territories through the medium of three languages: Spanish, French and Basque. However, most of the law schools follow single-medium education. French is the medium of instruction at the multi-disciplinary Faculty of Bayonne (France) which teaches law and forms part of the *Université de Pau et des Pays de l'Adour*, and Spanish is the medium of instruction at the law schools of the two Universities of Navarre (the Public University of Navarre and the private, Opus Dei-owned University of Navarre) and at the Spanish Distance University (UNED), which has premises in Portugalete and Bergara. Legal education is only bilingual (Spanish-Basque) at the law schools of the public University of the Basque Country and of the private, Jesuit-owned University of Deusto. There is a third private University, Mondragon University, that is highly committed to Basque-medium education but it does not include a law school.

It is not casual that both the University of the Basque Country and the University of Deusto have the only bilingual law schools. They are located in the Basque autonomous community, which, on the one hand, with 2.1 million inhabitants, is the most populated Basque territory and, on the other hand, constitutes a region (or 'autonomous community' in the terms of Spanish constitutional law) that has used the devolution of power from 1978 onwards to advance the legal status and the social use of the Basque language. In contrast, in Navarre legislation explicitly only recognises Spanish and Basque as the languages of instruction with regard to teacher training; although it does not exclude the use of Basque as a language of instruction in other areas, there is a lack of clear commitment on the part of regional autonomous authorities to bilingual education in the higher education.[1] Therefore, this paper will deal in practice with Basque-medium legal education offered in the Basque autonomous community.

With the exception of a very short autonomy period during the Spanish civil war (October 1936-June 1937), Basque has never enjoyed the status of language of law in the Basque-speaking territories. Languages such as Latin, Navarre's Romance, Occitan, Castilian or French were used to write legal and political documents, even if the majority of the population was Basque-speaking.[2] The early presence and knowledge of regionally important languages in the Basque-speaking territories and the strong links with external institutions may explain that even the 'Old-Laws' of the Basque-speaking territories were not written in Basque.[3] Nevertheless, the Basque language was not totally absent in modern times when there was a need to communicate directly with the population. Thus, Basque was used in some municipalities' documents for communicative reasons, especially in regulations addressed to the local population and in cross-border official post between Basque-speaking municipalities on both sides of the Spanish-French border.[4] Similarly, some political texts (for instance, the official texts of the French Revolution) were translated into Basque to gain the support of Basque-speaking people. In any case, the proclamation of the Spanish constitution in 1978 and the devolution of powers that took place on that basis is the starting point of the revitalisation of the Basque language and of its emergence as a language of law.

B. Legal Framework of Universities and Legal Education in Spain

The legal framework is especially complex in Spain with regard to bilingual higher education in the legal context. Four kinds of competence

---

[1] X. Arzoz, 'Universidad y pluralismo lingüístico', in J. V. González García (ed.), *Comentario a la Ley Orgánica de Universidades* (Civitas 2009) p. 1125 at p. 1179; I. Agirreazkuenaga, 'Universidad y lengua: Universidades multilingües para una Europa multilingüe', 86 (II) *Revista Vasca de Administración Pública* (2010) p. 17 at p. 39–45.

[2] A. Urrutia and A. Lobera (eds.), *Euskara, Zuzenbidearen hizkera* (Universidad de Deusto 1995) p. 57–86.

[3] For the Old-Law of Bizkaia see G. Monreal, *The Old Law of Bizkaia (1452). Introductory study and critical edition* (University of Nevada 2005).

[4] I. Trebiño, *Administrazio zibileko testu historikoak* (Instituto Vasco de Administración Pública 2001).

and spheres of legislation are involved according to the Spanish constitutional order:

Firstly, higher education is a competence shared by the central state and the autonomous communities. In general terms, the central state establishes the basic legislation and autonomous communities have the power to develop it and the power to execute all legislation.[5] In practice, however, basic state legislation can be very detailed. In 2001 the central state passed the University Act, which was amended in 2007. Most autonomous communities have approved their own university legislation, since all have at least one public university within their territory. With all but two exceptions,[6] all Spanish public universities are dependent upon regional authorities. Private universities need to be authorised by regional authorities.

The Basque autonomous country passed the Basque University System Act in 2004. The Basque university system embraces a public (UPV/EHU) and two private universities (Deusto, Mondragon). In addition, the Spanish Distance University and the San Sebastián Campus of the University of Navarra offer teaching to students living in the Basque Country.

Secondly, access to all legal professions is a matter regulated exclusively by the central state.[7]

Thirdly, the Spanish University Act (2001) does not rule on language use within the university. Officially bilingual autonomous communities have the competence to establish the legal status and to rule the use of official languages other than Spanish. This is a so called horizontal competence that permeates all other competences and binds all regional and central state authorities based on an officially bilingual autonomous community. In that respect, public universities as other public services must abide by language legislation. The main piece of legislation in this field in the Basque Country is the Basque Language Act (1982).

---

[5] A. Nogueira, 'Distribución de competencias y organización administrativa en materia de universidades', in Julio V. González García (ed.), *Comentario a la Ley Orgánica de Universidades* (Civitas 2009) p. 129–166.

[6] The Spanish Distance University (UNED – *Universidad Nacional de Educación a Distancia*) and a postgraduate University (UIMP – *Universidad Internacional Menéndez Pelayo*).

[7] Law 34/2006 and Decree 775/2011 rule access to the profession of lawyer. For an accurate description see E. Merino-Blanco, *Spanish Law and Legal System*, 2nd ed. (Sweet & Maxwell 2006) p. 74–96; P. Leith and F. Galindo Ayuda, 'Legal education in Spain: becoming a lawyer, judge and professor', 8 *International Journal of the Legal Profession* (2001) p. 169–186.

Finally, public universities in Spain have constitutionally entrenched autonomy.[8] This autonomy, which must be exercised according to the law, includes the power to manage their organisation and functioning as public administrations. The use of official languages both in internal and external relations is a matter belonging to the organisation and functioning of public universities, which they may rule upon either in their university constitution (*estatutos*) or in specific language regulations.

Summing up, the structure and organisation of higher education is rather uniform across Spain. However, the state legislator has not ruled on the linguistic aspect of higher education in the officially bilingual autonomous communities. Therefore, officially bilingual autonomous communities may opt for different linguistic models. The higher education language policy does not need to follow primary and secondary education language policy. In the next section, an outline of the organisation of Basque-medium higher education in the University of the Basque Country will be given.[9]

C. The Organisation of Basque-Medium Higher Education in the University of the Basque Country

Since 1982, all students of the Basque autonomous community have a legally entrenched right to "receive education both in Basque and in Spanish in all education levels".[10] The Basque Country is the only Spanish autonomous community that has opted for the same freedom of language of education for primary, secondary, and tertiary education. At primary and secondary levels of education, there are three linguistic educational models: Spanish as the medium of education, with Basque as a compulsory subject ("A" model); both Basque and Spanish as mediums of education ("B" model); and Basque as the medium of education, with Spanish as a compulsory subject ("D" model). In higher education there are two general languages of instruction: Basque and Spanish.

In 1985, the first constitutions (*estatutos*) of the University of the Basque Country, created in 1980, were finally approved. For their time,

---

[8] Art. 27 (10) of the Spanish Constitution.

[9] For Catalonia and Galicia see the chapters by E. Pons and A. Nogueira López, respectively.

[10] Art. 15 of the Basque Language Act of 1982.

those constitutions were the most committed text of its kind in Spain with regard to minority language higher education.[11] As is typical for Basque language legislation, university constitutions combine two legal techniques to advance the status of the Basque language: the recognition of language rights and the establishment of language planning to gradually give full effect to those language rights. On the one side, all members of the university community were granted the following rights: a) the right to express themselves in any official language; b) the right to address themselves to all university bodies in any official language; c) the right to receive and teach in any official language; d) the right to write essays, tests and exams in any official language; e) the right to write, publish and defend research in any official language.[12] On the other hand, a sophisticated institutional structure was designed to plan and advance Basque-medium higher education: a vice-chancellor for the Basque language, a university-wide interdepartmental Institute for Basque language (*Euskara Institutua*), a university-wide commission for Basque language, and a Basque language commission in each faculty or school.

The above mentioned rights do not imply correlative duties for other members of the university community: all teachers do not have to speak both official languages in order to comply with the students' right to express themselves or receive education in any official language. It is the university as a whole which has to guarantee that right, not every single member of its staff: "all bodies of the University of the Basque Country will guarantee, within their competences and with regard to the situation of each of its three campuses, the exercise of the above mentioned rights and will avoid their infringement".[13] In any case, knowledge of both official languages is generally considered as a merit in access to any university position.

The enactment of the abovementioned educational rights imposes the splitting of teaching into at least two 'linguistic streams', Basque and Spanish groups, according to the language of education.[14]

---

[11] X. Vilhar Trilho, 'A consagracáo da universidade bilingüe ou as bases jurídicas para a náo normalizacáo das línguas propias das comunidades autónomas no ensimo universitario', 14 *Revista de Llengua i Dret* (1990) p. 255 at p. 256.

[12] Today, these rights are stated in Art. 116 (1) of the Constitutions of the University of the Basque Country approved by Decree 17/2011 of Feb. 15, 2011.

[13] Art. 116 (3) of the Constitutions of the University of the Basque Country (2011).

[14] There may be more groups to match the demand for certain studies (law, business, etc.).

Students may register for tuition in either Basque or Spanish in all undergraduate studies. Nevertheless, same faculties (including the law faculty) have traditionally allowed students that had enrolled in a given language track at the beginning of the academic year to take any subject in the other language. This is now a general policy of the University of the Basque Country, in order to foster mobility of students between the two language tracks and to promote a more inclusive and multilingual formation of students. Even if the timetable and, in some cases, the morning/afternoon separation of both language tracks condition in practice the linguistic mobility of students, in general it seems that few students take advance of this possibility: the majority seem to be Basque-track students and for a rather opportunistic purpose, to circumvent a particular Basque-medium lecturer.

To guarantee the students' right to receive education in their preferred official language, the university as an institution has to have enough members of its teaching staff that are able and willing to teach in both languages. Since all Spanish citizens speak Spanish and the Basque language is spoken by around a quarter of the population in the Basque Autonomous Community, the legal and institutional problem lies in the guaranteeing of the right to choose Basque as the language of instruction.

There is only one public university for the whole Basque autonomous community, but it is organised into three campuses (Bizkaia, Gipuzkoa and Araba/Alava), which correspond with the Basque autonomous community's administrative division. At the beginning of devolution, the Basque authorities responsible for university issues had two dilemmas, the creation of a single vs. various universities and the choice of the language of instruction. It was opted for a campus-based single university model and for dual instruction: i.e., in both cases, the option was aggregation, and territory or language-based separation or division was excluded. Parallel-medium education was an objective to be achieved gradually, but for the time being Spanish was the primary medium of instruction. The law school was established in San Sebastián-Donostia, but in the 1990s a second unit was created in Leioa (outside Bilbao). In both headquarters, legal education is offered in Spanish and in Basque.

Therefore, the University of the Basque Country combines "institutional bilingualism" to conduct its university business, with parallel-medium education or 'double monolingual education' at the instruction level.[15] There is neither splitting nor doubling of universities, faculties or departments according to the language of instruction, but rather a functional splitting of all teaching into (at least) two groups. The teaching staff is organised in departments according to scientific fields, not according to the language of tuition. At the beginning, the option to aggregate languages of instruction was also a decision to consolidate and make sustainable the Basque language as a language of higher education.

The right to receive education in both official languages has been progressively implemented. The Basque Language Act combines two legal techniques to advance the status of the Basque language: the recognition of language rights and the establishment of language planning to gradually give full effect to those language rights. When the University of the Basque Country was created in 1980, the Basque language was at the margins of the higher education system. A few activities mostly of informal character were voluntarily organised by some teachers. Twenty-five years later, in 2007, two thirds of all main and obligatory courses (that is, with the exception of optional subjects) were being offered through the medium of the two official languages. Certainly the offer of Basque-medium higher education still varies from scientific area to scientific area: experimental sciences, technical studies and health care sciences are below the average, and they only offer one quarter of all obligatory credits in the second cycle of education.[16] As regards legal studies, a couple of lecturers started to teach in Basque in 1985 at the Law Faculty of San Sebastián-Donostia: some more lecturers joined them in the following years, and the Basque stream began to take form. In 1999, all courses of the old law degree (*licenciatura*) were taught in Basque.[17]

---

[15] T. Du Plessis, 'From monolingual to bilingual higher education: The repositioning of historically Afrikaans-medium universities in South Africa', in 5 *Language Policy* (2006) p. 87 at p. 89.

[16] Those scientific areas are also those which show a lower average of full-time bilingual teachers. See the 2007 approved Master Plan for the Basque Language in Vicerrectorado de Euskara, *Plan Director del Euskara en la UPV/EHU (2007/08–2011/12)* (University of the Basque Country Press 2007) p. 21–24.

[17] I. Alkorta, 'Zuzenbidearen irakaskuntza eta euskara, itzulpenaren ikuspegitik: Euskal Herriko Unibertsitatea (UPV/EHU)', in S. Larrazabal and E. Oregi (eds.), *Hizkera juridikoa eta itzulpengintza: euskararen norabideak* (Universidad de Deusto/IVAP 2005) p. 209 at p. 210.

D. A Community of *Alumni* and *Profesores*

1. *Students: Linguistic Requirements and Fidelity to Basque-Medium Education*

Access to higher education is not linguistically conditioned, neither in general[18] nor in the field of legal education. Students are not screened for their Basque or Spanish language proficiency. Language competency in the chosen language of instruction is not required. It has been sometimes reported that some law students' Basque language abilities were so limited that neither interactive participation nor even effective communication could be expected from them;[19] nevertheless, this viewpoint is becoming more and more marginal as long as the Basque language proficiency of the new generation has improved notably.

The lack of language requirements seems to be based on two ideas. Firstly, one of the most sacred principles of Basque language policy is freedom of choice within the linguistic educational model. This applies both to primary and secondary education and to higher education. Secondly, Basque education policy aims at students achieving 'enough practical knowledge' of both official languages by the end of obligatory education. Whatever the language of instruction they choose in primary and secondary education, they have always to learn the other official language as a compulsory subject. Whether 'enough practical knowledge' of the Basque language is enough to attend higher education in Basque may be disputable, but no entrance test is imposed on students coming from the "A" model in comparison with those coming from "B" and "D" models.

Evolution of the Basque-medium schools has been very positive in the last twenty five years. Today, the majority of pupils are enrolled in those linguistic educational models that operate partially or fully in Basque (so-called 'B' and 'D' models): in 2008/09, the distribution was 18.65 percent, 23.12 percent and 57.60 percent in 'A', "B" and "D" models, respectively. Figures for enrolment in the "B" and "D" models in primary education in the last years are even more favourable, so a further increase of those models' weight within the educational system

[18] The only exceptions are translation and interpretation studies, in which a certain level of competency in the relevant foreign language(s) is required.

[19] J. A. Tamayo, 'De la enseñanza bilingüe en general y de la docencia del Derecho romano en lengua vasca en particular', 8 *Anuario da Facultade de Dereito da Universidade da Coruña* (2004) p. 909 at p. 917.

will occur in the coming years. In 2009/10, 61.96 percent of children were enrolled in the "D" model, 29.27 percent in the "B" model and 8.05 percent in the "A" model. Certainly, according to the IV Sociolinguistic Map published in 2009, in 2006 67.5 percent of the 15–19 years-old population was considered to be officially bilingual.

However, this positive development cannot hide that a significant part of students that have studied in Basque at primary and secondary education do not opt for Basque-medium higher education at the University of the Basque Country, when this is available (see Table 1). To some extent, there is a student drain from Basque-medium schooling to Spanish-medium higher education. We can but speculate about the possible reasons.[20] Firstly, there has been societal prejudice about the quality of Basque-medium higher education, especially in the initial years. Certainly, as will be argued below, Basque-medium higher education had to be organised from scratch and exhibited deficiencies and instability in the founding years until it could be progressively consolidated. Secondly, some students might also be afraid of the politicisation (shorthand for the perceived influence of extreme nationalist students) of Basque stream groups. Basque stream groups have been sometimes identified with ideology and conflict: as a matter of fact, they often had to mobilise in order to claim more Basque-medium education when, for instance, at the beginning of the academic year enough bilingual teachers had not been hired by the University. In any case, ideologisation is a double-edge sword: without some degree of ideologisation or socio-political awareness, even less students would have attended Basque-medium education in the prevailing social, linguistic and political circumstances. Thirdly, tertiary education is supposed to prepare students for professional life, and all professions outside administration and the education sector are Spanish-dominated: some students may see no point in receiving a

[20] There is neither research about the level of migration of Basque students to universities outside the Basque Country, nor about the social and linguistic characteristics of participation of Basque students in the private and the public higher education sectors of the Basque Country. On the effects of language planning initiatives on the language attitudes and language practices of Basque university students, see M. Moriarty, 'The effects of language planning initiatives on the language attitudes and language practices of university students', 34 *Language Problems & Language Planning* (2010) p. 141–157; on the linguistic options of Basque university students, see B. G. Abad and I. Martinez de Albeniz, 'Quiebras y discontinuidades en la socialización, un análisis de la opción lingüística en los universitarios del País Vasco', 21 *Revista Internacional de Sociología* (1998) p. 129–146.

Table 1: Law graduates and language of instruction at the University of the Basque Country (2001–2010)

	2001	2002	2003	2004	2005	2006	2007	2008	2009	2010	Total
Basque	62	67	65	56	50	30	38	30	25	26	449
Spanish	384	292	390	216	191	117	170	143	74	62	2039
Total	446	359	455	272	241	147	208	173	99	88	2488

Source: My elaboration with data provided by the administrative services of the Law School of the University of the Basque Country.

formation they will not be using later. It is clear that many students prefer to avoid any difficulties additional to those inherent in higher education, be it derived from the linguistic dimension, the ideological component or logistical aspects (lack of materials and instability of education).

2. *Bilingual Teachers: Legal and Sociological Conditions of Recruiting and Work*

There are three ways to recruit teachers who are able to teach in both official languages. Firstly, teachers who were or have become fluent in both languages may voluntarily accept to teach in both language tracks. The first lecturers who started to teach in Basque belonged to this group. Secondly, teachers may be granted a six-month long paid leave to learn Basque with the obligation to become 'bilingual teachers' at a given point in time. And thirdly, the university may create specific teaching positions in which the knowledge of both official languages is a prerequisite (so called 'bilingual positions'[21]). In Spanish politico-legal jargon it is said that those positions have a 'linguistic profile'. All teaching positions existing within the Spanish university system may be assigned a 'linguistic profile'. A great number of 'bilingual positions' have been progressively created to match the demand of Basque-medium higher education. The proportion of bilingual lecturers among those holding permanent positions has increased from 13 percent in the late eighties to 40 percent in 2010. The 2007 University

[21] In this paper we will use the administrative notion of 'bilingual lecturers' to refer to those lecturers who hold teaching positions in which they are obliged to teach in both official languages of the Basque Country. Of course, many officially 'monolingual' lecturers are bilingual in the sense that they are proficient in two or more languages, whether official or not, and could teach in them.

Master Plan for the Basque Language aims at increasing the proportion to 43 perent in 2012.

In 2009, there were 56 bilingual lecturers (40 percent) and 83 monolingual lecturers (60 percent) affiliated to the law faculty.[22] In addition, affiliated to other faculties (business, social sciences, etc.) but teaching also in the law degree, there were around approximately 13 bilingual and 10 monolingual law lecturers.[23] However, the status of bilingual lecturers is in general lower than the one of monolingual lecturers: they are less represented in the highest academic positions. There are 29 monolingual full professors against 3 bilingual and 12 bilingual associate professors against 20 monolingual.

While the objective has long been offering all graduate studies in both official languages, for many years only a third or less of the lecturers have been bilingual. The unequal proportion of monolingual and bilingual lecturers demonstrates two sociological realities. Firstly, the fact that the Basque track has not been fully implemented in some studies. Secondly, Basque-medium lecturers have had in practice more teaching obligations (more groups and more different courses) than their monolingual colleagues. Teachers holding 'bilingual positions' do not limit themselves to teaching in Basque. Departments assign teaching tasks: according to departmental needs and within their teaching duties, bilingual lecturers may also have to teach in Spanish and may be responsible for teaching the same subject in both official languages, which is often the case.

Table 2: Language of instruction and status of teachers at the law school of the University of the Basque Country (2009)

	Full professors	Associate professors	Lecturers	Assistants	External lecturers	TOTAL
Bilingual	3	12	12	18	11	56
Monolingual	29	20	3	15	16	83
TOTAL	32	32	15	33	27	139

Source: My elaboration with data provided by the administrative services of the Law School of the University of the Basque Country.

[22] Source: Administrative Services of the Law School of the University of the Basque Country.

[23] These data are based on my own estimations.

Until recently, senior teaching positions in Spain constitute a civil service corps (made up of full and associate professors) as happens to be the case in other countries (France, Italy, Germany, etc.). Legislation sets down the formal responsibilities of full and associate professors in their capacity as public servants, scholars and scientists. University professors form a civil service corps and their individual members are ascribed to the existing universities, some of which happen to be bilingual. The creation, selection and appointment of those civil servant positions need to fulfil the requirements and procedures formally laid down within the national context by the weight of national law. These requirements have changed twice in the last decade. Currently, candidates to a civil servant teaching position have to go previously through an accreditation procedure managed by the National Agency for Quality Assessment and Accreditation (ANECA). The accreditation procedure consists of peer-review and a panel assessment: two anonymous experts from the same field, out of a public list of approved referees, have to evaluate the publications and other merits of each candidate with the help of some guidelines (an assessment rubric); each expert writes a separate rapport, on the basis of which the accreditation commission made up of distinguished professors will take the final decision, if necessary after a third rapporteur's contribution. Individuals that have successful gone through the accreditation procedure are conferred an eligibility to be considered for a civil service place at a public university. But the right falls to the university to select one candidate out of the eligible ones. Currently, according to the diversification of higher education institutions, individual universities (or departments) have greater scope to define the scientific profile of the most suitable candidate to occupy the vacancy.

Civil servant positions are created by universities, within their financial resources basically provided by the authorities of the autonomous community. From the very beginning, the University of the Basque Country respected general requirements established by state legislation, but established an additional linguistic requirement for certain posts (so-called positions with a 'linguistic profile'), as far as it was necessary to match the demand for Basque-medium education. Although linguistic requirements in other fields of public administration were challenged before the courts, this legal scheme has consolidated at the University of the Basque Country. Today, a candidate must obtain the accreditation from the National Agency for Quality Assessment and Accreditation (ANECA) in order to be allowed to apply for a public law position in a university. The traditional system is unfair for candidates engaged in Basque-medium education: they are engaged in Basque-medium education, even obliged through their appointment or initial contract to teach in Basque, but their Basque-medium research or teaching publications cannot be fairly assessed. Therefore, a candidate involved in Basque-medium higher education has to develop strongly his or her non-Basque publications if he or she wants to go through the research assessment or the accreditation exercise.

Since 2007, Spanish legislation allows also for contract-based appointment in public universities, from the bottom to the top. This reform, which runs counter to a two centuries old tradition of 'nationalisation of academia',[24] involves two dimensions. The first one is the regionalisation of higher education, that is, the 'repatriation' to the regional level of functions that, beforehand, were centralised. The conditions of employment of contract-based teachers are laid down by regional legislation. This opens the door to regional differentiation.[25] The second issue is that control over professorial appointment has been decentralised back to individual universities. Nevertheless, for access to those new contract-based positions, an accreditation procedure is still required; but new regional accreditation agencies are also empowered to award the accreditation required for a contract-based position. Since this new legal status of lecturers is regulated by regional legislation and the accreditation for all contract-based positions, including those which are bilingual in character, may be obtained from the Basque accreditation agency, this would seem to create a wholly 'Basque academic career'. Most law lecturers that have followed the new appointment system are officially bilingual lecturers.[26] The new system has advantages and risks. It is more flexible than the old one in order to answer regional needs in general and the needs of Basque-medium education in particular, but it has the risk of parochialism:

---

[24] G. Neave, 'The European Dimension in Higher Education: An Excursion into the Modern Use of Historical Analogues', in J. Huisman, P. Maasen and G. Neave (eds.), *Higher Education and the Nation State – The International Dimension of Higher Education* (Emerald 2007) p. 13 at p. 30.

[25] The creation of an independent professor faculty system for the Basque Country has been a recurring demand from certain nationalist sectors: some lecturers even refused to become Spanish civil servants and were dismissed from the University for that reason. See J. R. Etxeberria, N. Xamardo and J. Zalakain, 'Irakasle-antolakuntza propioa euskal unibertsitatean', 50 *Bat. Soziolinguistika aldizkaria* (2004) p. 141–150.

[26] In 2009, in the law school they were 12 bilingual *agregados* against only 2 monolingual ones.

candidates compete within a small circle of possible candidates and are assessed within a small circuit of "regional" peers and, consequentially, the applying standards might decrease. A second risk is that a type of 'inner exile' or 'semi peripheral existence' – a relative marginalisation – is imposed upon the new body of lecturers by an academic community whose status and standing are wholly determined by criteria that lie solidly beyond the region. In any case, a new, non-nationalist Basque government has changed the rules governing the accreditation procedure, and it has established that scientific evaluation boards assisting in the accreditation procedure must be made up of Spanish and international senior scholars from outside the Basque university system.[27] This implies that Basque-medium teaching and research will be assessed by scholars who lack knowledge of the Basque language. While this may aim at quality assurance, it will leave no room for considering the achievements of Basque-medium scholarship. Be it in the strong or in the weak version, one may also debate the exact repercussions which the 'regionalisation of academia' will have upon particularistic identity or upon the multiple loyalties of the teaching body.

In the first two decades of Basque-medium education, bilingual teachers were appointed generally at a very young age, often without previous teaching or research experience, predominantly on the basis of their linguistic skills and their degree marks. Teachers spanned a range of Basque language proficiencies, skills and abilities, relating to general communicational purposes relevant to their disciplines as well as to their teaching as subjects. Some lecturers, whether junior or senior, had to rely on a limited Basque language proficiency in order to enact discursively their content expertise and to mediate it to students. Inexperienced graduates had to start teaching in Basque immediately after being hired or appointed. No policy or planning was developed to select and train future bilingual lecturers, for instance organising a program to train future bilingual lecturers in issues like legal translation, legal terminology and innovative teaching methods, or to accommodate appointed lecturers. Recruitment of Basque-medium lecturers was driven by the existence of a massive demand, specifically as the first wholly Basque-medium educated secondary education cohorts started to arrive at the university.[28] In practice, departments dictated

---

[27] Art. 16 (2) of Decree 349/2010 of Dec. 28, 2010, which amends the rules governing the Regional Evaluation and Accreditation Agency Uniqual.

[28] M. Aizpuru and R. Jimeno, 'Euskal Unibertsitatearen Historia', in UEU and EIRE, *Euskal Unibertsitatea 2021* (Udako Euskal Unibertsitatea 2002) p. 21 at p. 40.

the rhythm of implementation of Basque-medium education at their convenience, whilst even opposing it with filibusterous practices;[29] (in general, bilingual posts became a much queried booty, a way to strengthen departmental weight and distribute posts among in-house candidates. How the university's language policy was interpreted and applied systemically varies according to departmental cultural models, as in many complex organisations. Since the whole process of expansion (even duplication) of provision was mainly based on new recruitments, no relevant tensions have been reported when transforming the University through language policy. Some senior academics complained from time to time about the ease of recruiting new staff using linguistic criteria, while supposedly highly talented researchers had to migrate elsewhere due to their lack of Basque language competence.

The responsibility upon those young bilingual teachers was enormous, and it has no comparison with the similar responsibility put upon bilingual teachers at primary and secondary education. Firstly, they had to teach a subject they had to learn for themselves.[30] Secondly, they had to prepare their lessons in Basque and eventually produce from scratch their own rudimentary teaching materials: in practice this means that they were, consciously or not, de facto responsible for the corpus planning of their assigned scientific fields, without assistance or help from older colleagues, university services or external standardisation institutions. They had to fulfil the task of elaborating teaching materials, or translating textbooks into Basque, thus creating unknowingly a standardised language and technical terms for their subject. Most did and still do this work in a purely amateurishly way;[31] support from linguists began later. In general, the process of modernising the Basque language (especially technical terms for politics, administration and law) went hand in hand with the gradual introduction and use in official spheres. Thirdly, they usually had responsibility for many different teaching subjects at the same time, while their

---

[29] J. I. Pérez and P. Salaburu, *Unibertsitatea eta euskal gizartea, gaur* (Pamiela 2003) p. 196.

[30] In their first year, many newly recruited teachers might have to learn their subject only one week or even a couple of days in advance before they had to mediate it to students.

[31] This is from my personal experience as a teacher of administrative law. But I think that it is also the experience of my colleagues. From the perspective of another bilingual lecturer appointed in the early 90s of the twentieth century, see Tamayo, *supra*, n. 19, p. 914: 'Likely with more will than skill, we began to teach the subject [Roman law]. The problems were many. The solutions improvised – as anyone can guess, they were very intuitive'.

non-bilingual colleagues had most probably less teaching obligations. Finally, as these tasks were rather time- and energy-consuming, there remained little time to do research, progress in their academic career and obtain an appointment as a full-time professor or lecturer.

After two decades, things have improved globally. If new bilingual teachers are now recruited, it is very likely that they have already studied fully or mostly in Basque at the university, and that they have some previous teaching and/or research experience, even a PhD.[32] Secondly, they enter departments that count on older colleagues who previously went through the same process and may help them, with counsel, assistance and, more importantly, with materials produced by them. Thirdly, although neither the Basque language[33] nor the scientific language is completely standardised,[34] the most basic scientific terminology and phraseology have been spread across the school system and the new generations of students and teachers. Fourth, special programmes have been devised to foster the production or the translation of basic materials and textbooks. Fifth, as other public institutions, the University of the Basque Country has also established its own language services, which have done a huge amount of work creating and implementing advisory services, training plans, instruction, etc.[35] Finally, new technologies facilitated the production and dissemination of non-commercial texts, especially for non-dominant languages.[36]

E. Teaching Methods and Materials in Legal Studies

1. *Teaching in Basque: Handicap or Opportunity?*

One of the handicaps of Basque-medium higher education has been the attempts to reproduce the traditional magisterial teaching method,

[32] From a different perspective, it can be said that there are increasingly better prepared candidates for bilingual vacancies or new positions.

[33] Recently, a colleague asked my opinion about the Basque translation of the expression "digital divide", since the available dictionaries and reference works provided different solutions: "zulo digitala", "bretxa digitala", "hesi digitala", "haustura digitala"...

[34] J. I. Hualde and K. Zuazo, 'The standardization of the Basque language', 31 *Language Problems & Language Planning* (2007) p. 143–168; J. Irazusta, 'Euskara sustatzeko politika UPV/EHUn: Plan Gidaria', 75 *Bat. Soziolinguistika aldizkaria* (2010) p. 73 at p. 80.

[35] I. Ugarteburu, 'Hizkuntza zerbitzuak Unibertsitatean (EHU)', 50 *Bat. Soziolinguistika aldizkaria* (2004) p. 31–50.

[36] Citing my own experience, the first multiple choice test I prepared for my university students in June 1993 was made with an electronic typewriter.

according to which lecturers know all about their topic and students nothing, and the only purpose of the course was the memorisation of a textbook. This was the way all lecturers in Spain were educated in, and this was in principle the easiest way for most newly appointed or hired lecturers to fulfil their teaching obligations.

Each problem creates an opportunity. The advantage of Basque-medium higher education compared with the Spanish-medium one was, on the one hand, the small size of the groups, at least in most cases. For a young lecturer it would be a surreal proposition to reproduce the traditional distant and paternalistic approach in a room of twenty or less students. Moreover, how to insist on the memorisation of a thick Spanish textbook the young lecturer was not fully conversant with? On the other hand, young lecturers were granted freedom to follow their intuition and even negotiate the course rules with students. In this critical situation, some lecturers suggested the idea that a more dynamic approach should be fostered in the classroom and that demands to students should be coherent with what was delivered in the courses. Abstract theories continental European legal doctrine is very keen on and which are less useful for practice could be excluded. This did not merely imply a significant quantitative shortening of the syllabus, but its qualitative adaptation to what a student needs to know and is able to assimilate through the medium of a non-dominant language.

2. *Legal Texts and Teaching Materials*

There are two basic kinds of materials necessary for legal education: collections of statutes and textbooks. In both regards, there is still an enormous lack of texts.

a) It should be noted that Spanish central institutions (Parliament, Government, Supreme Court, Constitutional Court, Council of the Judiciary, and so on) operate only in Spanish and that their norms, decisions and case-law, which affect the whole state, are not translated into Basque. A 1997 legal provision allows for translating new legal texts into official languages other than Spanish in cooperation with officially bilingual autonomous communities, but unlike other autonomous communities and for unknown reasons, Basque authorities never signed an agreement to implement that cooperation.[37] In contrast, the

[37] Reasons may include: reluctance to cooperate with central state authorities and/or an objection on principle to the absent legal status of the translated versions:

new options to translate European Union norms which came into force in 2005 have been taken advantaged of. 80 EU legal acts adopted by the European Parliament and the Council have been translated so far. These translations are not official, and they do not have legal force.[38] Therefore, the greatest part of the legal order that law students have to work with is neither originally written nor translated into Basque.[39]

Certainly, statutes and subordinate legislation passed by the Basque autonomous institutions (as well as those passed by Navarre's institutions) are published in both official languages in the Official Journal. Today, all legal acts can be downloaded from the electronic edition of the Official Journal. These official bilingual norms are relevant for some fields of law, such as administrative law and environmental law.

b) In 1990s, some universities initiated the translation of main codes and statutes with funding from Basque institutions. These initiatives have two characteristics in common: translations are the joint effort of philologists and lawyers, and the texts are published in bilingual editions. The University of Deusto has been actively promoting this type of projects.[40] Within the law faculty, a Basque Legal Workshop was established in 1993: it started to translate and publish the principal Spanish codes and compilations of statutes, a total of 14 volumes (Civil Code [2nd ed., 2007], Criminal Code [2nd ed., 2004], Civil Procedure Act, Criminal Procedure Act) as well as several collection of statutes in constitutional law, civil law, commercial law, labour law, mortgage law, company law, bankruptcy law, etc. These editions have been very carefully and attractively edited. Translations have been coherently thought and carried out by a small group of dedicated people.

Some Basque-medium lecturers of the University of the Basque Country had initially shown reluctance to the idea of translating

---

translated versions lack binding force. However, other bilingual communities have taken advantage of the opportunity opened through Royal Decree 489/1997.

[38] 27 regulations, 26 directives, 12 decisions and 14 recommendations. All legal acts are of 2006; I do not know whether the translation practice has been interrupted. All translations were undertaken by the Translation Service of a governmental body, the Basque Institute for Public Administration.

[39] The only Spanish norm that the Spanish institutions translated in the past thirty-two years was the text of Spanish Constitution in 1978. Nevertheless, the quality of the Basque translation was so low that it was rendered completely useless. Both the University of Deusto and the University of the Basque Country have published Basque translations of the Constitution.

[40] See E. Urrutia, 'Zuzenbidearen irakaskuntza eta euskara, itzulpenaren ikuspegitik: Deustuko Unibertsitatea', in S. Larrazabal and E. Oregi (eds.), *Hizkera juridikoa eta itzulpengintza: euskararen norabideak* (Universidad de Deusto/IVAP 2005) p. 173–208.

authentic legal texts into Basque, since the translated texts would lack legal force. Nevertheless, their distrust was later overcome by the realisation that students and the legal community as a whole required Basque-medium legal texts and the university should match those expectations.[41] The University of the Basque Country started in 2003, with the help of lecturers from the school of law, to translate into Basque and publish its own series of translated statutes. Professional translators check the translation, and then they discuss the terminological options jointly with legal experts within an open seminar. Eleven statutes covering different legal areas have been published so far between 2006 and 2010,[42] and other titles are foreseen in the *Leyes-Legeak* collection.[43]

The third main promoter of translations and editions of legal texts has been a governmental body. The Official Translation Service of the Basque Institute of Public Administration[44] has translated the Local Administration Act (1992) and the Administrative Procedure Act (1999; an updated edition is in process) and has prepared collections of administrative forms and reference works for the internal use of public employees. In addition, all major European Treaties have been translated by the same body: the European Economic Community Treaty (1991), the European Single Act (1991) and the post-Amsterdam and post-Lisbon consolidated versions of the EU Treaties. Only the Constitutional Treaty was translated into Spanish official languages under the auspices of the Spanish government (2004), since a referendum on the ratification of the Constitutional Treaty was called in 2005.

The availability of a Basque edition of a relevant Spanish statute does not often avoid the need for using the more comprehensive collections of Spanish laws available in Spanish. As a matter of fact, many students find it awkward to have to buy and use so many materials.

c) With regard to textbooks, there have been two different approaches. In the nineties, the translation of Spanish textbooks was

---

[41] Alkorta, *supra* n. 17, p. 213.

[42] Spanish Constitution, Labour Procedure Act, Administrative Jurisdiction Act, Constitutional Court Act, Consumer Law, Judiciary Organic Law (excerpts), Intellectual Property Act, Employment Act, Land Use Act, Social Security Act.

[43] The completion of the Judiciary Organic Act, Mark Act, Temporal Joint Venture and Labour Infractions Acts, Antitrust Law, and Biomedicine Law.

[44] See E. Oregi, 'Itzulpenaren harian: Itzultzaileen Zerbitzu Ofizialaren ekarria', in S. Larrazabal and E. Oregi (eds.), *Hizkera juridikoa eta itzulpengintza: euskararen norabideak* (Universidad de Deusto/IVAP 2005) p. 161–171.

fostered at the university level. The University of Deusto translated an administrative law textbook in three volumes, several textbooks covering the complete civil law, a constitutional law textbook, a legal history textbook, a commercial law textbook, etc. Nevertheless, the translation policy has serious handicaps. Firstly, the resulting translations may not be palatable to the lecturers responsible for the corresponding courses,[45] either because they dislike the translation for its quality or for its difficulty or because they prefer to follow another Spanish textbook. The fundamental right to academic freedom protects the choice of those lecturers. Sometimes it is students who oppose the extra task of deciphering what they consider a cryptic translation. Secondly, translations of Spanish law textbooks become obsolete very quickly, while the principal Spanish textbooks are updated almost yearly. For instance, an important reform of administrative law at the end of the nineties of the 20th century left the 1996/1997 published translation of a three volume administrative law textbook very much *touché*. Last but not least, translations are very expensive.

The University of the Basque Country has also translated a few Spanish textbooks: a constitutional law textbook in two volumes (1994/1995) and a family law textbook (1996). Yet, the University's general policy and many lecturers' firm belief has been that lecturers should produce themselves their own teaching materials and textbooks most adequate for their courses.[46] Translations may be adequate for those works that are internationally relevant and/or not time-bound, for instance in the field of legal history or legal philosophy, but for most fields of legal studies the elaboration of specific teaching materials in Basque by lecturers seems a more realistic approach. At the University of the Basque Country, there is a yearly general call for the production of teaching materials in Basque. The University funds the extra costs that the elaboration of certain teaching materials may involve (such as formatting, specific illustrations or other materials required in certain scientific fields) and assumes or pays for a general language and style revision of manuscripts. This support has encouraged the production of textbooks directly in Basque. After the manuscripts are produced and revised, they can be published electronically with an ISBN number. They can be downloaded by any member of the

[45] Alkorta, *supra* n. 17, p. 21.
[46] Alkorta, *supra* n. 17, p. 212 and 215.

university community; other interested people may ask for an invitation. Eighty-seven electronic teaching materials exist so far, twenty-one of them from law. Certainly there are asymmetries between legal areas: the most productive areas are civil and procedural law, while no title covers commercial law or international law. The intranet application also allows for terminology searches and for consulting glossaries made out of the electronic resources. Authors are free to publish their materials wherever they want. To be printed by the university press, however, manuscripts need the authorisation of the Basque language services of the university: those services supervise more carefully the language and style of the manuscript than in texts aiming at an electronic publication. Textbooks on trade union law (2000), administrative law (2006) and inheritance law (2008) have been published by the university press.

Some lecturers from the University of the Basque Country have taken their manuscripts to other publishers, like the Basque Institute of Public Administration (a legal philosophy textbook), the Society for Basque Studies (introductions to labour law sources, public services law, and civil procedure law), or the Basque Summer University (an introduction to advertising law). The University of Deusto has published three textbooks (on finance, tax and constitutional law) produced by its lecturers.

The Basque Summer University (*Udako Euskal Unibertsitatea*) is an association, founded in 1978, that started organising a Basque-medium summer university and which, more generally, promotes higher education teaching and research in Basque.[47] They have published approximately one hundred titles from all academic genres (dissertations, textbooks, essays, translations of reference works, divulgation, etc.). In addition, this association has its own yearly program for fostering the production of Basque textbooks: selected projects are awarded a small grant to finalise a textbook. But the pioneer work is the two volume law dictionary—actually a Basque-Spanish-French glossary and a Basque-medium law dictionary— published in 1985 by the Basque Centre for University Services (UZEI).[48]

---

[47] See I. Torregarai, 'Udako Euskal Unibertsitatea (UEU)', 50 *Bat. Soziolinguistika aldizkaria* (2004) p. 83–96.

[48] Social movements, associations and initiatives have been very relevant in the defence and promotion of the Basque language and culture in all social fields: education, culture, media, press, etc. This also applies to the field of Basque-medium higher

The translation and elaboration of Basque-medium textbooks is promoted by the Basque Government. The Basque Ministry for Education makes a yearly call for the translation, elaboration or adaptation of textbooks and other scientific works related to the studies being offered in the universities and other higher education centres of the Basque autonomous community. Commercial publishers, universities and research centres, and non-profit private institutions can apply for funding in that call. Financial assistance covers the costs of translation and the costs of the technical publication. As the public administration has responsibility for the standardisation of the Basque language, all funded books must previously obtain the linguistic conformity from that Ministry: in the case of the Basque universities, the corresponding vice rector responsible for Basque-medium education will issue a statement that the manuscript conforms to the norms and guidelines established by the Basque Language Academy.[49]

Finally, in the last decade, many classics from political thought and political philosophy have been translated into Basque within different translation projects: Plato's *Republic*, Locke's *Second treatise on civil government*, Hobbes' *Leviathan*, Montesquieu's *The Spirit of the Laws*, Rousseau's *The social contract*, Maquiavelo's *The Principe*, Tocqueville's *Democracy in America*, John Rawls' *A theory of justice*, etc.[50] These translations have been carefully carried out and edited.

education: the Summer Basque University (UEU), the Basque Centre for University Services (UZEI), the Society for Basque Studies, and the Association of Basque-medium University Lecturers (EIRE). Despite maintaining their original denominations, the missions of UEU and UZEI have evolved. The former understands its mission as helping the creation of the Basque University; the latter as the production of field-specific dictionaries. However, unlike primary and secondary education, the high complexity and cost of higher education provision explains why in this sector the public university has remained unrivalled as the main provider of Basque-medium formal higher education.

[49] See Official Bulletin of the Basque Country (EHHA/BOPV), no. 178 of Sept. 16, 2009; no. 93 of May 19, 2008, etc. The first call of this kind seems to be from 1989.

[50] These titles form part of an extraordinary collection called *Klasikoak*, launched in 1991, with more than one hundred classic titles from the history of ideas, published by Klasikoak, S.A., a non-profit association supported by the three Basque saving banks, the BBVA foundation, the University of the Basque Country and the University of Deusto. Other relevant collections are the *Limes* series published by the University of the Basque Country (twelve titles), and the *Jakin irakurgaiak* collection published by *Jakinkizunak*. The *Limes* collection focuses on classics that have literary value (Plato, Rousseau, Burke, etc.), and *Jakin irakurgaiak* on philosophical short pieces.

F. Research

The Constitutions of the University of the Basque Country proclaim the right of researchers to conduct research and disseminate their research results both in Basque and Spanish. This declaration gives a linguistic dimension to academic freedom. However, linguistic academic freedom must confront the many practical and socio-professional difficulties involved in its implementation.

On the one hand, in Spain there are individual research assessments under the responsibility of a national research council. These research assessments covering a period of at least six years of research, although voluntary in character, are having increasingly consequences, including for law lecturers. Firstly, researchers are granted a small bonus for each positive research assessment. Secondly, the number of positive research assessment periods a researcher has obtained is a crucial criterion in order to undertake many relevant academic and career decisions: to assess the quality of a master program in general terms, to qualify for accreditation as a professor (the main promotion in an academic career), to appoint referees within the many assessment, accreditation and audit systems now in work within academia, etc. The research assessment system largely conditions the decisions of researchers about what and in which language to publish. Basque-medium early academics working at the University of the Basque Country are not, and should not be, blind to the career advancement system ruling in public universities.[51]

Therefore, Basque-speaking lecturers are in a paradoxical situation: as academics, they are socially well-recognised; but as Basque-medium researchers, they are located far from the sources of symbolic capital in academia – both at their university and within the scientific community. This poses a dilemma for Basque-speaking scholars, especially in social sciences: they have to opt between the commitment to Basque language and culture on the one side, and their advancement in academic career on the other.[52] In some social sciences, scholars may

[51] Although most of them have produced their own teaching materials in Basque and have even published some articles in Basque, they try to publish in the best Spanish legal journals and publishing houses.

[52] X. Isasi, 'Unibertsitario euskaldunen egoera zaila', 50 *Bat. Soziolinguistika aldizkaria* (2004) p. 131 at 133; A. Larrinaga, 'Unibertsitate esparrua, gatazka sinbolikoen agertoki: akademiko euskaldunen pertzepzioak', in A. Larrinaga and M. Amurrio

adopt some kind of compromise: for instance, they can publish the same or different pieces of research in Basque and in other languages. But in highly hierarchised legal studies, the option of publishing mainly in Basque is materially infeasible. In fact, no legal scholar publishes mainly in Basque. Basque-medium legal research is very marginal in quantitative and qualitative terms – even within the Basque-medium scientific production. In the future, this could change, not only thanks to the new possibilities of electronic publication, but also because of the regionalisation of higher education: some researchers might look at the new regional system of research and teaching assessment. However, the option of linking one's academic career to a regional agency may not be attractive for many researchers in legal studies. Only a positive assessment awarded by the national agency will score high in the eyes of the academic community.

On the other hand, it is obvious that the Basque-speaking legal community, including both academics and practitioners, is very small. The effectiveness of the use of Basque as the language of legal research depends not only on the institutional and economic support of the authorities, including both policymakers and university managers, but also on the availability of a critical mass of legal experts who are able and willing to carry out their work in Basque. Currently, books other than textbooks in Basque have no market at all, and there are no referred quality journals for Basque-medium legal writings.[53] A few authors have opted for publishing simultaneously a Basque and a Spanish version of their research work, in the same volume or separately: dual publication is an expensive option that requires publication grants and which could only be justified in special cases.

The above mentioned reasons attempt to explain why the most underdeveloped area of Basque-medium legal education is research. Scientific production is very scarce. According to the Data Base of the Basque Scientific Community (*Inguma*),[54] in the field of legal studies

(eds.), *Hezkuntza Euskal Herrian aztergai. Hurbilketa soziologikoa* (Utriusque Vasconiae 2006) p. 123 at 152–161.

[53] There is a Basque-medium legal journal, *Eleria. Euskal Herriko Legelarien Aldizkaria*, grounded in 1996. This journal is published by the Society for Basque Studies (*Eusko Ikaskuntza*). In 2011, it had reached the twenty-first issue. The majority of the articles are written by lecturers and researchers of the University of the Basque Country. Another legal journal, called *Revista Vasca de Administración Pública*, also publish articles in Basque, and the social sciences Basque-medium journal *Uztaro* includes occasionally articles on legal issues.

[54] For a presentation of the *Inguma* Data Base in English, see http://www.inguma.org/indexen.php#zer_da

395 articles have been written and published in Basque as of 2010 (all but two after devolution in 1979). In any case, that number includes many chronicles, purely informative or non-academic texts published in non-legal journals. In all scientific fields, a total of 371 doctoral theses have been written in Basque in the history of the Basque language.[55] Yet, the number is significantly reduced in the field of legal studies: only four even with a flexible thematic approach, three of which are related to Basque legal issues (cooperatives, Basque 'Old-Laws' and Basque legal language) and the other to music education law. The first generation of Basque-medium legal scholars who graduated in Basque had to establish priorities, and the priority of even those most committed to Basque-medium education was the production of teaching materials in Basque, while they understood that their career advancement depended on a PhD written in Spanish.

To promote an increasing Basque-medium research, apart from ordinary calls for PhD scholarships that are available regardless of the language of research, a specific programme of the University of the Basque Country yearly awards five scholarships to write a dissertation in Basque in any scientific field. Financial assistance is also given to avoid the practical problems of a dissertation in a non-dominant language, i.e. that a doctoral candidate has no language-based difficulties in undertaking doctoral viva consisting of five members: to that effect, funding is granted to translate parts of the dissertation for non-Basque-speaking members or to provide for an interpreter at the dissertation defence.

G. New Challenges: Trilingualism, Europeanisation and Globalisation

Legal education faces many challenges: the emergence of English as a language of instruction, the Europeanisation of higher education and the globalisation of legal practice and legal studies. Very few seem to be aware of the challenges with regard to minority language higher education in particular. In this section, I will comment on some of those implications.

Scholars and private schools have been analysing and exploring the possibilities of trilingualism (Spanish, Basque, and English) in the

[55] Data from the Inguma Data Base.

educational system for a long time.[56] The current Basque government has decided to introduce a trilingual educational model in primary and secondary public education. A similar trend seems to be gradually emerging for higher education. It is clear that trilingualism has not the same implications for early education or for higher education. In 2005, the University of the Basque Country approved a multilingualism plan to promote the use of foreign languages in optional courses as well in conferences and seminars. In 2009/10, 126 optional courses were offered in languages other than Spanish or Basque, mainly in English, at the whole University: this is still a small percentage of courses, even of the total of optional courses. At the law faculty, optional courses such as genome and law, environmental law and history of international relations have been offered in English in the past years. The extra work for lecturers involved in the initial preparation of an English course is rewarded with double the amounts of credits for the relevant course over two years. Lecturers are screened for their language proficiency, while students are not. Some lecturers facilitate the enrolment of less adventurous students, allowing them to write exercises and exams in their preferred language, Spanish or Basque.[57]

For the future, Basque legislation states that 'when implementing new degrees funded by public resources, groups will be established taking the Basque language as a preferential criterion"; in other words, it will always be required that a Basque group will also be created.[58] A subsequent decree has further established more specific objectives according to the different type of studies and subjects: a) the University of the Basque Country 'will adopt measures to achieve that in all degree studies main and compulsory subjects may be taken in Basque and in Spanish'; b) 'with regard to optional and freely elective subjects multilingualism will be fostered, and the offer of subjects in Basque will be at least as broad as in other languages'; c) 'when degrees are enacted in accordance with the European Higher Education Space, the offer of

[56] L. Joaristi, L. Lizasoain, J. F. Lukas and K. Santiago 'Trilingualism (Spanish, English and Basque) in the educational system of the Basque Country', 6 *International Journal of Multilingualism* (2009) p. 105–126; J. Cenoz, *Towards Multilingual Education: Basque Educational Research in International Perspective* (Multilingual Matters 2009).

[57] J. Cenoz, 'Elebitasunetik eleaniztasunera Euskal Herriko Unibertsitatean: Eleaniztasun Plana', 75 *Bat. Soziolinguistika aldizkaria* (2010) p. 39 at p. 45.

[58] Art. 46 (3) of Basque University System Act (Act 3/2004).

postgraduate studies in Basque as a whole must be equivalent to that in Spanish'.[59]

The philosophy that emerges from the abovementioned provisions aims at combining equal parity of status of Basque and Spanish in the main and compulsory subjects at the undergraduate level, with a balanced trilingual approach (Spanish, Basque, and English) for optional subjects of degree and for postgraduate studies. In other words, English should not be introduced to the detriment of Basque.

In general, Basque-speaking academics are in favour of the introduction of English as a language of instruction. They regard it as an inevitable consequence of the relevance of English in science, global economy and international politics. They see no contradiction that the use of English is being expanded and promoted even before fully implementing the legally entrenched Basque-medium provision of higher education. Differences seem to lie with regard to the space that should be offered to English, not to the desirability of that introduction. Some argue that, if further languages of instruction are to be introduced, more flexibility is required. For instance, Ludger Mees advocates what he calls a flexible scheme of "asynchronic uses".[60] The current strict parallel-medium education model in undergraduate studies should be tempered: the Basque track should be opened to Spanish and other languages, and vice versa, the Spanish track should be opened to Basque-, English- and French-medium courses. In postgraduate studies, which should foster the mobility of students and try to catch foreign students, the use of English should be increased and be significant. In contrast, the use of other languages could not be established in general terms but would depend on several criteria: the provenience of students, the market for the relevant studies, the relevance of studies for the Basque Country, and so on. The use of Basque in research should be promoted with special measures, although it is clear that Basque will be a secondary or even a tertiary language in

[59] Art. 23 of Decree 40/2008 of Mar. 4, 2008 on the legal regime of teaching and research staff at the University of the Basque Country (Official Bulletin of the Basque Country no. 55 of Mar. 18, 2008).

[60] L. Mees, 'Eleaniztasuna eta euskalduna, baita mundu akademikoan ere: posible ote?', 75 *Bat. Soziolinguistika aldizkaria* (2010) p. 83 at p. 91–92. Born and educated in Germany, Ludger Mees is a professor of history at the University of the Basque Country very much committed to the Basque language; he has been vice chancellor for Basque-medium education at the University of the Basque Country (2004/08) and is a member of the Consultative Board of the Basque Language of the Basque Government.

scientific production. The focus should be directed, therefore, to its role in scientific dissemination and divulgation.

In my view, there is an additional argument for a flexible multiplicity of languages in the curriculum. As experts indicate, bi- or multilingualism in the twenty-first century must be more than the knowledge of two or more languages. Abilities such as translation, language switching and designing information bilingually will be increasingly important.[61] In fact, Basque-medium provision of legal education has ever been very much a bilingual practice discourse, in which classroom explanations and, perhaps, some rudimentary teaching materials can be available in Basque, but the whole legislation and case-law is in Spanish only.[62] Of course, the same situation applies to an ever greater extent to legal practice. A Basque-medium lawyer, whether scholar or practitioner, must be equally proficient in two languages, Basque and Spanish. This is nothing peculiar to the Basque case: as it happens often in bilingual societies, lawyers must be not only lawyers, but also 'jurilinguists'.[63] Similarly, the European, transnational and comparative dimension of law in Europe should increasingly lead to a multilingual practice discourse in legal education, in which, for instance, classroom explanations may be given in the local languages but cases, teaching materials and case-law are given and analysed in foreign languages.

The second challenge of legal education is the Bologna process. Duration and content of almost all studies have been reformed. It is not clear why legal education should have been included within the Bologna process. Law is a field in which national traditions and practices are still determinant. The whole process seems to have been guided by one idea, that of simplification: to foster mobility of consumers and services within the European Area of Higher Education, every national higher education system has to offer its products in three kinds of packaging: carton (degree), tetrabrik (master) and glass (PhD). This idea has been also extended to higher education through the medium of non-dominant or lesser used languages. What German,

---

[61] O. García, *Bilingual Education in the 21st Century – A Global Perspective* (Wiley-Blackwell 2009) p. 297.

[62] Alkorta, *supra* n. 17, p. 213.

[63] A. Urrutia, 'Jurista euskalduna, jurista elebiduna', in S. Larrazabal and E. Oregi (eds.), *Hizkera juridikoa eta itzulpengintza: euskararen norabideak* (Universidad de Deusto/IVAP 2005) p. 147 at p. 150.

French, English, Italian, Polish etc. student is going to study law through the medium of Basque or Welsh? What kind of mobility may Basque-medium education reasonably expect: only a one-way mobility? The Bologna process's slogan is flexibility, but the result is increasing uniformity. The decisions to adopt the Bologna process were top-bottom decisions, and the new syllabus was decided by central state institutions and by university centres. Neither the former nor the latter seem to have considered the specific needs of Basque-medium legal education. As a result, the same syllabus applies to Spanish-medium and Basque-medium legal education; that is, to an education that may cater for more and more foreign students and to an education that cannot attract students outside its linguistic community and which has enough problems in retaining Basque-speaking students.

The implementation of new degrees in accordance with the European Area of Higher Education started in the academic year 2010/11 at the University of the Basque Country as in most Spanish universities. In addition, new regulations concern the access of students to higher education. Now, there is no a unique final mark for access to higher education, whatever the studies the student wants to apply for, each faculty may regulate the 'basket of marks' they will consider to decide on the admission of candidates.

The third challenge is the globalisation of higher education. Universities are more and more regarded as suppliers of services in a global market. Their customers do not need to come from the same region or even the same state. This opens new opportunities for those universities whose languages of instruction happen to be an international language, such as English or Spanish. This can be detrimental to those universities that teach through the medium of a non-dominant language, especially those inserted in an English- or Spanish-speaking majority. Welsh- or Basque-medium legal scholars are all bilingual. Why offer Welsh-medium legal education if any English-medium master on commercial or international business law, with no or little investment, will attract flows of students every year and be profitable both for the responsible institution and its lecturers?[64] To a lesser extent, the same dilemma will face other scholars speaking lesser used languages.

Spanish universities have also started to look at the Spanish-speaking market in Latin-America. Many South-American states are lacking the

[64] See the chapter on Welsh-medium education by G. Parry.

physical/human infrastructure and the financial resources to offer post-graduate education (master degrees and doctoral programmes). Those countries are interested in importing education programmes and institutions for nation-building purposes: i.e., in order to have an educated, trained and knowledgeable citizenry and workforce. The University of the Basque Country's law school has been very active offering doctoral programmes in Latin-American universities. As a result, every year at least half a dozen of doctoral theses are defended by candidates who are enrolled in those programmes. The number of PhDs written in Spanish by those 'external' students is growing while the number of Basque-medium theses is not increasing.[65] The 'market' opportunities do not limit to masters and doctoral programmes. In 2007, a group of 33 Colombian undergraduates moved from their home university (*Universidad Javierana de Bogotá*) to Donostia-San Sebastián to finish their law degree at the University of the Basque Country's law school, following an agreement between both institutions.

H. Conclusions

Basque is a language of law in the Basque autonomous community. Moreover, bilingual legal education has been introduced and established in two Basque law schools, fully at the public University of the Basque Country and widely at the private Deusto University. The most relevant change in legal education (and in higher education in general) in the last three decades has been the introduction of Basque-medium education. In that period, the Basque language has moved from the farm to the law school. This huge transformation of legal education through policy has not raised significant conflicts and resistance – as always happens, some would have preferred to go faster. But what is relevant is that some hundreds of students have studied all or part of their law degrees through the medium of Basque. The objective of Basque higher education policy—the extension of parallel-medium education—seems to have been accomplished.

However, the whole process has been driven by duplication of education provision. Basque-medium education needed to be provided,

[65] The same happens in Galicia. There, the number of thesis written in Portuguese and defended in Galician universities by Portuguese or Brazilian PhD candidates exceeds by far the number of Galician-medium thesis. See the chapter on Galician-medium education by A. Nogueira López.

and bilingual lecturers were progressively appointed to meet that demand. The majority of candidates were fresh graduates with no professional, teaching or research experience. Since the whole process of expansion (even duplication) of provision was mainly based on new recruitments, no relevant tensions can be reported when transforming the University through policy. After three decades of development, an evaluation of the existing parallel-medium education is necessary to assist in making recommendations regarding the role of different languages in higher education including the role that should be accorded to English.

For the time being, the result is *weak* parallel-medium education: only the instruction and some study materials are in Basque. It cannot be said that there a mature Basque-medium legal scholarship exists. Bilingual (or Basque-medium) university education produces bilingual graduates and academics, but it is far away from creating a Basque-medium legal environment. After three decades of democratisation, devolution and language legislation, access to legal professions in officially bilingual autonomous communities does not require any linguistic skill. Judges, prosecutors, court registrars, notary and other legal professions are still regulated by the central state. Regional authorities cannot control language use in legal professions. The Spanish-dominated legal profession and scholarship keep their hegemony at the state and substate level. This significant mis-match between Basque-medium legal education and Spanish-medium legal practice may result in a migration of potential Basque-speaking students away from Basque-medium legal education.

The option for a single university and for parallel-medium education was carried out until the last consequences. When a new section of the law school was created in Leioa (Bilbao), it had to offer the same teaching as in San Sebastian and the same languages of instruction (Basque, Spanish). Similarly, since 2010/2011 a new degree of criminology is offered in Donostia-San Sebastián also in both languages. As a result, Basque-medium scholarship is not concentrated and appears weaker and diluted in the shadow of substantial departments that, moreover, are scattered across two distant campuses. It is not an accident that, at the present, the heads of the seven large law departments of the University of the Basque Country do not hold bilingual positions and, as a result, do not teach in Basque, although they may be more or less bilingual in family situations or in the community.

Parallel-medium education has been a crucial strategy for gradually setting and developing Basque-medium education. Now, Basque-medium education is very much developed, and the question is whether the sustainability of Basque in general and the advancement of Basque-medium legal education in particular should not be better served through a different strategy, that of creating monolingual centres, which could ensure visibility of Basque-medium legal education. The creation of a Basque-medium centre is difficult, since it seems to break a sacred institutional principle of Basque university policy: that of aggregation of campuses and cohabitation of both official languages. However, it does not need to take the traditional form of a new law school, but it could take the legal form of a university institute or an interdepartmental institution responsible for co-ordinating and promoting Basque-medium legal research and Basque-medium postgraduate and life long legal education, to which lecturers and researchers from different faculties and departments could be ascribed functionally, which could establish their own research masters and programmes for practitioners and which could serve the professional stakeholders of the Basque-speaking territories. The centre should be a hub for scholars and practitioners at the forefront of research, debate and practice in legal issues. It should draw on the strength of the University of the Basque Country's legal scholars across a wide range of disciplines, and it should bring scholars and practitioners together to ensure that Basque-medium scholarship is informed by rigorous theoretical work as well as hands-on experience.

CHAPTER SEVEN

BILINGUAL LEGAL EDUCATION IN CATALONIA

Eva Pons

A. Legal Framework

According to Article 27(10) of the Spanish Constitution, "the autonomy of universities is recognised under the terms established by law". Two legislatures are concerned with this mandate, since the central state and autonomous communities—regional authorities endowed with political autonomy—share powers over the universities.

On the one hand, the Constitution confers to the central state the power to establish "regulations of the conditions for obtaining, issuing, approving, and standardising academic and professional degrees and basic norms for carrying out Article 27 in order to guarantee compliance with the obligations of the public powers in this matter".[1] In addition, the State may regulate other aspects of universities, such as: the "promotion and general coordination of scientific and technical research";[2] "the bases of the legal system of the public administrations and the statutory system for its officials";[3] and with regard to students, "the regulation of the basic conditions which guarantee the equality of all Spaniards in the exercise of their rights and fulfilment of their constitutional duties".[4]

Organic Law 6/2001 on Universities (OLU), reformed by Organic Law 4/2007, is the basic norm in this field adopted by the State. Universities are defined by this Law as institutions that develop scientific and technical functions, preparation for professional activities, social transfer of knowledge and training throughout life.[5] There are two types of institutions: public universities, created by State or Autonomous Community legislatures; and private universities, defined in negative

[1] Art. 149 (1) (30).
[2] Art. 149 (1) (15).
[3] Art. 149 (1) (18).
[4] Art. 149 (1) (1).
[5] Art. 1 and 2 OLU.

terms and which must be recognised by the same legislative bodies.[6] Spanish universities operate under the principles of autonomy and coordination: the *Council of Coordination* and the *General Conference for University Policy* are the two main state coordination bodies.[7] In addition, the Law regulates some aspects of the structure, governing bodies, assessment and accreditation (*National Agency for Quality Assessment and Accreditation*), degrees and diplomas, research, student access, teaching and administrative staff and finances of the universities.

On the other hand, regional governments hold legislative and executive powers in the higher education sector. The Statute of Autonomy of Catalonia (SAC)—defined as the basic institutional norm of the Autonomous Community—recently reformed by Organic Law 6/2006, incorporates an exhaustive enumeration of the powers of the *Generalitat*—institution of self-government of Catalonia—over universities. Article 172 SAC distinguishes three types of power devolved to the *Generalitat*, notwithstanding university autonomy: *executive power* (basically, the planning and coordination of the Catalan university system within the framework of general coordination, the approval of university constitutions, the system of remuneration of teaching and research staff employed by universities and the establishment of additional remuneration for teaching staff in permanent public employment, among others); *shared power* (mainly, the establishment of a legal system for the organisation and functioning of public universities, including governing and representative bodies, regulation of the system of access to the universities, regulation of the system governing contracted and permanent teaching and research personnel, evaluating and ensuring the excellence and quality of university education, and also of teaching and research personnel); and *executive power over the issuing of official university qualifications*. The University Law of Catalonia (ULC, Law 1/2003), adopted under the previous Statute of Autonomy of 1979, establishes regional powers in these fields. According to this Law, "Catalonia's university system is made up for the existing public and private universities and those subsequently created or recognised by the Parliament of Catalonia" (Art. 2).

---

[6] Art. 3 OLU.

[7] Art. 2 and Title IV OLU.

Regarding language matters, the Constitution states that "Castilian is the official language of the Spanish state" and that "all Spaniards have the duty to know it and the right to use it".[8] With regard to languages other than Castilian, Article 3 (2) establishes that "the other languages of Spain will also be official in the respective autonomous communities, in accordance with their Statutes". At present, the Statute of Autonomy of Catalonia establishes that the official languages in Catalonia are Catalan, Castilian and Occitan,[9] although the official status of Occitan, a language spoken in the Aran Valley in the Pyrenees, must be defined by legislation. Article 143 (1) SAC states that "the *Generalitat* of Catalonia has exclusive power with regard to Catalonia's own language. This power includes, in every case, determination of the scope, uses and legal effects of its official status, and also the linguistic normalisation of Catalan". Though the State does not have explicit powers over linguistic matters, the Constitutional Court admits that such powers are implicit in legislative powers over other matters assumed by the State, who in doing so must respect the statutory and legislative autonomic regulation of the official languages different from Castilian.[10]

In general, since 1983 state university's laws have ignored language matters. In practice, this lack of attention favours Castilian language, which official status cannot be denied in any part of the territory of the State.[11] According to the duty established by Article 3 (1) of the Spanish Constitution, knowledge of Castilian by members of the universities is also implicitly guaranteed by the State regulation of various central aspects of the university system. In 2007 a first mention to multilingual character of the university system was included in the OLU, where is said: "Public authorities and universities, through their statutes, must introduce mechanisms to endow members of the university community with sufficient knowledge of co-official languages through adequate instruction and initiation processes in order to faster the use of these languages".[12]

In a different way, within the framework of the Statute of Autonomy, the Catalan legislature has paid special attention to the linguistic

[8] Art. 3 (1).
[9] Art. 6 (2) and (5).
[10] Judgments 74/1987 and 87/1997.
[11] Judgment 82/1986 of the Constitutional Court.
[12] Art. 6 (2) OLU.

elements in the above mentioned University Law of Catalonia (ULC) and, more obviously, in the linguistic regulation which is contained in the Language Policy Law (Law 1/1998, LPL). We can draw from these laws four main principles on which the university language policies in Catalonia are based:

Firstly, the definition of Catalan as Catalonia's *own language*. As such, Catalan is the language of normal and preferential use in Public Administration bodies –including universities- and is also the language of normal use for teaching and learning in the education system.[13] This principle implies that universities "must make Catalan the normal vehicle for expression in their educational and administrative activities, both internal and external".[14] It must be said that Judgment 31/2010 of the Constitutional Court on the 2006 reform of the Statute of Autonomy has overruled the adjective "preferential" to qualify Catalan language as Catalonia's own language, to preserve the official status of Castilian, but the concrete consequences of this decision are uncertain at the present time.

Secondly, and connected to the previous one, is the principle of *linguistic normalisation of Catalan*. In that sense, "the incorporation of the Catalan language in all spheres of knowledge and the contribution to the normalisation process of scientific, social and cultural uses of Catalan" is defined as one of the goals of the university system of Catalonia.[15] Government, universities and higher education institutions, according to their respective powers, "must take appropriate measures to ensure the use of Catalan in all spheres of teaching activity, non-teaching activity and research".[16] These norms are consistent with the objectives of protection and promotion assumed by the European Charter for Regional or Minority Languages, an international treaty made in the context of the Council of Europe and ratified by Spain in 2001. Nevertheless, the international commitments assumed by Spain with regard to university education are limited,[17] below the level of protection provided by internal regulations.

Thirdly, the principle of *double official status of Catalan and Castilian* means that legal acts and formal communications of university bodies

---

[13] Art. 6 (1) SAC; Art. 2 (1) and 20 (1) LPL.
[14] Art. 20 (2) LPL; Art. 6 (1) ULC.
[15] Art. 3 (1) (d) ULC.
[16] Art. 50 (2) SAC; Art. 22 (2) LPL.
[17] Art. 8 (1) (e) (iii) of the Charter.

or their members executed in either of the two official languages have, in linguistic terms, fully validity and effects.[18] At present, Article 6 (2) SAC tends to equate the basic rights and obligations derived from the official status of these two languages.[19] As regards to higher education, Article 35 (5) SAC stipulates that "teachers and students of universities have the right to express themselves orally and in writing in the official language of their choice".[20] At the same time, public universities as Public Administrations must respect language rights and the duties of citizens.[21] According to Article 5 (6) SAC, universities must also recognise the right to use Occitan, and also other additional rights and obligations relating to Occitan that will be determined by law.[22]

And, finally, since 1998 one may deduce from the Catalan legislation a principle of *internationalisation*, which has several expressions: the ability of the universities to establish "specific criteria for language use in activities related to international commitments";[23] the mandate "to establish programmes to promote knowledge of third languages which may include both the use of these languages in academic activities of the university and a number of specific subjects to each program";[24] and also measures to "secure that the admission and the incorporation of new members in the university community do not alter the teaching language used and the process of linguistic normalisation of the universities".[25]

In the above-mentioned legal framework, Catalan universities have regulated the use of languages in their statutes and other provisions. According to Judgment 75/1997 of the Constitutional Court, these linguistic provisions may be included in the "ordinary content" of university autonomy, which is not explicitly determined in Article 2 (2) OLU, and where only a legal negative limit can be found. The linguistic

[18] Art. 32 SAC.

[19] However, this provision has been the object of a consistent interpretation by the Constitutional Court in Judgment 31/2010, in which the equivalence between the constitutional obligation to know Castilian and the obligation to know Catalan for citizens of Catalonia was denied.

[20] This was already in Art. 22 (1) LPL.

[21] Art. 6 (2) and 33 (1) SAC; Art. 4, 9 and 10 LPL; Art. 54 (11) of the State Law 7/2007 on the Basic Statute of the Public Employees.

[22] Art. 36 SAC.

[23] Art. 22 (4) LPL.

[24] Art. 6 (6) ULC.

[25] Art. 6 (5) ULC.

content of the university statutes in force is quite similar, since they ratify the legal principles and may specify some linguistic rights and obligations arising from them. The differences are more important in the regulatory sub-statute level: firstly, not all universities have adopted the linguistic regulations called for Article 9 (3) LPL to "regulate the use of Catalan, within their respective powers"; and, secondly, some institutions have adopted special plans or documents in order to formalise their institutional language policy (since 2010, the Catalan Government encourages the adoption of multilingual plans by universities through the provision of additional funding).

B. Organisation of Legal Education with Regard to Official Languages

The political and administrative organisation of language use at the universities of Catalonia has been largely based on the *principle of language conjunction*. In its strictest terms, this principle postulates the joint education of students of different native or initial languages as a way to prevent the production and reproduction of intra-societal limits or boundaries. In its philosophical base we can find the Republican tradition that ignores the potential communitarian attachment of citizens when building the common institutions. Nowadays, Article 35 (3) SAC recognises the right of students "not to be separated into centres or different class groups on the basis of their habitual language of use." But beyond that, the non separation has become a structural principle of an educational system in which Catalan is defined as the language of normal use of teaching and learning,[26] without excluding Castilian as a teaching language.[27]

Additionally, the political and administrative organisation of languages use in the university is based, which originated in the nineties, upon a *principle of coordination*. This principle has allowed the building of a globally unique linguistic university model, despite geographical location, public o private dependency or the legitimate interests of each of the institutions involved. Therefore, in principle, inside this system there is no place for the distinction between Catalan and

[26] Art. 6 (1) and 35 (1) SAC.

[27] See Judgment 337/1994, on non-university education, and more recently Judgment 31/2010 for all educational levels.

Castilian universities and even the existence of linguistic lines in a given university is the exception rather than the rule.

The university system of Catalonia is composed of a total of eleven universities, including public (since 1983 the Central State has not exercised the power to create new universities in Catalonia) and private; ten of them offer legal studies: the public universities of Barcelona, Autónoma de Barcelona, Girona, Lleida, Pompeu Fabra (Barcelona) and Rovira i Virgili (Tarragona); the private universities of Ramon Llull-ESADE, International of Catalonia and Abat Oliva-CEU (all located in Barcelona); and finally the non-presential Open University of Catalonia (Universitat Oberta de Catalunya), that is of a mixed nature, both public and private. There are no other higher education institutions that provide law studies programmes.

In accordance with the above-mentioned legal principles, Catalan and Spanish are used interchangeably, as official languages in the teaching of law in Catalan universities. The official status of both languages is manifested in an *emissive freedom*, according to which "the teaching staff and pupils of universities have the right to express themselves, orally and in writing, in the official language of their choice".[28] Certainly, with regards to the language of instruction, this freedom can be modulated in accordance with the provisions of Article 35 (1) SAC, which states that "each individual has the right to receive an education in Catalan". So the need to guarantee the rights of students, in an institutional context where Catalan is the universities' own language, can justify the imposition of limits on the teacher's right to linguistic choice (such limits could be derived also from other principles or criteria, like the principle of internationalisation). In practice, departments or faculties, as well as university structures in charge of the organisation of teaching, are concerned with practical implications of this issue.

In summary this legal framework supports a dynamic relationship between rights and responsibilities: namely, individual rights are protected and collective responsibilities are imposed on universities; at the same time it is possible that, under some circumstances, the possibility of individual action being restricted and even some linguistic obligations being imposed on individuals exists since this is the only way to guarantee the enjoyment of linguistic rights for the large majority of individuals.

---

[28] Art. 35 (5) SAC; Art. 22 (1) LPL.

The translation of this linguistic model into quantitative data is not immediately apparent, because the distribution of Catalan and Spanish in teaching varies in each university and within the same institution among different courses. Overall, Catalan maintains the position as the official language most commonly used as a vehicle of education within the university system of Catalonia (around 62 percent of class groups, according to data from the academic year 2006–07)[29]. In general, the rate of use of Spanish is higher in private universities (while Catalan is used in 65 percent of class groups in public universities—none of which has a lower percentage than 50 percent—; the average of 60 percent use of Catalan in private universities shows a high variation from 36 percent—in UIC—to 87 percent—UVic—) and this can be explained, among other reasons, by a weaker adherence of such institutions to the legal linguistic provisions. Although the comparison between the linguistic percentages of Catalan/Castilian teaching in various universities should be taken with caution, given the absence of a common methodology or regularly updated data, it could be argued that the use of Catalan in legal studies is lower than the overall rates of use for this language: UPF: 42.91 percent Catalan, 52.61 percent Spanish (academic year 2007–08);[30] UAB: 53.09 percent Catalan 46.91 percent Spanish (2006–07);[31] UB: 40.9 percent Catalan; 59.1 percent Spanish (2004–05);[32] UdL: 58.23 percent Catalan, 30.38 percent Spanish, 11.39 percent Catalan and Spanish.[33]

For some time, Catalan universities have adopted measures to promote multilingualism in their institutional activities. Regarding organisation of language teaching, the precedent division between the two official languages will be altered by the gradual introduction of a third language of instruction (mainly English). The increased presence of English as language teaching in legal studies is currently located in the master's and postgraduate courses, where the presence of Spanish was for a long time much more widespread than Catalan (previous data on PhD courses in the UB Faculty of Law, for the year 1996–1997, indicated that 84 percent of academic subjects were taught in Spanish and 16 percent in Catalan). Masters and postgraduate are now divided into

---

[29] http://www.gencat.cat/diue/doc/doc_28796434_1.xls

[30] http://www.upf.edu/gl/sociolin/dadesdoc/dret.html

[31] http://www.uab.cat/Document/LlenguesDocenciaUAB.pdf

[32] http://www.ub.es/slc/socio/curs0405/uni.htm

[33] These data are of 1995–96 and include the faculties of law and economy; http://www.udl.cat/serveis/sl/catala/dades#cos

official masters and universities' own masters, where there is not enough information about the use of languages. For example, among the 140 master degrees offered by the UB during the academic year 2009–2010 the use of English—usually along with Spanish, or Catalan and Spanish—was established in 74 and the use of Catalan was established in 81, always together with other languages except in the master of secondary teachers training in Catalan. With regard to law degrees, the presence of English as a teaching language has been very limited until now. In any case, there is a lack of quantitative data illustrating the use of languages of instruction; the only available data is from the Faculty of Law of UPF, where English was used in 4.48 percent class groups during 2007–08.

Finally, it is worth noting that from the beginning of the academic year 2009–2010, the use of English as a language of instruction (in undergraduate studies and master) has been established by the Government as a general goal of the Catalan university system, specifically driven by the establishment of financial university incentives. Consequently, universities must implement the use of English in some knowledge areas or class groups in the next few years through specific planning measures. Thus the current trend seems to point to a more marked differentiation between university multilingual models, through which universities will be able to define their own profile in a more competitive context.

C. Students

With regard to students, State legislation outlines a general framework that covers the requirements that applicants must meet and the establishment of the so-called *open university district*.[34] This means that any student who has passed baccalaureate studies and the selectivity exam (general exam previous to the entrance to university established by autonomous communities following the state guidelines) is guaranteed equal access to any Spanish university. This norm has been established without taking into consideration its impact on the multilingual character of the university system. For example, the Ministry of

[34] Royal Decree 69/2000, of Jan. 21, regulating the selection procedures for admission to the universities for students who meet the legal requirements for access to universities; and Orders of July 26, 2000 and Sept. 21, 2001.

Education and Science has specified that this legislation prevent communities or universities from setting linguistic examinations or any other type of test of knowledge to their own regional official language because it may prevent the access of students from other territories of Spain or from Europe.[35] Only when regulating the specific procedures for access to university for people over twenty-five years old, State legislator has provided that autonomous communities can establish compulsory test of knowledge of the own co-official language.[36]

The State has applied different criteria when implementing European directives that require the promotion of student mobility. In these cases the new conditions for access to Spanish universities for students from EU states and from other states which have signed an agreement with Spain[37] explicitly states that universities may require an adequate knowledge of the language in which the different academic subjects will be taught and set, if necessary, a test to assess the language proficiency of foreign transfer students (as has been done, for example, by the Andalusian universities regarding the Spanish language).

In Catalonia, students who have completed primary and/or secondary education in the regional schools "have the right and obligation to have sufficient oral and written knowledge of Catalan and Castilian upon completing compulsory education", at sixteen years old.[38] The same norms specify that knowledge requirements be set according to "whatever the habitual language [of pupils] at the beginning of their education".[39] At the university level, the linguistic conjunction system involves double exposure of students to Catalan and Spanish as languages of instruction, without the recognition of a right to linguistic choice between the official languages (nevertheless, especially in big institutions, organisational solutions ensure the existence of different class groups where the same academic subject is taught in Spanish and

[35] *El País*, 04/10/2007, http://www.elpais.es

[36] Art. 2 of Royal Decree 743/2003, of June 20.

[37] Resolution of the Secretary of State for Universities and Research of May 7, 2007, in force since academic year 2007–2008.

[38] Art. 35 (2) SAC; Art. 21 (3) LPL.

[39] In the absence of specific data related to language of pupils in Catalonia, we can mention the results of the *General Population Linguistic Statistics Survey of 2008* (http://www.idescat.cat/cat/idescat/publicacions/cataleg/pdfdocs/eulp2008.pdf) for the age group 15 to 29 years: for the question of initial language: 30.7 percent Catalan, 50.6 percent Castilian, 5.3 percent both official languages and the rest other languages; for the question of language of identification: 33.4 percent Catalan, 45 percent Castilian, 10.4 percent both languages and the remaining other languages; and, finally, for the language more used: 31.5 percent Catalan, 44 percent Castilian, 14.4 percent both official languages and the rest other languages.

in Catalan). Likewise, the right recognised by Article 35 (5) SAC (and, previously, by Article 22 (1) LPL) allows students to express themselves, orally and in writing—in exams, presentations, assignments, papers and participation in university life—in the official language of their choice. This right admits exceptions in the so-called "integrated language teaching subjects", where the language used by pupils is determined depending on the content of this subject.[40]

Despite the lack of aggregated data on the number of foreign transfer students who are studying law in Catalonia,[41] it is clear that the implementation of the above described linguistic model in a context of mobility requires specific measures which address the pupils who join Catalan university system from abroad. Universities, through their language boards, and with the financial and technical support of the *Generalitat's* Government, carry out an important function in this area, including: sending prior information to interested student homes about the linguistic situation, free basic Catalan languages courses, the possibility of self-learning trough computerised language learning (*Intercat*, *Lingcat*, etc.), distribution of specific materials (vocabularies, conversation guides, brochures, etc.), language exchanges with native students (language partners) and the organisation of a wide range of activities so students can get to know the linguistic reality of Catalonia.

D. Teaching Staff

In 1983, when the first Organic Law on University Reform (Law 11/1983) was enacted, the state legislation already contained an almost

---

[40] Nevertheless, the legal formulation of this right do not entail a hypothetical right of students to ignore the own official language of universities of Catalonia, among other reasons for the possibility they have to freely choice of institution of higher education within the state university system.

[41] According to data published by the Government for the academic year 2006–07, the global number of students visiting Catalan faculties of social sciences—not all the universities offers these data—, computing only those included in mobility programmes of first and second cycle, was of 1,827, of which 1,173 from countries of the European Union, 59 from other European countries, 148 from the rest of Spain and 447 from the rest of the world. See http://www.gencat.cat/diue/doc/doc_60686141_1.xls (it should be noted that among the students from de rest of the State there are those from other Catalan-speaking territories). Data on social science university studies—only available for part of the universities—are, in global terms and for the four possible origins indicated (rest of Spain, EU, other countries in Europe, elsewhere in the world) are: UB 721 (93+485+8+135); URL 478 (9+229+19+221); UPF 332 (18+243+30+41); UdG 79 (3+74+0+2); URV 72 (23+40+0+9); UdL 68 (2+29+2+35); UAO-CEU 55 (0+54+0+1); UIC 22 (0+19+0+3).

complete regulation of university faculty and staff regarding the different categories of teachers, the access system and its juridical regime; later, in 2001, the new Organic Law on Universities (OLU) bestowed certain powers on the autonomous communities over the new categories of teaching and research staff employed by the universities. A subsequent reform of OLU in 2007 also conferred to autonomous communities certain legislative and regulatory power over teaching staff in permanent public employment,[42] but the central State retained the power to establish regulation over the general status of teaching and research staff.[43]

At first glance, the language issue seems absent from state regulation on the university teaching staff (with the only exception of linguistic requirements established for foreigners who access permanent public employment in the areas of education and research, which are required to prove knowledge of the Spanish language[44]). However, as it has been previously showed, the organisation of the Spanish university system is structured such that there is a general *de facto* prerequisite of linguistic knowledge of Spanish for all its members. Thus, in the access to permanent public employment, a substantial part of the proceedings must be conducted in Castilian and commissions responsible for assessing the suitability of the candidates are elected among the whole state teaching staff, so that the oral and written examinations must almost always be done in the Spanish language. In addition, the *National Agency for the Evaluation of Educational Quality* (ANECA), which believes composition and functioning are not established formal criteria for multilingualism (Art. 31 and 32 OLU), assesses the suitability of teaching and research personnel in permanent public employment and employed by public universities,[45] grants supplements to income to the above mentioned personnel and assesses the quality of teaching staff at private universities. Many other procedures in university life also foster an active use of the Spanish language (for example, in order

[42] Art. 56 (2) OLU.

[43] Sixth additional provision of OLU.

[44] Art. 6 of the Royal Decree 800/1995, of May 19, implementing the Law 17/1993, of Dec. 23, on access to certain sectors of the civil service of nationals of other member states of the European Community.

[45] Royal Decrees 1312/2007 and 1313/2007, both of Oct. 5. With respect to teaching and research personnel hired by universities, there is concurrence between the ANECA and the University Quality Assurance Agency of Catalonia (Art. 137 and 140 ULC).

to participate in research projects or to obtain state economic aids of various kinds).

The described framework should include an evaluation of the need for a requirement stipulating the knowledge of Catalan for teachers assigned to Catalan universities, as provided in general legislation for public administration personnel: "The Public Administrations, in their respective powers, should provide for the selection of adequate personnel to cover public work posts in the autonomous communities with two official languages".[46] In Catalonia, Article 6 (4) ULC states more specifically: "In accordance with Law 1/1998, of January 7, on language policy, university teaching staff, except visiting professors and other similar cases, has to know both official languages in accordance with the requirements of their academic tasks. The Government, in accordance with current legislation and through the Interuniversity Council of Catalonia, must ensure that in the selection, access and assessment processes sufficient linguistic knowledge has been demonstrated."

In substantive terms, these linguistic requirements can be justified by the necessary guarantees of language rights of students to receive instruction in Catalan and to use both official languages in the learning process,[47] which may support restrictions on the teacher's right to linguistic choice, following the analogous regime established for other type of civil servants to guarantee the linguistic rights of citizens.[48] Although neither the law nor the university regulations have expressly provided that the university teachers must give lessons in both official languages,[49] the teacher's right to use the official language of his or her choice is not covered by the fundamental right to academic freedom guaranteed by Article 20 (1) (c) of the Constitution, and consequently the decision on this subject may be conditioned by these facts in order to protect other principles or legitimate interests. Moreover, the Government and university governing bodies are concerned with ensuring the principle of *linguistic transparency*: the language of

---

[46] Art. 56 (2) of State Law 7/2007, of Apr. 12, on the Basic Statute of Public Employees.

[47] Art. 35 (1) and (5) SAC.

[48] For example, in Art. 33 (3) and (4) SAC and in Art. 54 (11) of State Law 7/2007.

[49] However, is not uncommon that one teacher may give either lessons in Catalan and in Spanish depending on the subjects or during different academic years (for example, to balance linguistic offer of a department in both official languages, because a non Catalan-speaking teacher step towards the use of Catalan, etc.).

instruction of each subject has to be made public before it starts, and cannot be negotiated or changed later. As is evident from the characterisation of the system of linguistic conjunction, the Catalan model opposes the establishment of linguistically separate sections for teachers.

Pending approval of governmental regulation under Article 6 (4) ULC, some universities have regulated, through specific norms the requirement of knowledge of Catalan and have applied them as a prerequisite to fill a vacancy (UB, UVic, UdL), while others have established linguistic accreditation *a posteriori* (UAB, UPF, UdG). This conduct was authorised by an agreement by the Interuniversity Council of Catalonia, of June 11, 2008, on the accreditation of language knowledge in the selection and access processes of faculty to the universities in the Catalan university system, which provide linguistic requirements for university teachers, with some exceptions related to the timing (*post* certification for non-permanent teachers), teaching in third languages or the need of attracting talent from abroad. Recently, by virtue of powers over academic staff conferred by the new Statute of Autonomy,[50] the Catalan Government approved a regulation with similar content, which allows the universities to specify the level of linguistic knowledge required to carry out academic tasks.[51]

Regarding linguistic training, language services at universities, with the support of the *Generalitat's* Government, promote knowledge of Catalan and provide training for non-Catalan-speaking teachers, both through courses and through e-learning. Universities also carry out the tasks of certification of knowledge of the Catalan language, and their certificates or diplomas are officially recognised by the Government. Consistent with actions that promote education in third languages, the availability of English courses for academic staff has increased. Public universities' administrative staff has the same status as staff from other Catalan administrations, and that implies the requirement of knowledge of Catalan language to gain the admittance to the post,[52] they also benefit from linguistic training offered by universities.

---

[50] Art. 172 (2) (e) and (f) SAC established a shared power over "regulation of the system governing contracted and permanent teaching and research personnel" and over "evaluating and ensuring the excellence and quality of (…) teaching and research personnel".

[51] Decree 128/2010, of Sept. 14, on the accreditation of linguistic knowledge by the academic staff of the university system of Catalonia.

[52] Art. 11 (3) LPL.

E. Teaching Methods and Materials

The application of the pedagogical criteria arising from the Bologna process (European Space of Higher Education) has revolutionised the teaching methods in all Catalan universities and, in similar terms, in law schools. Magisterial teaching and rote learning have largely been replaced by methods that focus on student learning and increase the use of practical exercises, seminars and group work. In this area, the academic autonomy of each university is very broad. Law faculties and academic departments, responsible for the organisation of teaching in the different areas of knowledge, enjoy significant freedom to plan teaching and learning methods (at the same time, this new trend reduces the scope of academic freedom for individual teachers).

In this context, the need for training future lawyers with abilities in both official languages, which can be rightfully maintained as a goal of the Catalan university system, does not translate into the adoption of strategic measures that go beyond the guarantee of a certain percentage of class groups in Catalan. In this sense, it's doubtful that the recognition of the students' right to use the official language of their choice guarantees their professional training in Catalan, especially given the strong Castilian juridical tradition of Spanish law. Thus, the objective of guaranteeing dual language skills can only be achieved if institutions provide the necessary conditions for law studies in Catalan. It is worth pointing out some positive experiences in this regard: in the UB Faculty of Law, all pupils study Catalan legal language during the first year as a part of a introductory subject about research and study techniques and communication; whereas in the UPF Faculty of Law students can choose to take the optional legal language course in Catalan, Spanish or English.[53] In the coming years, the introduction of English as a language of instruction, and the need to demonstrate a certain level of knowledge of the third language at the end of university studies, can indirectly encourage the addressing of language-policy issues with respect to both official languages.

[53] The recent Royal Decree 775/2011, of June 3, by approving the regulation of the Law 34/2006, of Oct. 30, on access to the profession of lawyer and solicitor of the Courts, establishes as a requirement of the degree of law the acquisition of a series of legal skills, including "handle with skill and precision the legal language and terminology of the various branches of law. Writing in an orderly and understandable manner legal documents and communicate orally and in writing ideas, arguments and legal reasoning using appropriate records in each context" (Art. 3 (1) (g)).

Another consequence resulting from new programmes and teaching methods within the framework of the European Space of Higher Education is a significant increase in the need for new teaching materials. Regarding this aspect, Catalan has a similar problem to other regional or minority languages, which is the lack of a complete offering of teaching materials. The situation in Catalonia is perhaps, less severe than the situation of other non-state languages. The number of textbooks written in Catalan, published by universities or private-publishers, is considerable (frequently legal text books appear simultaneously in Catalan and Spanish, while there are less text books written only in Catalan), and there is a programme of public subsidies for publishing text books in Catalan. The main problem, however, is the lack of systematic action in the editing of university texts in Catalan -that is usually justified because the Spanish language is understood by all students and has a wider market-, which causes the scarcity of the latter texts. The use of texts and other types of materials published in other Catalan-speaking areas (Valencian Community and the Balearic Islands) do not encounter such problems (recently a vocabulary of law in Catalan-Castilian was published jointly by the University of Barcelona and the University of Valencia). The online resources for learning and consultation of terms and expressions in Catalan legal language are quite numerous.[54] Syllabi, notes, diagrams and other teaching materials are reviewed by university language boards, which ensure good linguistic quality.

A specific task force undertaken by Spain in accordance with the European Charter for Regional or Minority Languages now ensures the availability of legal texts in Catalan.[55] Since 1998,[56] State laws and general regulations have been published in Catalan, in a separate Catalan edition of the Official State Bulletin (BOE). But this publication has not solved all the problems of accessibility to state legislation, since there is a delay in the Catalan translation and as a result of the

[54] Especially the *Curs d'autoaprenentatge de llenguatge jurídic* (http://www.gencat.cat/justicia/llengjur/index.html) and the *Curs de llenguatge jurídic* (http://www20.gencat.cat/docs/Adjucat/Documents/ARXIUS/doc_88604569_1.pdf); and also dictionaries, vocabularies and syllabus in Catalan.

[55] Art. 9 (3).

[56] Royal Decree 489/1997, of Apr. 14, on the publication of the BOE in the co-official languages of the Autonomous Communities and the subsequent agreement of 1998 between by the State Government and the *Generalitat*.

fact that it is not a consolidated text. Thus the initiative by the Department of Justice of the *Generalitat* to maintain an updated online Catalan translation of the main legal texts, in a consolidated version (*Lexcat*) is valuable. Universities have also published, in a non-systematic way, annotated translations into Catalan of some basic State laws (civil code, criminal code, procedural law, etc.). Regarding norms enacted by the Parliament and the Government of the *Generalitat*, there is a bilingual official publication in Catalan-Spanish in the Official Journal of the *Generalitat* (DOGC).

Judgments issued by national courts (including the Constitutional Court) appear only in Spanish and are not usually translated into the other official languages. As for judicial courts located in Catalonia, the overall percentage of sentences in Catalan has varied the last years between 15 and 20 percent, given that the concerned citizen has the right to request the translation of judgments into Catalan. Correction and updating of Catalan legal language is dealt with by the official body of terminology set up by the *Generalitat* (TERMCAT) in close collaboration with universities and other linguistically specialised staff of the Catalan Public Administrations.

F. Research and the Dissemination of Results

The general problems surrounding scientific research in Catalan, as a non-dominant language, are complex and they cannot be analysed here in depth. Regarding research in the legal areas, this situation is also characterised by a strong element of statehood and by the difficulties of penetration to the new European and international research forums. Subject to these limiting factors, the situation of the Catalan language in the field of research presents some promising aspects—at least in comparison with other linguistic realities of non-state languages—that should be emphasised and evaluated appropriately.

Firstly, the maintenance of important institutional support, focusing on the existence of a significant number of journals, supported by the Catalan government and other public or semi-public institutions, through which scientific research in public and private law is disseminated (*Revista Jurídica de Catalunya*, *Revista Catalana de Dret Públic*, *Revista d'Estudis Autonòmics i Federals*, *Revista de Llengua i Dret*, among others). As for books, institutional publishers and editorial services of universities have also published legal works in Catalan, frequently with digital versions, which sometimes replaced paper versions. Private publishers receive financial support from the Government to publish legal works in Catalan, but the presence of the language in this sector has been almost anecdotal, given that Castilian is the prevalent language for accessing the Spanish and Latin American markets.

Secondly, with regards to the language of doctoral theses, it is difficult to conclude from general data (available for 2006–2007, which show the general percentage of use of Catalan as 25 percent) about the presence of Catalan in law theses. Additionally, it seems inadequate to compare the percentage of the UB, with hundreds of doctoral dissertations every year, with other small universities with less than five. As for the UB, the general data of the 2006–07 academic year show a significant use of Catalan in doctoral theses (168 in absolute numbers, representing 31.4 percent of the total, while 54.95 percent were in Spanish, 13.46 percent in English and 0.19 percent in Portuguese), but during the same course the use of Catalan in the theses ascribed to the Faculty of Law is lower (only one thesis among seven, which represents a rate of 14 percent, while five were in Spanish and one in English). The evolution of law theses language shows, after the maximum growth in the mid nineties (20 percent of use of Catalan), a clear and sustained trend of decline during the current century (with percentages below 15 percent for the use of Catalan, sometimes with students opting to use English but usually opting to use Spanish).[57]

The explanation for this decline in the scientific use of Catalan, apart from the relationship with to social perception of the current advance in the normalisation of Catalan, lies basically in the negative influence of new assessment and accreditation criteria introduced by state (ANECA) or regional (AQCU) specialised bodies that, either implicitly or explicitly, damage or undervalue the research done in the Catalan language (often without considering its intrinsic scientific value). Additionally, the assessment and recognition of research linked to journal rankings tend to undermine the position of Catalan journals, which have additional difficulties in fulfilling criteria set at state or international levels.

---

[57] A link to the study of the evolution of the language of doctoral theses in the legal field at the UB from 1993 to 2007: http://www.ub.edu/sl/ca/socio/dades/docs/tesis_evo.pdf

G. Cooperation with Same-Language Universities and within the Same-Language Community

In Catalonia, cooperation in the field of university policy language is a phenomenon that developed especially in the nineties. First in an informal way, this cooperation took place at meetings of university leaders to tackle together and formulate plans of action for issues of common interest (such as linguistic legislative reforms, judicial challenges to linguistic university regulations or linguistic issues raised by the implementation of the European higher education standards). Later, this cooperation was institutionalised with the creation of the Language Policy Committee of the Interuniversity Council of Catalonia.[58] Among its functions, this Committee proposes political guidelines in linguistic matters and ensures the coordination of various university models for managing multilingualism. Since the discontinuation of activity of the Language Policy Committee, the interuniversity cooperation has maintained its practical importance and often played a substantial role in the lack of governmental initiative. University language services and the personnel of the Linguistic Policy Office (technical body set up inside the relevant Department of the Government) have played an important role in sustaining these collaborative dynamics.

In a broader context, the most important inter-university cooperation is the *Xarxa Vives*, a network that was created in 1994 to promote relations between the universities of the Catalan linguistic area, which extends to Catalonia, Valencia, Balearic Islands, Northern Catalonia (in France) and Andorra. Currently the *Xarxa Vives* includes 20 universities, representing a collective of more than 440,000 people: 400,000 students, 30,000 teachers and 10,000 administrative and services staff. The Strategic Plan of the association establishes the linguistic unity of the academic community members as a value to promote. Among its functions, covering various aspects of university life, there are: The promotion of the use and the normalisation of the Catalan language,

[58] Resolution IUE 135/2007, of Apr. 27, which established the standing committees of the Interuniversity Council of Catalonia (Art. 5). The composition of this body includes one representative from each university, both public and private, with the rank of vice-chancellor or general secretary (and also two students appointed by the Commission of Students of the same Interuniversity Council of Catalonia) and is headed by a university chancellor appointed by the Government.

the establishment of guidelines on language policy and the management of training activities and exchanges between the language boards of the network members. Two committees are responsible for the promotion of the language activities: the Language Commission, made up of the directors of language boards at the universities;[59] and the Language Policy Committee, made up of vice-chancellors responsible for language policy. Sometimes joint initiatives or proposals in linguistic matters face difficulties, because of the different sociolinguistic and political contexts where universities members are enrolled, that cover three States (Andorra, Spain and France) and three different regions (Catalonia, Balearic Islands and Valencian Community).

Notwithstanding the general significance of the *Xarxa Vives* for the articulation of universities included in the Catalan linguistic area, the institutionalised collaboration between the faculties of law of Catalonia, Valencian Community and the Balearic Islands is not favoured by a university system organised in autonomous (or regional) communities and where permanent teachers are assigned to a fixed university. However, this doesn't prevent regular academic exchanges and the mobility of students and faculty, enhanced by the linguistic connection, based on individuals, research groups and institutional relationships.

H. Impact of the European Space of Higher Education on Catalan Legal Education

The management of the linguistic impact of the European Space of Higher Education on the university system of Catalonia is now a central question for the majority of university language policies. Initially, the marginalisation of linguistic diversity as one of the main objectives of the Bologna process, launched by the States and the European Union, gave rise to concern about the future of Catalan in this new European framework. While subsequent documents of the European Space of Higher Education have formally taken into account "linguistic diversity" as an objective and a value to promote, the *Generalitat's* Government and the universities have adopted a more pragmatic approach with regard to the introduction of multilingual criteria. At the same time, political and university leaders are conscious of the

[59] There is a united Internet portal of linguistic resources of the universities participating in the *Xarxa Vives*: http://www.llengua.info/

vagueness of linguistic discourse developed within the European Space of Higher Education, where the messages in favour of multilingualism are often in reality directed to favour the spread of English as a lingua franca which facilitates mobility within the European Area, role that the Spanish language can also play to some extent.

Spain has followed the same trend observed in previous legislation when incorporating the criteria derived from the Bologna process: no specific mention of languages was made in the norms containing the principles which underpin the new undergraduate and postgraduate programmes (where, for example, the principle of equality between men and women and the forecast of studies related to this issue was expressed). An existing regulation regarding doctorates mentions the need to register the language of writing and defence of the doctoral thesis, since the total or partial use of a European language other than those that are official in Spain is required to obtain a European doctorate mention.[60] Other linguistic reference can be found inside the regulation governing the European Diploma Supplement, which is set to be issued in Spanish and another official language of the European Union determined by the university, with the possibility for universities of autonomous communities with a regional official language to adopt a trilingual model.[61]

As mentioned above, Catalan university legislation has been sensitive to the need for openness and internationalisation in higher education. In 2010 the Catalan Government established a funding program that aimed to promote the use of the English (in a certain percentage of class groups or in a certain number of academic subjects) as a teaching language in bachelor's and master's degrees adapted to the European Space of Higher Education. This funding program also envisages that universities establish mechanisms to accredit or test the knowledge of the third language for students completing bachelor's studies. New developments seem to lead to a greater diversification of multilingual university models, as opposed to the precedent of linguistic homogeneity. Language can become a differentiating feature for singular universities in a more competitive context. Lastly, at the core of all these changes lies a desire for a more efficient use of resources, the results of which should be contrasted in the future.

---

[60] Royal Decree 1393/2007, of Oct. 29, on the arrangement of the official university studies.

[61] Royal Decree 1044/2003, of Aug. 1, which establishes the procedure for the issuance by the universities of the European Diploma Supplement.

I. Access to and the Practice of Legal Professions

Regarding the organisation of the legal profession, the central government reserves the power to regulate access to the professions of lawyer, notary and registrar and the whole range of judges.[62] The existence of such a state regulated professional environment (the only exceptions to this principle derive from the principle of free movement of workers and professionals inside the European Union, for which an obligation of knowledge of Spanish language to gain admittance to research or teaching public sector is established[63]) assures that the access to and exercise of legal professions in Catalonia already imply the mastering the Spanish language. With regard to lawyers and solicitors this is also a consequence of the silence regarding official languages in the recent regulation of access to the legal profession.[64] Additionally, the organisation in unitary state bodies of judges, registrars and notaries, together with the guarantees of territorial mobility and the frequent corporate attitudes among these professional groups, favour the continuity of the historical inertia of the use of Castilian (it must be noted that, within the contemporary period, excluding only the Second Republic 1931–1936, the Catalan language was forbidden and rejected for such official uses).

Currently, the Statute of Autonomy of 2006 establishes several mandates of linguistic knowledge of both official languages for judges and magistrates, notaries, registrars and administrative staff in the Administration of Justice and the Civil State Administration in Catalonia.[65] However, the effectiveness of these provisions depends on the reform of state legislation regulating these bodies.[66] The resulting paradox is

---

[62] Art. 36 and 122 of the Spanish Constitution.

[63] Royal Decree 800/1995, of May 19, implementing Law 17/1993, of Dec. 23, on access to certain sectors of the civil service of nationals of other member states of the European Community.

[64] Royal Decree 775/2011, of June 3, by approving the regulation of the Law 34/2006, of Oct. 30, on access to the profession of lawyer and solicitor of the Courts. The only mention, in the list of skills of training courses for access to lawyer profession, is 'knowledge of languages' (Art. 10)

[65] Art. 33 (3), 34, 102 and 147 (1) (a) SAC.

[66] Since the entry into force of the Statute of Autonomy a first legislative reform, adopted in 2007 and concerning Public Prosecution, considers knowledge of Catalan a "deciding merit" to gain admittance to the post of General Prosecutor of Catalonia. More recently, the Regulation 2/2011 on the judicial careers, approved in Apr. 28, 2011, by the General Council of the Judiciary, maintains the consideration of language as a

that although citizens have the right to use the official language of their choice in all administrative, judicial, notary or registrar activities,[67] knowledge of Catalan is counted only as a non deciding merit for candidates in admittance to posts that performs these functions in Catalonia.[68] On this point, the Council of Europe has issued two reports (in 2005 and 2009) on the application in Spain of the European Charter for Regional or Minority Languages, and subsequently the Committee of Ministries concluded that state authorities do not fulfil the guidelines stipulated under Articles 9 ("Judicial authorities") and 10 ("Administrative authorities and public services"), and has proclaimed the need to modify the structure and the training career for administrative and judicial staff depending on the State.[69]

To counteract some of these legal and socio-political unfavourable factors, the *Generalitat* of Catalonia has set up policies to promote the normal use of Catalan within the legal professions including: the provision of free language courses to judicial and administrative staff of the courts and tribunals; the setting up of a linguistic board with the task of promotion of use and translation of documentation in the courts and tribunals established in Catalonia; the signing of linguistic conventions with professional associations of lawyers, notaries and registrars; special programmes to offer linguistic support to law firms, etc. The exercise of powers assumed under Articles 33 and 147 SAC has also allowed the *Generalitat* to regulate the requirements of knowledge of the Catalan language in the appointments of notaries.[70] A future line of action would be to strengthen the connection between universities and legal professions, for example through the joint organisation of a new training master for lawyers.

no preferential merit to fill judicial vacancies in Autonomous Communities with another official language.

[67] Art. 33 (1) and (2) SAC.

[68] Despite of this, data of 2007 shows a highly expanded basic knowledge of Catalan between judges (55.6 percent) and administrative staff (80.6 percent). Contrasting this data with the low rates of sentences and proceedings conducted in Catalan (see the a general survey of language use in the Administration of Justice in Catalonia (*Enquesta d'usos lingüístics a l'Administració de Justícia 2008,* http://www20.gencat.cat/docs/Adjucat/Documents/ARXIUS/informe_enquesta_2008.pdf), one may conclude that this basic or passive knowledge is not enough to guarantee a practical and normal use of Catalan in judicial tasks.

[69] See the reports on the implementation of the Charter in Spain in the web site about Charter's monitoring in www.coe.int.

[70] Resolution JUS/319/2008, of Febr. 7, by which a public competition for posts in vacant notaries is announced.

J. Concluding Remarks

If bilingual higher education can be defined as that which takes place in an environment where two or more languages are normally used and that aims to ensure the training of graduates in both languages, the Catalan university system is surely one of its most perfect expressions. This is at least the aim of the organisation of language use at the universities in Catalonia which is largely based on the principles of language conjunction (joint education of students of different native or initial languages) and emissive freedom in both official languages, Catalan and Castilian. Despite this, the legal and practical position of the two official languages is not identical within the Catalan university system, where other languages, namely English, are increasingly present.

The knowledge and use of Castilian by university members, as the only official language of the State according to the Spanish Constitution, is mainly implicitly guaranteed by State regulation of various central aspects of the university system. Not only do many aspects of university life provide for an active use of Spanish language (competitive examination, academic evaluation, application forms for grants and research projects, etc.) but a state organised of professional environment also (with some exceptions deriving from the European Union), determines that access to and exercise of legal professions in Catalonia imply a mastering of the Spanish language. The current situation reinforces the strong Castilian juridical tradition of the Spanish law.

In this context, the objective of guaranteeing dual language skills can only be achieved if political and higher education institutions provide the necessary conditions for the law studies in Catalan. The legal framework of universities in Catalonia pay specific attention to linguistic elements: in an institutional context where Catalan is defined as the universities' own language, Catalan and Spanish can be used interchangeably by teaching staff and students in their academic tasks. We can summarise this legal framework as supportive of a dynamic relationship between rights and responsibilities: namely, individual rights are protected and collective responsibilities are imposed on universities; but at the same time, under some circumstances, individual action may be restricted and even some linguistic obligations imposed on individuals, as this is the only way to guarantee the enjoyment of linguistic rights for the majority of individuals. A significant use as a language of instruction in the degree of law (not in the masters and postgraduate studies), the institutional support for the dissemination of juridical research and the inter-university cooperation alongside the Catalan area must be stressed as positive elements of the current situation of Catalan in this field as compared to other non-State languages.

Since the nineties, the university system in Catalonia has followed the principle of internationalisation, which implies the ability of the universities to establish specific criteria for language use in activities related to international commitments and the establishment of programmes to promote knowledge of third languages. Given the vagueness of linguistic discourse developed within the European Higher Education Area, the implementation of the general Catalan linguistic model in the context of greater mobility requires specific measures to assure that the incorporation of new members in the university community do not alter the process of linguistic normalisation in the universities.

Thus the current trend seems to point to a more marked differentiation between multilingual university models, as opposed to the precedent of linguistic homogeneity, through which universities can try to define their own profile in a more competitive context. Thus, the introduction of English as language of instruction in graduate legal studies (currently located in the master's and postgraduate courses) indirectly promotes government and universities to address language-policy issues also with respect both official languages through new instruments of language planning and management through objectives. Language can become a differentiating feature for singular universities in a more competitive context. Lastly, at the core of these changes lies a desire for a more efficient use of resources, the results of which should be contrasted in the future.

CHAPTER EIGHT

LIVING ON BORROWED TIME: BILINGUAL LAW TEACHING IN GALICIA OR THE URGENT NEED TO RECOVER PRESTIGE[1]

Alba Nogueira López

A. Introduction

In 1983, with devolution and the early passing of a Language Act (the third non-financial Act passed by the Galician Parliament after those regulating the symbols, President and Government of Galicia), there were grounds for optimism concerning education in Galician. In particular, a number of considerations suggested that degree courses in law would soon be taught in Galician or bilingually: apart from the millions of speakers of languages of the Galician-Portuguese family worldwide, a large proportion of law students at what was then the only Galician university were Galician speakers, and non-Galician students were few. However, long-standing prejudices, inadequate support for teaching in Galician, and the dependence of teaching staff on central government decisions (recruiting requisites; research assessment) have thwarted these hopes. Because of the significant differences between legal systems, also those of Spain and Portugal, it has not even been possible to take full advantage of teaching materials available in the closely related language Portuguese.

More generally, Galician is a good example of how a language that is widely spoken in its native area but is not backed by a nation-state or strong political support can suffer an acute loss of speakers due to lack of self-esteem and the irresistible pressure of the majority language of the State to which its area of use belongs. In the absence of political will to implement a systematic language recovery policy, sweeping social changes (accelerated industrialisation, a shift from a rural to an urban society, universal access to education) have hindered the transmission

[1] I thank Isabel Vaquero of the University of Santiago Linguistic Normalisation Service for data and helpful comments.

of Galician to rising generations, resulting in a progressive decline in the number of speakers. It may seem paradoxical that this crisis has occurred during a period – the past 30 years – in which, within the Spanish State, Galicia has had the status of an Autonomous Community, with a regional government empowered to promote Galician. Proactive policies of support for Galician may still stop the rot; but we are living on borrowed time.

B. The Basic Legal Context of Galician Universities and Law Teaching

Galicia, with a population of about 2,800,000, has three public universities: Santiago de Compostela, Vigo, and A Coruña. Together they have four Law Schools, one belonging to Santiago, one to A Coruña, and two to Vigo (one located in Vigo and the other in Ourense). There are no privately run higher education institutions other than two single-degree centres (one offering Architecture and the other Business Studies). The Galician government has the power to found new public universities and authorise private ones.

The linguistic position of higher education in Spain differs from that of primary and secondary education, because it is not so subject as compulsory education to provisions for the use of co-official languages as a "key factor in the promotion and protection of regional or minority languages".[2] Nevertheless, universities have a central role in the training of professionals, and the co-official status of Galician in Galicia implies that in this Autonomous Community it can be used by citizens in all their relationships with public authorities, including those involved in higher education.

The general legal framework of universities comprises both central and regional provisions, while a principle of "university autonomy" also allows each university to establish its own organisational regulations.[3] The use of languages in higher education is subject, at least

[2] Council of Europe, *The Committee of Experts' interpretation and evaluation practice concerning the implementation of articles on education of the European Charter for Regional or Minority Languages (Strasbourg, 5 October 2005)*. MIN-LANG (2006) 3, Strasbourg, 6 March 2006.

[3] For an in-depth study see A. Nogueira López, "Distribución de competencias y organización administrativa en materia de universidades", in J. González García (ed.), *Comentario a la Ley orgánica de universidades* (Civitas 2009); A. Nogueira

potentially, not only to educational legislation but also to public employment legislation and to specific legislation on language use.[4] Thus the relevant or potentially relevant legislation includes:

(1) general provisions on language status established by Autonomous Communities (though in Galicia the 1983 Galician Language Act is the only such measure affecting higher education);
(2) central and regional regulations governing public employment, which apply to the teaching staff of public universities and include provisions for training all public employees in Autonomous Communities in the co-official language other than Castilian Spanish, if any.
(3) Autonomous Community legislation on higher education.

The Galician Language Act (1983) is the only Galician legislation on language protection that deals with universities.[5] Article 15 establishes the right of teachers and students to use the official language of their preference, leaving to the university authorities and the Galician government the adoption of measures making the use of Galician normal in higher education. Language should not hamper the exercise of students' right to learn. It must be borne in mind that this Act was passed in the early days of Galician self-government, not long after the advent of Spanish democracy and the Constitution of 1978. In the political context of the early 80's, following a long period during which Galician had been persecuted, this Act was a starting point for the protection of the language, and many of its provisions were non-prescriptive promotional mandates. It established Galician as co-official with Castilian Spanish in Galicia, but compulsory education and the Administration were the only two areas in which it provided for measures to ensure protection of the rights of Galician speakers. In other areas, such as

---

López, *Régimen jurídico de la selección del profesorado universitario* (Atelier 2004) p. 129–166.

[4] See X. Arzoz, "Universidad y pluralismo lingüístico", in J. González García (ed.), *Comentario a la Ley orgánica de universidades* (Civitas 2009) p. 1125–1192.

[5] "Article 15

1. Teachers and students at university level have the right to use, orally and in writing, the official language of their choice.
2. The Galician government and the university authorities shall arrange appropriate measures to make the use of Galician in university education normal.
3. Education authorities shall adopt appropriate measures with the aim that language not be an obstacle to the exercise of students' right to receive knowledge."

business, the media or higher education, it merely called for actions to promote Galician; and Galicia – unlike Catalonia – has not subsequently proceeded to enact more positive legislation affecting sectors other than compulsory education and the Administration.

In particular, the provisions of the Language Act concerning university education, unlike those concerning primary and secondary education, have not been fleshed out by any further legislation. Nevertheless, the Act declares Galician to be an official language in consideration of its being the autochthonous language (*lingua propia*) of Galicia, and this applies to all the institutions of the Autonomous Community, including universities. Thus in all dealings with these institutions the use of Galician is legitimate, and its normal use by public authorities in their dealings with citizens is encouraged.

The principal self-approved ordinance of each of the three Galician universities is its Statutes. In each case, Galician is declared to be the language of the university.[6] The more detailed provisions of other texts promote the use of Galician in teaching and establish the exclusive use of Galician for internal and external administrative and formal institutional purposes (including, for example, matriculation and public procurement), except as required by higher-ranking legislation or in communications with organisations not belonging to the Autonomous Community of Galicia.[7] Thus Castilian Spanish is not "visible" in dealings with most university services. However, this general predominance of Galician in the administrative area is not echoed in teaching or research.

The case of Galicia illustrates the limitations of the Kingdom of Spain's undertakings as regards universities in its 2001 ratification of

[6] *Estatutos de la Universidad de Santiago de Compostela* (Decreto 28/2004, BOE 22-04-2004), http://www.usc.es/gl/normativa/normas_xerais/estatutos2004.html). *Estatutos de la Universidad de Vigo* (Decreto 7/2010, DOG 02-02-2010), http://secxeral.uvigo.es/secxeral_gl/normativa/universidade/estatutos/index.html. *Estatutos de la Universidad de A Coruña* (Decreto 101/2004 (DOG 26-05-2010) modificado por Decreto 194/2007 (DOG 17-10-2007)), http://www.udc.es/sobreUDC/documentos/LOU_estatutos/. All visited Nov. 9, 2011.

[7] For the University of Santiago de Compostela, see *Regulamento do Uso do Galego na Universidade de Santiago de Compostela* (1993) (http://www.usc.es/gl/normativa/normalizacion/regusogl.html) and *Plan de Normalización Lingüística* (2002), http://www.usc.es/gl/normativa/normalizacion/index.html; for the University of Vigo, *Plan de Política Lingüística* (http://anl.uvigo.es/?cat=2); for the University of A Coruña, *Regulamento de Usos da Lingua Galega na Universidade da Coruña* (22-07-2004) and *Plano de Normalización Lingüística da Universidade da Coruña* (2006), http://www.udc.es/snl/plano.html, visited Nov. 9, 2011.

the European Charter for Regional or Minority Languages. Whereas the paragraphs of Art. 8.1 that it applies to pre-school, primary and secondary education are respectively a.i, b.i and c.i (the highest level of protection), the paragraph applied to higher education is e.iii, which was originally conceived for private universities and, according to the *Explanatory Report on the ECRML*[8], constitutes a further solution (alternative to teaching in the regional or minority language and teaching that language as an object of education) "for those cases in which the public authorities have no direct competences for the type of education concerned". The reason why Spain chose to act in this way seems to lie in the distribution of competences between central and regional government, central government having been willing for Spain to subscribe to the highest standards in compulsory education, which was not its immediate responsibility, but not in higher education, which was.[9] Jean-Marie Woehrling has argued that States with competence in higher education should not apply Art. 8.1.e.iii.[10]

Thus the Galician universities have not been subjected to the normalisation undergone by primary and secondary education, at least as far as teaching is concerned. Galician is used by teachers at their own discretion, and in none of the three universities are more than 20 percent of classes given in this language. This effective confinement of Galician to the administrative services ignores the linguistic rights of the users of higher education.

C. The Organisation of Law Courses in Galician and Castilian

In principle, the linguistic policies of the three Galician universities can be coordinated and regulated by regional government. According to the Report of the Committee of Experts on the initial monitoring

---

[8] http://conventions.coe.int/Treaty/EN/Reports/Html/148.htm, visited Nov. 9, 2011.

[9] However, Xabier Arzoz has argued that higher education *is* the responsibility of Autonomous Communities, and that since their language policies in this field are quite different, the State opted for an undertaking demanding no more than the lowest common denominator of these diverse policies. See X. Arzoz, 'The implementation of the European Charter for Regional or Minority Languages in Spain', in *The European Charter for Regional or Minority Languages: Legal Challenges and Opportunities* (Council of Europe Publishing 2008) p. 98.

[10] J.M. Woehrling, *The European Charter for regional or minority languages. A critical commentary* (Council of Europe Publishing 2005) p. 154.

cycle of the ECRML in Spain,[11] "This leads to various actions being carried out, such as promotion campaigns, traineeships, research, conferences, financial support for activities involving the use of Galician, prizes for literary works, publication of the programmes in Galician and the joint publishing, by the administration of Galicia and the three universities, of books and research magazines in Galician." Notwithstanding, government action in this field has been limited to promotional activities that have had a very limited effect on teaching or on the negative attitude of many university lecturers towards teaching in Galician. It is only quite recently that the constitution of the European Higher Education Area and the increasing number of foreign students has forced the universities to envisage the formulation of a coherent, comprehensive policy regarding the use of language – Galician, English and Castilian Spanish – in university courses.

The General Plan for the Normalisation of Galician that was approved by the Galician Parliament in 2004[12] identified several interrelated weaknesses of, or threats or obstructions to, the process of normalisation of Galician in university education: its never having been considered as a high-priority or strategic goal by the universities; the traditional predominance of Castilian, and resistance to the use of Galician, in higher education, and the resulting very small percentage of classes taught in Galician; the predominance of Castilian and English in research; the particularly low implantation of Galician in science and technology; the lack of formal plans for linguistic normalisation in the Universities of Vigo and A Coruña, and the understaffing of their linguistic normalisation services; lack of coordination among the universities; and the lack of training enabling future teachers to teach in Galician. The strengths, achievements and propitious circumstances that were identified were the favourable treatment of Galician in the statutes of the universities; the predominance of Galician in the administrative and other university services; the predominance of Galician-born teachers and students; the increasingly satisfactory knowledge of Galician by new intakes; the positive example of the University of Santiago as regards both the establishment of a linguistic

[11] ECRML (2005) 4, pp. 140–141; available on-line at http://www.coe.int/t/dg4/education/minlang/Report/EvaluationReports/SpainECRML1_en.pdf, visited Mar. 15, 2011.

[12] http://www.xunta.es/linguagalega/plan_xeral_de_normalizacion, visited Mar. 15, 2011.

normalisation plan and the operation of its linguistic normalisation service; the possibility of this lead being followed by the Universities of Vigo and A Coruña (the University of Vigo was at that time drafting its linguistic normalisation plan, and the University of A Coruña would follow suit in 2006); and the availability of regional government resources for linguistic normalisation in the universities. However, the actions that were proposed in the General Plan for exploiting these strengths and remedying the aforementioned weaknesses are scarcely ambitious, and fail to establish verifiable objectives in terms of the actual use of Galician in university teaching; they include the publication of teaching materials, the organisation of language courses, organisation of the means to coordinate the initiatives of the three universities, and the organisation of volunteer-based promotion of Galician.

In May 2007, one of the goals set by the four-year plan of the University of Santiago for 2007–2010 was that the proportion of classes taught in Galician should be the same as in secondary education, i.e. at least 50 percent. Likewise in 2007, the committee monitoring the University of A Coruña's linguistic normalisation plan insisted on consideration of proficiency in Galician in recruiting procedures.[13] However, none of the linguistic normalisation plans of the three universities include measures that really incentivise the knowledge and use of Galician by teaching staff – measures such as requiring new staff to be proficient in Galician, compensating teachers for time spent on preparing teaching materials in Galician, or the establishment of appropriate pay bonuses. Recruiting procedures currently treat proficiency in Galician as a merit but not as a requisite; there have been no provisions guaranteeing the existence of courses taught in Galician, or taught in Galician to interested groups of students (a partial dual-language scheme in the Pharmacy Faculty at Santiago in the late 1980s petered out due to lack of support and assessment); and there is no institution of higher education in which Galician is employed exclusively. The language in which a course is taught – Castilian or Galician – is still the personal choice of each individual teacher, unconstrained by the demand for one or the other by students, by the relative proportions of Castilian- and Galician-taught courses in the teacher's department or faculty, or in the university as a whole, or by the general

[13] http://www.udc.es/snl/plano.html, visited Mar. 15, 2011.

policies adopted by the university or the Galician government. Currently, around 20 percent of courses are taught in Galician and 80 percent in Castilian, although there are differences among universities. At Santiago, 26.79 percent of all first degree course time, and 36.36 percent of all Master's degree course time, is occupied by courses taught in Galician.[14] At A Coruña and Vigo, the proportions appear to be smaller, although the data for these two universities are survey-based rather than exhaustive.[15]

There are also differences among different faculties or areas of knowledge as regards the use of Galician in teaching. In general, it is more common in the social sciences and humanities,[16] but this tendency is not contributed to by law courses, among which the scant available data show the use of Galician to be much less frequent. Furthermore, Master's courses in law, especially the courses most directly concerning professional activities, are almost exclusively offered in Castilian. Paradoxically, it is not only the presence of many Latin American students that has been used as an argument against the use of Galician in Master's courses, but also the presence of students from Portugal and Brazil, whose native language is more closely related to Galician than to Castilian.

That the percentage of law courses in Galician is so small is attributable to a lack of proactive policies, lack of support for teachers, and the low standing of Galician in academic legal circles. Although official surveys place the proportion of students capable of understanding Galician at 90 percent and the proportion of teachers self-reported as able to speak it at 75 percent, many of the older faculty members never studied Galician and do not feel confident enough to use it in their lectures. There are almost no teaching materials in Galician apart from

---

[14] http://www.usc.es/snl/dinamiza/docencia_datos.htm. Data of academic year 2010-2011.

[15] A survey carried out at the University of A Coruña in 2003 found only 10 percent of courses to be taught in Galician; see *Análise sociolingüística da UdC*, available at http://www.udc.es/snl/analise_socio.html. At Vigo, the linguistic normalisation plan of 2003 quotes figures of 26.7 percent for oral use of Galician, and 29.2 percent for its use in teaching materials (http://anl.uvigo.es/?p=19. Both visited 15 March 2011.

[16] At the University of Santiago, the departments with an above-average proportion of courses taught in Galician mostly belong to the Faculties of Economics, Geography and History, Psychology, Philosophy, Journalism, Political Science, and Education. Only eight other departments are in this situation: three in the Faculty of Mathematics, two in Veterinary Science, and one each in the Polytechnic College and the Faculties of Physics and Medicine. The situation is similar as regards Master's degrees, most degrees with above-average use of Galician belonging to the disciplines of education, economics or psychology.

vocabulary lists. At Santiago, among other measures affecting all areas of academic life, the linguistic normalisation service is trying to change the situation by designing pilot schemes specific to each faculty; the Law Faculty should be the first. Changes in views on plurilingual degree syllabuses are in fact being forced by the progressive internationalisation of most universities in recent years, which has led to a gradual increase in the numbers of Master's courses and others that are delivered in English. In fact, all three universities are not only offering progressively more courses in English, but are introducing systems to promote the proficiency of teaching staff in English and to take into account the effort involved in the development of courses taught in English.

D. Students: Statistics and Requirements Concerning Language Use

Most students at the three Galician universities are Galician. In 2008, for example, 95.8 percent of the intake at Santiago and 92 percent of all students at A Coruña were domiciled in this Autonomous Community. These students should have received bilingual primary and secondary education with 30–50 percent of classes in Galician. Indeed, in terms of the Common European Framework of Reference for Languages, students completing their secondary education in Galicia are understood to be of at least level B2 in Galician, and passing a general examination of knowledge of Galician, Castilian and English (among other subjects) is a pre-requisite for admission to university. No further specific linguistic requirements have been established for applicants to Galician universities, but the construction of the European Higher Education Area has led the University of Santiago to require level B1 in a foreign language for graduation, and A Coruña and Vigo will probably follow suit. Students from outside Galicia can also obtain credits for attaining level B1 in Galician.

There are no recent statistics on the linguistic skills and preferences of students at Galician universities. However, for Galicia as a whole there are quite detailed statistics on language use stratified by age, location and linguistic background.[17] Comparison of the data for 2003 and

[17] http://www.ige.eu/web/mostrar_actividade_estatistica.jsp?idioma=gl&codigo=0206004&num_pag=4, visited Nov. 9, 2011.

2008 shows a reduction in the proportion of the population who are monolingual Galician speakers and an increase in the proportion that use both Galician and Castilian Spanish. Although the proportion who claims to be able to speak Galician "well" or "fairly well" has remained stable at around 90 percent, the proportion in the latter category has risen by about 13 percent at the expense of the former. Furthermore, the proportion who actually use only Galician outside school or family has fallen by 6–10 percent, and the proportion who only ever speak Galician by 10–17 percent, depending on age group (11.8 percent among 5–14-year-olds, 9.9 percent among 15–29-year-olds, 14.5 percent among 30–49-year-olds, 16.9 percent among 50–64-year-olds, and 13.2 percent among those aged 65 years or older); and although the decrease among the under-30s has been somewhat smaller than among older groups, it has left the former with particularly small proportions of persons speaking only Galician (15.3 percent among 5–14-year-olds and 18.6 percent among 15–29-year-olds as against 22–53 percent for older age groups). The situation is especially dramatic in certain urban areas: in A Coruña, Vigo and Ferrol the proportions of inhabitants claiming to speak exclusively or mostly in Galician are respectively 27 percent, 25 percent and 19 percent, in contrast to figures of around 50 percent in other urban areas (Lugo, Santiago, Ourense) or around 90 percent in areas such as Costa da Morte or the most rural areas of the provinces of Ourense and Lugo.

The most recent broad survey of linguistic habits and proficiency in any of the Galician universities was carried out in 2003 at the University of A Coruña.[18] It found that students were most likely to speak exclusively or mainly in Galician with their teachers if they were male; if they came from small rural hamlets; if their parents had had at most primary schooling; if they were studying for a degree in the area of humanities; and if they conceived of Galicia as a nation State. However, since the previous survey, carried out in 1994, the proportion of students speaking exclusively or mainly in Galician with their teachers had increased from 4 percent to 13 percent, while the proportion of students who never spoke in Galician with their teachers had decreased from 76 percent to 53 percent. The trend here was thus the opposite of that described in the previous paragraph.

[18] *Análise sociolingüística da UdC*, Section 6.4. Función laboral. Available at http://www.udc.es/snl/analise_socio.html, visited Mar. 15, 2011.

At the University of Santiago de Compostela the most recent comprehensive survey was carried out in 1995–96.[19] In the Law Faculty around 20 percent of students spoke Galician (as against 30 percent in the whole university), and although 80 percent of these Galician-speakers felt they spoke Galician well, they gave their knowledge of Galician legal terminology an average mark of only 1.6 on a scale of 1 to 3. Importance was given to "the issue of Galician in the University" (3.9 on a scale of 1 to 5), and there was a demand for more teaching in Galician: the insufficiency of existing lectures in Galician was assessed as 2.6 on a scale of 1 to 3, and 76 percent of students were willing to have more classes in Galician. The students' ideal proportion of lectures in Galician was about 50 percent (3.13 on a scale ranging from 1 (all in Castilian) to 5 (all in Galician)).

The 2003 survey at the University of A Coruña showed no significant differences among students of different areas of knowledge as regards the exclusive or more habitual use of Galician: 21 percent for law and social science, 18 percent for experimental and health sciences, 25 percent for humanities, and 22 percent for technological disciplines.[20] By contrast, there were striking differences among the teaching and research staff: 8 percent for law and social science, 15 percent for experimental and health sciences, 35 percent for humanities, and 12 percent for technological disciplines. Furthermore, the proportion of students who generally spoke in Galician with their teachers (13 percent for law and social science, 12 percent for experimental and health sciences, 19 percent for humanities, and 11 percent for technological disciplines) was in all areas smaller than the proportion who generally spoke in Galician, whereas only for technological disciplines and the experimental and health sciences was there an analogous difference between the proportion of teachers who generally spoke in Galician with their students (7 percent for law and social science, 6 percent for experimental and health sciences, 35 percent for humanities and 6 percent for technological disciplines) and the proportion who generally spoke in Galician. In particular, the data for law and social science suggest that the scant use of Galician by teachers in

[19] M. A. Rodríguez Neira (coord.): *O idioma na Universidade de Santiago de Compostela (resultado dun inquérito realizado no curso 1995–1996)* (Servizo de Publicacións da Universidade de Santiago de Compostela 1998).

[20] *Análise sociolingüística da UdC*, Section 7. Idioma empregado maioritariamente. Available at http://www.udc.es/snl/analise_socio.html, visited Mar. 15, 2011.

this area may have a significant influence on the linguistic habits of their students, consolidating prejudices about whether Galician is appropriate for formal and legal uses, and hampering the acquisition in Galician of the legal vocabulary that is so important for professional performance in the legal field.

As regards actual teaching through the medium of Galician in Galician law faculties, at Santiago there has been a rise from 3–4 percent of class hours during the period 2003–2006 to 9–12 percent since then[21], though the volatility of these figures is illustrated by the Department of Special Public Law, where the replacement of just one lecturer in 2009 resulted in a decrease from 28 percent to less than 16 percent.[22] At the University of A Coruña the situation is similar: only 7 percent of teachers of law or social sciences teach always or mostly in Galician, as against 87 percent in Castilian, and only 4 percent draw up their examinations in Galician, as against 84 percent in Castilian and 9 percent in both Galician and Castilian.[23]

Most of the efforts of the linguistic normalisation services of the Galician universities have concentrated on developing the proficiency of students in Galician by means of courses and awards, and on fighting linguistic prejudice. Since 2008 the normalisation service at Santiago has been working for the implementation of a specific plan of action for the Law Faculty that is mainly directed at increasing the ratio of Galician to Castilian in teaching.

E. Teaching Staff: Recruiting and Research Constraints That Favour Teaching in Castilian

The 1983 Language Act recognised the right of both students and lecturers at Galician universities to use either of the official languages of Galicia. However, the only Decree adopted by the Galician government to implement the Act does not concern universities[24]; and deep-rooted prejudices about the use of Galician in formal contexts and at work, together with the inactivity of Galician authorities as regards

[21] http://www.usc.es/snl/dinamiza/docencia_datos.htm, visited Mar. 15, 2011.

[22] http://www.usc.es/snl/dinamiza/docencia_datos.htm, visited Mar. 15, 2011.

[23] *Análise sociolingüística da UdC* http://www.udc.es/snl/analise_socio.html. 6.4. Función laboral; visited Mar. 15, 2011.

[24] Decree 247/1995, *Diario Oficial de Galicia* 15/9/1995.

intensification of the linguistic normalisation process, have resulted in the Galician law faculties ignoring the official status of the two languages, the desire of students for more teaching in Galician, and the fact that most graduates will work as civil servants in a bilingual society in which citizens have the right to be attended in either Galician or Castilian in their dealings with public authorities. Teachers use mainly Castilian in their lectures, and no significant incentives or recruiting policies have been adopted to alter this situation, even though the (admittedly scant) data on opinions suggest that teachers would favour an increase in the use of Galician in teaching if there were positive support for it by the universities.[25]

The language used by Spanish university staff in the workplace is in principle subject to regulation by both public employment legislation and legislation on universities. The Spanish Statute of Public Employees (Act 7/2007), which regulates the situation of the majority of Spanish public employees, including university staff, instructs public employees to guarantee that citizens be attended in the official language of their choice; and it is in keeping with the doctrine of the Spanish Constitutional Court[26] that Article 56 (2) of the Statute, which instructs public authorities in Autonomous Communities with two official languages to employ staff that are properly qualified for the posts they occupy, be interpreted as concerning all public employees. Teachers at public universities, as public employees, should therefore be required to speak both official languages, and legislation regulating their selection should specify how their linguistic proficiency should be assessed. Nevertheless, linguistic requisites have been introduced into teaching staff recruitment by neither State nor regional legislation on higher education, nor by the Galician universities themselves, in spite of the fact that the Spanish Universities Act of 2001, as amended in 2007, places no impediment on the establishment of such requisites. Thus no

---

[25] M.A. Rodríguez Neira (coord.): *O idioma na Universidade de Santiago de Compostela (resultado dun inquérito realizado no curso 1995–1996)* (Servizo de Publicacións da Universidade de Santiago de Compostela 1998). In this survey, Law Faculty teaching staff awarded the issue of Galician a mark of 4.07 on a scale of 1 to 5 as regards its importance for the University of Santiago de Compostela. Some 27 percent of teachers were willing to teach in Galician, a further 55 percent would have been willing if helped with teaching material, courses or vocabulary, and only 18 percent were unwilling to switch to Galician even with appropriate asistance. On a numerical scale ranging from 1 (Castilian) to 5 (Galician), Law Faculty lecturers described their teaching language preference as 3.37, i.e. they came down 6:4 in favour of Galician.

[26] Judgments 87/1997 and 46/1991.

concrete steps have in fact been taken to ensure that, with regard to their linguistic proficiency, teaching staff recruited by the Galician universities are properly qualified in accordance with Article 56 (2) of the Statute of Public Employees; and thus no steps to extend the right of students to use the official language of their choice (Art. 15 of the Language Act) to a right to be taught in the official language of their choice.

By virtue of the autonomous powers recognised by the Spanish Constitution, Spanish universities can themselves establish the methods and means by which relevant central and regional legislation is implemented, and also impose their own language requirements in the absence of relevant central and regional legislation. However, although knowledge of Galician is considered favourably in the recruitment procedures of all three Galician universities (see, for example, Art. 4(4) of the Statutes of the University of Vigo[27]), teachers have no obligation to teach in Galician.[28] Indeed, although the establishment of knowledge of Galician as a requisite in teacher recruitment has been pressed for by one of the labour unions[29] involved in the 2010 round of collective bargaining on non-functionary teachers' pay and conditions, this initiative has been rejected by the Galician universities and by other labour unions.[30]

In defence of their failure to impose rules that would enable students to study in the language of their choice, the Galician universities have argued difficulties that include staff mobility, lack of support from regional government, and the fact that teachers' recruitment, pay bonuses and promotion all depend heavily on central government evaluation of research activity. In this latter regard, Article 1 of the Universities Act describes universities as performing the public service

[27] "In personnel selection procedures, knowledge of Galician and of other official languages of the European Union shall be granted positive value."

[28] Art. 16 (d) of the Statutes of the University of Santiago de Compostela actually sanctions the establishment of linguistic requirements for selected teaching posts as a means of achieving a personnel structure appropriate for progressive linguistic normalisation and respect for linguistic rights; but this clause has never been put into effect, probably because of failure to plan for a certain proportion of courses to be taught in Galician.

[29] Confederación Intersindical Galega (CIG).

[30] Art. 26 of the agreement about to be signed establishes, *inter alia*, that schedules of merit for use in teacher recruitment must include knowledge of Galician, but without imposing this as a requisite; and that the universities must adopt such measures as may be necessary for the teachers recruited to acquire familiarity with Galician.

of higher education through teaching, study, and research; and indeed, the concept of a knowledge society undoubtedly requires that higher education establishments, as providers of a public service, should not only supply training but also produce research results. More specifically, the increasing efforts of universities to disseminate research results and transfer know-how to the rest of society should in the first instance address their most immediate social environment, as should their research efforts themselves. Yet the methods used by certain institutions to assess research are seriously hindering this objective in regard to both the lines of research that are pursued and the language in which research results are presented. In particular, the criteria employed by the Spanish National Research Evaluation Committee, a body reporting to the Ministry of Education, practically boil down to the examination of citation index impact factors. Among the numerous inequities of this system is the sidelining of research published in languages other than English, an effect that is particularly pernicious in the area of law and social science, in which many of the most demanding journals have and continue to be published in other languages. Researchers are accordingly incentivised to publish in English, in "high-impact" journals, on subjects that are favoured by those journals rather than on subjects that are more immediately relevant to their own social context.[31] While journal impact factors – which were originally developed merely to provide orientation for librarians – may have a legitimate role in the evaluation of research output, it is intolerable that they constitute the sole criterion; there are other criteria that are more accurate measures of the contribution of more locally oriented research to society.

Although the evaluation system described above discriminates against publication in Castilian as well as against minority languages such as Galician, it is Galician that is most affected in the Galician law faculties, which publish research almost exclusively in Spanish or foreign languages. At the University of Santiago, for example, only two of the fifty PhD theses read in the Law Faculty between 1998 and 2007 were written in Galician, in spite of the production costs of theses in Galician having been subsidised by the university throughout this period; and although eight theses were written in the closely related

[31] See A. Nogueira López, "Avaliación da actividade investigadora e dereitos lingüísticos", in *Lingua e Investigación. II Xornadas sobre lingua e usos* (Universidade da Coruña 2006).

language Portuguese, they were written by Brazilian or Portuguese students, whose number has increased at Santiago in recent years.

F. The Impact of Globalisation, European Higher Education Policy and Portuguese

In line with WTO/GATS promotion of a liberalised global higher education market, and in spite of concerns regarding consequences for the exercise of language rights,[32] the EU Services Directive includes private and commercial higher education services within its scope, and this is putting pressure on public higher education to adopt a similar market-oriented attitude.[33] The OECD predicts that higher education establishments will in future have a more international intake and that there will likewise emerge an international market for academics, even though national circumstances constrain academic activity.[34] This trend is particularly strong among research-intensive universities,[35]

---

[32] On language rights and the Services Directive see: A. Nogueira López, "Simplificación administrativa y régimen de control previo administrativo de actividades de prestación de servicios", 52 *Revista Llengua i Dret* (2009) p. 205–226. The right of EU Member States to subject teachers coming from other EU Member States to the same linguistic criteria as their own nationals was made clear as early as 1989; see De Witte, B., "La influencia del Derecho Comunitario en los sistemas nacionales de enseñanza superior", 17 *Autonomies* (1993) p. 44, the author already pointed out that if higher education was considered as a market (with private providers) then it should be open to EU providers with non-discrimination rules.

[33] EU documents such as *The Financing of Higher Education In Europe* (European Commission, Directorate General for Education and Culture, December 2004; http://ec.europa.eu/education/higher-education/doc/studies/financing1_en.pdf), visited Mar. 15, 2011, or *The role of the universities in the Europe of knowledge* (COM(2003) 58 final, Brussels 05.02.2003 (http://europa.eu/legislation_summaries/education_training_youth/lifelong_learning/c11067_en.htm), visited Mar. 15, 2011, call for an increase in private funding of universities, and for universities to enhance their attractiveness for foreign students.

[34] OECD, *Higher Education to 2030*, vol. I, 2008, p.15. According to this report (p. 215), whereas "in the past one could assume that most students were citizens of the country in which they studied", it is now the case that "in some highly developed countries ... student mobility can no longer be viewed as marginal."

[35] S. Marginson and M. Van der Wende, *Globalisation and Higher Education*, Education Working Paper No. 8, EDU/WKP(2007) p. 3, OECD Directorate for Education, p. 5 (http://doc.utwente.nl/60264/), visited Mar. 15, 2011: "in a networked global environment in which every university is visible to every other, and the weight of the global dimension is increasing, it is no longer possible for nations or for individual higher education institutions to completely seal themselves off from global effects. But research-intensive universities, and the smaller number of vocational universities organised as global international businesses, tend to be the most implicated in globalisation. Typically they are more internationally networked than the bulk of the

and the Spanish university system is for various reasons – among them the influence of national and international rankings, and the need to attract funds – placing rising stress on competitive research. This brings with it an increasing emphasis on the publication of research results in non-minority languages – mainly English, followed by Castilian and other major European languages.

The internationalisation of student intakes and of the labour market is leading universities worldwide to increase their offer of courses taught in majority languages, especially English. Galician universities are not foreign to this trend; even though they have not yet adequately recovered the autochthonous language of Galicia as a teaching medium, they are increasingly programming courses in English that are granted the facilities – training for lecturers, time off for the preparation of teaching materials in English – that are often denied to teachers wishing to teach in Galician. Paradoxically, a significant part of the demand for teaching in English comes from exchange students studying in Galicia under the Erasmus programme and similar schemes originally conceived of as favouring multilingualism: since many would-be incoming students cannot speak Castilian, let alone Galician, the desire to attract them results in universities providing English-language courses. Even when courses are not taught in English, the presence of a significant number of foreign students with some proficiency in Castilian but not in Galician can lead to teachers choosing to teach in Castilian rather than Galician. On the other hand, formal multilingual teaching language policies can potentially be positive for Galician: the University of Vigo's plan to encourage faculties to teach in English, Castilian and Galician – each language to be used for between 25 percent and 40 percent of all teaching time – would increase the use of Galician in many faculties.

Somewhat curiously, the use of Galician in the Galician universities appears not to have been furthered by their increasing numbers of undergraduate and postgraduate Portuguese and Brazilian students, in spite of the close relationship between Galician and Portuguese as members of the same subgroup of West Iberian languages. This may partly be due to lack of appreciation for the common historical roots of

---

societies in which they sit. Research-intensive universities that downplay global connectivity pay the price in diminished effectiveness. On the other hand, with some exceptions, predominantly teaching institutions, community colleges and traditional vocational sectors are less engaged and affected".

these languages, and to the standardisation of Galician following the advent of Spanish democracy not having pursued uniformity with Portuguese as regards spelling. Galician has not been able to attract the support of the strong Portuguese-language publishing industry, and those wishing to teach in Galician have largely been unable to make use of Portuguese teaching materials.

G. Bilingual Citizens, Monolingual Law Practitioners

Language skills are important in the legal profession. On the basis of a survey carried out among law graduates working in the legal field, a Spanish white paper on the adaptation of Spanish law degrees to the requirements of the European Higher Education Area found that, together with capacity for analysis and synthesis, capacity for oral and written communication was the most valued professional quality, scoring 3.63 on a scale of 1 to 4. In acknowledgement of this importance, the new EHEA-adapted law degree programmes of the Universities of A Coruña and Santiago have introduced courses on Legal Communication to develop expertise in speech and writing. Nevertheless, it is only at A Coruña that these courses are partly delivered by the Department of Galician in order to promote proficiency in this language. Most Galician law students can speak Galician, but their law courses, in general, fail to enable them to use Galician in legal practice; and on the basis of official survey data it has been found that among Galician law practitioners Galician achieves a usage score of only 1.75 on a scale of 1 to 4, the only lower score (1.70) being found among the military.[36] Although the practice of law in Galician could be facilitated with relatively little effort (establishment and dissemination of appropriate standardised vocabulary, translation of all relevant legal texts into Galician), it is clear that university courses are not at present producing bilingual law professionals. Since most Galician law graduates will work in the public administration, and since in regional government 95 percent of written communications and about 65 percent of oral communications are in Galician,[37] this means that the Galician

[36] H. Monteagudo and A. Lorenzo, *A sociedade galega e o idioma. A evolución sociolingüística de Galicia (1992–2003)* (Consello da Cultura Galega 2005) p. 41–44.

[37] http://www.observatoriodalinguagalega.org/?q=node/116&a=6&miga=Administraci percentF3npercent3AXunta+de+Galicia, visited Mar. 15, 2011. As noted

universities are not producing law graduates capable of fulfilling their probable employer's obligation to guarantee that citizens can exercise their linguistic rights.[38]

The lowest prevalence of Galician in Galician legal practice is found in the law courts. According to the regional government's Galician Language Observatory, law courts constitute one of the public service arenas with least overall institutionalisation of Galician, around 30 percent (60 percent in the health services and 78 percent in regional and local public administration), with scores for individual factors ranging from 43 percent for the proficiency of staff in Galician (some 55 percent of court staff believe that increased use of Galician in the courts would require more training) to as low as 25 percent for the promotion of Galician and its use in internal and external communications.[39] The finding that usage of Galician was lowest among judges and public prosecutors is in keeping with data from an official database that show that no more than 8 percent of judicial decisions are emitted in Galician.[40] The reasons for this situation are several. Entry into the judiciary is administered by central authorities; the high degree of mobility among judges results in many of those assigned to Galicia being non-Galicians who spend only a few years in this Community (legislation requiring that judges be proficient in all the official languages of their jurisdiction has been contested in the courts[41]); and the lack of electronic forms and basic legal texts in Galician doubles the workload of the few who strive to use it in the courts – although regional government is empowered to support the judiciary, it has not

previously, the co-official status of Galician and Castilian in Galicia means that in this Autonomous Community all public administrations (central, regional and local) must be able to work and attend the public in both languages, and knowledge of Galician is tested in recruiting all staff for regional and local administrations.

[38] The new degrees in Law of the University of Coruña and Santiago have placed a new subject on Legal Communication trying to promote oral and writing skills. Coruña's Galician Philology department is in charge of part of the teaching in an attempt to combine expression proficiency with the use of Galician.

[39] http://www.observatoriodalinguagalega.org/?q=node/116&a=6&miga=Adminis traci percentF3n percent3AXunta+de+Galicia, visited Mar. 15, 2011.

[40] See http://www.observatoriodalinguagalega.org/?q=node/116&a=9&miga=Adm inistraci percentF3n percent3AAdministraci percentF3n+de+Xustiza, visited Mar. 15, 2011.

[41] The Constitutional Court passed in June 2010 a ruling (no. 31/2010) on the Autonomous Statute of Catalonia on that matter. The Statute of Catalonia stipulates that all judges working in Catalonia have to speak Catalan. An Act of the central legislator has to rule the methods to accomplish that obligation.

as yet tackled this kind of issue. However, it is hard to avoid the impression that the scant use of Galician by the judiciary is due not only to lack of appropriate training and other promotional aids, but also to prejudice.

It may be stressed that the scant use of Galician by judges naturally influences the practice of lawyers appearing before them. Although some bar associations have a positive attitude towards Galician, most lawyers believe their clients' interests can be harmed if they use Galician before judges biased against Galician. Indeed, the use of Galician has originated conflict in several Galician courts.

H. Conclusions

The importance of the use of Galician by law graduates working in Galicia does not only reside in its allowing Galician citizens to exercise their linguistic rights, but in its reinforcing confidence in Galician as a language that is valid for all purposes, including formal and institutional uses. Indeed, since most high-ranking posts in the administration and in politics are occupied by persons with law degrees, their use of Galician would help dispel the notion that the language of leadership in Galicia, and the language that is appropriate for all formal intercourse, is necessarily Castilian – a notion that has been favoured by the lack of vigorous promotion of Galician by the political party that has been in power in Galicia for most of the period since the advent of democracy in Spain. So far, no measures have been adopted to promote Galician as a medium for economic or business affairs or labour relations, and there is a stark contradiction between its widespread use in public administration and its avoidance by prejudiced social elites that include the judiciary, the media and business associations. One of the factors that is holding back the use of Galician for teaching in Galician law faculties is thus an identity problem.

Within the Galician universities, this identity problem has given rise to an analogous contrast between the almost exclusive use of Galician in the institutional and administrative spheres (including interaction with the public in the course of recruitment, matriculation, etc.) and its much less widespread use for teaching – especially in law faculties. Linguistic normalisation services have focused mainly on translation and non-specialised courses; specific measures to promote the use of Galician in teaching and research have been until recent times few, incomplete, uncoordinated, and devoid of pre-defined improvement objectives, with the result that no monitoring has been performed to see whether improvement has actually been accomplished. Most importantly, proficiency in Galician has been granted only secondary value in teacher recruitment policy.

Another major obstacle derives from the changing social and economic situation of universities everywhere. One aspect of these changes, a labour market with an increasing demand for English speakers, is leading universities to offer courses taught in English, and to provide training and related facilities for the teachers of these courses, even though teaching in Galician is still precarious. Added to this, the weight of research evaluation in the promotion of teachers and the funding of universities themselves is impelling scholars to publish in higher-impact Spanish- or English-language journals.

Students at Galician law faculties are desirous of more teaching in Galician, and most will find employment in the Galician public sector, where the ability to attend the public in both the official languages of Galicia is obligatory. To meet these wishes and needs, Galician universities and the corresponding regional authorities should adopt clear linguistic planning measures. Recruitment procedures should require teachers as well as administrative staff to be proficient in Galician, and a goal should be set for the proportion of teaching performed in Galician: around 50 percent, the same as in secondary school. Specific policies should address prejudice against or avoidance of Galician in certain key areas –notably the law courts, where lawyers jealous of their clients' interests are currently wary of Galician.

After thirty years of letting providence guide the way, urgent action is required if Galician is not to be lost for future generations. We are living on borrowed time.

CHAPTER NINE

BILINGUAL LEGAL SCHOLARSHIP IN WALES: HISTORICAL AND CONTEMPORARY PERSPECTIVES

R. Gwynedd Parry

A. Introduction

It is arguable that there has never been a better time to establish bilingual legal scholarship as a vibrant force within Welsh universities than the present. The development of the legislative competence of the National Assembly for Wales[1] and the strengthening of statutory bilingualism,[2] have facilitated the creation of bilingual Welsh law as a distinctive and dynamic phenomena in contemporary Wales.

Bilingual law-making, legal practice and official bilingualism generate a need for educated and skilled bilingual lawyers.[3] Moreover, the creation of a Welsh-Medium Federal College, *Y Coleg Cymraeg Cenedlaethol*, to drive forward the cause of Welsh-medium university scholarship could well turn out to be a historic opportunity. Without a doubt, the current constitutional, political and legal environment is supportive of the cause of Welsh-medium legal scholarship.

Yet, despite these important initiatives and notwithstanding the political rhetoric, whether institutional ethos and academic culture within Welsh universities can embrace this politically driven impetus remains a question. Indeed, it is arguable that university legal scholarship in Wales is in a state of post-colonial transition, a transition which

[1] In accordance with the provisions of the Government of Wales Act (UK) 2006, which defines the powers of the National Assembly of Wales. In a referendum held on Mar. 3, 2011, the Welsh people voted for the National Assembly to exercise primary law making powers in those twenty policy fields devolved to it.

[2] The Welsh Language Measure (Wales) 2011 confirms the status of Welsh as an official language in Wales and creates a new framework for the implementation of this principle.

[3] The implications of legal bilingualism were considered by Robert Bergeron, 'Co-Drafting: Canadian Experience of the Creation of Bilingual Legislation in a Bijural System', *The Law Making Powers of the National Assembly for Wales* (Elfen 2001) pp. 54–58.

poses significance challenges of orientation and focus for law schools in Wales.

This paper claims that the prosperity of legal scholarship in the Welsh language depends on addressing difficult social, linguistic, educational, cultural, historical and economic challenges. Only by confronting these challenges can the potential breakdown between national policy and national aspiration, as articulated by the National Assembly for Wales and the Welsh Government, and the culture and mindset of Welsh universities be avoided.

Many of the challenges arise as a result of the globalisation of higher education. The Welsh experience is thus presented as a case-study which highlights some universal challenges to the relationship between university scholarship and a minority language.

B. The Historical Context of Welsh Legal Scholarship

To understand the nature of the challenges facing bilingual legal scholarship in contemporary Wales, some appreciation of the historical background is necessary.

The history of Welsh legal scholarship can be considered within the context of three distinct periods of development. The cultured reader of this paper will be familiar with Titian's renowned painting, "The Three Ages of Man", which hangs at the National Gallery of Scotland in Edinburgh. This renaissance painting depicts the three stages of life: infancy, adulthood and old age.[4] Borrowing the symbolism of Titan's painting, what follows is a historical overview of the three ages of legal scholarship in Wales.

1. *The Age of Endeavour*

The first age, as in Titian's painting, was the infancy of Welsh legal scholarship. It was what I shall describe as the age of endeavour, because this was an age when a new venture was beginning and the idea of university legal scholarship in Wales was becoming an accepted

[4] To the right, the painting portrays infancy represented by Cupid keeping watch over sleeping babies. Adulthood is portrayed by the young lovers to the left of the composition. Their short-lived summer will eventually be interrupted by the autumn of life, which is symbolised by two skulls and an old man in the background. In this painting, Titian invites us to meditate on the transience or passage of human life.

fact. Of course, the genesis of legal scholarship in Wales was part of a wider movement during the late nineteenth century to establish law as a recognised university discipline in Britain as a whole. But, in Wales, there were also some local imperatives which inspired the development of university legal scholarship.

Let us turn briefly to the history of university education in Wales. There is no doubt that, for historians, the Welsh university movement was the climax of the national rebirth of the nineteenth century, when the very idea of Welsh nationhood was re-discovered and proclaimed.[5] National institutions were established to nurture this renewed sense of national identity, and the establishing of the University of Wales in 1893 was a climax in this process.[6] 'A powerful symbol of popular achievement and national status' was one historian's verdict on its significance.[7]

The University of Wales had provided a focal point for university education in Wales, and was to be the degree-awarding body for the constituent colleges located throughout Wales for more than a century.[8] This important national institution was 'a binding, centripetal influence',[9] and provided a national intellectual forum for Wales, promoting scholarship which had a distinctively Welsh outlook through its academic press, the University of Wales Press, and its specialist research centres, in particular its Centre for Advanced Welsh and Celtic Studies. Without a doubt, '…the creation of a national university was a symbol of devolution, not in any political sense but in that it recognised the separate cultural identity of Wales and the intellectual aspirations of its people'.[10] It formed a component within a portfolio of national

[5] See J. Gwynn Williams, *The University Movement in Wales* (University of Wales Press 1993); J. Gwynn Williams, *The University of Wales 1893–1939* (University of Wales Press 1997); P. Morgan, *The University of Wales 1939–1993* (University of Wales Press 1997).

[6] See K. O. Morgan, *Rebirth of a Nation: A History of Modern Wales* (Oxford University Press 1981) pp. 106–12.

[7] *Ibid.*, p. 110.

[8] The constituent colleges at the time of founding the University of Wales were Aberystwyth, founded in 1872, Cardiff, founded in 1883, and Bangor which was founded in 1884. See, further, E. L. Ellis, *The University College of Wales Aberystwyth 1872–1972* (University of Wales Press 1972); J. Gwynn Williams, *The University College of North Wales: Foundations 1884–1927* (University of Wales Press 1985).

[9] D. E. Evans, *The University of Wales, A Historical Sketch* (University of Wales Press 1953) p. 36.

[10] See G. E. Jones, "The Welsh Universities and Devolution", 14 (1) *The Welsh Journal of Education* (2007) p. 21 at p. 37.

institutions, including the national museum and national library, established at this time.[11]

However, although the Welsh university movement was the product of a resurgence in an expression of Welsh identity, it was also conceived at a time when the British Empire was at its zenith, and when English civilisation and its values was being exported to the four corners of the globe. From the start, the Welsh universities were more about producing good British subjects to serve the empire than meeting Welsh national aspirations. They became vehicles for maintaining English civilisation in a particular part of the empire. Unsurprisingly, Welsh-medium studies were consigned to a few subjects, and were never part of the mainstream of university life.[12]

Perhaps it is in the historical genesis that Welsh universities can be distinguished from those of Scotland. The ancient Scottish universities were established in the fifteenth and sixteenth centuries,[13] long before the union of the crowns of England and Scotland in 1601 and the union of the parliaments in 1707.[14] They were products of an indigenous Scottish national movement and were created to serve a nation with a stronger sense of national identity, an identity which had been secured on the field of Bannockburn in 1314.[15] Although the linguistic element may not have been a straightforward matter in the Scottish experience, Scottish universities have and continue to promote Scottish studies, including the laws and legal traditions of the country.[16]

Wales's story was different. The war for independence was lost in 1282, and with the Statue of Wales of 1284, a process of assimilation into the English realm and the consequent eradication of national autonomy was to accelerate.[17] Of course, there was that remarkable historical moment between 1400 and 1415, when the vision of an independent Welsh state found dramatic, but, ultimately, short-lived expression.[18] Owain Glyndŵr's political manifesto included the founding of two universities in Wales, one in the north and the other

[11] See J. Davies, *History of Wales* (Penguin 2007) p. 482.

[12] See S. Lewis, *Ati Wŷr Ifainc* (University of Wales Press 1986) pp. 62–64.

[13] That is, of course, the ancients of St. Andrews, Aberdeen, Glasgow and Edinburgh.

[14] See M. Lynch, *Scotland: A New History* (Pimlico 1992) p. 102, 104–105.

[15] *Ibid.*, pp. 124–26.

[16] See N. MacCormick, 'Law', in P. H. Scott (ed.), *Scotland: A Concise Cultural History* (Mainstream Publishing 1993) pp. 343–56.

[17] See T. G. Watkin, *The Legal History of Wales* (University of Wales Press 2007), ch. 5 and 6.

[18] See R. R. Davies, *The Revolt of Owain Glyndŵr* (Oxford University Press 2005) p. 171.

in the south. The early fifteenth century was a time when the universities of Europe were becoming more secular, and were being regarded as important symbols of national expression by rulers who were conscious of their political significance. Owain Glyndŵr had also recognised the importance of having universities in the cause of maintaining national identity. Had he succeeded in his aims, it is possible that Wales would have had a university before St Andrews was established in 1412. Alas, the story of this lost historical opportunity is one of these fateful episodes in the story of the Welsh people.[19]

Be that as it may. Centuries later, the late Victorian period witnessed a national rebirth in Wales culminating in the creation of great national institutions, chief among which were the university colleges and the federal University of Wales.[20] In addition, greater democratisation led to the growth in local government and would-be clients for the lawyers of Wales.[21] Furthermore, the needs of commerce and industry generated a need for legal services on a hitherto unprecedented scale. The resulting expansion in the legal profession heralded greater professionalisation, and with this came the recognition of the importance of education and training.

Demand for a Welsh law school found mounting support and a campaign was launched in the late 1890s to establish such a school. Lord Justice Vaughan Williams, a Welshman by descent,[22] was one of the main orchestrators of the project, and saw to it that Aberystwyth became the base for the newly founded Welsh law school in 1901.[23] The University College of Wales, Aberystwyth had a distinctive place in the national makeup, and, in the context of the north-south divide, its location gave it the egalitarian merit of mutual inconvenience.[24]

The Aberystwyth law department's founders were Thomas Levi and Jethro Brown, both of whom were awarded chairs upon the Department's launch.[25] Whereas Brown's tenure proved to be short, as

---

[19] See, further, Davies, *supra* n. 11, p. 197.

[20] The history of the development of university education in Wales has been well-chronicled. See, for example, Evans, *supra* n. 9.

[21] See Morgan, *supra* n. 6, pp. 106–112.

[22] The Welsh origins of Sir Rowland Lomax Bowdler Vaughan Williams (1838–1916) are considered in *The Dictionary of Welsh Biography down to 1940* (Honourable Society of Cymmrodorion 1959) p. 1050.

[23] See J. A. Andrews, 'A Century of Legal Education', 34 *Cambrian Law Review* (2003) pp. 3–26.

[24] Its first hundred years was surveyed by Ellis, *supra* n. 8.

[25] See, also, J.A. Andrews, 'The Aberystwyth Law School, 1901–1976', 7 *Cambrian Law Review* (1976) pp. 7–10.

he departed for a Chair at Adelaide in 1906,[26] Levi's proved to be enduring. Thomas Arthur Levi should surely be acknowledged as the founding father of Welsh legal scholarship.[27] A native of Aberystwyth, he had impressive scholarly credentials and had practised at the Bar at the Inner Temple before being appointed to the chair at Aberystwyth in 1901.[28] Levi was to remain in post for nearly forty years, and, thanks to a dry wit and a streak of eccentricity, he became an integral part of the institution's folklore.[29]

For the first half century of its existence, the Aberystwyth Law School ran on a modest scale, with never more than a handful of teachers at any one time. This was typical of most of the provincial law schools in Britain during the first half of the twentieth century. However, in Aberystwyth's case, it was a case of quality if not quantity, and, for brief periods, it would claim the services of legal scholars of the calibre of Geoffrey Cheshire, David Hughes Parry and Glanville Llewellyn Williams.[30]

Although the needs of legal practice had provided the impetus for the creation of the Welsh law school, the scholars who would inhabit it recognised the distinction between learning and training and between scholarship and preparation for trade.[31] Although it provided courses for practitioners and collaborated with local law societies and associations in providing training for articled clerks, it was also wary of the 'trade school' label.[32] Hence, from the beginning, the curriculum included studies in subjects that had no immediate nexus with legal practice, such as jurisprudence and legal history. This need to have an intellectual identity was not lost on Levi, who in his inaugural lecture stated: 'the last function we would wish the present Faculty to fulfil is that of merely negotiating legal examinations'.[33]

---

[26] See R. Ireland, 'John Austin, H. L. A. Hart…Oh, and W. Jethro Brown', 34 *Cambrian Law Review* (2003) pp. 27–56.

[27] See his entry in *The Dictionary of Welsh Biography 1941–1970* (Honourable Society of Cymmrodorion 2001) p. 155.

[28] Levi was the son of the Revered Thomas Levi [1825–1916], a renowned Calvinistic Methodist preacher; see the elder Levi's entry in *The Dictionary of Welsh Biography (down to 1940)* at p. 543.

[29] See Lord Elwyn-Jones, *In My Time* (Weidenfeld & Nicolson 1983) p. 23.

[30] See, further, Andrews, *supra* n. 25.

[31] Andrews, *supra* n. 23, pp. 11–12.

[32] See Ellis, *supra* n. 8, pp. 133–137.

[33] See Levi's inaugural lecture: T. A. Levi, *The Opportunities of a New Faculty of Law (The Opening Lecture of the Department of English Law, University College of Wales, Aberystwyth)* (Curtis and Beamish Printers 1901) pp. 5–6.

Levi retired in 1940, and was succeeded by D. J. Llewelfryn Davies, who had been a student of Levi's at Aberystwyth in the 1920s.[34] Whereas Levi was only twenty seven when appointed to the chair in 1901, Llewelfryn was thirty seven and, obviously, more experienced, with periods of teaching at the LSE and on the continent behind him. Llewelfryn was probably the better scholar too, and his election as president of the Society of the Public Teachers of Law in 1955 was well-deserved recognition of his important contribution to legal scholarship in Britain.[35] Llewelfryn would devote the next thirty years of his life to the cause of the Aberystwyth law school, gently nurturing and developing its reputation. However, even by the end of Llewelfryn's tenure in 1970, the department of law at Aberystwyth remained relatively small-scale, with no more than half a dozen academics and less than a hundred students. Indeed, Llewelfryn remained the only professor in the department until a second chair in law was created in 1967.[36]

This age of endeavour, when legal scholarship was in its infancy in Wales, can be said to have been dominated by two major challenges: academic acceptance and professional standards. Academic acceptance was an issue because legal scholarship was struggling to find acceptance in Britain generally, both within the academy and within the world of legal practice. The story of legal scholarship during the first half of the twentieth century was a struggle to establish law's credentials as a university discipline.[37] Internally, within the academy, legal scholarship was considered to be peripheral and insignificant.[38] Externally, legal practitioners were suspicious of its validity as an academic discipline, believing it to be a trade to be learnt 'on the job' rather than a scholarly discipline in the true sense.[39] Legal study at university,

[34] See C. Harding, 'Looking through Llewelfryn Davies' eyes: A Turn of the Century Retrospective of International Law in the Twentieth Century', 34 *Cambrian Law Review* (2003) pp. 83–102.

[35] This society's contribution to the development and maintenance of university legal scholarship is recorded by F. Cownie and R. Cocks, *'A Great and Noble Occupation!' The History of the Society of Legal Scholars* (Hart 2009).

[36] Professor John A. Andrews was appointed to the chair and became head of the Law Department at Aberystwyth in 1970, where he remained until 1992.

[37] See, for example, D. Sugarman, 'Legal Theory, the Common Law Mind and the Making of the Textbook Tradition', in W. Twining (ed.), *Legal Theory and Common Law* (Basil Blackwell 1986) pp. 26–61. See also, generally, W. Twining, *Blackstone's Tower: The English Law School* (Sweet & Maxwell 1994).

[38] A. Bradney, *Conversations, Choices and Changes: The Liberal Law School in the Twenty-First Century* (Hart 2003) pp. 2–9 and 109–112.

[39] See also F. Cownie, *Legal Academics: Culture and Identities* (Hart 2004) p. 31.

if undertaken, was considered to be something of a rite of passage, a phase that had to be endured, before sailing out into the 'real world'.[40] The dilemma was neatly encapsulated by Professor J. W. Bridge when he said, 'many practising lawyers regard academic lawyers as so remote from reality as to be irrelevant; many academics regard academic lawyers as involved in vocational training and not with liberal education and scholarship'.[41]

The practitioner's scepticism towards the academic lawyer gave birth to a principle whereby the works of living authors would not be referred to by the courts.[42] This cemented the perception of the legal scholar as a marginal and inferior creature, of little use to the practitioner.[43] This was somewhat paradoxical as the law curriculum was

---

[40] For the story of the establishing of law as a university discipline, see, further, J. H. Baker, 'The Inns of Court and Legal Doctrine', in T. M. Charles Edwards, M. E. Owen and D. B. Walters (eds.), *Lawyers and Laymen*, (University of Wales Press 1986) pp. 274–86; H. G. Hanbury, *The Vinerian Chair and Legal Education* (Blackwell 1958); F. H. Lawson, *The Oxford Law School 1850–1965* (Clarendon 1968); N. Duxbury, 'A Century of Legal Studies', in P. Cane and M. Tushnet (eds.), *The Oxford Handbook of Legal Studies* (Oxford University Press 2003) pp. 950–74; I. Fletcher, 'An English Tragedy: The Academic Lawyer as Jurist', in T. M. Charles Edwards, M. E. Owen and D. B. Walters (eds.), *Lawyers and Laymen*, *ibid.*, pp. 316–335.

[41] See J. W. Bridge, 'The Academic Lawyer: Mere Working Mason or Architect?', 91 *Law Quarterly Review* (1975) p. 488 at p. 489.

[42] The reason for the development of this convention is considered in some detail by N. Duxbury in *Jurists and Judges: an Essay on Influence* (Hart 2001) pp. 66–73. Sir Robert Megarry expressed the principle in the case of *Cordell v Second Clanfield Properties* [1968] 3 All E.R. 746: "...the process of authorship is entirely different from that of judicial decision. The author has the benefit of a broad and comprehensive study of his chosen subject. But he is exposed to the perils to yielding to preconceptions, and he lacks the sharpening of focus which the detailed facts of a particular case bring to the judge. Above all, he has to form his idea without the aid of the purifying ordeal of skilled argument on the specific facts of a contested case. I would therefore give credit to the words of any reputable author as expressing tenable and arguable ideas, as fertilisers of thought, and as conveniently expressing the fruits of research in print. But I would expose those views to the testing and refining process of argument". However, this cynicism towards legal scholarship was not universally shared. Lord Denning took a more positive view of academic writing, and said that, "...textbooks are not digests of cases but repositories of principles. They are written by men who have studied the law as a science, with more detachment than is possible to men engaged in busy practice" (Lord Denning, "Review of P.H. Winfield, A Textbook of the Law of Tort", 63 *Law Quarterly Review* (1947) p. 516). In more recent times, Lord Goff, sometime fellow of Lincoln College Oxford, and co-author of a leading textbook on the law of restitution, said in the case of *Spiliada Maritime Corporation v Cansulex Ltd*, that academic authors were, "... pilgrims with us on the endless world to unattainable perfection"; see [1987] A.C. 460.

[43] The thorny and unsettled relationship between the jurist and the practitioner is memorably described by P. Birks, 'The Academic and the Practitioner', 18(4) *Legal Studies* (1998) pp. 397–414.

often determined by the educational priorities of the Law Society, who paid many of the provincial universities to provide instruction for its professional examinations.[44]

If legal scholars were the victims of a lack of recognition and acceptance, perhaps they were themselves to blame for this rejection: professional standards for legal scholars were also in their infancy. Indeed, academic law was often a rather amateur activity, and many of the law teachers of the time invested very little effort in research and authorship. Indeed, in many cases, the legal scholar had nothing more than a dilettante interest in his subject. For some, research and authorship was an unwarranted interference with other more pressing commitments: it was claimed that Professor J. D. Ivor Hughes of the University of Leeds's law school felt that his time was better spent fishing in North Wales.[45]

Then again, the vast majority of the university law teachers were part-timers who, out of necessity, were driven to supplement their incomes through practice. Legal scholarship was rarely taken seriously by the universities, and the law schools, particularly in the case of the provincial universities, were populated mostly by fractional staff.[46] Furthermore, the law teacher had to shoulder a burden which entailed teaching across a broad range of different subjects.[47] The usual pattern was that of the lecturer teaching a great deal but doing little research. Even then, the teaching could often be uninspiring, with a technique which, according to one who had a brief period as law lecturer at Aberystwyth in the 1940s before departing for the London School of Economics, amounted to no more than reading "old style, dictated points, to be written down and learnt by heart for reproduction, much welcomed by the idle".[48] Another eminent Welsh lawyer and politician once told me how his tutor in Roman law at Aberystwyth in the 1950s gave the impression that the entire law had not changed much since Roman times.

---

[44] See Sugarman, *supra* n. 37, pp. 50–52; also B. Abel-Smith and R. Stevens, *Lawyers and the Courts: A Sociological Study of the English Legal System 1750–1965* (Heinemann 1967) p. 182 and 373.

[45] See Duxbury, *supra* n. 42, p. 71.

[46] See Abel-Smith and Stevens, *supra* n. 44, p. 183. See also W. Twining, '1836 and all that: laws in the University of London, 1836–1986', 40 *Current Legal Problems* (1987) p. 261 at pp. 275–276.

[47] See Twining, *supra* n. 46, p. 277.

[48] Recollections in a letter from the late Professor J. A. G. Griffith to R. Gwynedd Parry, Nov. 2, 2004.

Even so, the years after the Second World War would witness a drive to establish the British law school as a credible operation, where research and scholarship could flourish and law appreciated as an important international social phenomenon.[49] Gradually, the somewhat descriptive and uncritical analysis of cases made way for a broader, critical and more academic approach to legal scholarship. Rather than being in the shadow of the practitioner, legal scholars sought to establish their discipline as a genuinely intellectual activity within the academy.[50] Their ideas bore the obvious hallmarks of continental and American influences.[51] Their objective was to raise the status of law as a recognised intellectual discipline.

2. *The Age of Expansion*

The Aberystwyth Law Department had enjoyed a monopoly on legal education in Wales for more than sixty years. However, by the 1960s and 1970s, the educational climate was changing, and two major reports heralded the dawn of a new age in legal scholarship in Wales. This was to be the age of expansion.

The first of these reports was the Robbins Report on higher education, published in 1963, which recommended the expansion of higher education in the United Kingdom.[52] The existing universities were to expand dramatically and new universities were created to meet the growing demand for higher education (although, interestingly, none of the new 'plate glass' universities were established in Wales). The second report came in 1971, authored by Mr. Justice Ormrod, which made recommendations as to the role and purpose of the law degree in the training of lawyers.[53] Although its recommendations were never implemented fully, the Ormrod Report provided a basis for

[49] See L. C. B. Gower, 'English Legal Training', 13 *Modern Law Review* (1950), pp. 137–205.

[50] See, for example, C. Glasser, 'Radicals and Refugees: The Foundation of the Modern Law Review and English Legal Scholarship', 50 *Modern Law Review* (1987) pp. 688–708.

[51] For the continental influence, see, further, J. Beatson and R. Zimmermann (eds.), *Jurists Uprooted: German-speaking Émigré Lawyers in Twentieth Century Britain* (Oxford University Press 2004).

[52] *The Report of the Committee on Higher Education, chaired by Lord Robbins* Cmnd. 2154, (HMSO 1963).

[53] See Mr Justice Ormrod, *Report of the Committee on Legal Education: presented to Parliament by the Lord Chancellor* (HMSO 1971).

a more formal working relationship between the law school and the legal profession.

This expansion in higher education generally, and the development of the concept of a 'qualifying law degree', gave incentive for the expansion of legal education. In Wales, Cardiff's status as the national capital city, with governmental, legal and administrative importance given a significant boost with the creation of the Welsh Office in 1964,[54] meant that its university college became an obvious candidate for a new law school for Wales. Limited professional legal training had been offered by the Glamorgan Technical College in Pontypridd since 1949. However, its successor, the Polytechnic of Wales would not establish a law degree course until 1979, and a fully fledged law school would only be established in the 1980s.[55]

At Cardiff, in the meantime, the Cardiff Institute of Science and Technology (later, the University of Wales Institute of Science and Technology, UWIST) had been tentatively running legal courses as part of its degrees in social science and economics in the early 1960s. It soon established a law department, a process that was made easier by the fact that, at that point, it was not a constituent member of the federal University of Wales, and so did not face objections from Aberystwyth. Soon thereafter, University College Cardiff followed suit by setting up a law department, and in 1971 a formal partnership was established between the two Cardiff law schools.[56] That partnership would turn to merger in 1988, when UWIST and University College, Cardiff were merged.

Expansion continued into the 1980s. Unsurprisingly, Swansea, the second city, saw a need to respond to consumer demand for legal education, and law degrees were offered by the Institute of Higher Education, initially, followed by the University College, where a law department was established in 1994.[57] The founding of Bangor's law

[54] Its founding head as Secretary of State for Wales was James Griffiths, the Member of Parliament for Llanelli. His autobiography was published, *Pages from Memory* (J M Dent 1969).

[55] Information provided by Professor Gerwyn Ll. H. Griffiths, School of Law, University of Glamorgan.

[56] See L. A. Sheridan, 'University Legal Education in Cardiff', 4 *Cambrian Law Review* (1973) pp. 94–102.

[57] Although Swansea had a long history as a legal centre, it took more than seventy years for its university college to establish a law school. For a history of Swansea University see D. Dykes, *The University College of Swansea: an illustrated history* (Alan Sutton 1992).

school in 2004 meant that all of the big five universities in Wales now had a law school. In the space of a generation, legal education had gone from being a one horse race to having a pervasive presence at universities throughout Wales.

This period, from about 1965 to 1999, was thus an age of great expansion in legal education. Law became a popular subject within the UK university sector and in Wales the largest universities would develop law schools with an annual intake of between 150 and 200 students to the first year of study.[58] Indeed, by today, it is even arguable that, "the law degree (LLB) is possibly supplanting the Arts degree (BA) as the general degree of higher education".[59]

What were the features of this expansion in the specific Welsh context? In 1973, a law professor at Cardiff pondered on the purpose and mission of his newly established law school in an article in the *Cambrian Law Review*. Having delineated the school's ambitions, he then made these rather telling comments:

> It will be noticed that I have not said anything that gives a particularly Welsh flavour to the Cardiff Law School. That, I think, is an accurate impression. There is nothing particularly Welsh about the Law.[60]

Of course, his comment was a frank but completely accurate representation of the truth about legal scholarship and the administration of justice in Wales: it was overwhelmingly English in focus, orientation and language. It had been so since the Aberystwyth law school had been founded at the turn of the century, and although Welsh-speaking Welshmen had been at the helm for long periods, only in informal and social contexts would a student have heard a law professor utter anything in Welsh. Welsh was most certainly not the language of the lecture theatre or seminar.

The fact that the expansion in academic personnel during the 1970s and 1980s was marked by imported talent only served to dilute any potential for Welsh-medium legal studies. Most of the teachers in the Welsh law schools would be recruited from outside Wales (mostly from England). Only studies in medieval Welsh laws, led notably by Professor Dafydd Jenkins of Aberystwyth, provided relief to this

---

[58] For data, see <www.ucas.ac.uk>.

[59] See B. J. Richardson, 'Students as Stakeholders in Legal Education: Gaining Admission to Law School', in F. Cowine (ed.), *Stakeholders in the Law School* (Hart 2010) p.127–155 at p. 127.

[60] See Sheridan, *supra* n. 56, p. 101.

general trend of Anglo-centric legal studies.[61] Put simply, Welsh law schools were part and parcel of a network of English law schools.

3. *The Age of Engagement*

We now turn to the third age in the history of Welsh legal scholarship, what is described here as the age of engagement: but engagement with what?

Without a doubt, the creation of the National Assembly for Wales in 1999 was a momentous event in Welsh history and a watershed for Welsh democracy.[62] For the first time in history, the Welsh people have a national, elected, law-making body. Of course, the National Assembly is an evolving institution, and although it was initially the product of a somewhat clumsy political compromise,[63] it has organically and systematically normalised its practices and structures so that it now operates according to the standard model of a parliamentary democracy.[64]

From its inception, the National Assembly was responsible for higher education in Wales and for the maintenance and promotion of the principle of linguistic equality between English and Welsh, a principle which had been firmly established by an act of the Westminster parliament a few years earlier.[65] The Welsh Government initiated policy measures to safeguard and promote the policy of language choice, consistent with the principle of linguistic equality. Perhaps its first major initiative was the National Strategy for a Bilingual Wales: *Iaith Pawb*, which sought to establish a national language policy that would facilitate an increase in services delivered through the medium of Welsh.[66]

---

[61] See D. Jenkins, 'Legal History at Aberystwyth', 34 *Cambrian Law Review* (2003) pp. 27–56.

[62] Its significance was the subject of a detailed study by R. Rawlings, *Delineating Wales* (University of Wales Press 2003).

[63] For a critique, see V. Bogdanor, *Devolution in the United Kingdom* (Oxford University Press 1999) p. 254: also N. Burrows, *Devolution* (Sweet & Maxwell 2000), generally, and pp. 9–27.

[64] Especially following the Government of Wales Act 2006, which reformed its constitution and extended its law making capacity. For possible future developments, see *All Wales Convention - Report* (Crown Copyright 2009).

[65] By virtue of the Welsh Language Act (UK) 1993.

[66] See *Iaith Pawb - A National Action Plan for a Bilingual Wales* (Welsh Assembly Government 2002) and *Dyfodol Dwyieithog: A Bilingual Future* (Welsh Assembly Government 2002).

Universities were seen to have an important role in implementing the national language policy and in promoting the principle of linguistic equality, both in terms of enhancing the status of the Welsh language and extending the domains within which it operates. They were to have a vital role in opportunity, use and incentive planning,[67] and in developing the Welsh language as a language of work and social interaction by producing graduates who are capable of delivering services bilingually within the community.[68] Of course, the relationship between university scholarship and a minority language is much more than a means of producing linguistically skilled graduates. The university is the curator and the guardian of the nation's learning, its history, its culture, its identity, and the language through which it has articulated its collective experience, values and aspirations. Arguments for the claims of the Welsh language as a language of university scholarship have always been presented in the context of its contribution towards the maintenance of national identity.[69]

However, the implementation of linguistic equality through Welsh-medium university education also provided a practical and immediate policy objective. Subsequent policy initiatives on the part of the Welsh Government have reinforced the commitment of the body-politic to developing the Welsh language as a medium of university scholarship. A number of reports and reviews were commissioned to establish the nature and scope of the provision. What was established was that Welsh-medium provision within the higher education sector in Wales was in an impoverished state, with only 3 percent of all students at Welsh higher education institutions receiving *some* teaching through the medium of Welsh in 2002.[70] The Welsh Government thus initiated strategies to remedy the deficiency and extend the opportunities for university education through the medium of Welsh.[71]

---

[67] See C. Baker, "Language Planning: a Grounded Approach", in J.-M. Dewaele, A. Housen and L. Wei (eds.), *Bilingualism: Beyond Basic Principles* (Multilingual Matters 2003) pp. 88–111.

[68] See J. Cann, "Higher Education's Contribution to the Maintenance and Revitalization of Minority Official Languages: The Cases of Wales and New Brunswick", 13(1) *The Welsh Journal of Education* (2004) p. 95 at p. 113.

[69] See, for example, S. Lewis's writings in *Barn*, Dec. 1964.

[70] See, C. H. Williams, *Language Revitalization, Policy and Planning in Wales* (University of Wales Press 2000) p. 134.

[71] See "Universities in Move to Increase their Commitment to Welsh-medium Learners", *Western Mail*, Feb. 8, 2007.

A Welsh Medium Higher Education Sector Group, containing senior representatives of the institutions, the Welsh HE funding council and the representative body for higher education, was established in early 2007 to provide a new strategic framework for Welsh medium higher education. A national development plan for Welsh medium higher education was devised, and a reconstituted Centre for Welsh Medium Higher Education was established and assigned with the task of implementation.[72] The policy goals were to support "the development of Welsh-medium provision to meet the needs of a bilingual Wales",[73] to develop Welsh-medium learning, "further enabling universities to play their part ... in meeting the economic, cultural and social needs of Wales (including those associated with ... the Welsh language)",[74] and "in having a strong emphasis on ... collaboration ... to sustain improved performance of individual institutions and of the higher education system as a whole".[75] These core policy objectives remain and have found expression in subsequent policy documents.[76]

As part of the Centre for Welsh Medium Higher Education's action plan, subject panels were established to initiate developments, coordinate policy in specific subject areas and develop provision through collaboration across the institutions. These panels would consist of representatives of the relevant disciplines in all the institutions. Included among these subject panels was a law subject panel.

The specific case of legal education provides us with valuable insights into some of the difficulties in developing bilingual higher education in Wales, but also some of the compelling arguments in support of such development. The legal profession, arguably the chief consumer of law graduates, can make a significant contribution towards promoting linguistic equality. Indeed, with the well-established legal right to give evidence in Welsh in court proceedings, the legal community has been required to engage directly with the principle of linguistic equality for some time.[77] The Courts Service, the Crown Prosecution Service

---

[72] For more information, see http://www.mantais.ac.uk

[73] *HEFCW Corporate Strategy to 2010, The Deal for Students* (HEFCW 2005).

[74] *HEFCW Corporate Strategy to 2010, Benefiting the Community and Society* (HEFCW 2005).

[75] *HEFCW Corporate Strategy to 2010, Making it Work* (HEFCW, 2005).

[76] See *For Our Future: The 21st Century Higher Education Strategy and Plan for Wales, Department for Children, Education, Lifelong Learning and Skills, Welsh Assembly Government* (Crown Copyright 2009).

[77] Welsh Language Act 1993, s. 22, provided: "In any legal proceedings in Wales the Welsh language may be spoken by any party, witness or other person who desires to

and other public legal bodies were required to devise and implement language policies in accordance with the 1993 Act. The National Assembly for Wales and the Welsh Government also have a statutory duty to observe the principle of linguistic equality in the conduct of their business, including the preparation of legislation.[78] The principle of linguistic equality therefore has a tangible impact on law-making and the administration of justice in Wales.

Devolution became the catalyst for the development of the "Legal Wales" movement, an expression which captures the process whereby the legal system in Wales has acquired its own distinctive identity in response to constitutional change.[79] Legal Wales potentially heralds the further evolution of an indigenous legal system to serve the needs of bilingual Wales.[80] Accordingly, lawyers provide an important professional sector that is required to operate bilingually within the context of devolution.[81] Naturally, the sector needs the training within an appropriate framework for skills acquisition and development in order to be able to respond effectively to the needs of the new constitutional settlement.[82]

In view of these significant developments, legal scholarship seems to have a vital role in supporting the objectives of Welsh democracy.[83]

---

use it, subject in the case of proceedings in a court other than a magistrates' court to such prior notice as may be required by rules of court; and any necessary provision for interpretation shall be made accordingly".

[78] The main provisions include Government of Wales Act 1998, s. 47 (1), s. 122 (1), Government of Wales Act 2006, s. 35(1). For commentary, see G. Griffiths, 'Her Deddfu'n Ddwyieithog', 38 *Cambrian Law Review* (2007) pp. 103–116; K. Bush, 'Deddfu yn y Gymraeg: Ail-gydio mewn Hen Ymgom', 38 *Cambrian Law Review* (2007) p. 83 at p. 95; K. Bush, 'Deddfu yn y Gymraeg', 4 *Wales Journal of Law and Policy* (2006) pp. 374- 381.

[79] See Sir John Thomas, "Legal Wales: Its Modern Origins and its Role after Devolution: National Identity, The Welsh Language and Parochialism", in T. Watkin (ed.), *Legal Wales: Its Past, Its Future* (Welsh Legal History Society 2001) pp. 113–165.

[80] See, for example, T. H. Jones and J. Williams, 'Wales as a Jurisdiction' [2004] Public Law 78; Sir Roderick Evans, "Legal Wales- Possibilities for the Future", Bangor University Law Lecture, Feb. 22, 2008.

[81] See 'Legal Directions in Wales', *Directions in Legal Education* (UK Centre for Legal Education, March 2010) pp. 4–5.

[82] See P. Leighton et al., *Mapping Legal Education in Wales Project 2002/03: The Key Findings* (University of Glamorgan 2003); see also P. Leighton, 'Is the Legal Education System in Wales Measuring up to Contemporary Challenges? Some Research Evidence from the MaLEW Project', 2 (4) *Wales Law Journal* (2003) p. 386 at p. 388.

[83] See T. Watkin, *How the Law is Taught in Modern Wales*, Law Society Lecture, National Eisteddfod of Wales, Eryri a'r Cyffiniau, 2005.

There is an opportunity, indeed, a *need* for engagement with this process on the part of university law schools.[84] Law schools could be the main generators of intellectual debate and of research and learning on the Welsh constitution and its impact on Welsh society. This might pose a challenge of realignment for many of the Welsh law schools. The old values and perspectives seem outdated: the nothing Welsh about the law remark now appears like an old fashioned remnant of a colonial by-gone age. Indeed, to make such a statement today would be plainly wrong.

Moreover, besides the need to respond to the challenges of public policy on bilingualism, there are also economic arguments for strengthening the bilingual skills of the legal community in Wales.[85] Devolution and the development of Legal Wales can offer lawyers the opportunity to make a unique contribution to the Welsh economy and to develop expertise and skills that will improve their ability to retain high quality work that hitherto has been lost to lawyers in the large cities of England.[86] If bilingualism is a cardinal tenet of legal life in Wales, bilingual lawyers operating in Wales have a further claim to retain legal work that is otherwise exported to the English legal conurbations. This need to appreciate the economic implications and benefits of bilingualism applies to the legal sector as it does across all sectors in the Welsh economy.[87]

With this strong political, social and public policy impetus in support of the development of bilingual legal scholarship, surely university law schools would seize the initiative and devise an innovative strategy to put the bilingual policy into effect? Law has become a pervasive subject within the UK university sector and, in Wales, each of the big five universities have a law school: law schools are therefore major undertakings within the Welsh institutions.

Leaders of the legal profession in Wales, many of whom concurrently hold positions of influence within the universities, have recognised the

---

[84] See Winston Roddick QC, '*The Role of the Law Schools of the University of Wales in the development of Legal Wales*', Aberystwyth University, 13 November 2000.

[85] See I. Davies, *The Challenge of Legal Wales*, Law Society Lecture, National Eisteddfod of Wales, Denbigh, 2001.

[86] The contribution of the legal profession to the development of the economy in Wales is considered in detail in I. Davies and L. Mainwaring, *The Supply of Private Practice Legal Skills in Wales* (The Law Society Research Report 2005).

[87] See *Economic Development and the Welsh Language: The Second Progress Report of the Language-Economy Discussion Group* (Welsh Assembly Government 2007).

critical nexus between the development and nurturing of Legal Wales, with its bilingual dimension, and what goes on within the university law schools.[88] Some within the academic legal profession have also recognised that legal scholarship has a crucial role to play in the new national legal order.[89] Obviously, constitutional change created a need for expertise in constitutional and administrative law. How could such expertise be developed? There would surely be initiatives to develop research projects, learning pathways and other means of knowledge dissemination that would facilitate public understanding of the legislative functions of the National Assembly. This, it was thought, was a golden opportunity for the law schools of Wales to do national service by being a fount of knowledge and understanding of the devolution settlement and to act as expositors of legal aspects of the constitution. Through continuing professional development programmes, the legal profession in Wales would be guided by the university law schools in the legal ramifications of the National Assembly's statutory output.[90]

The initial response seemed very promising. At Aberystwyth, for example, a Centre for Welsh Legal Affairs was established to provide an intellectual powerhouse for the law in contemporary Wales. Cardiff University's law school initiated a Wales Governance Centre, which would, among other things, develop an on-line legislation resource to promote awareness of and facilitate access to the National Assembly's legislative programme. Swansea's law school established a new bilingual academic journal, the Wales Law Journal, to facilitate the intellectual discourse inspired by devolution.[91] Bangor University established a new law school with a distinctive commitment to meeting the needs of Legal Wales and, especially, the bilingual agenda. The founding of the Welsh Legal History Society, the Wales Public Law and Human Rights Association and the creation of specialist masters' courses in devolution were further examples of the academic community's enthusiastic response to the possibilities of Legal Wales.

The Welsh Law Schools therefore seemed to be responding to devolution in an innovative way. A divergence seemed to be emerging

---

[88] See W. Roddick QC, '*The Role of the Law Schools of the University of Wales in the development of Legal Wales*', Aberystwyth University, Nov. 13, 2000.

[89] See Davies, *supra* n. 85.

[90] For some observations on the role of universities, see R. G. Parry, "Hyrwyddo'r Gymraeg ym Myd y Gyfraith- Beth yw Cyfraniad Adrannau Cyfraith y Brifysgol?", 1 *Wales Law Journal* (2002) pp. 387–395.

[91] See Davies, *supra* n. 85, p. 12.

between English and Welsh law schools as professional legal education became a pervasive element in the Welsh provision. Whereas only Cardiff and Glamorgan provided post-graduate vocational courses for intending legal practitioners in 1999, the next decade would see provision being established in Swansea and Aberystwyth.[92] Indeed, at present, only one of the five Welsh law schools remains without a professional legal studies unit. This is in total contrast to England, where hardly any of the old university law schools offer post-graduate vocational courses for those intending to practice law, and where the emphasis is on traditional academic courses. There can be little doubt that the growth in this provision in Wales coincided with a growing recognition of the need for vocational legal training to take account of devolution, and a belief that vocational legal education provided an appropriate vehicle to develop the required legal skills base (including linguistic skills).[93]

In order to coordinate the development of bilingual provision within the Law Schools, the Law Panel, hosted and supported by the Centre for Welsh Medium Higher Education, devised a national strategy, that, among other things, would develop the provision and promote collaboration between the schools in order to ensure sustainability and growth. Periodic reviews by the law subject panel revealed a degree of apparent support for Welsh-medium teaching in most of the law schools throughout Wales. There seemed to be a process of mapping a way forward that would see the provision mature in years to come.

C. Threats to Engagement

Despite these encouraging signs and indications that a new chapter was opening in the history of Welsh legal scholarship, a chapter which could see university law schools becoming the engine of the devolution project and its legal aspects, there remains the risk of disconnection between the Legal Wales agenda and the strategic priorities of

---

[92] Those intending to practice as solicitors must undertake a one-year vocational course, the Legal Practice Course, the content of which is approved and validated by the profession's regulator. Likewise, the Bar has its equivalent, the Bar Professional Training Course.

[93] For the potential role of vocational legal education, see D. Miers, 'The Role of Universities in the Training of Lawyers in the United Kingdom', 33 *Kobe University Law Review* (1999) p. 55.

Welsh universities and their law schools. What follows is an attempt to analyse the causes of this disconnection.

1. *Globalisation and Economics*

Universities in Wales, as in the rest of the United Kingdom, and beyond, are institutions which are fighting on several fronts. In the current financial and economic environment, some are fighting for their very survival and are busy putting out the fires of insolvency.[94] Because of precarious public finances, universities in the United Kingdom can expect less financial support from the government in the future. The Browne Review points firmly in the direction of a market-led and market-sustained sector.[95] Inexorably, universities will be required to fend for themselves financially and to become economically independent. A process of privatisation is unavoidable.[96] In such a world, only that which pays can endure.

Welsh universities are part of a higher education market that has become increasingly more globalised, with most universities engaging in intense international recruitment. International recruitment matters because it has economic repercussions: overseas students pay large fees for their university education.[97] Law schools participate, with great enthusiasm, in this international market: little wonder, as one overseas student is worth three EU students in economic terms. Of course, the international market is volatile, and over-dependence on overseas students may turn out to be flawed short-termism. But it currently plays a major role in determining institutional strategy at most of the institutions.

The introduction of student fees has meant that home students in England and Wales must pay for their higher education. In a consumer-led market, universities must ensure that their provision is attractive to employers, placing the graduate-consumer in a strong position in the jobs-market. Further privatisation will inevitably lead to increase in

---

[94] The cuts in government spending in the university sector in Wales were reported in *Times Higher Education*, March 25–31, 2010.

[95] See Securing a Sustainable Future for Higher Education: An Independent Review of Higher Education Funding and Student Finance, Oct. 12, 2010: www.independent.gov.uk/browne-report

[96] See 'Another brick in the wall: private higher education is growing, often to the dismay of academics. Coming soon: the Lego university', *The Guardian*, Feb. 2, 2010.

[97] See the article, 'Overseas students 'are not cash cows', *Times Higher Education*, Mar. 26, 2010.

fees, to ever greater consumerism, to fostering a more competitive relationship between institutions, and to less interest in any teaching or scholarly activity which might be regarded as altruistic.[98] Although the National Assembly of Wales has sought to support Welsh-domiciled students through a relatively generous financial package, which will lessen the burden of tuition fees compared to English-domiciled students, it remains to been seen whether the Welsh exchequer can maintain this approach in the medium to long term.

Universities concentrate on areas where there is likely to be investment by government, certainly, but also industry, business and the private sector. Science, technology, engineering and mathematics (STEM), along with medicine are subject areas which are more likely to resonate with economic priorities than arts and humanities, whose traditional reliance on public investment is likely to become a source of weakness in future years.[99] This has major implications for Welsh-medium scholarship, which has traditionally flourished in arts and humanities areas such as history, theology and modern languages.

This has significance for Welsh law schools and their relationship with the Welsh constitutional agenda. Those running the business of higher education listen to what the market is telling them it wants. Nervousness, rightly or wrongly, surrounds any venture which appears to emphasise unduly the Welsh component at the expense of the international perspective. Moreover, the prospects for Welsh-medium legal scholarship must be evaluated in light of the fact that the international market is fuelled by a demand for English-medium higher education, where the financial stakes and rewards are high.[100] The economics of higher education dictate where money is spent and institutions invest where they believe they will find the highest returns. It is little wonder that managers at Welsh universities contemplate with gloom the profitability of Welsh-medium education, legal or otherwise.

Perhaps they are right to be cautious. The uptake of the Welsh-medium provision in law has not been encouraging. Not even in the

---

[98] See 'Growing student consumerism is inevitable, says NUS', *Times Higher Education*, June 15, 2007.

[99] http://news.bbc.co.uk/1/hi/education/7924765.stm

[100] Indeed, even official, majority state languages are facing pressures from this globalisation effect. For the position of Finnish within Finland's universities, and the demands of the international market, see Raili Seppanen, 'Funding and flexibility: keys to the future', *Times Higher Education*, Dec. 1, 2006.

heartland of Welsh-speaking Wales, at Bangor University, is there more than about twenty students studying law through the medium of Welsh in each undergraduate year. When it is appreciated that each year there is an intake of about 150–200 students, that 10 percent of the student body choose to study through the medium of Welsh hardly represents buoyancy. The story is the same throughout Wales. Having responded to the "new dawn" in Welsh democracy by establishing masters' courses in devolution, universities find that the student take-up can be counted on one hand. That, in an age of fiscal constraints, is just not economically sustainable.

2. *Resource Capacity*

The economics of higher education dictates where money is spent. Institutions invest where they believe they will find the highest returns. University investment has two key aspects: the human and the physical. For there to be any meaningful Welsh-medium provision, there needs to be appropriately qualified staff with the right tools to do the job.

At most of the institutions reviewed by the Law Panel, students who take up the Welsh-medium provision usually study legal subjects through the medium of Welsh which also contain elements of study through the medium of English within those subjects. The diet is thus literally bilingual, with code switching a normal part of the student learning experience. This, obviously, has its advantages in terms of skills acquisition and preparation for the real world of legal practice in Wales. However, necessity rather than design may be the true reason behind this formula. It was evident that, at every institution, the scarcity of legal literature in the Welsh language is proving to be the major factor in determining the quality of the provision, and, in many cases, a significant barrier to the provision of modules through the medium of Welsh. Of course, the *Welsh Dictionary of Law* supports the provision to some extent, but does not explain the legal principles, nor does it provide commentary on relevant cases.[101] After all, a dictionary is not the same as a monograph or textbook.

The Centre for Welsh Medium Higher Education has made efforts to address the learning resource issue by commissioning academics to produce literature, including legal literature, in Welsh, and its 'Porth'

---

[101] See R. Lewis, *Geiriadur Newydd y Gyfraith* (Gomer Press 2002).

internet initiative has provided a platform for collating resources and facilitating access to learning materials in Welsh.[102] However, too few academics engage in Welsh-medium authorship for this literature deficit to be remedied, even in the medium term.

The absence of the extensive learning resources, the textbooks and the primary sources, that one finds in the English-medium provision means that studying law through the medium of Welsh can be wholly unattractive to the student. The result is that a significant number of bilingual students chose not to study even elements of law through the medium of Welsh. The absence of learning resources is also a turn-off for potential teachers of law. It is not surprising that there are no more than two or three people responsible for Welsh-medium teaching in most law schools, even though the largest schools have more than forty teaching staff. This reinforces a perception that Welsh-medium scholarship is marginal and non-essential activity.

Of course, on an all-Wales basis, there are probably a sufficient number of legal academics who could collaborate to provide a more comprehensive programme of courses through the medium of Welsh in all core legal subjects. Developing staff capacity has been a priority for the national development plan, with the creation of Welsh-medium fellowships and PhD scholarships, funded by the national Welsh HE funding council, increasing the number of postgraduate research students and teaching fellows willing and qualified to teach through the medium of Welsh. But this is a medium to long term strategy, and is unlikely to make a substantial impact for some time. Already there has been criticism of certain institutions' over-dependence on postgraduate students to deliver teaching while experienced, senior scholars get on with their more pressing tasks (when I come to research, I will explain more fully).[103] There is nothing that can undermine Welsh legal scholarship more profoundly than the perception that it is done solely or mainly by post-graduate tutors or junior lecturers, with not a professor that would touch it with a barge-pole.

Some empirical research on the position at Aberystwyth Law School provides us with an interesting insight into the psyche of the Welsh-speaking law student, the potential consumer of Welsh-medium legal

[102] See <www.porth.ac.uk>.

[103] See 'Worst British universities ranked by disgruntled students', *Daily Telegraph*, May 17, 2009.

education, and his or her response to the existing provision.[104] Among the reasons provided by students for the very low uptake in the Welsh-medium provision offered (even at Aberystwyth, an institution with a relatively honourable tradition of Welsh-medium scholarship), the most prominent were: the low esteem attached to Welsh-medium studies; a belief that having studied through the medium of Welsh would not be helpful in the job market later on; insufficient numbers of teachers to support the provision; and, above all, the lack of teaching materials and textbooks.

Whatever may be the deeper, sociolinguistic factors at play, there can be no doubt that some of these are rational, common sense reasons for not studying law through the medium of Welsh. The fact that students took the view that the market was not calling out for Welsh-speaking lawyers contradicts the message from government and leaders of the legal profession about the value of bilingual skills. Somehow, the students are being put off Welsh-medium legal studies.

Developing high quality learning materials in the form of legal literature in Welsh is therefore essential. But it is also a resource intensive activity. Appointing staff with the necessary linguistic skills and aptitude to teach through the medium of Welsh may be an onerous investment. Indeed, allocating Welsh-speaking staff to teach through the medium of Welsh when they could be teaching on the lucrative masters to overseas students, or supervising English-medium doctoral students or teaching core undergraduate modules to the English-speaking masses, may be seen as uneconomic and a wasteful deployment of valuable and scarce resources. Have no doubt, university managers must operate within a tough financial environment and there is little room for indulgence in non-profitable ventures.

3. *Research Policy*

Government policy on higher education in Wales can often seem whimsical, contradictory and lacking holistic coherence, where the left hand does not seem to know what the right hand is doing. Even if there are positive messages from the Welsh Government about the importance of promoting bilingualism and the development of Legal Wales,

---

[104] See G. Williams, 'Legal Education in Welsh – an Empirical Study', 39 (3) *The Law Teacher* (2005) pp. 259–276.

universities are also told to strive to achieve excellence on the global stage and to be significant players on an international level. One important means of measuring research excellence has been the periodic research assessment exercises, coordinated jointly by the HE funding councils of the UK, with which all research-active university institutions have to engage.

The UK government's research assessment exercise (now termed 'research excellence framework') is a periodic review undertaken every five years or so[105] on behalf of the four UK higher education funding councils in order to evaluate the quality of research undertaken by British higher education institutions.[106] Submissions from each subject from each institution (or "unit of assessment") are given a grade by a subject specialist peer review panel. The rankings are used to inform the allocation of quality weighted research funding each higher education institution receives from their national funding council. The precise grading mechanism or criteria have been slightly altered over the years, but its essential function is the same, as it seeks to provide a rating for departments on the basis of their collective research output and research culture. The principal factor which dictates the grading which each academic school receives is the research output of individual academics. Normally, academics submit four publications which are individually graded and which then contribute to the overall grading of their academic school or department.

The submissions and results of RAE 2001 and RAE 2008 can be accessed on dedicated websites which, according to every institution and particular unit of assessment, give details of each individual academic's return in that particular assessment.[107] A group of researchers at the University of Stirling analysed the 2001 data in order to establish significant patterns in law journal output, and so determine the relative popularity of law journals.[108] Their research demonstrated that certain law journals were favoured outlets for academics in the more successful departments. Based upon the facts emerging from the

---

[105] Previous RAEs took place in 1986, 1989, 1992, 1996, 2001 and 2008. The REF is scheduled for 2014.

[106] Each of the UK's 'nations' has its own funding council: HEFCE in England, SHEFC in Scotland, HEFCW in Wales and DELNI in Northern Ireland.

[107] <www.hero.ac.uk/rae>.

[108] See K. Campbell, A. Goodacre and G. Little, 'Ranking of United Kingdom Law Journals: An Analysis of the Research Assessment Exercise 2001, Submissions and Results', 33 (3) *Journal of Law and Society* (2006) pp. 335–363.

survey, they drew up a league table of legal journals, taking into account a combination of factors which might be relevant to the formulation of the table, including the correlation between the journals and the successful departments. Perhaps their research simply reinforced what was suspected already, namely that certain journals are more highly regarded than others, and that legal academics know that they should endeavour to publish in those journals if they are to have professional credibility.[109]

This RAE data has revealed one significant fact about Welsh-medium legal scholarship. None of the publications returned in either the 2001 or the 2008 RAE was written in the Welsh language. For the purposes of the RAE, even if legal academics in Wales published through the medium of Welsh in the relevant period, they, or their institutions, did not think it appropriate for that scholarship to form a part of their return for the RAE.

What is the significance of this for Welsh-medium legal scholarship? The importance of these research assessments and their overwhelming influence on the working culture of universities cannot be exaggerated.[110] They have become, "a major part of the culture of the academy",[111] and, as it was also said, "the RAE is the principal means by which institutions assure themselves of the quality of the research undertaken in the H. E. sector".[112] If the RAE, and its successor, has become the principal method by which university institutions assess the quality of the research produced by their academics, then the absence of Welsh-medium publications is highly significant.

What it tells us is this: the few legal academics who publish through the medium of Welsh do not regard this work as being appropriate for inclusion in the RAE. Perhaps they held a view that the RAE panel would not have been favourably disposed towards such work. Their professional culture, their colleagues and their academic community may have convinced them that research and publication through the medium of English, including in the prestigious English-medium law

---

[109] The undesirable and distorting effect of journal ranking was considered by D. Svantesson, 'International Ranking of Law Journals – Can it be done and at what cost?', 29 (4) *Legal Studies* (2009) pp. 678–91.

[110] Its influence on the culture of the contemporary law school is considered extensively in Cownie, *supra* n. 39; see also, generally, A. Bradney, *Conversations, Choices and Changes: The Liberal Law School in the Twenty-First Century* (Hart 2003).

[111] See Cownie and Cocks, *supra* n. 35, p. 247.

[112] See <www.rae.ac.uk/aboutus/history.asp>.

journals, was the surest way to impress the panel.[113] Then again, despite sporadic efforts to promote Welsh-medium research and publication, there are no referred quality journals for Welsh-medium legal writings, certainly none that would score highly in the eyes of the academic community as a whole. It follows that research and publication through the medium of English is the best route to career advancement. Accordingly, legal academics in Wales invest their energies in writing and publishing through the medium of English because that is where the highest returns are to be found.

Even for the unambitious, this is not simply about self-promotion and success versus patriotism or a duty to promote one's language. Generating research outputs that are RAE/REF returnable forms an important condition of most academics' contract of employment. Indeed, if academics do not demonstrate the potential to produce research outputs at the desired level, they are unlikely to be appointed to an academic post in the first place. Those in post who fail to deliver face the spectres of redundancy and dismissal. This research culture drives the academic market and determines how appointments are made and where promotions are awarded. It also determines who is retained when the need to economise on staffing is required.

Of course, this impacts on Welsh-medium scholarship in a host of ways. If academics do not generate research and publish through the medium of Welsh, the learning resource deficit which is such a major impediment to the development of the provision is not remedied and the library remains empty of Welsh legal literature. Because there are no books or journals, students are discouraged from studying through the medium of Welsh. No student demand means that there is no incentive to instigate new provision…and so it goes on.

The RAE, and its potentially adverse effect on Welsh-medium scholarship, appears irreconcilable with HEFCW's strategic aims of supporting the development of Welsh-medium provision. The Standing Committee for Legal Wales was set up in 2001 by the Counsel General of the National Assembly in order to represent the legal community in Wales and promote the Legal Wales agenda. It provided a robust response to the consultation on the publication of the RAE guidelines,[114] calling on the RAE administration to declare that "publications on law

---

[113] This was a view held by a former vice-chancellor of Aberystwyth, D. L. Morgan, 'Rhethreg a Realiti', *Barn*, Feb. 2002, pp. 17–19. See also Watkin, *supra* n. 83.

[114] <www.rae.ac.uk/pubs/2005/04/consult>.

in the Welsh language shall also be treated as capable of making a substantial scholarly contribution to knowledge and eligible for the highest ratings, and it shall not be counted against them either that they are expository in nature or that their originality derives in whole or in part from the fact that they are written in Welsh".[115]

In response, the funding council published a *Welsh Language Mainstreaming Strategy*, where it stated that research through the medium of Welsh would be treated with equal parity as that submitted through the medium of English.[116] As an official position, this met the argument that Welsh-medium scholarship would not be 'returnable'. However, rhetoric and reality rarely match, and with the task of evaluating the research firmly in the hands of a specialist subject panel consisting of academics from outside Wales, it is clear that Welsh law schools were not going to take any risks by submitting Welsh-medium publications.

Perhaps they had been given a contradictory message from another source. A law professor at Cardiff's experience of an exercise carried out at his institution in preparation for RAE 2008 should give rise to grave concern. Two external academics had been asked to review the research outputs of members of the school with a view to identifying areas for improvement. According to this particular participant's evidence, their report commented,

> ...on the merits of work which addressed the specific needs of lawyers in Wales in the wake of Devolution. Their conclusion was that Welsh law schools could not plead what they termed the 'Belfast Principle', that is to say there was no argument to be made in Wales along the lines of that made by academic lawyers in Northern Ireland to the effect that they had a special calling to service the needs of law students and lawyers within the context of Northern Ireland's separate jurisdiction. In effect, this view denies to Wales and its lawyers any claim to being seen to be a distinct legal entity in the wake of Devolution.[117]

A final point which reinforces the extent to which the research culture inhibits the development of bilingual scholarship is the fact that the UK research councils remain undevolved. As the UK's government's agencies responsible for coordinating and funding particular areas of

---

[115] *Law in Wales and the next RAE* (Standing Committee for Legal Wales 2005).

[116] See HEFCW, *Welsh Medium Mainstreaming Strategy* (HEFCW 2006) at para. 2.3.7

[117] Watkin, *supra* n. 83, p. 14.

research, including the arts, humanities, all areas of science and engineering, their funding priorities can influence considerably the orientation of research carried out at UK universities. There is a well-founded perception that they are not particularly disposed towards funding research that has an overwhelmingly Welsh focus. If so, this is another disincentive to those wishing to see a more robust academic engagement with Welsh legal issues and Welsh-medium legal scholarship.

4. *Demography*

Thus far we have reflected on some of the economic, political and academic preoccupations of the present which pose threats to scholarly engagement with Legal Wales and, in particular, Welsh-medium legal scholarship. But that engagement may also be threatened by the legacy of history.

Perhaps that it is history which explains why universities in Wales, including their law schools, have suffered from a mentality which has undervalued activity with a Welsh perspective. After all, historically, English law was the law of Wales, and Wales was firmly wedded to the English legal system. There was little resistance to a process of Anglicisation, and Welsh universities and their law schools became virtually indistinguishable from their English counterparts. But, in addition to this mindset, history has bequeathed a certain demographic legacy.

Compared with the universities of the other nations of the United Kingdom, Welsh universities have an unusual demography.[118] Wales exports its talented young people to a very high degree, and the proportion of students studying in their home country is far lower in Wales than in the rest of the UK. More specifically, when we examine the demography of the Welsh law schools, we find that the majority of law professors at Welsh universities have come from outside Wales and do not speak Welsh. In fact, a cursory review of each Welsh law school's website indicates that there are approximately 50 full law professors currently active at the Welsh law schools (discounting honorary professors or emeritus professors who are either retired or engaged

---

[118] Statistical data shows that Wales is a net importer of students because it imports more students from outside than it exports to external institutions. About 56 percent of undergraduate and 67 percent of postgraduate full-time UK enrolments at Welsh universities are Welsh domiciled: see *Statistics for Wales: Statistical Bulletin*, SB 13/2009, Feb. 26, 2009: http://wales.gov.uk/docs/statistics/2009/090226sb132009en.pdf

primarily in another occupation). Of these, only one or two are Welsh-speaking and able to teach through the medium of Welsh. These, obviously, are the people who are the leaders of legal scholarship in Wales and who determine its intellectual direction. Of course, it would be absurd to suggest that Welsh universities should adopt isolationist policies by appointing Welsh or Welsh-speaking academics only to teach in their law schools. Like all the great universities throughout the world, Welsh universities benefit greatly from imported talent, which can bring fresh and innovative ideas and perspectives to academic life. New blood can bring about renewal. It is more a question of balance. However, at the moment, there is arguably an imbalance which, in turn, poses a risk of disconnection.

Compare this demography with that of the judiciary in Wales. The senior judiciary is now dominated by home-grown talent with a keen understanding of the Welsh legal and linguistic context and who are ready to promote a legal culture which serves the distinctive interests of Wales. As the senior presiding judge of Wales was able to announce in a recent public lecture, no less than twelve circuit judges, ten district judges, fifteen deputy district judges and thirteen recorders are able to conduct hearings in Welsh.[119] In addition, there are some 350 Welsh-speaking magistrates serving in Welsh courts,[120] and several tribunal judges and chairpersons with competence in the Welsh language. This represents a silent revolution in the composition of the Welsh judiciary and a successful transition from the colonial past. This demographic profile is in stark contrast to that of the university law schools, and it would be naive to think that the demography has no bearing on the way in which Welsh law schools engage with both Legal Wales generally and the Welsh language in particular.

According to the Irish historian, Professor Joseph Lee, Ireland faced similar demographic challenges in the fifty years which followed independence. Most of the Irish universities, like Welsh universities, were created in the nineteenth century, a time when Ireland was firmly under English control as it had been for centuries.[121] On the matter of the balance between Irish and foreign academics at Irish universities,

[119] See Mr Justice David Lloyd Jones, "The Machinery of Justice in a Changing Wales", *Law Society Lecture*, National Eisteddfod of Wales, Blaenau Gwent, 2010, at p. 21.

[120] *Ibid.*, at p. 22.

[121] See A. Jackson, *Ireland 1798–1998* (Blackwell 1999) pp. 156–58.

Professor Lee commented that, "Irish thinking has been dominated by imports", but warned that, "importing intellectual produce is a highly skilled activity. Ireland's experience is paradoxical in the extreme. It has imported much, but it has learned little'.[122]

The Irish experience was that an excessive use of imported intellectuals had created a schism between universities and their society. There was a disconnection, the product of what was described as a "dependency syndrome", which caused a failure on the part of Irish universities to provide appropriate intellectual engagement with issues of national concern.[123] It is an experience that may serve as a warning for the Welsh law schools and, indeed, Welsh universities in general, as they reflect on their engagement with the Welsh legal and political context. But changing engrained social attitudes is not an overnight affair, and the historical legacy can be stubbornly enduring.

D. The European Charter for Regional or Minority Languages: An External Perspective?

The cause of bilingual legal education in Wales might have found a champion in the form of the European Charter for Regional or Minority Languages (ECRML), which was ratified by the United Kingdom on March 27, 2001.[124] The treaty is unique in that it is wholly concerned with linguistic minority rights, and requires states parties to take resolute action in the interests of minority languages within their territories.[125] Its fundamental rationale is that it regards;

---

[122] J. J. Lee, *Ireland 1912–1985, Politics and Society* (Cambridge University Press 1989) p. 627.

[123] Why were the Irish universities so keen on imported talent and why was there a failure to promote and nurture the natural genius of the Irish people? Perhaps this extract from Professor Lee's book gives us a brief insight to some of the fundamental causes: "The incapacity of the Irish mind to think through the implications of independence for national development derived largely from, and was itself a symbol of, the dependency syndrome that had wormed its way into the Irish psyche during the long centuries of foreign dominance. The Irish mind was enveloped in, and to some extent suffocated by, an English mental embrace. This was quite natural. A small occupied country, with an alien ruling class, culturally penetrated by the language and many of the thought processes of the coloniser was bound in large measure to imitate the example of the powerful and the prosperous", Lee, *supra* n. 122, p. 627.

[124] European Charter for Regional or Minority Languages (ECRML), Strasbourg Nov. 5, 1992, which can be found at http://conventions.coe.int/Treaty/EN/Treaties/Html/148.htm

[125] I have considered the ECRML's significance to the debate in some detail before: see G. Parry, "Higher education and Article 8.1.e of the European Charter for Regional

> ...the right to use a regional or minority language in private and public life is an inalienable right conforming to the principles embodied in the United Nations International Covenant on Civil and Political rights, and according to the spirit of the Council of Europe Convention for the Protection of Human Rights and Fundamental Freedoms.[126]

The languages that are to be protected by the Charter are those which are not 'official languages' of the state and which are spoken by a minority. Minority languages are defined within the Charter as being languages traditionally used by part of the population of a state but which are not languages of migrants, dialects or artificially created languages.[127] The focus is entirely on the historical or indigenous languages.[128]

In Part III, there are a series of provisions in the form of specific measures that states should implement in support of their regional or minority languages. Articles 8 to 14 provide detailed particulars of obligations for states in the fields of education, law, public administration, media, culture, and economic and social life. Party states enjoy quite an extensive freedom to tailor their subscription to suit their circumstances. Of the range of specific obligations set out in Part III, party states are required to apply a minimum of 35, roughly half of the entire range of obligations within the Charter, in accordance with the Charter's a la carte approach. States can therefore pick and chose those obligations that are most palatable for them, subject to a few qualifications and limitations.[129]

Our interest here is Article 8 of the ECRML. It deals with the subject of education and contains a series of potential obligations, from

---

or Minority Languages: a Welsh 'opportunity avoided'?", in R. Dunbar and G. Parry (eds.) *The European Charter for Regional or Minority Languages: Legal Challenges and Opportunities* (Council of Europe Publishing 2008) pp. 253–75.

[126] *Ibid.*, Preamble.

[127] ECRML, Art. 1: "the term regional or minority languages means languages that are, i. traditionally used within a given territory of a State by nationals of that State who form a group numerically smaller than rest of the State's population, and, ii. different from the official language(s) of that State; it does not include either dialects of the official language(s) of the State or the languages of migrants."

[128] For comment, see R. Dunbar, 'Implications of the European Charter for Regional or Minority Languages for British Linguistic Minorities', 25 *ELRev Human Rights Survey* (2000) p. 46 at p. 50; T. Cheesman, 'Old and New Lesser-Used Languages of Europe: Common Cause?', in C. C. O'Reilly (ed.), *Language, Ethnicity and the State, Volume 1* (Palgrave 2001) pp. 147–166; R. G. Parry, 'History, Human Rights and Multilingual Citizenship: Conceptualising the European Charter for Regional or Minority Languages', 61 (4) *Northern Ireland Legal Quarterly* (2010) pp. 329–348.

[129] ECRML, Part I, Article 2, para. 2: as a minimum subscription, states must choose at least three from each of Art. 8 and 12 and one each of Art. 9, 10, 11 and 13.

preschool education to adult education, in relation to the relevant minority or regional language. Paragraph 8.1.e specifically deals with higher education and provides three alternative undertakings, namely:

> i. to make available university and other higher education in regional or minority languages;
> or
> ii. to provide facilities for the study of these languages as university and higher education subjects;
> or
> iii. if, by reason of the role of the State in relation to higher education institutions, sub-paragraphs i and ii cannot be applied, to encourage and/or allow the provision of university or other forms of higher education in regional or minority languages or of facilities for the study of these languages as university or higher education subjects.

In the case of the Welsh language, the UK has adopted article 8.1.e.iii rather than article 8.1.e.i. According to a leading commentator, paragraph e.iii is appropriate where the state does not determine the language policy of its universities, where universities enjoy a considerable degree of autonomy, or in the case of private universities.[130] In such cases, encouragement is all that can be expected. However, paragraph e.iii should not be used to avoid having to adopt and comply with the more demanding provisions of paragraph e.i, which, of course, expects the state to *make available* higher education in the minority language.

Accordingly, it is doubtful whether the UK's current undertaking is appropriate and adequate in the case of the Welsh language. The state plays a key role in higher education planning in the UK. Through the funding councils, the state is a major contributor towards the financing of higher education institutions. In Wales, the Welsh Government has responsibility for higher education policy and planning, and so establishes educational priorities and strategic direction.

During the course of the ECRML's second monitoring cycle in the UK, the Welsh Language Board (the public body with statutory responsibility for monitoring the Welsh Language Act 1993) responded to the consultation on the UK's second periodical report by arguing that the UK should review its commitment by substituting paragraph e.i for its

---

[130] See J.-M. Woehrling, *The European Charter for Regional of Minority Languages: A Critical Commentary* (Council of Europe Publishing 2005) pp. 154–155.

current undertaking.[131] In its second periodical report, the UK's explanation of its compliance with Article 8.1.e.iii had amounted to no more than, "Welsh-medium provision for Higher Education is allowed in higher education. It accounts for 1.5 percent of the total provision. In 1999–2000 3 percent of students undertook at least part of their degree through the medium of Welsh".[132]

This was clearly inadequate, especially as the ECRML's Committee of Experts, in their report following the first monitoring cycle in 2004, considered that the undertaking had only been partly fulfilled and that more information would be expected in the subsequent monitoring exercise.[133] A further report was provided by the UK on the 23 August 2005, which mentioned the Welsh Government's target of ensuring that 7 percent of students will be studying through the medium of Welsh by 2010, and ancillary investment in scholarships and fellowships to increase the numbers of those teaching through the medium of Welsh.

However, despite the Welsh Language Board's submission about the adoption of paragraph e.i, the Committee of Experts' report was disappointing.[134] Noting that there had been a slight increase in Welsh-medium provision so that 3.2 percent of students study at least part of their studies through the medium of Welsh, and that the government had promised to invest 2.9 million pounds, over seven years, in developing Welsh-medium teaching (which, incidentally, represented about 1 percent of the total higher education budget in Wales), it concluded, "The Committee of Experts notes the positive initiatives taken and looks forward to the implementation of the envisaged measures. Based on information received and the nature of the obligation, it considers the undertaking fulfilled".[135]

There was no response to the argument that there is a defect in the UK's current undertaking and no comment on the Welsh Language

---

[131] See *The European Charter for Regional of Minority Languages, The Second Review of the Implementation of the Charter in Wales: A Draft Document for Public Consultation* (Welsh Language Board 2005) pp. 19 and 77.

[132] See *Second Periodical Report Presented to the Secretary General of the Council of Europe in accordance with Article 15 of the Charter* – United Kingdom (Council of Europe 2005) p. 76.

[133] See *Application of the Charter in the United Kingdom: Report of the Committee of Experts on the Charter* (Council of Europe 2004) para. 118–121.

[134] See *Application of the Charter in the United Kingdom, Second Monitoring Cycle: Report of the Committee of Experts on the Charter* (Council of Europe 2007) para. 205–210.

[135] *Ibid.*, at para. 210.

Board's recommendation to substitute it for the more rigorous and, arguably, technically more appropriate alternative. Of course, the Committee of Experts cannot engage in a "quasi-judicial complaints procedure" and it is not a "judicial appeal body".[136] It is limited in its ability to provide authoritative guidance on the interpretation of the ECRML. The international treaty jurisprudence within which it functions inhibits the sort of definitive ruling that would have been beneficial to the cause of bilingual higher education in this particular case.[137]

As it transpired, the third monitoring cycle proved to be a spectacular non-event as far as this particular matter is concerned. In its third periodical report, the UK reported on the funding of various initiatives to develop the Welsh-medium provision, and in particular the work of the Centre for Welsh Medium Higher Education, but made no mention of substituting its present undertaking.[138] In return, the Committee of Experts took the view that this was not a problematic area which required comment, and announced that it did not deem it necessary to assess the implementation of this particular provision.[139]

These experiences of the monitoring process with regard to the specific matter of Welsh-medium higher education are, of course, symptomatic of the ECRML's generic weakness. Although it employs the language of rights, it cannot grant or uphold rights and it does not have the status of law. Its monitoring exercise and consequent reports, although contain an element of judgment-making in as much as the Committee of Experts is required to determine whether undertakings are fulfilled, partly fulfilled, or not fulfilled, do not contain legally binding rulings.

The general conclusion must therefore be that the ERCML, regrettably, has proved to be an uninspiring, marginal and unhelpful contributor to the debate on the future of Welsh-medium university scholarship. Although it strengthens somewhat the normative case

---

[136] See ECRML, Explanatory Report, para. 129.

[137] See R. Dunbar, "Definitely Interpreting the European Charter for Regional or Minority Languages: the Legal Challenges", in R. Dunbar and G. Parry (eds.), *The European Charter for Regional or Minority Languages: Legal Challenges and Opportunities* (Council of Europe Publishing 2008) pp. 37–62.

[138] *Third Periodical Report Presented to the Secretary General of the Council of Europe in accordance with Article 15 of the Charter* – United Kingdom (Council of Europe 2009) pp. 172–73.

[139] See *Application of the Charter in the United Kingdom, Third Monitoring Cycle: Report of the Committee of Experts on the Charter* (Council of Europe 2010) para. 139.

for Welsh-medium university scholarship and provides a degree of externality to it, it cannot convert that normative position into resolute practical measures. The prescription to the deficient state of bilingual higher education in Wales would, therefore, need to come from within.

E. *Y Coleg Cymraeg: A* Prescription?

If in Titian's painting the third age was the age of mortality, it is hoped that the prognosis for bilingual legal scholarship in Wales is a little more optimistic. It is here that we turn to the Welsh Government's latest initiative to develop Welsh-medium university scholarship, *Y Coleg Cymraeg Cenedlaethol* (The National Welsh College).

The creation of a dedicated Welsh-medium federal college to promote Welsh-medium studies had been demanded by Welsh-language activists on a sporadic basis for many years.[140] Left to their own devices, the universities had failed to promote Welsh-medium scholarship sufficiently, and, therefore, major structural reform the only way forward. The idea seemed to be doomed until the outcome of the May 2007 elections for the National Assembly for Wales. The ensuing coalition between Labour and Plaid Cymru brought about a renewed political appetite for the idea of the Welsh-medium federal college.[141] The coalition government's manifesto, *One Wales, a Progressive Agenda for the Government of Wales*, made a clear commitment to the setting up of a Welsh-medium higher education network, that is, a federal Welsh-medium college.[142]

In July 2008, the Welsh Government's Minister for Children, Education, Lifelong Learning and Skills announced the establishment of a Planning Board to consider the Coleg Ffederal commitment in *One Wales*. A former vice-chancellor of Swansea University, Professor Robin Williams, was invited to chair a board consisting of a broad representation of university institutions, Welsh language activists and

---

[140] See, in particular, D. G. Jones, *Problem Prifysgol a Phapurau Eraill* (Gwasg Carreg Gwalch 2003).

[141] See *Western Mail*, June 29, 2007.

[142] See *One Wales: A Progressive Agenda for the Government of Wales, An Agreement between the Labour and Plaid Cymru Groups in the National Assembly*, June 27, 2007, at p. 22.

other potential stakeholders. The planning board met, deliberated and submitted its report to the Minister in June 2009.[143]

The 26 page report supported the concept of a federal institution, *Y Coleg Ffederal*, and evaluated the potential models that it might adopt. It recommended the creation of a new legal entity, which would not be a single geographical entity and a degree awarding body in its own right, but would work with and through the existing higher education institutions in Wales (thus, the federal concept). It would have branches located at the universities, and its function would be to "maintain, develop and oversee Welsh medium provision in higher education in Wales".[144]

The Welsh universities would be corporate members of the Coleg Ffederal with representation on the governing body. Staff and students who participate in Welsh medium teaching and learning would be members of the Coleg. The governing body of the Coleg Ffederal would consist of representatives of the universities, students' unions, teaching staff, officers of the Coleg Ffederal, HEFCW, schools, school parent associations, employers and others.[145]

The Report hailed the creation of *Y Coleg Ffederal* as a means of providing "unity of purpose, coherence and leadership" for Welsh-medium scholarship, of ensuring "motivation and drive" and "supporting and reinforcing national identity and promoting the national life of Wales".[146] It also set out the level of government funding that is necessary to ensure that *Y Coleg Ffederal* has the capacity to deliver change and finance the future development of Welsh-medium scholarship within the university sector.

The political response was encouraging. In a major strategic document for the university sector, the Welsh Government confirmed its commitment to implement the Williams Report's recommendation for *Y Coleg Ffederal*, and said:

> The Coleg Ffederal will provide an independent oversight, management and development of Welsh medium higher education across Wales delivering the recommendations of Professor Williams' report. This will help deliver social justice for those who seek to learn through the medium of

---

[143] See Professor Robert Williams CBE, FRS, *Y Coleg Ffederal: Report to the Minister for Children, Education, Lifelong Learning and Skills* (Welsh Assembly Government 2009).

[144] *Ibid.*, pp. 6–7.

[145] *Ibid.*

[146] *Ibid.*, pp. 7–8.

> Welsh, but also carries potential economic benefit through wider access to workforce development, and business opportunities which exploit the potential offered by a bilingual environment.[147]

The venture was subsequently renamed as *Y Coleg Cymraeg Cenedlaethol*, a setting-up process was initiated and the new institution was launched in 2011.

Of course, the devil is in the detail, and there remain challenges which may yet prove problematic. The Report, quite rightly, emphasises the importance of 'buy-in, drive and ownership' by the universities.[148] At the moment, *Y Coleg* is more of a politically driven initiative than an intellectual one. There were very few academics within the universities who were calling for its establishment. There is a risk that the 'buy-in' is less than wholehearted and that *Y Coleg* becomes a ghetto on the margins of institutional life unless its place at the heart of the governance and academic life of each institution is guaranteed.

There is also a risk that *Y Coleg* becomes nothing other than an administrative, co-ordinating body, and that it offers another layer of bureaucracy to burden Welsh-speaking staff. The Report provides some detail on the governance of *Y Coleg* and its administration, but says little on how its objective to increase the Welsh-medium provision is related to the core business of universities. It would be a serious error to believe that the problem with Welsh-medium provision is a lack of co-ordination or poor management, and that what is needed are a few more committees and a few more bureaucrats to manage the delivery. For all the reasons outlined in this paper, it should be clear that Welsh-medium scholarship faces serious challenges posed by the intellectual culture and general outlook of universities in Wales. In simple terms, the problem is with the substance not the form. Unfortunately, in the public life of Wales, too much emphasis is often placed on process; as one Welsh economist has pithily remarked, "... the problem is the focus on developing long-winded strategy documents without any underlying action plan –an obsession with process rather than outcomes".[149]

---

[147] See *For Our Future: The 21st Century Higher Education Strategy and Plan for Wales, Department for Children, Education, Lifelong Learning and Skills, Welsh Assembly Government* (Crown Copyright 2009) p. 14.

[148] *Y Coleg Ffederal: Report to the Minister for Children, Education, Lifelong Learning and Skills*, p. 8.

[149] See Professor Brian Morgan's article in the *Western Mail*, Apr. 28, 2010.

Y Coleg and its contribution to develop teaching capacity is said to occur through the funding of "lecturing and teaching assistant posts".[150] How does the creation of such posts facilitate the mainstreaming of Welsh-medium scholarship? Will it also fund senior appointments, including chairs? What career paths for young academics will it seek to develop? How will it ensure continuity in the Welsh-medium provision if and when its funding of staff appointments comes to an end at the end of the five year period of funding which it recommends? It mentions absorption of funded posts into the normal staff complement, but there are no guarantees that this will happen in the unstable higher education economy.

The Report fails to reassure that Welsh-medium teaching does not become the province of the peripheral, the unambitious and the exploitable, in particular the early-career academic. There may well be 'buy-in' of sorts by institutions at management level, but not individual academics at the coal-face, nor, crucially, by heads of schools or departments who continue to enjoy considerable autonomy in setting out their units' strategic direction. One can but wonder at the responses of the heads of the law schools to the report's recommendations that *Y Coleg* would fund teaching posts at universities on condition that "the contracts will be for Welsh medium provision only".[151] It is hard to imagine that all of the law school managers will readily agree to the appointment of Welsh-medium only teaching staff who after five years would need to be fully integrated within their law schools.

For it to be more than a side-show on the margins of academic life, it must engage with university scholarship in its entirety. Its remit must be holistic, for otherwise it will fail to have the real, long-term and transformational impact which it aspires to achieve. It must be capable of developing an intellectual agenda of its own that embraces fully the academic vocation in all its aspects. It must, for example, define Welsh-medium scholarship's relationship with research quality, the world of work and the broader, international context. It must have a vision that is capable of refuting the inevitable accusation of it being insular, parochial and inward-looking.[152] Government policy provides us with the rhetoric, when it declares;

---

[150] *Y Coleg Ffederal: Report to the Minister for Children, Education, Lifelong Learning and Skills*, p. 9.

[151] *Ibid.*, p. 9.

[152] See Watkin, *supra* n. 83, p. 4.

> As well as driving economic transformation, we expect higher education to champion Welsh cultural awareness and identity in an environment of global awareness; upholding opportunities to learn through and explore the Welsh language, while promoting appreciation of cultures and traditions from across the world.[153]

Of course, in all of this, sufficient funding is going to be critical. The main stakeholder in the new initiative should be the Welsh people, and, in the legal context, representatives of the legal profession in Wales. In the case of legal education, the views of the legal profession and the judiciary can determine the nature and content of the degree syllabus. They have an influential role to play in determining the priorities of legal education. A law degree that is not recognised and validated by the relevant professional bodies is worthless. As we have seen, many of the Welsh law schools also offer professional courses for those intending to practise law. In what will become increasingly a user-led or consumer-driven higher education economy, the voice of the legal profession will be crucial. Increasingly, the emphasis is on universities meeting the economic and social priorities of Wales and ever-increasing pressure on the public finances will result in greater scrutiny and the search for best value for investment. Active engagement with the Welsh consumer of legal skills may therefore be vital for legal scholars working within the *Coleg* if they are to have the expected impact on Welsh society.

Yet, although partnership with stakeholders and responsiveness to government education policy must be at the centre of the strategic aims of the *Coleg*, if it is to have intellectual credibility, it must maintain academic rigour and secure academic independence. In a democratic society, intellectuals and academics must have the freedom to say things that the government of the day or any other affected party may not like to hear. History teaches us that to deny this freedom is the beginning of totalitarianism.[154] Academic freedom, according to one observer, concerns,

> the right of the teacher to present his views without interference or fear of persecution from inside or outside the university...freedom within

[153] *For Our Future*, p. 7.

[154] In 1933, when Adolf Hitler was elected Chancellor of Germany, he set upon those intellectuals whose views he did not share. He persecuted them or, if they were lucky, drove them out. Many came to Britain, among them jurists and lawyers, and their contributions to intellectual life were to prove remarkable. Their experiences and life-stories are chronicled in Beatson and Zimmermann, *supra* n. 51.

> the university also involves the right of the scholar to control his research and publish his results, as well as freedom for scholarly bodies or the institution as such to publish opinions and criticism, even of the state, and even if the state is the sponsor.[155]

The maintenance of academic standards is also going to be absolutely critical. Doing things in Welsh must not be seen as an excuse to avoid qualitative issues which would otherwise apply were English to be the medium of expression.[156] The *Coleg* must not be seen as a language campaigner whose function is "to serve and assist the language community".[157] It must not loose sight of its intellectual mission and of its membership of a world-wide scholarly community.

Simon Blackburn recently observed that, "universities should be about the attempt to see things that matter and see them as they are".[158] This captures the importance of freedom in the pursuit of truth, of honesty and integrity in that pursuit, and of scepticism of momentary fads and distaste of the shallow nomenclature of that which is temporary or politically expedient. If it is the legal academic's duty to seek out and examine the "things that matter", then surely the nature of democracy and social justice in Wales is among these things. But he must carry out his examination by applying the highest academic standards and in the spirit of intellectual freedom, free to criticise and expose that which he or she feels is deficient without political interference or political pandering. In a small country like Wales, observing and maintaining these boundaries can be a challenge because politicians, lawyers and academics live in a 'cheek by jowl' society. Vigilance must therefore be a watchword. The *Coleg* must be more than a government

---

[155] See S. Egerod, 'Freedom and Equality in the Universities', in P. Seabury (ed.), *Universities in the Western World* (The Free Press 1975) p. 12.

[156] As a Scottish Gaelic scholar observed with reference to Gaelic and Irish scholarship: "There must be an unapologetic insistence on academic rigour and excellence, and vigorous resistance to any culture or special pleading. That is to say, there should be no room at all for excuses for things being second-best because they are done through Gaelic or Irish, or treating Gaelic- or Irish-medium academic projects as sacred cows of some kind that cannot be judged by general standards of quality. Delivering courses through Gaelic or Irish cannot be seen as an end in itself, a project effectively immune to criticism with regard to its conceptualisation, management, or academic quality" – see W. Mcleod, 'Lessons from Gaelic-medium Higher Education in Scotland', in C. Nic Phaidin and D. ui Bhraonain (eds.), *University Education in Irish: Challenges and Perspectives* (Dublin City University 2004) p. 43 at p. 49.

[157] *Ibid.*, p. 49.

[158] See *Times Higher Education*, Feb. 4–10, 2010, p. 36.

department or a language pressure group if it is to win the hearts of Welsh scholars.

F. Conclusion

Devolution made it possible for the people of Wales to devise internal solutions to issues of national concern. The *Coleg Cymraeg Cenedlaethol* is the creation of the Welsh Government, and it is presented as the vehicle through which bilingual scholarship, including legal scholarship, is to flourish. It derives considerable legitimacy in that it is the product of Welsh democracy in action. Universities would be well advised not to disregard this powerful expression of democratic will.

The case of bilingual legal scholarship is given further impetus by the fact that it can be an important contributor to meeting the challenge of developing a bilingual legal system in Wales. Whether or not it is right to start employing the term 'jurisdiction' to describe the future administration of justice in Wales remains a matter of debate and controversy. Even so, bilingualism means that the legal system in Wales must operate in a different way to that of England.[159]

For the *Coleg Cymraeg* to fulfil its potential, it must have a holistic vision of what university scholarship in the Welsh language means for the national future of Wales, and, in the context of law, what legal scholarship in the Welsh language means for Welsh democracy and justice. It must convert that vision into a strategy which will lift the intellectual depression, inspire Welsh-medium scholarship and give confidence to a new generation that they are engaged in a noble and honourable vocation which will make a valuable contribution to the task of nation-building in twenty-first century Wales.

The greatest risk facing *Y Coleg*, of course, is that it fails to deliver on its promise to generate the step-change in the fortunes of Welsh-medium university scholarship. If it is to provide leadership and direction for Welsh scholarship, it must be more that a cosmetic innovation, a bit of window dressing through committee. Partnership was a

---

[159] For further reflections on this issue, see Sir R. Evans, 'Devolution and the Administration of Justice', *The Lord Callaghan Memorial Lecture 2010*, Swansea University, Feb. 19, 2010; T. H. Jones and J. Williams, 'Wales as a Jurisdiction', 78 *Public Law* (2004); Sir R. Evans and I. Davies, 'The Implications for the Court and Tribunal System of an Increase in Powers' (Richard Commission 2003); W. Roddick, *The Development of Devolution and Legal Wales* (Aberystwyth University, Nov. 28, 2008).

keyword in the Williams Report.[160] Because it will inevitably rely heavily on government funding, at least for the foreseeable future, partnership with government will be critical. Failure to give *Y Coleg* the financial support that it needs will lead to failure. In return for investment, it must demonstrate its commitment to being an integral and dynamic force for social progress in Welsh society. But it must also promote scholarship that can be measured against the highest international standards.

Perhaps, above all, it must command the support and respect of the Welsh people, including parents, teachers, students, academics and employers, whom, ultimately, will be its primary stakeholders. The Welsh Government's policy agenda will form the basis of *Y Coleg* and its strategic direction. In particular, its directors should note that part of government policy which declares:

> The two pillars of social justice and supporting a buoyant economy form the basis of our refreshed national policy on higher education. There are many stakeholders whose needs, demands and potential drive this strategy. It is vital that in taking the next steps we take account of their needs, priorities and perspectives, but move forwards with pace and decisiveness.[161]

Pace and decisiveness must be the motto of *Y Coleg* in the coming years. Indeed, the very future of bilingual scholarship (including legal scholarship) in Wales depends on it.

---

[160] *Y Coleg Ffederal: Report to the Minister for Children, Education, Lifelong Learning and Skills*, p. 8

[161] *For Our Future*, p. 2.

CHAPTER TEN

LEGAL EDUCATION IN HUNGARIAN LANGUAGE IN TRANSYLVANIA: BETWEEN A GLORIOUS PAST AND AN UNCERTAIN FUTURE

Gyula Fábián

A. Minorities in Romania: Statistics

By constitutional law Romania is a unitary national state, but also the homeland of over twenty ethnic groups. The census of 2002 shows a population of 21.680,974 divided into the following ethnic groups according to native language:

Nationality	Number of people	Percentage
1. Romanian	19 399,597	89.4
2. Hungarian	1 431,807	6.6
3. Romany	535,140	2.4
4. German	59,764	0.2
5. Ukrainian	61,098	0.28
6. Russian – Lipovan	35,791	0.17
7. Turk	32,098	0.14
8. Serbian	22,561	0.10
9. Tartar	23,935	0.11
10. Slovakian	17,226	under 0.1
11. Bulgarian	8,025	under 0.05
12. Hebrew	5,785	under 0.05
13. Czech	3,941	under 0.05
14. Croatian	6,807	under 0.05
15. Polish	3,559	under 0.05

(*Continued*)

Nationality	Number of people	Percentage
16. Greek	6,472	under 0.05
17. Karaschoven	206	under 0.05
18. Csango	1,266	under 0.05
19. Armenian	1,780	under 0.05
20. Slovenian	202	under 0.05
21. Chinese	2,243	under 0.05
22. Italian	3,288	under 0.05
23. Albanian	477	under 0.05
24. Slavic – Macedonian	695	under 0.05
25. Ruthenian	257	under 0.05
27. Other	15,013	under 0.1
28. Of undefined nationality	1,941	under 0.05

Statistical data is very important for minorities. It is the grounds on which they can ask for certain rights to be granted, and it also reflects the decrease or growth of an ethnic group. This data is usually based on the results of the census, but it needs to be viewed with scepticism, for a state with an ethnic majority usually attempts to influence the declaration of nationality and thus distort data on the ethnic situation as much as possible.[1]

Nearly every ethnic group regards native language as one of the most important elements of its culture and identity. In many cases language is the most important unique feature distinguishing a minority from a majority. Linguistic identity stands also for cultural identity, since every language reflects the inner world of the group that speaks it and is a bearer of the history and cultural development of that group. Extinction of a language may mean also loss of the culture and identity of an ethnic group.[2]

[1] Gy. Fábián and P. Ötvös, *Kisebbségi jog [Minority Law]* (Cluj-Napoca: Korunk Kom-Press Kiadó 2003) p. 208.

[2] H. Hannum, *Autonomy, Sovereignty and Self-Determination: The Accommodation of Conflicting Rights* (University of Pennsilvania 1990) p. 459.

In society, language, taken in the larger sense, has not only a cohesive, but also a symbolic function. Assigning a minority language the status of an official language of the state also means that this particular ethnic minority is accepted by the state as a community, which plays an important role in that state. Equality of languages also reflects a good relationship between the various ethnic groups or even the equal status of these groups.

B. Historical Background of Legal Education at the University Of Cluj/Kolozsvár/Klausenburg, Romania

The work of the representatives of every profession and science is essentially determined by the education they receive. Quality of education is closely related to the institutions of education whose way of functioning cannot be understood unless one familiarises himself with their history and development.

Hungarian-language legal education in Transylvania (Romania) is caught at present between concepts of the glorious past and the uncertain future. Transylvania has been a part of the European higher education system since the establishment of the first Transylvanian *universitas*. In the period between the 12th and the 16th centuries nearly three thousand Transylvanian young people studied at various European universities.

The Diet of Cluj (formerly Hungary, present-day Romania) adopted in 1565 the decision to establish an institution of higher education. Under the rule of István Báthory the College was opened in 1581 in Cluj, and the next year it was granted the rank of academy by Pope Gregory XIII. The language of education was Latin and staff members included Jesuit professors and priests. This was the first university to provide legal education (apart from courses in theology and philosophy). As Protestantism gradually spread, the establishment of a Reformed College in Alba Iulia/Gyulafehérvár was necessary in 1622. Many renowned teachers and scientists from Europe taught in this newly established institution. In 1658, during the invasion of the Tartars the College and its library were destroyed.

After the dissolution of the Jesuit Order under Pope Clement XIV in 1766, the College in Cluj was taken over by the Piarists. They officially used the name "University". The institution had four faculties: Theology, Law, Arts and Medicine. In 1703 the institution had 50 students, while by 1770 their number reached 493. In 1784 Hungarian was introduced as the language of education in primary and secondary school. In the same year the number of universities in the Habsburg Empire fell back to three. The University of Cluj was first reduced to a "secondary school having the rank of an academy", then to a "secondary school". At these academies, philology and law could be studied for two years each; the study of philology was considered a preparatory course for legal studies.

After the *Compromise* between Austria and Hungary in 1867, and the re-enactment of the union between Hungary and Transylvania, it became obvious that in addition to the University of Budapest, Hungary needed a second university.

In 1872 the Monarch signed Act No. 19 ordering the establishment and operation of the University of Cluj. At the beginning the University had four faculties: History and Arts, Law and Political Science, Mathematics and Natural Sciences, and Medical Sciences. The language of education was Hungarian. The Faculty of Law had first 12, than 16 departments.[3] The University initially had 258 registered students. The official name of this University of Cluj was changed to "Franz Joseph University" in 1881.

In 1918, the National Assembly in Alba Iulia proclaimed the union of Transylvania with Romania. Negotiations to establish a Romanian-medium university started. Under military supervision the new government closed the Franz Joseph University. On September 1, 1919 a Romanian-language university called King Ferdinand I University was established. In 1921 the Franz Joseph University, extruded from Cluj, was taken in by the city of Szeged in Hungary and it continued to function there.

As a result of the Second Arbitration of Vienna, in 1940 Transylvania was re-annexed to Hungary and the Hungarian-language Franz Joseph University moved back to Cluj and started to function again. King Ferdinand I University moved to Sibiu/Szeben/Hermannstadt in Romania.

In 1944 Romania changed sides, decided to fight against Germany and sided with the Soviet Union. The Communist power forged ahead. The Soviet power decided to maintain the existing institutions.

[3] Zs. Nagy, "A magyar jogi oktatás történeti áttekintése a második világháborúig" [Historical Review of Hungarian Legal Education until the Second World War], 2 *Jogelméleti Szemle* (2003) p. 53.

In 1945 Romanian administration was re-introduced in North Transylvania.

Regulation No. 407 regarding this issue[4] provided for the establishment of a Hungarian-language university at Cluj effective on June 1. The bill established the Faculty of Law and Economical Sciences among other three faculties. The provisions of this Regulation were completed by a Decision of December 11, 1945, stating that this institution of higher education should bear the name Bolyai University. This new state university, which continued the old traditions, assumed the name of János Bolyai, a great mathematician born at Cluj. Thus, Franz Joseph University has a 73 year long history, of which 52 years are associated with the city of Cluj, 19 years with Szeged and 2 years with Budapest[5].

In Paris on February 10, 1947 the victorious powers signed the peace treaty with Romania whose text had been already prepared between July 29 and October 15, 1946.[6] One of the conditions imposed by the great powers in order to accept the peace treaty was the establishment of a Hungarian-language university. Romania established the Bolyai University for this sole reason. Afterwards the Romanian government was just waiting for convenient circumstances to have the chance to dissolve this institution and during the next few years, the one-party Socialist regime made use of the situations that arose to carry out this plan.

At the beginning of the 1955/1956 academic year, a rumour started to circulate in the Ministry of Education according to which the Bolyai University was "over productive" because a number of its graduates could not find employment. After the suppression of the Hungarian Revolution in 1956, many of the teachers and students were brought to justice and sentenced to 10 to 20 years of imprisonment or forced labour without reason.

The government plan was openly revealed at the national conference of the Romanian student association held in Bucharest at February 18–22, 1959. Among other things, Gheorghe-Gheorghiu Dej, the General Secretary of the Communist Party urged the audience to

---

[4] Published in the Official Journal of Romania no. 119 on May 28, 1945.

[5] Gy. Gaal *The Franz Joseph University of Cluj*, at 'www.bolyai.eu/fj_tortenet_en.php?m=8'.

[6] S. Balázs, "A Bolyai egyetem…lett, hogy ne legyen" [The Bolyai University … Born to Non-Existence], 3–4 *Magyar Kisebbség* (1997) pp. 3–11.

eliminate any efforts to isolate nationalities and ethnic groups, citing Lenin who said that students of different nationalities should go to the same school in order to be educated in the spirit of Socialist internationality. He also set one of the goals of the conference as the review of how Lenin's idea could be carried out in Romania.

Students of Cluj expressed their solidarity in 1956 with the principles of the Hungarian Revolution. In the period between February 26 and March 5, 1959 upon an order, given at the Communist government meetings promoting the idea, the unification of the two Universities was initiated leading to the full merger of these Universities in only a couple of months. The merging process was led by Nicolae Ceausescu and Ion Iliescu[7], the president of the Association of Young Communists at the time. Under the psychological pressure caused by this forced unification both the Vice-Rector and one of the professors of the Bolyai University committed suicide. As Babeş-Bolyai University emerged from this unification, Hungarian-language groups gradually ceased to exist.

Since Bolyai University was the main institution of higher education that supported the Hungarian intelligentsia, with this action, the Communist regime, obviously well-established by then, intended to crush and eliminate the Hungarian intelligentsia by dissolving this institution of higher education. The attack on the intelligentsia intended to create the proper conditions for an unstoppable assimilation of the Hungarian community.[8]

Minister's Order no. 168 of July 19, 1959 ordered Victor Babeş University and Bolyai János University of Cluj to merge (*se contopesc*) on July 1, 1959. The name of the new institution would be Babeş-Bolyai University. The order indicated the departments and sections within the departments that would have a place in the new institution, one of these being the department of law, and referred to the fact that the sections that were functioning in the 1958/1959 academic year, but had not been mentioned in the order, would be gradually dissolved as the groups of students presently studying there graduated.

The basic principle was that the unification of these two universities served to build Socialism because it eliminated isolationism and

---

[7] The same Ion Iliescu who was president of Romania in the periods 1990–1996 and 2000–2004.

[8] K. Vekov, "Újabb adatok a kolozsvári egyetemegyesítésről" [New Data on The Merger of the Universities in Cluj], 5 *Korunk* (2009).

nationalism and set the foundation for the true completion of the culture of a Socialist people.

During the entire history of Transylvania, only during the period 1945–1959 has this region had two state universities, a Romanian and a Hungarian one, and it was the first time that the principle of *cuius regio eius lingua et eius universitatis* was not taken into consideration. This fact simultaneously reflects historic tradition, demographic reality and political thought.[9]

After the merger, there was no Hungarian-language legal education at the university and by the eighties even Romanian-Hungarian legal terminology was eliminated from the curriculum. Thirty years were time enough for the Hungarian-speaking teachers of the faculty of law to reach retirement age and retire, while no new Hungarian-speaking teachers were employed. The leaders of the Ceausescu regime aimed for an incomplete minority society with no intelligentsia, which would be easier to assimilate. The primary and most dangerous pillar of the intelligentsia, the legal profession, was nearly eliminated by 1989. The communists did not manage to eliminate this ethnic group, but they succeeded in preventing Hungarian-language legal education from taking place and thus legally and practically stopping new teachers from joining the Hungarian-speaking educational staff of this department.

C. The Basic Legal Framework of Universities and Legal Education

As expressed in the Constitution, Romania is a sovereign, independent, unitary and indivisible National State.[10] As viewed by the majority of the members of the Romanian political class this phrasing does not allow even for the establishment of ethnic-based forms of autonomy. Moreover, in the 20 years since the abolition of the Communist regime, no parliamentary majority has agreed to enact a master law regarding the rights of ethnic and national minorities.

The little importance minorities bear in the country is also demonstrated by other provisions of the Constitution that emphasise that

[9] S. Tonk, *A magyar nyelvű felsőfokú oktatás Romániában [Hungarian-Language Higher Education in Romania]* (1998) pp. 1–47.

[10] Art. 1 of the Constitution of Romania (republished) published in the Official Gazette no. 767 of Oct. 31, 2003.

"(T)he State foundation is laid on the unity of the Romanian people".[11] However this provision is followed by another that includes an interdiction from general discrimination and which guarantees that "Romania is the common and indivisible homeland of all its citizens, without any discrimination on account of race, nationality, ethnic origin, language, religion, sex, opinion, political adherence, property or social origin."[12]

The main provision of the Constitution that ethnic minorities may cling to is Article 6, which provides that "(T)he State recognises and guarantees the right of persons belonging to national minorities, to the preservation, development and expression of their ethnic, cultural, linguistic and religious identity." But even though the text of the Constitution mentions development of ethnic identity, conditions for such a development are fundamentally limited by the "fatidic" Article 13, which declares that: "In Romania, the official language is Romanian." Therefore in Romania there are not two or more official languages, a fact that theoretically undermines any attempt to teach and study the law in any other language than the official language and seriously questions the utility of such a legal education.

The Constitution stipulates that education of all grades shall be in Romanian, but that education may also be conducted in a foreign language of international use, under the terms laid down by law. At the same time it guarantees the right of ethnic minorities to learn in their native language and the right to have suitable conditions conducive to education in their native language while methods of exercising these rights are left to provisions of special laws.[13] State education is free from taxes, and autonomy of the universities is guaranteed.[14]

Even if at first sight there seems to be no major impediments for studying any subject in the language of an ethnic minority from the point of view of education organisation, perspectives change when the aim of legal studies in the language of a minority is analysed knowing that the language of legal proceedings is Romanian.

As stipulated in the Constitution, legal proceedings are performed in Romanian. Romanian citizens belonging to the group of ethnic minorities have the right to speak in their native language before the

---

[11] Art. 4 (1) of the Constitution of Romania: Unity of the people and equality among citizens.

[12] Art. 4 (2) of the Constitution of Romania.

[13] Art. 32 (2) and (3) of the Constitution of Romania: Right to education.

[14] Art. 32 (4) and (6) of the Constitution of Romania: Right to education.

court, observing the provisions of the organic law, one of the options being to employ interpreters and translators in this process. Methods of using one's native language, other than Romanian, have to be provided in such a way as not to interfere with the legal activity and not to imply additional costs for the parties concerned.[15]

The prospects for the improvement of this situation are not very hopeful considering that Article 152 of the Constitution stipulates that the provisions of the Constitution with regard to the national, independent, unitary and indivisible character of the Romanian State, the Republican form of government, territorial integrity, independence of the judiciary, political pluralism and *official language* shall not be subject to revision.

D. The Power to Establish Universities: State and Private Initiative

The law of national education of Romania[16] states that in Romania education is a national priority (Art. 2); it pursues the ideal education established on humanistic grounds, values of democracy and the aspirations of Romanian society, and it contributes to maintaining the national identity (Art. 3). Education provides for fostering love of the homeland, of the history and traditions of the Romanian people (Art. 4).

Romanian citizens have equal rights to all levels and forms of education, regardless of their social and material condition, sex, race, nationality, political or religious affiliation.[17]

It is mandatory to teach Romanian as the official language of the state for all Romanian citizens regardless of their nationality and to provide proper conditions for learning the official language of the state. Both in state and private education, all documents of the school or university drawn up under the Minister of Education and Research's order will be drawn up in Romanian. All the other documents of the school or university can be drawn up in the language of education.[18]

---

[15] Art. 128 (1) to (4): The right to have an interpreter.

[16] Law no. 84 of 1995, republished in the Official Gazette of Romania, Part I, no. 606 of Dec. 10, 1999, updated based on the modifying laws published in the Official Gazette of Romania, Part I until Dec. 22, 2009.

[17] Art. 5 of Law no. 84 of 1995.

[18] Art. 8 (3) and (4) of Law no. 84 of 1995.

Management of education and pedagogical content cannot be drawn up on criteria that exclude or discriminate ideologically, politically, religiously or ethnically.

Duration of studies in higher education for day courses is established by Governmental Decree depending on specialisation at 4–6 years. Studies in long-term higher education are followed by a final or diploma examination. General criteria of organisation of the final or diploma examination are determined by the Ministry of Education and Research, while the content and specific criteria of the examination by the senate of each university. Graduates who have passed the final examination are awarded the title of licensee in the specialisation and specialty they studied.[19]

In order to establish higher education institutions in the field of legal education, it is necessary to provide teachers with scientific titles, such as a PhD degree. All graduates of a long-term specialty of an institution of higher education who have earned a degree can apply for a PhD course. PhD tutors can be tenured or associated university professors or consultants or academics who have earned a PhD degree. The right to be a PhD tutor is approved for each person individually by the *National Council for University Title, Degree and Certificate Attesting* (CNATCDU) if the person is proposed by the organising institution, and it is awarded by minister's order of the minister of education and research. PhD courses are organised as day and extramural courses in the institutions of higher education approved by the Ministry of Education and Research and proposed by the CNATCDU.[20]

An unfavourable and costly alternative to this for minorities is the private university. Accredited private institutions and units of education are part of the national education system and are subject to the relevant legal provisions. Private institutions and units of education have organisational and functional autonomy as provided by legal provisions regarding organisation and functioning of the educational system. Accredited private institutions and units of education can receive state subsidies.[21]

---

[19] Art. 67 (1) to (3) of Law no. 84/1995.
[20] Art. 73 (2) to (4) of Law no. 84 of 1995.
[21] Art. 103 (2) to (4) of Law no. 84 of 1995.

Private education is lawful if:

(1) it is organised and functions as a non-profit entity;
(2) it is organised based on non-discrimination principles and rejects antidemocratic, xenophobic, chauvinist and racist ideas, trends and attitudes;
(3) it is in accordance with national standards.[22]

Private universities are free, open, academically, economically and financially independent institutions of higher education, being based on private propriety guaranteed by the Constitution.[23] In order to be approved and given permission to function, institutions of higher education have to pass all the phases of authorisation and accreditation as provided by European and national legislation on higher education. Private universities are established by law, which means that all efforts of a minority to establish a university depend on the vote of the majority in Parliament. This aspect is not negligible in the case of Romania since so far no private minority university has been accredited by law.

As a matter of fact, the law of national education, like the Constitution, is generous on a general level, but not in the matter of regulating concrete problems with regard to the study of the law.

According to Article 118 of the above mentioned law, "National minorities have the right to study and be tutored in their native language *at all levels and forms of education, and also at the forms of education* for which there is a sufficient demand as provided by the law."

Article 123 provides that, within state institutions of higher education, there can be organised, as provided by the law and if requested, groups, sections, colleges and *faculties having the language of national minorities as their language of education.* In this case, study of the specialised terminology in Romanian must be provided. If requested and under the conditions established by law, multicultural institutions of higher education can be created. The language of education in these

---

[22] Art. 104 of Law no. 84 of 1995.

[23] As provided by Art. 116 (3) of Law no. 84 of 1995: if a private university established under the law is abolished, dissolved or wound up, its founders are entitled to its patrimony.

institutions of higher education is established by law. The right of national minorities to create and manage their own private institutions of higher education, according to legal provisions, is also acknowledged.

The law expressly provides that institutions of higher education with multicultural structures and activities be encouraged in order to promote harmonious interethnic cohabitation and national and European integration.[24]

All forms of education with the language of education in Romanian or in the language of national minorities are open to any Romanian citizen regardless of his or her native language and the language of education during his or her former studies. In all degrees and levels of education, admission examinations and final examinations will be performed in the language of education of the respective subjects, according to legal provisions.

One of the most important elements of minority language education is teacher training. Even the UNESCO report *The Use of Vernacular Languages in Education*[25] mentions the lack in sufficiently qualified teachers as one of the most frequent impediments. Romanian law stipulates that the Ministry of Education and Research provide tuition and continuous education of teachers in the language of education and also textbooks and other teaching materials for institutions and units of education where there are groups, classes or sections using the language of national minorities as the language of education and that a proportionate representation of minority teachers be present in the management of these institutions, considering also professional competence. In fact, applications for teacher's jobs in the graduate and post-graduate departments of higher education are approved by faculty councils following the proposals of application councils and are then validated by the senate of the university. Titles of tenured and associate professors are confirmed by the CNATCDU through its specialised commissions. Based on this confirmation the Minister of Education and Research issues an order for the titles of associated professor and tenured professor to be awarded. Applicants for a teacher's job in a place where the language of education is different from the language they completed their higher education studies take a test in

[24] Art. 123 (3) of Law no. 84 of 1995.

[25] UNESCO, *The Use of Vernacular Languages in Education, Monographs on Fundamental Education* (Paris 1953) pp. 50–54.

front of a specialised committee to prove that they speak the language that is going to be the language of education.[26] Thus the success of attempts the member of a minority makes in order to obtain the title of tenured professor depends on decisions by the faculties, universities and ministries managed by members of the majority. Moreover, in Romania there are no PhD graduate schools: some of the professors are awarded by the Ministry of Education and Research the right to tutor PhD students who are admitted into graduate schools based on an admission examination organised by these professors.

Another, equally important problem is infrastructure and financing. As it is shown in the historical data that has been presented, when carrying out the dissolution of the Hungarian university in 1959 the Romanian state also ordered its infrastructure to be directed to the succeeding university. After 1990 the Hungarian minority requested not only that the Hungarian university be re-established but also that its former buildings be returned.

However, Article 166 of the Law on national education stipulates that material items needed in the instructional and educational process originating from state funds or funds of state institutions or companies before December 22, 1989 will be included in the patrimony of the Ministry of Education and Research, of the institutions and units of education and of scientific university research and occasionally of the public domain of the communes, towns and municipalities, of the districts of the municipality of Bucharest, without granting any payment for them. Material items of state institutions of higher education and scientific university research rightfully belong to them.

Institutions of higher education are allotted a specific fund for scientific university research from the global budget for scientific research. Allotment of funds to finance scientific university research occurs according to competitive criteria, depending on national priorities and obtained or projected results. Competition for funds for financing scientific university research is open for all accredited institutions of higher education and for research and development units and institutions that are authorised to perform research and development activities. Funds for financing scientific university research are allotted by the Ministry of Education and Research following the proposal of the National Council for Higher Education Scientific Research.

[26] Art. 154 (4) and (5) of Law no. 84 of 1995.

As provided by Article 171, state institutions of higher education function as institutions financed by funds allotted from the state budget and by other funds, according to legal provisions. The main financing is provided from the state budget, on the basis of the number of students and PhD students admitted under a tax-free regime, on the number of participants in each course, on the level and specialisations of theoretical and practical education and other indicators specific to the educational activity, especially quality indicators.

E. The Possibility to Use Minority Languages in Court and in Administration

As it has been shown before, the Constitution theoretically allows the use of minority languages in the judicial system in accordance with the legislation. The matter is ruled by the law on judicial organisation, which has been modified several times. The present regulation on judicial organisation[27] provides that the language of judicial procedure is Romanian. Romanian citizens belonging to a minority ethnic group have the right to speak in their native language in court and if one or more of the parties must speak in their native language the court has to provide, free of charge, an authorised interpreter or translator.

In the case that all parties require or agree to speak in their native language, the court has to ensure exercising of this right and the proper administration of justice also minding that principles of an adversarial system, orality and publicity be respected. Petitions and documents of the proceedings are to be written exclusively in Romanian. Debates of the parties carried out in their native language will be recorded and then registered in Romanian. Objections of the interested parties regarding the translation and records on these objections will be solved by the court until the debates on the case file come to an end and then these will be recorded in the conclusions of the trial.[28]

A more recent means of detailing was introduced by Law no. 282 of October 24, 2007 regarding the ratification of the European Charter for Regional or Minority Languages adopted at Strasbourg at

[27] Law no. 304 of 2004, republished in the Official Gazette, Part I, no. 827 of Sept. 13, 2005.

[28] Art. 14 (1) to (6) of Law no. 304 of 2004.

November 5, 1992.[29] The provisions of the Charter are to be applied for the following minority languages used in Romania: Albanian, Armenian, Bulgarian, Czech, Croatian, German, Greek, Italian, Yiddish, Macedonian, Hungarian, Polish, Romany, Russian, Ruthenian, Serbian, Slovakian, Tartar, Turkish, Ukrainian. Still Hungarian and German are considered more important, since these are used most in education and in the judicial system. Only German[30] and Hungarian[31] are provided as languages of education in higher education, the same languages that can be used to a greater extent in the judicial system as well. According to the law of ratification, provisions of the Charter will be applied according to provisions of the Constitution of Romania and of Article 14 of Law no. 304 of 2004 regarding organisation of the judicial system.

Concretely, by ratification of the Charter, Romania began to provide lessons in the regional languages or the languages of the minorities, i.e. German and Hungarian in universities and other forms of higher education, respectively to provide basic and continuing education to the teachers needed to provide education in these languages.

As far as the judicial system is concerned, Romania began to allow minority languages to be used in legal proceedings within the judicial district where the number of people using regional or minority languages justify such measures, depending on the situation of each of these languages and on the condition that exercising this right is not

---

[29] Published in the Official Gazette no. 752 of Nov. 6, 2007.

[30] As stipulated in provisions of Art. 5 of the ratification law Romania agreed to the following provisions of the Charta in regard to usage of German:

(1) Article 8 – Education:
 (a) paragraph 1 subparagraphs a) (i), b) (i), c) (i), d) (i), e) (i), f) (iii), g), h), i);
(2) Article 9 – Judicial system:
 (a) paragraph 1 subparagraphs a) (ii), a) (iii), b) (ii), b) (iii), c) (ii), c) (iii), d);
 (b) paragraph 2 subparagraph a);
 (c) paragraph 3.

[31] As stipulated in provisions of Art. 5 of the ratification law Romania agreed to the following provisions of the Charta in regard to usage of Hungarian:

(1) Article 8 – Education:
 (a) paragraph 1 subparagraphs a) (i), b) (i), c) (i), d) (i), e) (i), f) (i), g), h), i);
 (b) paragraph 2.
(2) Article 9 – Judicial system:
 (a) paragraph 1 subparagraphs a) (ii), a) (iii), b) (ii), b) (iii), c) (ii), c) (iii), d);
 (b) paragraph 2 subparagraph a);
 (c) paragraph 3.

considered by the judge as being an impediment for the proper administration of justice. Such cumulative conditioning gives the greatest possibilities to Hungarian and German, but even in the case of these languages use is limited to the following situations:

(1) During penal proceedings:
  (a) guarantees the defendant the right to speak in his or her own regional or minority language; and/or
  (b) provides that written or verbal petitions and evidence should not be considered inadmissible only on grounds of being formulated in a regional or minority language.
(2) During civil proceedings:
  (a) allows for the party in litigation who is required to present himself or herself personally in front of a tribunal to speak in his or her regional or minority language, without having to bear further expense; and/or
  (b) allows management of documents or evidence in regional or minority languages, if necessary by contracting the services of an interpreter or translator.
(3) During proceedings of the legal department for administration proceedings:
  (a) allows for the party in litigation who is required to present himself or herself personally in front of a tribunal to speak in his or her regional or minority language, without having to bear further expense; and/or
  (b) allows handing in of documents or evidence in regional or minority languages, if necessary by contracting the services of an interpreter or translator.

Furthermore, by accepting the above mentioned provisions of the Charter, Romania began to provide interpreting and translation free of charge for the parties in civil and commercial legal cases, if necessary. Until the ratification of the Charter, only translation in penal cases was provided free of charge.

Romania also began to not contest the validity of legal documents drawn up in the country if the only reason for contestation would be that they have been drawn up in a regional or minority language and to provide the most important part of the national legislation and the legal provisions in which the users of these languages are especially interested in the regional or minority languages, if these legal provisions are not already accessible otherwise. It is to be mentioned that since 1990 in Romania a group of translators whose task is to translate the most important pieces of legislation into Hungarian has been working within the institution handling the publication of the Official Gazette (*Monitorul Oficial*).

One of the main deficiencies of this situation is that Romania has not accepted that tribunals have legal proceedings and procedures in the regional or minority languages if so requested by either of the parties in any of the procedures.

On the other hand, by provisions of the Law of local public administration[32] in administrative-territorial units where citizens belonging to the group of a certain ethnic minority constitute a percentage over 20 percent of the local population, they are granted the right to address the local public administration, the specialised apparatus and subordinated organism of the local council verbally or in writing in their native language and to receive an answer to their address both in Romanian and in their native language. In places where working with the public is also required persons who speak the language of the minority concerned will be employed. Local authorities are required to provide inscriptions with the name of the settlements and public institutions under their authority and a translation of public announcements in the language spoken by the minority. However it is mandatory that official documents be drawn up in Romanian.

Considering the fact that the law provides that the secretary of the local public administration to be a graduate of a faculty of law[33] or public administration and comparing this provision to the provisions regarding minority language usage there are both *de facto* and *de iure* sufficient grounds for legal specialists in the native language of the minorities to be formed in the fields of e.g. constitutional law, administration law, family law, labour and social services law and civil proceedings law.

General provisions of the law of local public administration regarding minority language usage have been detailed by a governmental decree[34] that refers also to the Framework Convention for the

[32] Art. 19 and 76 of Law no. 215 of 2001 regarding local public administration, republished in the Official Gazette of Romania, Part I, no. 123 of Feb. 20, 2007.

[33] Art. 116 of Law no. 215 of 2001.

[34] Governmental Decree no. 1206 of Nov. 27, 2001 on approval of applications of provisions regarding the right of citizens belonging to the group of an ethnic minority to use their native language in relations with the local public administration stipulated by the Law of local public administration no. 215 of 2001, published in the Official Gazette no. 781 of Dec. 7, 2001.

Protection of National Minorities.[35] That decree provides the following possibilities for members of ethnic minorities:

(1) The right to be notified on the agenda of the meetings of the local or county councils and on the decisions of these councils in their native language.
(2) The right to address the authorities of the local government and the apparatus of the local or county councils verbally or in writing also in their native language and to receive an answer both in Romanian and in their native language.
(3) The right to use their native language in the meetings of the local or county councils where councillors belonging to the group of an ethnic minority have a ratio of at least one third of the entire number of councillors. In these cases mayors and presidents of the county councils have an obligation to provide full-length simultaneous translation of the meetings from Romanian.
(4) The right to have public announcements posted also in the native language of the respective minority according to legal provisions.
(5) The right to have the draft decisions of the local or county councils and all the other documents to be discussed and approved by the council, which are mandatorily drawn up in Romanian in each case, translated into the language of the minorities that have this right by law.
(6) The right to be publicly notified in their native language on the normative decisions of the local or county council.
(7) The right to use the language of the respective minority at official ceremonies organised by authorities of the local public administration, along with Romanian.
(8) The right to celebrate their marriage in the native language of the parties if requested and if the registrar speaks that language.

Last but not least, legal professionals of the Hungarian minority can also use their knowledge of Hungarian legal terms before the three judicial organs of the EU: the European Court of Justice, the General Tribunal and the Civil Service Tribunal. The issue whether ethnic minorities of an EU member state who speak the official language of another EU member state can or cannot present their case in that

[35] Ratified by Romania by Law no. 33 of Apr. 29, 1995 on ratification of the Framework Convention for the Protection of National Minorities concluded in Strasbourg on Feb. 1, 1995, published in the Official Gazette no. 82 of May 4, 1995.

language is debated in EU law. The question may be answered positively in the light of the European Court of Justice's case-law.[36]

F. Attempts to Establish a Hungarian-Language Faculty of Law in the Last Twenty Years

After the events of 1989 (so called Revolution) one of the main demands of Hungarians of Transylvania was the establishment of an independent Hungarian-language state university. This has not been realised up to the present day. Mother-tongue education is one of the most important means of preserving identity; a Hungarian-language university is a key institution of high symbolic meaning in this respect.

After 1989 the Hungarian community had to face the fact that students have a great interest in studying law, but it was doubtful whether the Hungarian community has the capacity to provide the other pillar of Hungarian-language legal education, i.e., the teaching staff. It should not be disregarded that without Hungarian-language higher education there is no viable, high standard Hungarian-language secondary education either, since the latter will be chosen by a great number of students only if it is of further use.

After the fall of the Ceausescu regime, the first initiative for legal education came from the Protestant churches. The Romanian government issued operating license no. 4805 of 1991 for an extension of the Protestant Theological Institute of Cluj-Napoca in Oradea and thus the university extension known non-officially also as the Sulyok István Reformed College was established. In the 1991/92 academic year, there were three day course promotions of 25 students each enrolled in the following double degrees: religion teaching and social work, religion teaching and German language and literature, and religion teaching and legal studies. These disciplines were selected according to the needs of the Hungarian community in Romania (determined by the increasingly severe lack of professionals, an inheritance of the Communist regime) and to the diminishing human resources in place. In Romanian higher education the number of Hungarian-speaking lecturers had decreased to a critical level in most disciplines and the average age of active Hungarian-speaking academic scholars was

[36] ECJ, Judgment of Nov. 24, 1998, case C-274/1996, *Bickel and Franz*.

above 55. One of the disciplines suffering from this situation was legal education. There were two possible solutions: the recruitment of invited teachers from Hungary in the case of the disciplines suffering a severe lack of professionals and the promotion of post-graduate education among young graduates in order to assist them in earning scientific degrees.

In the 1993/94 academic year, Sulyok College applied for accreditation of the college for the above mentioned three day course double degrees. The National Accreditation Council made several on the spot examinations and refused to issue an interim operating license for any of the degrees, on the basis that "the institution has degrees that do not fit into its profile".[37] After discussions with the Minister of Education the direction of the faculty was given the following option: the College should give up Hungarian-medium legal education and it would be accredited for the other degrees. The direction of the College and the Church District decided to give up the double degree of religion teaching and legal studies. Students studying these disciplines were given financial assistance to enrol for the same studies in Romanian-language private universities in the form of a stipend to cover the first year tuition fee.

This College integrated in 2002 in Sapientia Hungarian-language private university which will be discussed later.

Hope for the re-establishment of Bolyai University faded away in time, especially after the new law of education approved by the neo-communist parliamentary majority in 1995 failed to provide possibilities for creation of independent Hungarian-language higher education.

In 1997, for the first time Romania was led by an anti-Communist majority. In March 1997 Prime Minister Victor Ciorbea promised a Hungarian branch of Babeş-Bolyai University and a study group to be established at the University of Cluj-Napoca, which would include also Hungarian-language legal education".[38] Within three days after this promise, Minister Virgil Petrescu declared that such a plan needed the approval of the University of Cluj-Napoca for the "autonomy of the

[37] I. Szűcs, *Magyar nyelvű felsőoktatás Nagyváradon: A Partiumi Keresztény Egyetem [Hungarian-language higher education at Oradea: The Christian University of Partium]*, pp. 1–26, available at http://cherd.unideb.hu/terd/cd/pke.rtf.

[38] *Szabadság* (daily paper of Cluj), 10/03/1997.

institution needs to be observed".[39] By this declaration the minister of education questioned even the right of the government "to take the first step" by protecting the autonomy of the university. It took only one day for the Minister of Education to write a letter of appreciation and support to the University regarding the "linguistic multiculturalism" of the institution functioning in an exemplary manner on the verge of this turn of the century, students of Romanian, Hungarian and German origin studying alongside one another; the letter was also sent to the press.[40] And within another two days an official statement of the Rector's Office of Babeş-Bolyai University made public that "the board of directors of the Babeş-Bolyai University approved a decision regarding multicultural development structures of the university approved unanimously by the Senate of the University".[41]

The enrolment plan for the Hungarian branch in the academic year of 1997–1998 foresaw the enrolment of 30 Hungarian-speaking students in the law department. This number meant an act of positive discrimination, not a *numerus clausus*, subject to an admittance examination. Unfortunately this "ethnolinguistic ratio" was not applied also to the teaching staff and without such an action it was nearly impossible to form a new, Hungarian-speaking teaching staff.

These places have been provided by the University to Hungarian students every academic year, but neither a Hungarian-language faculty of law nor a Hungarian-language branch of the existing faculty of law was formed at Babeş-Bolyai University. At present Hungarian-speaking students can study 3 subjects in the law degree and 8 subjects in the master's degree in Hungarian.[42] These 11 subjects are but the remnant of the whole Hungarian-medium legal education that the same university used to have until the 1960s.

In the case of Babeş-Bolyai University, bilingualism and multiculturalism prevailed instead of the model of Turku (Finland) or Louvain (Belgium) where the Swedish and the Finnish and the Flemish and the French university, respectively, split into two different institutions, and in the faculty of law of Babeş-Bolyai University, proper bilingualism is not applied either. Furthermore interchanging of the linguistic and

[39] *Szabadság*, 15/03/1997.
[40] J. Faragó, "A Bolyai-ügy 1997 tavaszán ..." [The Status of the Bolyai University in the spring of 1997...], 3–4 *Magyar Kisebbség* (1997) pp. 28–35.
[41] *Szabadság*, 07/04/1997.
[42] Details on these subjects in the next section.

ethnic criteria is quite inconvenient. Minorities regard the language of education as relevant, since application of the ethnic principle is manipulated. The Ministry of Education decided on the enrolment plan on ethnic and not linguistic basis. Thus the "minority" or "Hungarian" part of the enrolment plan mostly addresses the ethnic group, for Hungarian-language education is only partially provided at graduate level.[43]

After such precedents Hungarians of Romania saw the establishment of a private university as the only chance to reintroduce extensive Hungarian-medium higher education. One of the main arguments for creating a private university is free initiative, which means that political, legal and professional disputes regarding the division of the University of Cluj can be eliminated as well as the wrangling caused by the division. Another advantage of a private university is that it is organised by neutral, entrepreneurial logic instead of a dividing defensive political thinking.

Establishing a private university meant the following. Since the university was not supported by a private person, a public foundation needed to be incorporated to finance the university, as required by legislation. The statutes of the university needed to be drawn up. The program and the internal regulation of the university needed to be organised.

The most important argument against a private university is the economic aspect, while the second most important its unofficial status. This is not only the dilemma of the private university, but of the entire minority problem. Civil autonomy means also leaving the state institution status, i.e. renunciation to a certain kind of "institutionalisation".[44]

On October 3, 2001 the Sapientia – Hungarian University of Transylvania (EMTE) started functioning with assistance from the government of Hungary. The university was established by a foundation comprised of the eight representatives of the historical churches of Transylvania, having registered offices in Cluj-Napoca, Targu Mureş and Miercurea Ciuc. The first students graduated in June 2005.

---

[43] J. Péntek, "Közelkép a kolozsvári egyetemről ..." [A Close-up on the University of Cluj-Napoca ...], 9 *Educatio* (2000) p. 338.

[44] T. Kozma, "Magánegyetem" [Private University], 3–4 *Magyar Kisebbség* (1997) p. 57–59.

In Romania, private universities need to first obtain an "interim operating license" which guarantees the institution the right to organise admittance examinations, to set up various faculties, to teach and to conduct research. The accreditation process has two phases:

1. The ability to be able to teach depends on obtaining an interim operation license, while final accreditation can be requested only after three promotions have graduated. This means that if the period of study is 4 years, the duration of accreditation is 7 years minimum. In the meantime graduates can earn diplomas at other universities based on their studies.
2. For the university to be accredited at least 3 faculties of the university need to be accredited.

In 2009 the direction of this private university decided to set up a bilingual (Romanian-Hungarian) faculty of law. After providing the necessary finances and having promises from competent teaching staff from Hungary and Romania, the university petitioned for an interim operating license in February 2009 at the Romanian *Agency for Quality Assurance in Higher Education* (ARACIS).

The authority decided to reject[45] the petition for an interim operating license for the university program for licensees in Law on the grounds that the department did not meet the mandatory normative requirements, the performance standards and indicators and the specific standards. A challenge to this decision was also rejected[46] mainly on the following grounds:

(a) The syllabus was not properly drawn up
(b) There are some overburdened teaching positions in the staffing schedule, which demonstrate that the course or seminar teachers lack deep knowledge in particular specialties
(c) Lack of practical course agreements
(d) The concrete time table of the teaching activities have not been presented
(e) Book funds in the library of the faculty to be set up is insufficient
(f) Salary expenses represented 72 percent of the total income for 2007.

[45] Decision of ARACIS no. 6745 of July 9, 2009.
[46] Decision of ARACIS no. 8619 of Sept. 28, 2009.

The Hungarian minority and the private university did not give up, they handed in another petition in May 2010 and the ARACIS approved an interim operating license for the faculty of law at the university. Teaching is bilingual: Romanian-Hungarian. The mastery of the Romanian legal terminology is indispensable for a successful completion of legal studies; and the mastery of the Hungarian legal terminology enables law graduates to practice law using two EU official languages, apart from the positive impact on the implementation of the right to use minority languages provided by Romanian law. The high proficiency level of the teaching is guaranteed by Romanian and foreign qualified lecturers, and the 40-membered classes make possible a good interaction between lecturers and students.

G. Some Facts on Minority-Language Legal Education

The status of legal studies is at present somewhere between a theoretically extensive provision of higher education for minorities and a practice that makes it impossible to use a minority language for those who would graduate from a faculty of law having a minority language as their language of education. In the case of the Hungarian minority, one of the major impediments in restarting legal education was the lack of teaching staff professionally competent by university standards. Thus in the period of 1990–2005 in Romania there were about 25 legal professionals who regularly published specialised literature, only 10 of these had a PhD degree and only 5 taught at a university.[47]

At the beginning of 2010 in Romania, there were 16 state and 25 private universities with a faculty of law for a population of 21.680.974.[48] Out of all of these universities, there is only one that at present provides the opportunity to study subjects taught at a faculty of law in one of the 24 minority languages, i.e., Hungarian. This is

---

[47] Zs. Kokoly and Gy. Fábián, "Összefoglalás a romániai magyar jogászok kutatásairól 1990–2005" [A Summary of the Research of Hungarian Legal Professionals of Romania 1990–2005], 2 *Romániai Magyar Jogtudományi Közlöny* (2006) pp. 75–96.

[48] Governmental Decree No. 749 of June 24, 2009 on approving the Classification of fields, structures of institutions of higher education and specialisations/study programmes studied for a diploma or licence at universities that are accredited or have an interim operation licence. Published in Official Gazette no. 465 of July 6, 2009.

Babeş-Bolyai University of Cluj-Napoca, the de facto successor of the Hungarian university of 1872.

Students are motivated to choose to study law by the social prestige of the legal professions, the desire to know the law and the opportunity to obtain a higher income than in other fields. After graduating from a faculty of law, the graduate must have the ability to assimilate and understand legal documents, to obtain pieces of information from various sources, to synthesise and identify legal problems raised by the situation and to subordinate the situation to a legal provision. Also a well prepared legal professional must have the ability to find a solution to a new legal problem, to make a reasonable and motivated choice from among several possible solutions to the problem, to critically examine legal provisions and to make proposals for their alteration, if necessary.

For legal studies the Bologna system structure applied in Romania is "4+1+3", 4 years of graduate studies, 1 year for a Master's degree and 3 years for a PhD degree.

The subjects taught in Hungarian within the law degree at Babeş-Bolyai University of Cluj-Napoca are:

1st year: Romanian-Hungarian legal terminology and Institutional law of the UE, with optional courses in Philosophy, Sociology and Economy.

2nd year: Public international law

Since 2005 this faculty provides studies for Master's degree in Hungarian in the subject of "European private law" with 9 budget-financed and 25 tuition fee places in the enrolment plan. The subjects during these studies are: EU procedural law, European labour law, Environmental law and policy of the EU, the legal status of private persons in the EU, European private law, European intellectual propriety law, international family law, and European civil proceedings law. In addition, three subjects are taught in English: Computer science and communication law, Restructuring Enterprises under the Law of the European Community, and The Internal Market in the Current Practice of the European Court of Justice.

Also within Babeş-Bolyai University, the Faculty of Geography and of Economic Sciences teach subjects such as the general theory of the law, administration law, business law and environment law in Hungarian.

Sapientia Private University provides Hungarian-medium education in the following legal subjects:

(1) Faculty of European Studies: Public and private law, The law of the EU, Public international law, Administration law, Constitutional law, Public administration and the status of civil servants, Romanian and European business law.
(2) Faculty of Environment Sciences: Environment law
(3) Faculty of Media: Audiovisual law
(4) Faculty of Economic and Human Sciences: Civil law, EU law, Commercial law, International commercial law, Tax law, Competition law.
(5) Faculty of law (to be set up):
    1st year: Civil (Roman) law, Public international law, Universal and Romanian history of law, Applied computer science: Draft techniques.
    2nd year: EU Institutional law, with optional courses in Philosophy, Sociology and Economy.
    3rd year: International human rights protection, Criminology.
    4th year: EU law, Criminalistics
    In addition, following subjects will be taught in English: Romanian and EU consumer law, European competition law, Free movement of persons and the right to migration.

H. Conclusion

Viewed from the perspective of the effective legal provisions, it seems that in Romania a member of a minority group does not have "any reason" to study law fully in a different language than the only official language, and if that member would still insist on doing so, he or she must study at his or her own expense in private institutions created at the expense of the minority group he or she belongs to. These institutions are forced to operate under the severe supervision of the state, as a condition for obtaining an operating license, a process by which the state obstructs the creation and functioning of such institutions as heavily as it can. On the other hand, in the judicial system and public administration the use of minority languages is limited to oral usage, since the state stipulates that all proceedings and administration documents need to be drawn up in the official language. Therefore the current examples mentioned above can hardly provide members of minorities an opportunity to learn Hungarian legal terminology; instead of providing conditions for Hungarian to be revitalised to the level of an official language or at least at the regional level, they can only postpone the completion of the assimilation process.[49]

[49] In Feb. 2011 a new Law of Education in Romania (published in Official Gazette no. 18 of Jan. 10, 2011) came into force: it does not bring substantial modifications to what concerns bilingual education in legal studies. Among the few general positive changes the guarantee of the right to the "development" of ethnical identity can be mentioned, while in the preceding Law this right referred only to the preservation and expression of the identity. Another modification consists of granting financing based on an increased multiplier for students who attend courses held in a minority language. According to the new law, the length of academic service doesn't represent a condition for promotion in a didactic degree anymore unless other scientific and performance conditions are fulfilled, hence the facility of more rapid promotion for young university staff members who hold their lectures in a minority language.

CHAPTER ELEVEN

CREATING, STUDYING AND EXPERIMENTING WITH BILINGUAL LAW IN SOUTH TYROL: LOST IN INTERPRETATION?

Elisabeth Alber, Francesco Palermo*

A. Introduction

The Autonomous Province of Bolzano/Bozen in northern Italy is generally considered to be one of the most successful examples of the accommodation of minorities through territorial self-government. According to the census in 2001, South Tyrol's population of about half a million people consists of 69.15 percent German speakers, 26.47 percent Italian speakers, and 4.37 percent Ladin speakers.

In the province (hereinafter "South Tyrol") the German language has the same standing as Italian, the official language of the state, and can be used in the whole public sphere. The effective use of a minority language in administration and courts, however, depends not only on the status of the language, but also on more specific problems that might constitute practical obstacles to its full use. While German is the most spoken European language, a legal language is very specific to the country it refers to. In practice, it is difficult to find the appropriate legal terms in German to describe concepts of the Italian legal system, because they differ from Austrian and German law. For this reason, the use of standardised legal terminology and the quality of bilingual post-secondary education are of the utmost importance. With regard to legal terminology, in 1988, a special committee was set up to agree on and standardise the official legal terminology in German related to the Italian legal system. In the field of tertiary legal education, the neighbouring Austrian University of Innsbruck, located just 120 kilometres from the capital city of South Tyrol, Bolzano/Bozen, has played and

* In the course of the common elaboration of the present article, parts B and C were written by Francesco Palermo, parts D and E by Elisabeth Alber, and parts A and F by both.

still plays a fundamental role in training legal experts for public administration and, in general, bilingual lawyers.

This chapter begins by providing an overview of the history of South Tyrol, the settlement of the conflict, and the minority regime (B.), the essential features of South Tyrol's institutionalised linguistic regime (C.1.) and the use of languages (C.2.). The analysis shortly outlines the specific rules regulating the individual right to use (minority) languages in the "core areas" of relations with administrative and judicial authorities, in political bodies, and in other sectors of public and private life. Furthermore, the collective dimension of the linguistic rights will be briefly addressed, illustrating the South Tyrolean model on issues such as the topography, media, and economic life.

The second part of the chapter analyses the legal framework and practice of the Joint Terminology Commission, stressing the importance of such an instrument and pointing out difficulties in standardising legal terminology (D.). Further, the analysis focuses on higher legal education for South Tyroleans (E.) by examining both the development and current status of the "integrated curriculum in Italian Law" at the University of Innsbruck (Austria) and, where relevant, the law school of the neighbouring University of Trento (Italy). The latter is located in the almost 100 percent Italian-speaking Autonomous Province of Trento, which, together with the Autonomous Province of Bolzano/Bozen forms the Autonomous Region of Trentino-Alto Adige/Südtirol. Currently, tertiary education in South Tyrol at the Free University of Bolzano/Bozen does not include a law curriculum.

The chapter concludes by pondering what the future holds for South Tyroleans and the provincial territory in the field of bilingual legal higher education (F). Increased cross-border cooperation and Europeanisation aimed at the promotion of a European system of higher education and the establishment of the European Higher Education Area are just two of the current challenges.

B. History, Settlement of the Conflict and South Tyrol's Minority Regime within Italy

From the 14th century onwards, the current territory of the Autonomous Region Trentino-South Tyrol was part of the crown province (*Kronland*) Tyrol within the Habsburg Empire. In what is currently South Tyrol, there was a clear predominance of German- and

Ladin-speaking inhabitants. The southern part of this region, the current province of Trento, has always been predominantly Italian speaking.

After World War I, with the peace treaty of St. Germain (1919), both Trentino and South Tyrol were annexed to Italy. The Italian government promised to protect the German-speaking minority through territorial and cultural autonomy, but any such effort stopped in 1922, when the fascist regime came to power. During the fascist dictatorship a number of repressive measures were taken against the German-speaking minority. In 1939 Hitler and Mussolini agreed on a "final solution" for the South Tyrolean question: accordingly, the German-speaking South Tyroleans had to choose between keeping their identity (thus becoming German nationals and being forced to move to Hitler's Reich) and keeping their home (thus agreeing to assimilate, which would include changing their names). Around 86 percent of the German-speaking population decided to leave, although only a small part of them really left, due to the outbreak of war, and many returned after the war.[1]

In 1946, the peace treaty confirmed South Tyrol as part of Italy, but it provided for an international anchoring of minority rights, ensuring for the German-speaking population special provisions guarantying "complete equality of rights with the Italian-speaking inhabitants" and the safeguarding of "the ethnic character, and the cultural and economic development of the German-speaking element".[2] In 1948 the Italian Parliament issued by constitutional act an Autonomy Statute (hereafter ASt; regional constitution), which ensured far-reaching autonomy but essentially at a regional level (including Trentino), where the Italians were the majority. In the early 1960s the tension kept growing and many bomb attacks marked the beginning of difficult years. The Austrian government urged the United Nations to take a position on the South Tyrolean case, and in two resolutions (in 1960 and 1961), the U.N. General Assembly recommended that a friendly solution be found through further negotiations. A special commission

[1] E. Lantschner, 'History of South Tyrol Conflict and its Settlement', in J. Woelk et al. (eds.), *Tolerance through Law. Self-Governance and Group Rights in South Tyrol* (Martinus Nijhoff 2008) pp. 3–15.

[2] The smallest (and oldest) linguistic group, the Ladins, are technically not covered by the peace treaty. The claims of the Ladin minority group has been traditionally put forward by the German-speaking group's most representative party, the South Tyrolean People's Party.

was established,[3] which finally led to the so-called "package" of legislative measures. In December 1969 the package was approved by the South Tyrolean People's Party and by both the Italian and the Austrian Parliaments.

The most important consequence of the negotiations was the reform of the ASt and the transfer of essentially all legislative and administrative powers from the region to the two "Autonomous Provinces" of South Tyrol and Trentino. The implementation of the specific measures lasted until 1992, when the conflict was formally closed by the handover to the UN Secretary General of the "deed of discharge" by the Austrian government.

Today's South Tyrol is the top of the inverted pyramid of Italy's asymmetric minority-rights protection, it being the territory which enjoys by far the most extensive self-government and the territory in which minorities enjoy the highest degree of protection and broader range of rights. Within the Italian territory approximately three million people (5 percent of the population) belong to (at least) 12 minority groups.[4] This places Italy among the EU countries where the most minorities live. It is important to stress that the Italian Constitution mentions only language as a distinctive feature to be used to identify minorities. This means that special measures are constitutionally mandatory only for linguistic groups,[5] whereas other criteria, such as religion, "ethnicity", gender, are covered "only" by the non-discrimination provisions.[6] As a rule, minority rights can be enjoyed only in specific territories, at the regional (for the more numerous and better-protected minorities) or municipal level (for the smaller groups).

South Tyrol enjoys a very broad legislative and administrative autonomy, which includes nearly all competences except the military, administration of justice, the police, and a few minor issues. Even more importantly, the relationship between South Tyrol and the Italian state is essentially bilateral: all bylaws to the Autonomy Statute (which prevail over laws of the national Parliament) are negotiated by a joint

---

[3] The Commission comprised 19 members: 11 Italian speakers (representing the national government, the regional and the provincial governments, and parliament), seven German speakers (appointed by the regional and the provincial authorities), and one Ladin (appointed by the Province of Bolzano).

[4] The groups recognised as "historic linguistic minorities" by Art. 2 of Law no. 482/1999 are "Albanians, Catalans, Germans, Greeks, Slovenes, Croatians and the groups speaking French, Provencal, Friulian, Ladin, Occitan and Sardinian".

[5] Art. 6 of the Constitution.

[6] Art. 3 of the Constitution.

commission comprising six people, representing on an equal footing (three each) the state and South Tyrol, as well as the Italian-and German-speaking groups.[7] This makes the basic rules immutable against the will of South Tyrol and, ultimately, of its dominant population, the German-speaking minority.[8]

C. South Tyrol's Institutionalised Linguistic Regime

1. *Essential Features*

The whole institutional setting in South Tyrol is a power-sharing system based on strict separation and forced cooperation of the two main linguistic groups, German speakers and Italians.[9] The composition of the provincial government shall reflect the ratio of the groups as represented in the Assembly,[10] and the same goes for the municipal bodies.[11] In some circumstances, votes can be cast in the Assembly by language groups.[12] To not upset the ethnic balance in elections, four years of uninterrupted residence in the territory is required for exercising the right to vote.[13]

In the civil service, according to Article 89 ASt, jobs are assigned to the linguistic groups "in proportion to the size of the groups

[7] The joint Commission comprises three members representing the state (appointed by the national government) and three representing the autonomous province (two appointed by the provincial parliament and one by the regional parliament). One of the representatives of the state must belong to the German-speaking group and one representative of the province must belong to the Italian group (Art. 107 of the Autonomy Statute). This appointment procedure guarantees the parity of representation between both territories and groups and the acknowledgment of the ethnically composite character of both the state and South Tyrol. The Commission drafts all relevant bylaws of the autonomy statute, including the most relevant provisions on the exercise of minority and group rights. The drafts are subsequently adopted by the national government and enacted as presidential decrees. They thus bypass the Parliament and cannot be amended by an ordinary law.

[8] J. Woelk, 'What it Means to be Special in Relations with the Central State: Institutions and Procedures', in J. Woelk et al. (eds.), *Tolerance through Law. Self-Governance and Group Rights in South Tyrol* (Martinus Nijhoff 2008) pp. 121–142.

[9] S. Wolff, 'Complex Power Sharing as Conflict Resolution: South Tyrol in Comparative Perspective', in J. Woelk et al. (eds.), *Tolerance through Law. Self-Governance and Group Rights in South Tyrol* (Martinus Nijhoff 2008) pp. 329–370.

[10] Art. 49 ASt.

[11] Art. 62 ASt.

[12] Art. 56 ASt.

[13] Art. 25.4 ASt.

themselves, as they appear in the declarations of the official census".[14] This rule stretches to privatised institutions such as the railroad and the postal service and aims to guarantee both the representation of the groups as such and the provision of bilingual services (trilingual in the Ladin-speaking area) throughout the territory of South Tyrol.

Separation is also the rule in education. Each group runs its own schools, from the nursery to secondary schools. This means that in Italian-language schools, all subjects are taught in Italian, and, conversely, the schools with German language of instruction only teach in German. Teachers must also prove their mother tongue to be entitled to teach in the school of the respective group. Teaching of the "second language" (this is the official name of Italian in German schools and of German in Italian schools) is compulsory for at least 6 hours per week.

As to language, in South Tyrol, "the German language has parity with the Italian language, which is the official language of the State".[15] Every person can also use Italian or German (in limited areas also the Ladin language) in relations "with the judiciary and with the organs and offices of public administration located in the Province [...], as well as with private companies with concessions to provide public utility services".[16] In other words, the whole administration (broadly interpreted) has an obligation to "use [...] the language of the applicant and to reply in the language in which documents have been started".[17] When documents are "started by the offices themselves, the correspondence must be carried on in the language presumed to be the mother tongue of the citizen to whom it is directed", and documents directed to the public must be bilingual.[18] The civil servants (and persons working for companies charged with the provision of public utility services, such as pharmacies, transport companies, agencies) must

---

[14] E. Lantschner and G. Poggeschi, 'Quota System, Census and Declaration of Affiliation to a Linguistic Group', in J. Woelk et al. (eds.), *Tolerance through Law. Self-Governance and Group Rights in South Tyrol* (Martinus Nijhoff 2008) pp. 219–234; F. Palermo, 'Un système de «proportionelle ethnique»: le secteur public du Trentin-Haut Adige', 118 *Revue française d'administration publique* (2006) pp. 321–334. Through this declaration the strength of the linguistic groups can be ascertained, and it therefore forms the legal foundation of public life. Those who do not make the declaration are excluded from applying for public posts, offices, public housing, and various other social contributions.

[15] Art. 99 ASt.

[16] Art. 100.1 ASt.

[17] Art. 100.3 ASt.

[18] Art. 100.3 ASt.

also be bilingual (trilingual in the Ladin valleys), which has to be proved by a public examination.[19]

All these provisions and, even more importantly, all the stipulations on the use of language are enforced through strict legal remedies. The Autonomy Statute and its bylaws contain numerous and detailed guarantees in the case of an alleged violation of the minority (rather, "group") rights, available to individuals and groups as a means to strengthen mutual confidence. These guarantees include, inter alia, the right of linguistic groups represented in the provincial Parliament to veto a draft law they consider in breach of the equality between the groups ("alarm-bell procedure", which can ultimately end in front of the Constitutional Court, Art. 56 ASt); the same right extends to administrative acts (Art. 92 ASt); the right to challenge decisions of non-admission to schools on grounds of insufficient language skills (Art. 19 ASt); and rules on the ethnic composition of the ordinary and administrative judiciary (Art. 89 and 91 ASt).

2. *The Individual and Collective Right to Use Languages*

Each person has the right to address the administration in Italian or German. The general rule established by the Autonomy Statute is that administration must be bilingual in the whole territory of South Tyrol[20] and the choice of language is made by the individual. While these basic principles have been ensured since the beginning of South Tyrolean autonomy in 1948, most of the details took much longer to be fully implemented. For instance, the use of language in relations with the administration could be regulated in its main parts even before the new ASt was adopted in 1972, whereas the establishment of a fully bilingual judiciary was postponed until 1988, when the fundamental

[19] It is worth noticing that this system has been questioned by the European Court of Justice. In ECJ 6 June 2000, Case C-281/98, *Roman Angonese v Cassa di Risparmio di Bolzano SpA*, ECR I-4139, the Court held that the EC Treaty precludes an employer from requiring persons applying for employment to provide evidence of their linguistic knowledge exclusively by means of one particular diploma issued only in one particular province of a member state. This principle has only recently been implemented in South Tyrol: legislative decree 86 of May 14, 2010, indicates all other accepted evidence of proficiency in both Italian and German. The official portal of the Department for Bi(tri)lingualism Examination is at <www.provinz.bz.it/zdp/service/gesetzgebung.asp>, visited Oct. 22, 2010.

[20] And trilingual in the two Ladin valleys—this means that, in South Tyrol, the use of the two official languages is based on the personal principle, whereas the use of Ladin follows the territorial principle.

bylaw on the use of languages[21] was eventually enacted.[22] Among the reasons for the delay in fully implementing these rules, there are at least two, the first one being of a political nature. The administration of justice belongs to the powers of the state, and for quite some time there has been some resistance (especially in Rome) to accepting the very idea and the practical consequences of a fully bilingual regime. The second reason is technical in character. To set up a fully bilingual judicial system is undoubtedly a complex exercise, especially in terms of human resources. Only in 1976 did the compulsory hiring of bilingual judges and prosecutors (and support staff) start, and it took several years before the bilingual personnel was numerically sufficient to guarantee an effective service. Furthermore, it took years to start developing a consistent legal terminology in German and, not least, to allocate and guarantee sufficient financial resources for the functioning of a bilingual regime, including salaries and training for interpreters, translators, and other personnel. Since 1976, judges and prosecutors have been recruited through a special competition in which only persons who can prove their fluency in both languages can participate, and the quota system applies to them, as well as to all the personnel of the courts. Until 1988, however, the official language in trials was Italian, but German was allowed through the assistance of an interpreter. The 1988 bylaw on the use of languages finally enacted the principle of equal standing of the two languages in the judiciary, by creating the conditions for a trial to be conducted entirely in German. Like for the use of languages in relations with the administration, the general principle for the judiciary is the separate use of languages: as a rule, trials are conducted either only in Italian or only in German. Conversely, and as with the administration, there are several exceptions to the rule, allowing for a bilingual trial in some circumstances and safeguarding the free choice of language by the different parties. Understandably, the principle of the free choice of language is crucial in criminal

[21] Decree (dPR) 574/1988.

[22] F. Palermo and J. Woelk, 'Il diritto all'uso della lingua nei confronti dell'amministrazione e nei procedimenti giudiziari', in J. Marko et al. (eds.), *L'ordinamento speciale della Provincia autonoma di Bolzano* (Cedam 2001) pp. 717-745; F. Palermo and J. Woelk, 'Die Regelungen zum Sprachgebrauch vor Gericht und Verwaltung', in J. Marko et al. (eds.), *Die Verfassung der Südtiroler Autonomie* (Nomos 2005), pp. 332–350; C. Fraenkel-Haeberle, 'Linguistic Rights and the Use of Language', in J. Woelk et al. (eds.), *Tolerance through Law. Self-Governance and Group Rights in South Tyrol* (Martinus Nijhoff 2008) pp. 259–278.

proceedings, in order to guarantee the best chances for the defence, but it is partly attenuated in the civil proceedings, where it is balanced against the interest in a speedy procedure. As a matter of fact, although usually the trial is conducted in one language only, it is very common for both languages to be used. This is possible because all judges, prosecutors, and personnel are fluent in both languages due to bilingual legal education (see part E).

All in all, the system proves to work well, and no particular delays are created by these rules. Of course a bilingual judicial system is more expensive than a monolingual one: beside the possible use of interpreters (especially for parties coming from outside South Tyrol), which are employed anyway by the courts as part of the staff, the real costs are related to the translation into Italian of all documents and acts of the proceeding when it goes to the final stage in the Supreme Court, which is based in Rome and works only in Italian. All costs for translations are barred by the courts' budget. While the dominant language in the administration is German, Italian still prevails in the judicial system. The trend is increasing as to the use of German in court cases, and at present the number of trials conducted in German amounts to about 40 percent of the total.

With a view to effectively guaranteeing the individual right to use the language of his/her choice in a bilingual territory, the legal framework in South Tyrol includes detailed provisions on the collective dimension of a bilingual regime. In the political arena, linguistic groups have a legal subjectivity as such, not only when it comes to the composition of the executive bodies, but also in the legislative process.[23] As far as administration is concerned, the requirement of proficiency in both languages is provided for in a number of jobs even outside civil service, as in the case of notaries and pharmacists.[24] Most of the private undertakings which pursue a public interest, such as telephone-book publishing, are subject to special regulations guaranteeing bilingualism.

An important aspect of the collective use of language is media. South Tyrol has the power to regulate media, especially by ensuring

[23] Art. 56 ASt.

[24] Art. 30 and 31 dPR no. 574/1988. It is worth noting that there is as such no bilingualism requirement for lawyers (although a non-bilingual lawyer has de facto limited opportunities). However, the bar exam can be held in either Italian or German and the bar commission has to comprise an equal number of Italian-speaking and German-speaking members (Art. 32 dPR no. 574/1988).

the reception of broadcast media in German (and Ladin). Since 1975 a provincial law regulates free reception of media from Germany, Austria, and Switzerland,[25] and a number of agreements between the government of South Tyrol and the Italian public broadcasting company (RAI) ensures a number of hours for programmes in German (and Ladin) on public television.[26] Media in minority languages are subsidised by the state.[27]

The official denomination of place names (toponymy) is one of the open wounds of the South Tyrolean conflict and is still an extremely sensitive issue. Article 8 ASt attributes to the Autonomous Province the exclusive legislative power on "place names, without prejudice to the requirement for bilingualism". However, no such law exists so far. The problem is political in nature: adopting such a law is seen by most representatives of the German-speaking minority as also implicitly accepting the official Italian toponymy, thus "legalising" the fascist imposition and admitting that South Tyrol is equally as Italian as it is German. The paradoxical consequence is that, legally, only the Italian place names are so far official, and the German ones, although widely used, do not yet have a fully-fledged legal foundation. For at least a decade a proposal has been discussed in the South Tyrolean Assembly regarding the distinction between so-called "macro-toponymy" and "micro-toponymy": the first (being the names of all the 116 municipalities of South Tyrol, the main rivers, and the most important mountains) should remain bilingual (and trilingual in the Ladin valleys), while the latter (all the rest, including streets and squares) should be decided by the municipalities themselves (which means that the German names would become the only official version almost everywhere). After heated political debates between the state and the province in late spring and summer 2010 on German-only mountain signposts, in September a compromise was reached and a joint

[25] Provincial law 16/1975. In the digitalisation era this provision has lost most of its importance. When it was adopted, however, it represented a turning point in the media landscape, making it possible to receive freely in South Tyrol all public television programmes from Austria, Germany, and Switzerland.

[26] G. Rautz, 'I Media in Alto Adige', in J. Marko et al. (eds.), *L' ordinamento speciale della Provincia autonoma di Bolzano* (Cedam 2001) pp. 815–820.

[27] The main daily newspapers are *Dolomiten* (average 57,000 copies/day, in German) and *Alto Adige* (average 23,000 copies/day, in Italian). Weekly papers are only in German (FF – Das Südtiroler Wochenmagazin and the supplement to the daily *Dolomiten*).

commission of four experts was set up to advise both parties on how to standardise bi(tri)lingual signs by spring 2013.

Overall, a bilingual regime can only work if terminology in the minority language is reliable. While this is not a problem with regard to everyday German, in some special fields, such as in particular legal terminology, the concepts and the terms may differ from those used in Austria or Germany, due to the difference in the legal system. Therefore, the bylaw on the use of languages has set up a special joint commission consisting of six experts, three Italian speakers and three German speakers.

D. The Joint Terminology Commission

The Joint Terminology Commission (hereinafter Commission) is tasked with the establishment, updating, and ratification of the legal terminology to be used by public entities and bodies, with a view to standardising the legal terminology in German related to the Italian legal system. Only 16 years after having set German on par with Italian language (Second Autonomy Statute in 1972), the bylaw (Presidential decree, dPR 574/1988) sets the rules for the use of the German and Ladin[28] languages by the public administration and in court proceedings. It binds all bodies of public administration, while the private sector is not affected by the bylaw unless it is in charge of services with public utility.

Thus, there is a need for a consistent German legal language that correctly reflects the Italian legal system and enables administrators to clearly communicate in both Italian and German with persons living in South Tyrol. Article 6 para 1 of dPR no 574/1988 foresees the establishment of a Joint Commission for Terminology, enacted via a decree of the Government's Commissioner.[29] Its task is to determine, update, and validate the legal, administrative, and technical terminology in use

[28] Art. 32 of the dPR no. 574/1988 determines that the Ladin citizen can use Ladin with the public and if located in the Ladin municipalities (within the two valleys Gröden and Badia). Additionally, Ladin can be used in contact with regional and provincial authorities if they are in charge of representing Ladin interests. However, there is no indication in the bylaw about standardising legal terminology in the Ladin language.

[29] Woelk, *supra* n. 8, pp. 128–131. The Government Commissioner is the institutional interface between the central state and the province. His position changed after the constitutional reform of 2001 and nowadays is of a merely consultative and monitoring nature.

by the public administration and judiciary as well as by concessionary agents of public utility services. Furthermore, the Commission has to draft and maintain a dictionary of the terminology in Italian and German.[30] In 1991, an expert commission of bilingual legal experts and linguists was entrusted with the official validation and standardisation of the German-language equivalents for existing Italian legal institutes. The Commission consists of six experts elected for a two-year term, three of whom are Italian speaking (nominated by the Government Commissioner) and three of whom are German speaking (nominated by the provincial government). The bylaw does not determine the working methodology of the Commission. Article 4, paragraph 1, of the rules of procedure (hereafter RoP) prescribes that the Commission can take up works independently or upon request of institutional bodies or concessionaries; also private persons may ask for the standardisation of single terms.[31] A quorum is reached if at least two representatives of each language group are present[32]; simple work sessions require the presence of a minimum of three members, with the restriction that they cannot all belong to the same language group.[33]

Standardisation of terminology comprises five work phases: (1) Experts first compare the Italian legal institutes with different German-language systems (mainly those of Austria and Germany, less so Switzerland because of its apparent difference in terms of language and legal institutes); the contrastive work between different legal systems also takes into account South Tyrolese terminology that is already in use. If no equivalent to the Italian legal term in one of the other systems can be found, a translation proposal is advanced. (2) The terms move on to sub-commissions of experts (one for each legal subject matter). (3) They revise them before they get standardised by the Commission, accepting or modifying the translation equivalents. Subsequently, (4) the decisions are sent to the Commissioner of the Italian government and to the provincial government. Both can claim modifications within a time span of six months. If no modifications are claimed, (5) the translation equivalents are published in the official journal of the Trentino-Alto-Adige/Südtirol region in forms of lists of German and Italian equivalents, and they become legally binding.[34]

---

[30] Art. 6 (1) (b).
[31] Art. 4 (2) of the RoP.
[32] Art. 10 (3) of the RoP.
[33] Art. 10 (5) of the RoP.
[34] The lists are available at <www.provincia.bz.it/avvocatura/0302/it/terminologia.htm>, visited at October 31, 2010.

The process of standardisation of legal terms usually comprises the search of German equivalents for Italian legal terms. In rare cases the contrary happens, for example in the case of legal terms whose origin lies in law enacted by the Tyrol assembly in Innsbruck, Austria. An example is the legal term *Erbhof*, standardised as *maso avito* (a long-time inherited farm).[35] In the gastronomy sector it sometimes also happens that experts look for Italian equivalents, especially if in terms of content the term is relevant for legislation.[36] Specialised dictionaries, legal texts from foreign systems, foreign jurisprudence, and specialised manuals support this first work phase. The preparatory work is, inter alia, done by researchers of the European Academy of Bolzano/Bozen.[37]

It has to be pointed out that foreign legal systems (especially the Austrian, German, and Swiss) can be used as a reference point but not as real models for transposing Italian terminology into German. This is so for a twofold reason: Italian legal institutes are not always equivalent to Austrian or German ones, and South Tyrolese terminology has on occasions been born spontaneously by transposing Italian words. Thus, in order to justify, in the case of content equivalence, the adoption of foreign German legal terms or the modification of legal terms that are already of consolidated use, pointing out analogies and differences is unavoidable.[38] Once accepted by the Commission, the translation equivalents can be questioned by the government's commissioner or the provincial government. Article 6 dPR no 574/1988 refers to these two bodies and does not contain any other provisions on how to contest the Commission's decisions, which seems to be the only body for standardising German technical terminology. The Commission's

---

[35] G. Poggeschi, 'South Tyrol's Special Status in Private Law: the 'Entailed Farm' and the 'Grundbuch' Systems', in J. Woelk et al. (eds.), *Tolerance through Law. Self-Governance and Group Rights in South Tyrol* (Martinus Nijhoff 2008) p. 297. The *Erbhof* is a peculiar kind of entailed farm that has to be owned by the same family for at least two centuries.

[36] H. Zanon, 'Zur Problematik der Entwicklung einer deutschen Rechtssprache für Südtirol: Die Normierung durch die paritätische Kommission', in E. Chiocchetti and L. Voltmer (eds.), *Normazione, armonizzazzione e pianificazione linguistica/ Normierung, Harmonisierung und Sprachplanung/Normalisation, harmonisation et planification linguistique* (EURAC 2008) p. 56.

[37] N. Ralli and I. Stanizzi, 'Il dietro le quinte della normazione', in E. Chiocchetti and L. Voltmer (eds.), *Normazione, armonizzazzione e pianificazione linguistica/ Normierung, Harmonisierung und Sprachplanung/Normalisation, harmonisation et planification linguistique* (EURAC 2008) n. 66.

[38] F. Mayer, et al., 'Zwischen Skylla und Charybdis? Drei Rechtsordnungen in zwei Sprachen: Terminologiearbeit und Rechtsvergleichung', 1 *Informator* (1996) p. 213.

RoP (Art. 6 (4)) prescribe that only the government's commissioner or the provincial government—also singularly—may question the decision in written form within six months. This indirectly excludes the Administrative Tribunal from being competent in cases of conflict.[39] Private persons are only allowed to ask for information and certification of approved terminology lists.[40]

As already pointed out, one of the Commission's tasks is to take into account already-existing terminology used in South Tyrolese public administration. In fact, Article 6, paragraph 1a, of dPR 574/1988 prescribes that the Commission has to decide on, confirm, or update terminology already in use. Additionally, the Commission's RoP establishes that before deciding on terms the expert group can consult with stakeholders, institutional bodies, and concessionary agents to clarify remaining questions.[41] Even if the terms are standardised and legally binding after such rounds of consultation, reality shows that rank growth continues, and room for manoeuvring is left to persons and institutions using the term. As a consequence, there are sometimes different terms for a single meaning in use. This is also due to the fact that the Commission was established very late and only started work in 1994. This firstly contributed to the creation of spontaneously born legal terms deriving partly from Italian, and, secondly, it raised "language political" problems on whether to stick to the legal terminology in Austria or Germany or to confirm the local legal terminology.[42] In other words, socio-economic, cultural, and linguistic conditions influence legal terminology, and thus it is rarely possible to encounter full equivalence between legal terms in two countries.

This is also of importance for countries using the same official language (for example Austria and Germany), because equal terms belonging to different legal systems might have different meanings (system bondage of legal terminology).[43] While searching for terms

---

[39] F. Palermo and E. Pföstl, 'Minderheitenschutz durch Sprachnormierung. Die Kommission für Rechtsterminologie in Südtirol', 1–2 *Europa Ethnica* (1997) pp. 12–29 at p. 22.

[40] Art. 7 (2) of the RoP.

[41] Art. 4 (3).

[42] Palermo and Pföstl, *supra* n. 39, p. 19.

[43] G-R. de Groot, 'Zweisprachige juristische Wörterbücher', in P. Sandrini (ed.), *Übersetzen von Rechtstexten: Fachkommunikation im Spannungsfeld zwischen Rechtsordnung und Sprache* (Narr 1999) p. 203; G-R. de Groot, 'Das Übersetzen juristicher Terminologie', in G-R. de Groot and R. Schultze (eds.), *Recht und Übersetzen* (Nomos 1999) p. 12. For example, the legal term *Naturpark* in Germany is not

fulfilling the demand of a "functional equivalence",[44] the comparison of terms coming from different legal systems has to be integrated with the comparison of the legal institutes and their functioning. Only by doing so can the standardisation of false friends be avoided. German standardised terminology can also lead to misunderstandings if the standardised legal terms are extrapolated from foreign legal systems, instead of resulting from a translation proposal or from terms already in use. An issue that has been contentious, for instance, was the use of the term *Landeshauptmann* to designate the president of the provincial government. In early times, the official translation was based on the Italian term and thus *Präsident des Provinzialausschusses* was used, for example in the Official Journal. Subsequently, the term *Landeshauptmann* was introduced, an adoption of the term used in Austria. While the Commission initially challenged the decision and proposed a different term (*Präsident der Landesregierung*), it did not have the "political" strength to change an already rooted (and politically supported) term. Even though the decree prescribes that all Italian and German texts of laws, deeds, and orders have to be drawn up or translated in consideration of the standardised terminology, in reality this does not always happen (an acceptance problem).[45] A mechanism guaranteeing the implementation of such an obligation is missing, but an introduction of sanctions would neither be practicable nor desirable. First, provincial administrators dealing with the public usually only pass along information and work on behalf of department heads. Second, the creation of "language watchdogs" contradicts the dynamic nature of language. Thus, the use of standardised terms remains largely subjected to the goodwill and sensitivity of the public administrator, legislator, and, with regard to higher legal education, to university staff teaching Italian law at the University of Innsbruck (Austria), partly in the medium of German. Article 37 of dPR 574/1988 envisages sanctions for public employees for infringement of the regulations guarding linguistic rights. Should public

---

equivalent to the legal term *Naturpark* in Austria. See E. Chiocchetti, 'Criteri di armonizzazione della terminologia della Convenzione delle Alpi', in E. Chiocchetti and L. Voltmer (eds.), *Normazione, armonizzazzione e pianificazione linguistica/ Normierung, Harmonisierung und Sprachplanung/Normalisation, harmonisation et planification linguistique* (EURAC 2008) p. 21.

[44] S. Šarčević, *New Approach to Legal Translation* (Kluwer Law International 1997) p. 236.

[45] Art. 6 (3) of dPR 574/1988.

administrators violate their official duties, the offence can be sanctioned through disciplinary measures, without prejudice to the possible application of Article 328 of the Criminal Code for neglect of one's official duties (no cased have so far been recorded).

Due to the predominance of German speakers in the political bodies, most of the provincial legislation is actually drafted in German. Thus, the Italian version, which is legally the official one and the one that prevails in case of divergences in interpretation, paradoxically is often a translation from German.[46] Article 4, paragraph 4, of dPR 574/1988 envisages the joint use of Italian and German, pointing out that both legal texts in both languages must be printed next to one another and have the same layout.

An information system for legal terminology serves as a final database and ensures that all results of the terminological work are made public (internet platform bistro).[47] It contains several thousand terms of the Italian legal system as well as of the Austrian, German and Swiss federal systems in their respective original languages, with equivalent translations. The compiling of legal terms in Ladin is an ongoing project with the financial support of the Office for Language Issues and Ladin municipalities and associations.[48] Experts also work for the standardisation of the terms in the field of university law and higher education.[49] To fulfil its tasks, the Commission depends on the personnel and facilities that the Autonomous Province allocates. The Commission is not granted own financial autonomy and has only the right to propose the appointment of experts in specific legal fields. A secretariat coordinates the work. Article 3 of the Commission's RoP also prescribes that the Commission, with the help of the secretariat, gives notice of the results and raises awareness in the South Tyrolean public sphere about standardised legal terms. Initially established in the provincial department for language issues, the secretariat was moved to the research centre European Academy but recently moved back to the provincial administration.

---

[46] Palermo and Pföstl, *supra* n. 39, p. 19.

[47] Available at <http://dev.eurac.edu:8080/cgi-bin/index/preindex.en>, visited Oct. 27, 2010.

[48] Information at <http://dev.eurac.edu:8080/index/32_TermLad_en.html>, visited Oct. 27, 2010.

[49] Available at <http://www.provincia.bz.it/avvocatura/0302/it/elenco_terminol.htm>, visited Oct. 27, 2010.

Overall, it takes much time to reach compromises on a terminology list and the Commission's decisions are thus often outdated very fast or do not reflect the latest linguistics or legislation in force (temporal bondage problem). In other words, standardised terms become easily outdated when a subject field undergoes an extensive process of reform. For example, state law no 30/2003 introduced numerous measures intended to foster the flexibility of the labour market. Many previously standardised terms have become outdated or changed. As a consequence decisions made by the Commission were not relevant for a long time.[50] The handling of abbreviations and acronyms is also quite problematic: usually they are not standardised in order to promote the highest degree of transparency and comprehensibility.[51] One could also question whether the composition of the Commission facilitates or hinders the speeding up of the work. It equally represents German and Italian speakers. However, most of the work consists in the transposition into German. Additionally, the fact that none of the members is working full time on standardisation doubtlessly explains why it takes so long to make delicate decisions about term lists that have already been made in the sub-commissions and prepared by specialists.

E. Higher Legal Education for South Tyroleans

Unlike in primary and secondary education, which substantially promotes a linguistic model of separation,[52] recently in tertiary education

[50] E. Chiocchetti and I. Stanizzi, 'Die Beschlüsse der Südtiroler Terminologiekommission: Problematiiken bei der Normierung von Rechtstermini', presentated at the 17th European Symposium on Language for Special Proposes, 'Methods and Aims—(Re)Conceptualising LSP Research', at University of Aarhus, Aug. 17–21, 2009. For example, the term *Libretto di lavoro* was standardised as *Arbeitsbuch* in German in 2001. This booklet containing all employee qualifications and working experience was, however, abolished in 2003.

[51] For example the *Istituto Nazionale di Statistica* was standardised as *Zentralinstitut für Statistik* in German; the Italian short form ISTAT is, however, also used by German speakers.

[52] Art. 19 of the Autonomy Statute is primarily concerned with the regulation of mother-tongue instruction in kindergarten and primary and secondary schools. It establishes two separate and parallel school systems, with pupils taught in their "mother tongue" by teachers of the same language, while for the Ladin-language schools it provides for instruction on equal terms in German and Italian alongside the use of Ladin as a language of instruction. Also the school governance is separated, with a triplication of school authorities, one for the German-language school and one for the Italian-language schools, plus one for the Ladin schools.

the path of linguistic integration has been followed, translating into an extensive use of English in addition to German and Italian. In 1992 the research centre European Academy of Bolzano/Bozen was established as a non-profit private entity aiming at the promotion of applied research and the creation of know-how in sectors of special relevance to South Tyrol. Furthermore, the trilingual (Italian, German, and English) Free University of Bolzano/Bozen was founded in 1997. The university breaks for the first time with the principle of segregated education and opens up—although still to a limited extent—a new model of education.[53] The foundation of the Free University of Bolzano/Bozen was highly controversial. Some feared that the relationship with the University of Innsbruck could be blurred; others were afraid of an increase in Italian immigration. In reality, the latter apprehension was in vain, because a large number of registered undergraduate and graduate students come from Germany. All this seems to indicate that, albeit slowly and not for the whole population, in South Tyrol "the collective idea is growing according to which language is no longer simply the symbol of a minority identity and culture but also an element for personal and community enrichment".[54]

With regard to higher legal education, neither of the abovementioned tertiary education institutions offers a full curriculum. Occasionally, both institutions offer specialisation courses in legal subjects, both through the medium of Italian language and also through the medium of German language. For the time being, a full curriculum of legal studies is only offered by universities outside of South Tyrol. Both the University of Innsbruck in the Land Tyrol (Austria) and the University of Trento in the neighbouring Autonomous Province of Trento offer a full law curriculum, which opens up for legal professions and academia. The law school in Innsbruck enables students to register for the "integrated curriculum on Italian law", which allows for the undertaking of necessary legal training in both countries—Austria and Italy—and is partly taught in German and partly in Italian. The law school of the University of Trento (55 km from Bolzano/Bozen)

[53] J. Woelk, 'Forschung und Lehre in Südtirol: Europäische Akademie und Freie Universität Bozen', in J. Marko et al. (eds.), *Die Verfassung der Südtiroler Autonomie* (Nomos 2005) pp. 435–448.

[54] C. Fraenkel-Haeberle, 'Die Anerkennung akademischer und beruflicher Titel zwischen Italien und Österreich', presented at "Rechtsvergleichung an der Sprachgrenze", at Universität Innsbruck, June 15, 2010.

offers a program on comparative and transnational law, which is taught almost entirely in Italian (some classes are in English).

The development nowadays of bilingual higher legal education at the University of Innsbruck has to be seen in view of history. During the Habsburg period, legal studies in Austrian law were also offered in Italian; albeit this is not comparable with the current situation of the bilingual integrated curriculum in Italian law, it nevertheless illustrates the tradition of the University of Innsbruck in training legal experts and lawyers. The Leopold-Franzens-Universität of Innsbruck was founded in 1669 and defines itself as "the modern tertiary education and research seat for Tyrol, South Tyrol, Vorarlberg and the principality of Liechtenstein" (author's translation).[55] Overall, in 2009, it counted almost 26,000 students.[56]

A majority of German-speaking South Tyroleans law students register at the University of Innsbruck, because of the fact that the faculty of law offers an integrated curriculum in Italian law (partly through the medium of the German language). Furthermore, South Tyrolean associations and the province itself facilitate the legal studies in Innsbruck by assisting the students, guaranteeing student dorm placement, and dispensing study grants. Generally, the University of Innsbruck has been considered the *Landesuniversität der Tiroler bzw. Südtiroler* (the university of the Tyrolese people of the German mother tongue) because of its cultural-linguistic bond and geographical proximity (120 km from Bolzano/Bozen and 30 km from the border).

As mentioned above (part B), during the fascist dictatorship a significant example of repressive measures against the German-speaking minority was the prohibition of the use of German language in public and private matters; with regard to higher education, no foreign degrees were recognised and post-secondary study at foreign universities was prohibited.[57] After 1945 mother-tongue education was anew enforced and re-introduced at the primary and secondary level. Even though the Italian government committed itself in Article 3b of the

---

[55] The self-concept of the University of Innsbruck is available at <www.uibk.ac.at/universitaet/profil/leitbild.html>, visited October 25, 2010. In fact, the University of Innsbruck was since 1669 the tertiary education institution for the greater Tyrol area; only in the twentieth century were the University of Trento (1962) and the University of Bolzano/Bozen (1997) founded.

[56] University of Innsbruck, <www.uibk.ac.at/universitaet/profil/zahlen>, visited Oct. 25, 2010.

[57] R. Seberich, *Südtiroler Schulgeschichte* (Edition Raetia 2000) p. 239.

peace treaty to the reciprocal recognition of the validity of certain study degrees and university diplomas for the sake of neighbourly relations, it was only in 1952 that the agreement to the promotion of cultural relationships between Italy and Austria was signed.[58] In the aftermath of World War II the schooling system quickly showed that there was enormous need for action. Teachers of the German mother tongue did not have an appropriate educational background and, due to the big demand, students themselves were employed as teachers. Also, the entry into force of the Second Autonomy Statute in 1972 highlighted the lack of graduates needed to fill positions in public administration (respecting the ethnic quota system). A series of specialisation courses was started by the Austrian University of Innsbruck in cooperation with the Italian University of Padua, counteracting the educational arrears. In 1979 German- and Ladin-speaking South Tyroleans were set on par with Austrian citizens for the sake of access to services in Austria, including access to university and students' benefits.[59] In concrete terms this implied that secondary-education diplomas were equated with those of Austrian high schools and that South Tyroleans were entitled to the same treatment with regard to study fees.[60] Additionally, the Austrian University system opened up for full and associate professorships for South Tyroleans.[61] In 1982 Austria and Italy finally agreed on the manner and extent to which cooperation between universities should become a reality. The Agreement between the Republic of Austria and the Republic of Italy entered into force on October 1, 1983.[62] According to Article 6, the agreement finds application to higher legal studies, albeit Article 1 authorises all universities of the contracting states to conclude agreements with regard to instruction and scientific research. This bilateral agreement paved the way for the 'integrated curriculum on Italian law' of the University of Innsbruck in cooperation with the Italian University of Padua. Since 1985 the integrated curriculum allows for the study of Italian law, partly through the medium of German and partly through the medium of Italian. This has contributed to the establishment of a class of bilingual lawyers and to an increase in German-speaking legal

[58] Bundesgesetzblatt (BGBl.) no. 270/1954.

[59] *Gleichstellungsgesetz, Bundesgesetz* 25.01.1979, BGBl. no 57 (federal law on equal status).

[60] Section 4, para. 1, Austrian Law on Equal status for South Tyroleans.

[61] Section 2 Austrian Law on Equal status for South Tyroleans.

[62] BGBl. no 423/1983.

experts employed in public administration as mandated by the ethnic quota system.

The integrated curriculum aims at training students in a legal system other than the Austrian one, namely the Italian legal system. With the help of the University of Padua, initial organisational difficulties were overcome: specialised teachers in Italian law took over classes at the University of Innsbruck and specialised in teaching legal subjects relevant to the Autonomous Province of Bolzano/Bozen (initially on the basis of annual assignments).

Although classes on Italian law and the peculiarities of the South Tyrolean legal system started in the early 1970s, just a few years later, in 1978, the *Rechtswissenschaftliches Studiengesetz*[63] (law on legal studies) entitled foreign students to sit a certain number of exams in Italian law offered at the University of Innsbruck. Finally, the agreement between Austria and Italy in 1983 generally allowed for the introduction of integrated study programmes (in particular, Arts. 1 and 2, paras. 1 and 3, and Art. 3). Article 9 of the agreement envisages the establishment of a joint commission of maximum seven representatives of each contracting state, aiming at facilitating the application of cooperation schemes and integrated study programmes. The integrated law curriculum was discussed in a joint commission and agreed upon on November 22, 1985.[64] The *Gemeinsame Einrichtung* (joint facility) was established on February 5, 1986, via decree of the Austrian Federal Ministry for Science and Research. In 2006 the joint facility was advanced to the Institute for Italian Law.[65] The degree of the integrated curriculum on Italian law (*Magister/a iuris*) is set on par with degrees obtained in Italian law schools (*dottore/dottoressa magistrale in giurisprudenza*), entitling graduates to undertake the required trainings for exercising legal professions. However, there are still difficulties and problems in terms of the equalisation of study degrees and the recognition of professional titles and careers between Austrian and Italian Universities.[66] Currently, the existing integrated curriculum in

---

[63] Section 18. *Bundesgesetz* no 140/1978, BGBl. no 140/1978.

[64] BGBl. no. 3/1986 and no. 189/1987. The current study plan of the integrated law curriculum is available in information leaflet no 343/2002 and is available at <www.uibk.ac.at/fakultaeten-servicestelle/pruefungsreferate/studien/c102_2001w.html>, visited Oct. 26, 2010. Its legal basis is the agreement on the integrated law curriculum between the University of Innsbruck and the University of Padua (BGBl. no 262/2001).

[65] <www.uibk.ac.at/italienisches-recht/>, visited Oct. 26, 2010.

[66] Fraenkel-Haeberle, *supra* n. 54.

Italian law at the University of Innsbruck trains bilingual legal experts and lawyers and is generally considered to be a cornerstone of the identity of the greater area of Tyrol.[67]

F. Current and Future Challenges

Europe is much less linguistically diverse than other regions of the world,[68] but it is definitely the area with the highest density of norms in this field. South Tyrol, a small region in the Alps, has significantly contributed to such a normative density, being one of the most regulated examples of coexistence between different ethno-linguistic groups. As this chapter has shown with regard to linguistic rights, there is hardly any area of public, and to a considerable extent private, life that is not covered by a complex network of norms, guarantees, and remedies. The overall success of South Tyrol in terms of the accommodation of minority rights, including linguistic rights, shows that law is actually the most effective instrument for guaranteeing peace and stability. Only clear legal guarantees and remedies can create mutual trust when such trust is lacking.

Law, however, is not an abstract and artificial artefact. Rather, it is essentially part of culture. For a bilingual administration to work effectively, bilingual lawyers are necessary, in order to take into account not only the laws and regulations, but also the culture that produces them. The autonomy and minority regime in South Tyrol has been built thanks to the fundamental contribution of lawyers familiar with both languages and culture

Traditionally, these have been mostly German-speaking lawyers, trained in Italy and able to use their legal and linguistic skills in the endless negotiations with the government in Rome. Recently, the extraordinary development of a considerable body of South Tyrolean law, produced by the autonomous institutions, even more requires bilingual and bi-cultural lawyers; these are increasingly Italian speakers, often trained in Austria. It can thus be said that a real class of South Tyrolean lawyers is developing in both linguistic groups (Ladins have

[67] P. Pernthaler, *Die Identität Tirols in Europa* (Springer 2007) p. 214.

[68] The EU has 7 percent of the world's total population but it includes only 1 percent of the world's linguistic diversity. See P. Juaristi et al., 'Language diversity in the European Union. An overview' in X. Arzoz (ed.), *Respecting Linguistic Diversity in the European Union* (John Benjamins 2008) pp. 47–72.

been the most intercultural since the beginning), also thanks to the improved opportunities for bilingual legal education. While the impact of bilingual law and bilingual education on conflict settlement and their role as mediators of social conflicts is difficult to measure in absolute terms, their contribution cannot be denied and represents an effective guarantee for the future. Bilingual law and bilingual lawyers will certainly be increasingly needed for the management of a complex and densely regulated autonomy- and minority-protection system.

As to bilingual legal education, however, the future is less predictable. The establishment of a Faculty of Law in the Free University of Bolzano/Bozen is being considered ever more seriously by the political elites. This would be a positive or negative development depending on what the curriculum might offer. To replicate what has already been offered in Innsbruck and Trento seems rather useless and even counterproductive, as students will lose the opportunity to study in a different place and to be trained in a different cultural environment. Conversely, future-oriented, multilingual legal training, adding to what neighboring universities already do, emphasising the comparative, trans-national and Euro-regional[69] component of law may allow South Tyrol not only to train its future civil servants, but also to export cosmopolitan lawyers in different and not less challenging environments.

[69] Trans-frontier cooperation is particularly developed across the Tyrolean border. A "Euro-region" has been in place politically for some time, and, in 2011 a European Grouping for Territorial Cooperation among Tyrol, South Tyrol, and Trentino has been started. In the future, it is likely that the "Euro-region" will create additional challenges for multi-lingual and multi-cultural lawyers.

PART III

THE EMERGENCE OF ENGLISH AS A LANGUAGE OF LEGAL EDUCATION

CHAPTER TWELVE

ENGLISH-MEDIUM LEGAL EDUCATION IN CONTINENTAL EUROPE: MAASTRICHT UNIVERSITY'S EUROPEAN LAW SCHOOL: EXPERIENCES AND CHALLENGES

Nicole Kornet

A. Introduction

The Europeanisation of law and legal practice calls for the education of a new generation of law graduates; "European" law graduates who are comfortable with different jurisdictions, who can quickly understand a new legal system, who can identify the common European or international origins of divergent national laws and who can solve transnational legal problems. With its focus on national law, the traditional law curriculum is ill-suited to educating such "European" law graduates. Legal education will therefore gradually need to undergo transformation to become progressively "Europeanised". This Europeanisation of the law curriculum can also have consequences for the language, or languages, in which the law is taught, and may call for a common language for teaching and scholarship. In the many new developments in legal education that aim to respond to globalisation and Europeanisation of law and legal practice, English is emerging as the common language. This is not without its problems and challenges, since there is an intrinsic connection between law and language.

This contribution will share the experiences and address the challenges of offering a European-oriented curriculum through the medium of English. Attention will be given first to the need to educate European law graduates and therefore for the need to 'Europeanise' legal education (B). This is followed by an overview of what a European-oriented law curriculum could look like (C). The focus will then shift to the role of language in that programme, and in particular the experiences with and challenges of teaching an English-medium European-oriented law curriculum (D). In this context, this contribution will take as a case study the European Law School at Maastricht University (E). On an individual institutional basis, Maastricht University has taken the bold step to introduce a fully-fledged European-oriented law curriculum aimed at training truly European law graduates, in its bachelor programme of the European Law School. This English language track of the European Law School (ELS-ELT), teaches law from a European and comparative perspective, entirely through the medium of English.

B. The Need for 'European' Law Graduates

1. *The Europeanisation of Law, Legal Practice, Legal Scholarship and Legal Education*

European integration and globalisation has a great impact on social, economic and political systems; the law has not remained unaffected by these changes. Consequently, the past decades are marked by the Europeanisation, and to some degrees globalisation, of law, legal practice, legal scholarship and legal culture. These developments, in particular the Europeanisation of law and legal practice, raise new challenges to legal education.

The harmonisation and unification of law as a result of ever-deepening European integration has led not only to the expansion of EU law, but also to the Europeanisation of national law. The influence of European law – in its broadest sense, also including for instance the European Convention on Human Rights – on the constitutional, administrative, private and criminal law of the Member States of the European Union cannot be denied.[1] A cursory look at, for instance, the company, competition, public procurement and consumer law of Member States of the European Union further demonstrates the depth of the influence of European law on national legal systems and the gradual development of a supranational European legal system. These days, there are few areas of law that are entirely free from European influence. Consequently, the study of law cannot be confined to the study of national law and one or two individual and separate courses on EU law that focus on the institutional aspects and EU substantive law. These developments demand a more integrated approach that gives due attention to the European and international origins of national law as well as the influence of European integration and

[1] See for example, D. M. Curtin et al., *European Integration and Law* (Intersentia 2006).

globalisation processes on national legal systems and the complex interrelationship between the two.

European integration has furthermore led to the Europeanisation of legal practice. In particular as a consequence of secondary legislation concerning the legal profession, legal practitioners can avail themselves of their free movement rights to practice a legal profession in another Member State.[2] EU Member States are required to recognise qualifications obtained by their citizens in another Member State. Furthermore, the Establishment directive for lawyers entitles a lawyer to practice the legal profession under his home title on a permanent basis in another Member State and lays down a procedure whereby the migrant lawyer can integrate into the profession of the host state. It is therefore no longer the case that a law graduate who studied law in one country is limited to practising law in that country. European integration has led to the Europeanisation of the labour market for legal practitioners; it has also necessitated it. Through the creation of the internal market, legal problems have become all the time more transnational, which requires lawyers who are capable of thinking across jurisdictional boundaries. Consequently, there has been a Europeanisation of (commercial) legal practice, which can also be evidenced by the intensified collaboration between law firms in European networks, mergers between law firms in different countries and the establishment of large international law firms.[3] It should be observed that these developments are not limited to the European Union; there is an internationalisation of commercial legal practice.[4]

---

[2] Council Directive 77/249/EEC to facilitate the effective exercise by lawyers of freedom to provide services, *Official Journal* L 78, 26.6.1977, p. 17 (Lawyers Services Directive); Council Directive 89/48/EEC on a general system for the recognition of higher-education diplomas awarded on completion of professional education and training of at least three years' duration *Official Journal* L 19, 24.1.1989, p. 16 (Recognition of Diplomas Directive); Directive 98/5/EC to facilitate practice of the profession of lawyer on a permanent basis in a Member State other than that in which the qualification was obtained *Official Journal* L77, 14.3.1998, p. 36 (Lawyers Establishment Directive). *See* S. Claessens, *Free Movement of Lawyers in the European Union* (Wolf Publishers 2008); H. Schneider 'The Free Movement of Lawyers in Europe, and Its Consequences for the Legal Profession and the Legal Education in the Member States', in M. Faure et. al. (eds.), *Towards a European Ius Commune in Legal Education and Research* (Intersentia 2002) p. 15.

[3] See e.g., H. P. Glenn, 'Comparative Law and Legal Practice: On Removing the Borders', 75 *Tulane Law Review* (2001) p. 977 at p. 982.

[4] See e.g., A. Bernabe-Riefkohl, 'Tomorrow's Law Schools: Globalization and Legal Education', 32 *San Diego Law Review* (1995) p. 137; A.T. Von Mehren, 'The Rise of Transnational Legal Practice and the Task of Comparative Law' 75 *Tulane Law Review*

The constant expansion of EU law has led to the emergence of a new discipline, distinct from national legal scholarship: European legal scholarship. This new discipline focuses not only on the law of the European Union, but also on the influence of EU law on national law, the necessity, desirability and feasibility of harmonisation, comparative law, and the divergence and convergence of national legal systems. The development of truly European legal scholarship is particularly strong in the field of private law, nevertheless it is growing fast in other fields as well. Furthermore, as a result of these interconnected developments (Europeanisation of law, scholarship and practice), it is possible to observe a new European legal culture emerging.[5] Since law is embedded in culture, European law must be embedded in an evolving European legal culture. Through the growing body of European law, a common European legal identity, European values and principles, a European legal methodology and mode of legal reasoning will gradually emerge. These developments will unavoidably affect national legal cultures.

2. *The Europeanisation of Legal Education*

The Europeanisation of law, legal scholarship, legal practice and legal culture must inevitably have an important impact on legal education.[6] This has two dimensions: the Europeanisation of higher education systems and a reorientation of the law curriculum towards a more European-oriented law curriculum.

(2001) p. 1215; Glenn *supra* n. 3; P. Roorda, 'The Internationalization of the Practice of Law' 28 *Wake Forest Law Review* (1993) p. 141.

[5] See e.g., M.W. Hesselink, *The New European Private Law. Essays on the Future of Private Law in Europe* (Kluwer Law International 2002) p. 11–71; B. Fauvarque-Cosson *The Rise of Comparative Law: A Challenge for Legal Education in Europe* (Europa Law Publishing 2007) p. 13.

[6] Also see the contributions in B. De Witte and C. Forder (eds.), *The Common Law of Europe and the Future of Legal Education* (Kluwer 1992); M. Faure et al. (eds.), *Towards a European Ius Commune in Legal Education and Research* (Intersentia 2002); B. Akkermans, 'Challenges in Legal Education and the Development of a New European Private Law' 10 *German Law Journal* (2009) p. 803; S. Chesterman 'The Evolution of Legal Education: Internationalization, Transnationalization, Globalization', 10 *German Law Journal* (2009) p. 877 at p. 879; M. Storme 'The Consequences of European Unification for Legal Education in the Member States' 9 *European Review* (2001) p. 135; P. Schlechtriem, 'The Growing Importance of European Law and How It Affects Teaching and Research in the Field of the Private Law of Obligations (Torts, Contracts and Restitution)' 36 *Texas International Law Journal* (2001) p. 531; and the contributions in A.W. Heringa and B. Akkermans (eds.), *Educating European Lawyers* (Intersentia 2011).

With respect to the influence of the European Union on higher education, initiatives have been taken at a European level to stimulate and facilitate student mobility. Through the Erasmus programme, for example, students are able to study a semester abroad, which allows them to gain a better understanding of another legal system, legal culture and legal language. Higher education institutions are also encouraged to cooperate through intensive programmes, networks and multilateral programmes.[7] In the 1999 Bologna Declaration, the Ministers of Education from 29 European countries jointly declared that a European Higher Education Area would be created by 2010, 'in order to enhance the employability and mobility of citizens and to increase the international competitiveness of European higher education'.[8] Through this Bologna process greater transparency and comparability of educational systems in Europe through, for example, the introduction of a bachelor-master structure throughout Europe, is pursued.

The creation of a European Higher Education Area is also directed at promoting the attractiveness and competitiveness of higher education institutions in Europe. Universities have reacted to these European initiatives by creating new courses and programmes responding to European integration and globalisation, which allows them to compete for (foreign) students. As a result of the impact of European and global developments on the law, they have included courses on international and European law in the basic law curriculum, often as a mandatory component of the curriculum. In response to the increased mobility of students as well as teaching staff, they increasingly offer other courses with European or comparative elements. It is also possible to observe a veritable explosion of LL.M. programmes in European and comparative law aimed at attracting students from around Europe, if not the world, as well as the emergence of double degree programmes between universities in different countries.[9]

---

[7] See <ec.europa.eu/education/lifelong-learning-programme/doc80_en.htm>, visited Oct. 26, 2010.

[8] See the Bologna Declaration of June 19, 1999, <www.ond.vlaanderen.be/hogeronderwijs/bologna/documents/MDC/BOLOGNA_DECLARATION1.pdf>, visited Oct. 26, 2010. Today the Bologna Process involves 47 countries, all parties to the European Cultural Convention 1954 of the Council of Europe. For up-to-date information on the Bologna process and the European Higher Education Area, see the official website: <www.ehea.info>.

[9] See A. Klebes-Pelissier, 'Double degrees in the context of the Bologna process', 4 *European Journal of Legal Education* (2007) p. 173.

To attract these foreign students, it is necessary to make such courses and programmes accessible. However, the limited ability of those foreign students to master the language of the host university often constitutes a barrier. To promote accessibility, and thereby to attract these foreign students, these elective courses or LL.M. programmes on European and comparative law are increasingly taught in English. English has developed as the common language shared by professors and students.[10] A consequent side-effect of these developments is the growing recognition of English as the common language for European-oriented legal education.

3. *A Reorientation of the Law Curriculum*

The initiatives mentioned above reflect steps in the direction of Europeanising higher education systems in response to European integration; but they only represent a small-scale Europeanisation of the law curriculum. The impact of European integration has not yet led to a general overhaul of the law curriculum to integrally adapt it to the Europeanisation of law, legal scholarship and legal practice. A European curriculum for legal education does not exist. New developments aimed at responding to ever-expanding European law are typically embedded in the traditional national law curriculum or follow on from a bachelor programme oriented on national law. These courses necessarily remain embedded in the traditional national law curriculum, because law is still primarily viewed as a national product, and legal education is consequently circumscribed by national borders. Not only is the subject-matter of the law curriculum regarded as 'national', the subsequent practice of law is also dependent on the national legislature and/or legal profession. It must be kept in mind that admission to the bar, and therefore access to the legal professions (lawyer, judge, prosecutor, and in some countries even legal advisor), remains subject to national regulation. As long as the requirements to enter the profession remain national, the study of law will remain oriented on national law and will consequently remain affected by national borders and by national (legal) languages. This in turn renders the achievement of the Bologna objectives particularly difficult for legal

[10] Also see J. House, 'English as a lingua franca: A threat to multilingualism?', 7 *Journal of Sociolinguistics* (2003) p. 556 at p. 570.

education.[11] Unlike other academic disciplines such as the natural sciences, medicine, economics, psychology, and other social sciences, which are not restricted by national borders in the knowledge required or to be acquired, or the language in which it is studied, law remains embedded in a national legal system, a national legal culture and a national (legal) language.

This national orientation of the law curriculum renders it difficult to respond adequately to the need for a new generation of law graduates who are less dependent on a single legal system. To practice law in this European legal environment, legal practitioners need to be capable of crossing national borders, not only physically but also intellectually. They must be able to adjust to ever-changing (European) law, to understand the European origins of an ever-expanding body of national law, and to communicate effectively with legal practitioners in other jurisdictions. Educating this new generation of law graduates requires a reorientation of the law curriculum and ever more calls for a European-oriented law curriculum.

A glimpse of a European approach to legal education can be caught from the past. National laws were not the central focus of university education until the nineteenth century. The 'reception' of Roman law from the twelfth century led to the development of a common law – *ius commune* – for continental European countries.[12] Received Roman law did not replace local and national customs and laws, rather it was supplementary; it was followed where no local or national rules existed, but it was also used to interpret local and national rules. This *ius commune* formed the basis for legal education and legal scholarship. Students and professors travelled from one country to another in order to study at different universities, basic scholarly works were written in one common language – Latin – and were used throughout the continent, and the qualifications obtained by law graduates were recognised in all countries.[13] With the rise of the nation state and the codification of law as a means to unite the nation in the second half of the eighteenth

---

[11] Also see C. Bortoluzzi, 'A New European Model of Legal Education as One of the Institutional Elements of the New European Common Law', 10 *Global Jurist* (2010) Article 3, <www.bepress.com/gj/vol10/iss1/art3>, visited Oct. 26, 2010.

[12] On the history private law see, R. C. Van Caenegem, *An Historical Introduction to Private Law*, trans. D.E.L. Johnston (Cambridge University Press 1992).

[13] *Ibid.*, p. 76 et seq.; G.-R. de Groot, 'European Education in the 21st Century', in B. de Witte and C. Forder (eds.), *The Common Law of Europe and the Future of Legal Education* (Kluwer 1992) p. 7 at p. 14–15.

century, law and legal education became nationally oriented and studying abroad became an extravagance.[14] Yet, looking to the future, law will increasingly be based on a new-style *ius commune*, comprising principles and rules that are common to EU member states as a consequence of harmonisation and unification measures.[15] This must inevitably have consequences for legal education and the language in which it is taught.

C. A European-Oriented Law Curriculum

This evolving European legal environment calls for "European" law graduates. Since European integration and the Europeanisation of legal practice require lawyers to increasingly deal across borders, they must be flexible enough to think across jurisdictional boundaries and to become "interpreters" of different legal systems and traditions.[16] They must be comfortable to work with divergent national legal systems, or at least be capable of collaborating effectively with their counterparts in other jurisdictions. To be able to communicate effectively with each other, they must be able to understand each other's legal backgrounds, including its traditions, concepts, institutions and style of legal reasoning as well as each other's legal language.

This profile of a "European" law graduate calls for a different type of law curriculum. Rather than focusing on the laws peculiar to an individual national system, it requires a European-oriented law curriculum that combines the comparative study of national legal systems with an intensified study of European law in all fields of law. A European-oriented law curriculum trains these European law graduates to swiftly understand new legal systems, to identify the common European or international origins of divergent national laws and to solve transnational legal problems. It takes both a top-down as well as a bottom-up approach, in the sense that it looks at the supranational influence coming from the European Union and its impact on the national legal systems of the Member States, as well as looking at the convergence of those national legal systems.

---

[14] *Ibid.*, p. 15.

[15] Also see Fauvarque-Cosson, *supra* n. 5, p. 11.

[16] Bernabe-Riefkohl, *supra* n. 4, p. 149, who also writes that these lawyers have the 'responsibility for bridging the gulf of disparate national experiences, traditions, institutions and customs' (p. 153); also see Von Mehren, *supra* n. 4; Glenn, *supra* n. 3.

A European-oriented law curriculum aims to educate "European" law graduates. This does not mean that it aims to create specialists in EU law, nor is the aim to create experts on all the national legal systems studied. The latter would, after all, be impossible in a bachelor programme. It is clearly not possible to achieve the same depth of knowledge of the law of a number of different national legal systems in a European-oriented law curriculum in the same period of time as a national-oriented law curriculum is able to achieve with respect to its national legal system. Consequently, the focus of a European-oriented law curriculum is different from the "ordinary" law curriculum since the primary aim is not to teach comprehensively details of the national, positivistic law.[17] This different focus of a European-oriented law curriculum is related to the different profile of a "European law graduate", who should be adept to deal with law that is undergoing constant transformation as a result *inter alia* of European integration and globalisation.

D. The Role of Language in a European-Oriented Law Curriculum

1. *The Selection of Language(s)*

The role of language in educating European lawyers is naturally a difficult one. Law and language are closely interlinked due to the system-specificity of legal terminology and concepts.[18] Although it is possible to observe the development of a body of European law with its own legal terminology and concepts that can be taught through the medium of English; in the context of teaching a comparative law curriculum, the situation is not so simple. Just as law and language are interlinked, there is an intrinsic connection between comparative legal studies and languages.[19]

---

[17] Also see De Witte and Forder, *supra* n. 6, p. viii-ix, who write that such a curriculum aims to foster the necessary 'dexterity of thinking across jurisdictional boundaries', albeit 'to the detriment of encyclopaedic knowledge of one single legal system'.

[18] G.-R. de Groot, 'Legal Translation', in J. M. Smits (ed.), *Elgar Encyclopedia of Comparative Law* (Edward Elgar 2006) p. 423.

[19] See B. Grossfeld, 'Comparatists and Languages', in P. Legrand and R. Munday (eds.), *Comparative Legal Studies: Traditions and Transitions* (Cambridge University Press 2004) p. 154.

Unlike scientific or technical terminology, legal terminology or legal language is bound to its own legal system. Even where a number of countries use the same natural language, the legal language may nevertheless differ since legal terminology and concepts can diverge. This diversity of languages and legal concepts would not be so problematic if national laws followed a common system, or would have strong common roots, but this is largely lacking.[20]

Due to the interconnection between law and language, the best way to study any legal system is to read the legal texts in their original language. However, to access foreign laws in their original language requires fluency not only in the natural language of that legal system, but also its legal language.

In the context of legal education, a truly European-oriented law curriculum would appear to require mastery of the 23 official languages of the European Union.[21] Such an approach is obviously unrealistic, and consequently a selection of languages should be made. In any event, such a curriculum should be taught by multilingual staff and its students should also master a number of European languages to enable them to study the laws of different member states in their original language. But which languages should be selected?

An initial restriction could be made by limiting the number of national legal systems to be compared, thus restricting the necessary language skills to the languages of those countries. This is also practical from an educational point of view, since there is little added value in educating students in all European legal systems. A curriculum in which all the legal systems of the Member States of the EU are addressed in all fields of law would be impossible to teach within the standard three or four year bachelor degree structure. Furthermore, it is not the aim of a European-oriented law curriculum to train law graduates with detailed knowledge of the national laws all EU Member States. Instead, the focus is on training law graduates who are capable of adjusting to different legal systems and who can think across national jurisdictional boundaries. Comprehensive knowledge of all national legal systems of

---

[20] Schlechtriem, *supra* n. 6, p. 535.

[21] Bulgarian, Czech, Danish, Dutch, English, Estonian, Finnish, French, German, Greek, Hungarian, Irish, Italian, Latvian, Lithuanian, Maltese, Polish, Portuguese, Romanian, Slovak, Slovenian, Spanish and Swedish: Art. 1, Regulation No. 1 determining the languages to be used by the European Economic Community, Official Journal L 17, 6.10.1958, p. 385, as last amended by Council Regulation (EC) No. 1791/2006 of 20.11.2006, Official Journal L 363, 20.12.2006, p. 1.

the European Union is not necessary to achieve that objective. A selection of legal systems, and thus a limitation of the number of languages that need to be mastered should therefore be made.

It is generally accepted that the major European legal systems representing the major legal families must be addressed in comparative law courses: English law, French law and German law.[22] This would make three languages relevant: English, French and German.[23] Students opting for a European-oriented law study tend to be more internationally-oriented and are often therefore generally better at languages.[24] Nevertheless, even the requirement that students are able to speak, write and read English, as well as read French and German at an academic level, is difficult to meet in practice. There is consequently a reluctance in countries where French and German are not the natural language, to make students read (lengthy) texts in French and German. English consequently tends to be chosen as the medium for teaching this European-oriented law curriculum. This choice is also reflected in the many English-medium LL.M. programmes that have been developed throughout Europe.

2. *The Choice for English*

That English is the chosen teaching language of a European-oriented law curriculum is related to a number of factors. First, English is emerging as the single, dominant language in the field of European and comparative law.[25] This can be seen in its dominance as the

[22] See K. Zweigert and H. Kötz, *An Introduction to Comparative Law* (Clarendon Press 1998).

[23] Alternatively: Storme, *supra* n. 6, p. 143: 'That several languages will have to be used in this process is equally obvious. English is not the first anywhere on the Continent mainland except Gibraltar, furthermore, this language, on account of the special features of common law, could be unsuitable as a lingua franca for law. I have in mind particularly, of course, but not exclusively, procedural law. Needless to say, one cannot learn to use all European languages, but the objective criterion should be languages that are spoken in more than one European country, which prompts the following selection: German, French, English, Dutch and Swedish!'

[24] I. Sieben and E. Lintjens, *English Language Bachelor European Law School: Recruitment and Labour Market Position* (Research Centre for Education and the Labour Market, Faculty of Economics and Business Administration, Maastricht University 2006). This survey revealed that the final grades in high school for Dutch, English, French and German of European Law School students are generally higher than the grades of their Dutch law counterparts.

[25] V. Grosswald Curran, 'Comparative Law and Language', in R. Zimmerman and M. Reimann (eds.), *The Oxford Handbook of Comparative Law* (Oxford University Press 2006) p. 675; Akkermans, *supra* n. 6, p. 803.

language of European legal scholarship: international conferences, books and journals targeting an international readership are primarily in English, or where they are bi- or multilingual, English is generally the primary language. Second, English is the generally-accepted language of international business. Third, English is also the most common working language in European and international organisations. In the area of private law, for example, the predominant working language of academic groups drafting common principles is English.[26] Fourth, English is the common language used in higher education when the professor and students do not share a native language.[27] In essence,

> English plays, nowadays, the role of the international *lingua franca*, whatever the domain; jurists from different jurisdictions, cultures and mother tongue, regularly communicate with people in other countries in English.[28]

The 2006 special Eurobarometer survey on 'Europeans and their languages' reveals that English remains the most widely-spoken foreign language throughout Europe.[29] The survey also reveals that the language abilities of European citizens are expanding. As the EU policies promoting multilingualism, which aim at European citizens learning two foreign languages from an early age, take effect and other languages gain ground, it may be more realistic to work towards a multilingual European-oriented law curriculum in the future. In the meantime, English remains the common language and it thus tends to be the chosen medium for teaching such a curriculum.

An important question raised by this type of English-medium legal education, however, is whether, in light of the intrinsic connection

---

[26] V. Heutger, 'Legal Language and the Process of Drafting the Principles on a European Law of Sales', 12 *Electronic Journal of Comparative Law* (2008), <www.ejcl.org/122/abs122-3.html>, visited Oct. 26, 2010. Also see for instance the comments and notes to the Principles of European Contract Law which are in English: O. Lando and H. Beale, *Principles of European Contract Law* (Kluwer 2000).

[27] Grosswald Curran, *supra* n. 25; A. Kocbek, 'The Cultural Embeddedness of Legal Texts', 9 *Journal of Language & Translation* (2008) p. 49 at p. 58; House, *supra* n. 10, p. 570.

[28] F. Maschio, 'The Importance of English Language in the Education of European Jurists: Recent Developments in the Italian Academic Scenario' 3 *European Journal of Legal Education* (2006) p. 135 at p. 139; Kocbek, *supra* n. 27; House, *supra* n. 10, p. 557.

[29] Special Eurobarometer 243, Wave 64.3, 'Europeans and their languages', Febr. 2006, <ec.europa.eu/public_opinion/archives/ebs/ebs_243_en.pdf>, visited Oct. 26, 2010. Interestingly, the number of non-native speakers of English is larger than the number of native speakers; *see* House, *supra* n. 10, p. 557.

between law and language, a legal system and legal texts can be studied effectively in any language but the original.[30] This type of comparative teaching requires constant translation of the original legal concept from the source legal language into English. Inevitably, something will be 'lost in translation' when for instance German or French legal concepts, principles and laws, are studied through the medium of English, since the English language cannot express the distinctive style or mode of thinking of a legal system that is conveyed by the original language.

This is particularly problematic since the language chosen as the medium for teaching is itself closely connected to a particular legal system(s). English is the language of the common law. Since English itself is embedded in its own national legal system(s), teaching and studying the law of various legal systems through the medium of English can consequently lead to numerous linguistic problems. Common law and civil law systems diverge extensively in their legal sources, legal concepts and principles, legal reasoning, legal culture, legal language, etc; but these differences also exist amongst civil law systems.[31] English legal terminology, stemming from the Anglo-American common law is very different from the terminology used on the continent.[32] This in turn is due to the different legal concepts and principles, but also the different sources of law and legislative drafting style as well as the style of legal reasoning, which all impact on the way a language develops into a legal language.

Nevertheless, as will be seen below, the experience at Maastricht University with the European Law School demonstrates that English as a medium for teaching and studying law can provide an effective common ground for students to analyse, discuss, and understand the law. English is used as 'a language for communication'.[33] It is an instrument or vehicle for communication, for making oneself understood in an international, multilingual setting. The English language is used as the

---

30 Also see Grosswald Curran, *supra* n. 25.

31 See Zweigert and Kötz, *supra* n. 22, p, 69; also B. S. Markesinis, 'Judicial Style and Judicial Reasoning in England and Germany', 59 *Cambridge Law Journal* (2000) p. 294, who highlights the differences between the English and German judicial style and technique which is very insightful for understanding the legal systems at hand, but also illustrates where legal systems can learn from each other, suggesting for instance that German legal academics and practitioners could benefit from studying how English judges 'craft' their judgments and how English judges could benefit from looking at German substantive law and its techniques of controlling litigation.

32 Maschio, *supra* n. 28, p. 135.

33 House, *supra* n. 10, p. 559.

medium for teaching a European-oriented law curriculum. This is not the same as teaching legal English, in the sense of teaching the legal language of the Anglo-American common law.[34] The key is to create a linguistic framework of legal concepts in the medium of English, but to neutralise or defuse those terms from traditional common law concepts and terminology. In this process, comparative law plays an important role. With English as the common language of discourse it is necessary to construct the comparative meaning to be given to the terms being used.

2. *The Comparative Methodology in Practice*

To illustrate how this could function, let us focus on the concept of a "contract". It is not possible to provide a single common, uniform definition of a contract that is the same in all legal systems studied. Although, for instance, the German *Vertrag*, Dutch *overeenkomst*, and French *contrat* are conventionally translated as being a "contract", they are not the same as far as their content is concerned, and certainly not the same as the English legal concept of "contract". The systemic qualification of contracts and the constituent requirements to form a valid contract differ among the various legal systems.

In the English law of contract, for example, the doctrine of consideration plays a very important role for determining whether a valid contract has been formed. This doctrine requires for the valid conclusion of a contract that the promises made by the parties be supported by consideration, in the sense that the promise is given in exchange for a promise, performance or forbearance by the other party. Consequently, the fundamental characteristic of the concept of a contract under English law is the element of exchange. In contrast, civil law systems do not know the doctrine of consideration for the valid conclusion of a contract; this element of exchange is not essential to form a valid contract. A gratuitous promise can also be regarded as a valid contract, provided the requisite agreement and intention to be legally bound is present.

A further illustration is provided by the systemic qualification of contracts. What is generally referred to as a "contract" in German law, is more correctly referred to as a "contractual relationship of obligation" (*vertragliches Schuldverhältnis*). An individual is able to voluntarily

---

[34] See C. Frade, 'Power dynamics and legal English', 26 *World Englishes* (2007) p. 48.

assume obligations and enter into a legal relationship with another individual by means of a legal transaction (*Rechtsgeschäft*), and to create a relationship of obligation (*Schuldverhältnis*) by means of a legal transaction (*Rechtsgeschäft*), parties must enter into a contract (*Vertrag*). This in turn is done through an exchange of declarations of intention (*Willenserklärung*). When looking at what a "contract" is under German law, it is consequently necessary to consider three basic concepts: contractual relationship of obligation, legal transaction and declaration of intention. In comparison, French legal doctrine classifies a "contract" as a juridical act (*acte juridique*), in the sense of a voluntary act that is intended to create legal relations, since a "contract" is a source of obligation that is founded on the parties' agreement. French law then distinguishes between the *contrat* and the *convention*. Whereas a *contrat* is an agreement that creates obligations, a *convention* is any agreement based on consent, and includes agreements to modify or terminate a contract or transfer an obligation. A *contrat* is therefore a sub-category of the larger category of *convention*.

These illustrations demonstrate the importance of the comparative teaching methodology. Although the English word "contract" is used to discuss a common concept in all legal systems, through comparative legal analysis it becomes clear that although we might attach the general label "contract" to a particular phenomenon, or translate *overeenkomst, Vertrag, contrat* with the word "contract", it would be incorrect to equate such national concepts with the English common law concept of "contract" since they do not mean the same thing. During the teaching process, it becomes necessary to neutralise the term "contract" when discussing, for instance, the German concept of *Vertrag*, the Dutch concept of *overeenkomst*, the French concept of *contrat* and the English common law concept of "contract". It becomes important to neutralise the English language to a certain extent, in the sense that it is made clear to students that the national concepts of a "contract" differ.

In this context, the international composition of the student body and an interactive learning environment can play an important role. Students should be encouraged, and even required, to prepare materials in other languages, in particular their own native language. It would be a bizarre and even counter-productive situation, for instance, if German-speaking students would study German law in English, and never look at the original German text. For this reason, in a European-oriented law curriculum students should be encouraged to read and study laws, cases and textbooks in the original language, if they are able, in addition to the English language material. Consequently, a German student, for instance, is able to explain to the other non-German speaking students, through the medium of English as the common language of communication, the details and nuances behind a particular German concept based on their readings in the original German language. Likewise, a French student can explain the French legal texts.

Where the teaching set up is small-scale and the class has a multicultural and multilingual composition, it is possible to exchange a variety of perspectives, which enriches discussions and learning outcomes and allows students to experience the true strength of the group's cultural and linguistic diversity. This adds richness to a European-oriented law curriculum. Through this process, students also experience the difficulty of comparative law and the ever-present danger of misunderstandings. A problem-oriented comparative teaching method is highly adept to facilitate and in fact aims at such interaction between students.

It should be noted that the students of a European-oriented bachelor curriculum generally would not have a background in the law or legal terminology of their own country. Like any first year law student, they must be initiated into a legal language. Through the medium of English, students of a European-oriented law curriculum are introduced to a developing European legal language, which focuses on EU law, but also on the comparison of legal concepts in different legal systems.

D. Case Study: The European Law School at Maastricht University

1. *Background*

In advance of general trends in Europe today, Maastricht University launched the concept of a European Law School already in 1991.[35] In contrast to the national orientation of the traditional law curriculum,

[35] The Faculty of Law of the then Rijksuniversiteit Limburg, now Maastricht University, organised a conference on the occasion of its tenth anniversary on "Legal Education in the Future" with the purpose of exploring the possibility of developing a wholly new curriculum in legal studies based on European and comparative law, the results of the conference can be found in De Witte and Forder, *supra* n. 6; *also see* the contributions to Heringa and Akkermans, *supra* n. 6.

the European Law School aims to bring together students from various European countries with a view to teaching them an innovative curriculum with a European and comparative law focus. At the time, a fully-fledged European-oriented law curriculum was still too ambitious, since European law was not yet sufficiently developed to form the foundation of a law curriculum. Nevertheless, a first step in the direction of such a European-oriented law curriculum was taken by introducing a post-graduate LL.M. programme in 1992, the *Magister Iuris Communis* (Master of European and Comparative Law). With the knowledge and experience gained from this LL.M. programme, it proved possible to set up the European Law School, which welcomed its first cohort of students in 1995.

The European Law School combines traditional legal education in the national law of the Netherlands taught in the Dutch language, with courses taught through the medium of English that approach the study of law from a comparative and European angle, looking for a common core and a developing European law. At that time, it was still thought that it would be 'unworkable and unwise' to introduce a truly European-oriented law curriculum, as the state of European law had still not ripened or developed enough to form the basis for such a curriculum.[36]

By 2006, however, the richness of European law in its broadest sense could no longer be denied, leading to a further innovation in legal education with the introduction of an English language track in the European Law School. This entirely English-taught law curriculum is detached from any one national legal system and provides a truly European-oriented law curriculum, teaching law entirely from a comparative and European perspective through the medium of English. Consequently, within the European Law School, there are now two tracks: the regular track that combines traditional legal education in the national legal system of the Netherlands in the national language (Dutch) with courses taught through the medium of English on comparative and European law (ELS-regular); and a new comparative and European law curriculum taught entirely through the medium of English (ELS-ELT).

---

[36] A.W. Heringa, 'Towards a European Law School! A Proposal for a Competitive, Diversified Model of Transnational Co-Operation', in M. Faure et al. (eds.), *Towards a European Ius Commune in Legal Education and Legal Research* (Intersentia 2002) p. 3 at p. 5.

2. *The Curriculum*

At Maastricht University, all bachelor law students, except the ELS-ELT students, follow a common first year which is grounded in the law of the Netherlands. After the first year, students make a choice between continuing their studies in Dutch law and opting for tax law or European Law School - regular track. The ELS-regular programme therefore only really starts in the second year. In this second year, students continue to follow foundational courses in Dutch law to give them a thorough knowledge of the national law of the Netherlands in order to allow them to graduate fulfilling the requirements to be admitted to the Dutch bar. However, they also take additional courses on comparative law, legal English, common law and moot court training taught through the medium of English. During the second year of their studies, the students therefore follow courses taught in Dutch and English. The third year of the bachelor and the master European Law School – which students can opt for after completion of the bachelor degree – reflect a fully-fledged European-oriented law curriculum.[37] In all areas of law (contract, property, tort, constitutional, administrative, company, labour and social security, criminal and procedural law), students are taught the European dimension and fundamental doctrines and concepts in the main European legal systems as well as advanced courses on European Union law. All these courses are taught through the medium of English.

In contrast, students enrolled in the ELS-ELT programme follow an entirely separate curriculum. Their courses are not embedded in a particular legal system, instead they follow a European-based curriculum from their very first day. Students of the ELS-ELT programme first follow an introductory course on law and legal English. This foundational course aims to teach them fundamental concepts and principles underlying various legal systems and to provide an understanding of what law is. At the same time, they learn English legal terms of art in various fields. Throughout the remainder of the curriculum, students follow courses on private law, constitutional and administrative law, criminal

[37] Pre-Bologna, the European Law School was a four year programme leading to the Dutch title *meester in de rechten (mr.)*.With the Bologna operation, the four year programme was divided into a three year bachelor programme and a one year master. Although students who have completed the ELS-regular bachelor are free to choose any master they wish.

law, international and European law, legal philosophy and legal history from a comparative and European perspective.

A core component of a European-oriented law curriculum is the comparative study of law. The approach, however, is not one of classic comparative law, looking at the details of national legal systems to identify similarities and differences. Studying the details of different legal systems is only one aspect, and not the defining attribute to this curriculum. The comparative approach goes further, exploring the role of law in society, the feasibility, desirability and necessity of measures taken by the EU, and the impact these have directly and indirectly on national legal systems. The focus is on teaching students the skills necessary to acquire knowledge about legal systems, to make them aware of foreign legal concepts, the existence of fundamental differences and similarities and the divergence in approaches and methods of legal reasoning. This should lead to open-minded and creative law graduates who have acquired a critical understanding of the complex interrelationship between European and national law.

Consequently, the comparative law methodology adopted in the European Law School is to view comparative law as a teaching method: law is taught comparatively.[38] Comparative law has been integrated in the teaching method by adopting a functional, problem-oriented approach. This approach to teaching is reinforced by the general teaching method at Maastricht University, which can be characterised as being problem-based, small-scale and skills oriented.[39] The focus on problems is well-suited to a comparative law teaching method, in particular, a functional approach to comparative law. Students are able to focus on how a particular problem is dealt with in different legal systems. The focus is on how different legal systems adopt different or similar approaches to deal with a particular legal problem common to all legal systems. Students are thus presented with hypothetical scenarios which involve various legal problems. In this way, they discover that all legal systems are confronted with the task of creating rules to deal with particular problems, but that the solutions they choose can differ significantly. Progressing through the curriculum, they are able

[38] *See also* Heringa, *supra* n. 36, p. 8.

[39] It should be observed that Maastricht University is unique in that the educational model of problem-based learning (PBL) has been at the core of teaching at Maastricht University since it was founded.

to deal with new problems, rules and complex situations. This teaching method emphasises the development of the legal skills needed in a changing world.

The small-scale set up of the problem-based learning teaching method and the international composition of the student body,[40] brings together students from divergent national backgrounds. Through this small-scale set up and multicultural composition, it is possible to exchange a variety of perspectives, which enriches discussions and learning outcomes and allows students to experience the true strength of the group's cultural and linguistic diversity.

3. *The Link with European Legal Scholarship*

The gradual development of a truly European-oriented law programme, in the sense of first creating an LL.M. programme in comparative and European law, followed by the establishment of the European Law School which combines national legal education with comparative and European courses before creating a fully-fledged European-oriented law curriculum, was necessary. It was necessitated by the pace of development of the law, since at the time the concept of a European-oriented law curriculum was launched, the state of the law in Europe was not quite ripe enough for such a curriculum.

Further factors necessitating such a phased introduction of a European-oriented law curriculum relate to the need to develop expertise in all areas of the curriculum. This has two important dimensions. In the first place, it is important to ensure that faculty staff are specialised to teach this new curriculum in the sense that they have conducted comparative law research in their fields into the national legal systems to be studied, the developments of European law, and the interaction between national and European law. It is evident that the interaction between the Europeanisation of legal scholarship and the Europeanisation of legal education is essential in this context.

Since the medium of instruction in the European Law School is English, the teaching staff must also sufficiently master that language to be able to teach effectively in it. For this reason, academic staff is

[40] In the ELS-ELT, the student population roughly comprises one third Dutch, one third German and one third rest of the world. The nationalities are diverse, coming from around Europe (e.g. Poland, Sweden, UK, Italy, Bulgaria, Finland) and the world (e.g. US, China, Brazil).

increasingly selected on the basis of their ability to teach courses from a European and comparative perspective through the medium of English and are encouraged to engage in legal scholarship at a European and international level through participation in European and international conferences and publication in European and international journals. As mentioned above, English is the dominant language of European, even international, scholarship, since European and international conferences, books and journals targeting a European and international audience are primarily in English.

In the second place, it is necessary to develop appropriate teaching materials which have a European and comparative law focus. A European-oriented law curriculum taught in English requires suitable teaching materials which have a European and comparative law focus, written in a common language. One of the challenges facing the implementation of such a curriculum is to acquire appropriate teaching materials. Unlike studying a national legal system, however, there is still a general lack of teaching materials to provide the foundation for such a curriculum. Although there is a vast amount of English language textbooks on the law, these books are primarily written by for instance English or American scholars for use in English or American law schools to teach English or American law. They use legal English to analyse and explain Anglo-American common law. It is clear that it is often ill-suited to teaching a European-oriented law curriculum which focuses on comparative law and the development of European legal concepts. Even when these textbooks engage in comparisons with other legal systems, or address the Europeanisation of law, this is often done from a common law perspective.

The past decades have been marked by a Europeanisation of legal scholarship, which has led to a vast array of eminent comparative law treatises, monographs, encyclopaedias, and academic journals devoted to European and comparative law; however, only a few of these publications can be used for teaching purposes. Much of what is written is not directed at the undergraduate student population, but is written by scholars for postgraduate students and academics. For this reason, it has become necessary to develop new teaching material that is suited to teaching a European-oriented law curriculum. However, developing these new textbooks is not without challenges of its own, as they need to find a common language, common legal foundations and principles in which to discuss the law. This is closely tied to the development of a European legal scholarship. Through the emergence of English as the common and dominant language in the field of European and comparative law, this has become possible.[41]

Firstly, it is necessary that the primary materials are widely available in their original language, but also, for teaching purposes, in the English language. This not only includes the primary texts on European law, such as treaties, directives and regulations, but also national legislative provisions.[42] Ideally, such a primary materials source book would include the legal provisions in the original language as well as in an English translation for teaching purposes. This allows students to become familiar with the original text, in its authentic form in the sense of style and syntax, which forms an important part of understanding a legal system. At the same time, the English translation allows students to understand the original text and develops a common linguistic framework for comparison.

Secondly, textbooks and treatises are needed on each field of the law. These textbooks need to address the field of law from a comparative and European perspective, by analysing the structure, rules, concepts, principles and institutions of national laws and comparing the similarities and differences between them. Such books might address the historical development of legal systems as well. When comparing legal systems, in particular those on the continent, an understanding of the historical development of those systems and the common legal heritage shared by many countries through the reception of Roman law can be enlightening to explain the similarities and parallel developments. The analysis could then develop to consider whether the similarities

---

[41] Grosswald Curran, *supra* n. 25; Akkermans, *supra* n. 6, p. 803.

[42] Collaboration in the context of the European Law School at Maastricht University has led to the publication of Ph. Kiiver and N. Kornet (eds.), *Selected National, European and International Provisions of Public and Private Law* (Europa Law Publishers 2010), which is a compilation of national, European and International provisions of public and private law covering all areas taught in the main curriculum and includes a selection of important legal provisions from France, Germany, the Netherlands and the United Kingdom which have proven particularly relevant in the European-oriented law curriculum. Sources are reproduced in the original English or are rendered as English translations. Unlike many other translations, the translations in this collection try to remain true to the content, style and syntax of the original texts. This allows students to appreciate, to the extent that a translation can do so, not only the substance but also the authentic form of foreign legal sources in the English language. The collection does not include the full text in the original source language of provisions that have been translated, however for easy reference, but also to familiarise students with original language terminology, key legal terms and proper names are added in the original language as in-text citations.

reflect a common core of rules and principles that could for instance constitute the basis for harmonisation or unification of the law, or whether the differences are so fundamental that they stand in the way of convergence between systems, therefore requiring choices to be made should harmonisation or unification be pursued. Further consideration would clearly need to be given to the necessity, desirability and feasibility of harmonisation in the particular field of law. Also an analysis of measures already taken at a European and international level, and the direct and indirect impact these measures have on national legal systems could be included.

A key example of this type of book is Hein Kötz' *European Contract Law*,[43] which discusses contract law dislocated from a national legal framework and describes a European law that does not (yet) exist. In doing so, it creates a framework for discussing and teaching the law of contract in a European perspective. Further examples of innovative textbooks that could be useful in a European-oriented law curriculum include Markesinis' comparative treatises on German contract law[44] and tort law.[45] In these textbooks, Markesinis and his fellow authors analyse and explain the German law of contract in English and with comparative observations from the perspective of the English common law. With *Constitutions Compared*,[46] Heringa and Kiiver have written a textbook for a European-oriented approach to teaching constitutional law. Each topic of constitutional law is first introduced in a general, comparative overview and then further elaborated on in separate country chapters on that specific topic.

Thirdly, in addition to primary legislative materials, it is necessary that compilations of relevant national case law are also available and accessible to students studying law from a comparative and European perspective. In this context, the Ius Commune Casebooks for the Common Law of Europe are an important source.[47] This project fosters cooperation among legal scholars from around European to develop teaching materials for use in comparative law courses. The casebooks

---

[43] H. Kötz, *European Contract Law. Volume I* (Clarendon Press 1997).
[44] B. S. Markesinis et al., *The German Law of Obligations. A Comparative Treatise* (Hart Publishing 2006).
[45] B. S. Markesinis and H. Unberath, *The German Law of Torts. A Comparative Treatise* (Hart Publishing 2002).
[46] A. W. Heringa and Ph. Kiiver, *Constitutions Compared. An Introduction to Comparative Constitutional Law* (Intersentia 2009).
[47] See <www.casebooks.eu>.

comprise extracts from national sources, in particular case law, and European sources, which are put in context through introductions, explanatory and comparative notes and questions. The objective of the casebooks project is to adopt a bottom-up approach in order to uncover common principles already underlying national legal systems.

It should be noted that the work of European legal scholars to develop sets of principles such as the Principles of European Contract Law[48] as well as the results of the Study Group on European Civil Code[49] and the Draft Common Frame of Reference[50] also play an important role in creating a framework for discussion in the field of private law through the medium of English. They establish a common legal terminology which facilitates analysis and discussion. Through their development they lay down an evolving common core of principles in Europe. The commentaries and comparative notes on the national legal systems also aid the comparative teaching methodology. However, it should be noted that there are still problems with respect to developing a common linguistic framework, since the use of English terminology in various international and European sources reveals differences and inconsistencies. Looking at the UN Convention on Contracts for the International Sale of Goods, the EC Consumer Sales Directive,[51] and the Principles of European Contract Law, for example, the use of different legal terminology for the same concept remains apparent.[52]

4. *Legal Barriers: Access to the Legal Professions*

The European Law School aims to graduate students who can work in the legal environment of larger companies and specifically the larger law firms as well as government ministries. Nevertheless, national law sets up a significant barrier to achieving the goal of educating truly "European" law graduates since to be admitted to the bar, graduates

---

[48] Lando and Beale, *supra* n. 26.

[49] Including various editions on Principles of European Law, such as Lease of Goods, Unjustified Enrichment, Service Contracts, Loan Contracts, published by Sellier.

[50] C. Von Bar and E. Clive (eds.), *Principles, Definitions and Model Rules of European Private Law. Draft Common Frame of Reference (DCFR)*, prepared by the Study Group on a European Civil Code/Research Group on EC Private Law (Acquis Group) (Sellier European Law Publishers 2009).

[51] Directive 99/44/EC on certain aspects of the sale of consumer goods and associated guarantees, Official Journal L 171, 07.07.1999, p. 12.

[52] Heutger, *supra* n. 26.

must meet the requirements of the national bar. In the Netherlands, that necessitates educating students in the national law of the Netherlands.

Not all programmes give access to the typical legal professions such as the bar and the judiciary. To become a lawyer, prosecutor or judge in the Netherlands, it is necessary to graduate with a law degree that satisfies specific requirements. This is governed by legislation and supplemented with further requirements for each profession by an order in council (*Algemene Maatregel van Bestuur*). Where the programme satisfies the requirements laid down, it will give civil effect for that particular profession in the Netherlands. "Civil effect" means that the law programme comprises those components that satisfy the requirements to be appointed to the bar and the judiciary. In other words, a law degree with civil effect gives graduates the possibility to start training to become a practicing lawyer (*advocaat*), a public prosecutor or a judge in the Netherlands. According to the law, to be admitted as a member of the bar (Article 2 of the Advocatenwet) or the judiciary (Article 1d of the Wet rechtspositie rechterlijke ambtenaren) it is necessary to complete both a bachelor's and master's degree in law at university. In addition, various orders in council specify the courses for each professional group that should be completed in these programmes.[53] In essence, this means that students must study the private law, constitutional law, administrative law, criminal law, civil and criminal procedural law of the Netherlands.

For students in the ELS-regular track, the civil effect requirement is not problematic. The mandatory courses in the first two and a half years of the bachelor programme ensure that, provided the student completes a master's degree in law, a student obtains civil effect. With respect to these students, a study has shown that they are more likely to find employment as a lawyer (40 percent) or a company lawyer (16 percent) than graduates from international and European law, and Dutch law. The majority of ELS graduates is employed in commercial services, followed by government.[54]

To facilitate access to the legal profession for students enrolled in the ELS-ELT, a minor in the national law of the Netherlands has been

[53] Art. 1 of the *Besluit beroepsvereisten advocatuur*; Art. 38b, para. 2 and 3, and Art. 38c, para. 2 and 3 of the *Besluit rechtspositie rechterlijke ambtenaren*; Art. 21a, para. 2 of the *Besluit opleiding rechterlijke ambtenaren*; Art. 1 of the *Besluit beroepsvereisten Raad van State*.

[54] Sieben and Lintjens, *supra* n. 24, p. viii.

developed. In the third year of the bachelor programme, those students who opt for acquiring civil effect follow a mandatory programme comprising the essential courses on Dutch law. These courses are taught in the Dutch language, which requires non-Dutch speakers to learn the Dutch language. In the second half of the second year, they are prepared for studying Dutch law in Dutch by means of three introductory courses on Dutch private law, Dutch administrative law and Dutch criminal and criminal procedure law. Although students who follow this Dutch law minor obtain civil effect once they have completed a master in law, students are encouraged to opt for a master in Dutch law in order to be competitive on the Dutch labour market. After all, before being able to avail themselves of their free movement rights to provide services and establish in another member state, they will first have to complete the three-year vocational training as an *advocaat-stagiare* with a law firm in the Netherlands.

This need to create a Dutch law minor to give students access to the legal profession demonstrates that in the absence of a European system of legal education and of European standards of access to the legal profession, the need to train lawyers in national law in the national language in order to give them access to the European labour market for legal services remains.

E. Concluding Remarks

Legal education in Europe has not remained unaffected by the Europeanisation of law and legal practice, this is apparent from the inclusion of courses on EU law and comparative law in many law curricula and the sudden increase in master programmes in European and comparative law. This European legal environment requires, in addition to specialists in national law, 'European' law graduates who are comfortable with different jurisdictions, who are flexible enough to adapt to and find their way around different legal systems, who can identify the European and international origins of laws, and identify legal issues and provide solutions to transnational legal problems. This calls for innovative programmes in which the law curriculum is integrally adapted to the Europeanisation of law and legal practice. The reorientation of the law curriculum towards a European-oriented law curriculum which teaches law from a comparative and European perspective has consequences for the way in which law is taught and the language in which it is taught.

Ideally, a European-oriented law curriculum would be multilingual, allowing students to more fully grasp the intricacies of individual national legal systems. However, this does not yet appear realistic to implement. Like in the days of the old *ius commune*, when students and professors came from different national and linguistic backgrounds and the law was taught from the same basic scholarly works written in the common language, we must now also find a common language for students and professors to use as a medium for their exchange. English has emerged as the common language for European legal scholarship, European legal practice and European legal education. This contribution has aimed to share some of the experiences and challenges of offering a European-oriented law curriculum through the medium of English.

PART IV

CONCLUSIONS

CHAPTER THIRTEEN

BILINGUAL LEGAL EDUCATION IN EUROPE AND CANADA

Bethan Sarah Davies

The articles incorporated into this volume provide the reader with a unique insight into very differing situations in relation to minority language provision within legal education across Europe and beyond. The authors of each chapter have very disparate experiences, and provide the reader with a wealth of knowledge and understanding of the issues affecting minority language provision, particularly within legal education across Europe and Canada.

The objective of this concluding chapter is to provide an overview of the overarching issues addressed within the chapters, identifying key obstacles that affect a number of countries with two state languages, and countries with a minority and majority language. The aim of this chapter is to distinguish means of successfully addressing these recognised obstacles to minority and second language provision within legal education, particularly across Europe, in order to attain a provision of legal education akin to that of the French language in Canada.

The significant obstacles to minority language provision within higher education as highlighted within the chapters of this volume appear to be, a deficient legal requirement within countries for minority language proficiency within the legal profession. An acute lack of resources, ranging from a lack of experienced teaching staff, a need for materials for both teaching staff and students; and a severe lack of minority language terminology within the legal discipline. The third key difficulty is that of the impact of globalisation. With the development of study abroad programmes and a political will, particularly within Europe, supporting the movement of students from one member state to another to study and broaden horizons – what is its impact upon minority language provision within legal education? The final aspect discussed within this chapter however, provides some hope for the future of minority language provision, within the field of legal education in the higher education sector. This portion of the chapter will focus upon solutions developed by individual countries to respond to the challenges facing minority language provision within legal education, and will discuss the possibility of adapting such resolutions within other higher education systems that provide minority language instruction, or provision in both state languages.

A. Key Obstacles

1. *Legal Obligation of Linguistic Attainment for Bilingual Legal Practitioners*

The case studies identified within this volume underline the concern regarding a lack of legal obligation demanding a level of linguistic attainment in both state languages within the legal profession, for those who profess to be able to work through the medium of both state languages, and high ranking legal officials who are required to deal with cases in both state languages, or the majority and minority language. Undoubtedly, this lack of legal obligation leads to the prolongation of the impression that the majority language or one particular language, is the language of the law, and that no respect and acknowledgement is given to the second or minority language. This in turn perpetuates the idea that legal training and education in the majority language only is required for successful entry into the profession.

This volume demonstrates that legislation requiring official recognition of an individuals' bilingual proficiency, should be a prerequisite for all lawyers intending to practice bilingually. Such requirements will in turn, ensure that the bilingual service offered within a legal system will be equal in its application and capacity, and will unquestionably intensify the need for greater bilingual provision within legal education. Such an obligation would further support the aim of the normalisation of minority languages within both the legal field, and within each community in its entirety.

This is identified within the Catalan case study, where an imbalanced situation currently exists. Catalan is recognised as an equal language to that of Spanish, and individuals have the right to use the minority language when dealing with the legal system. However, entrance into the legal profession is governed by central government, and access is dependent on mastering the Spanish language only.[1]

[1] Art. 36 Spanish Constitution and Art. 122 of the Statute of Autonomy of Catalonia.

Accordingly, this confirms that there is no corresponding requirement that legal officials be able to understand or speak the minority language. Although the Statute of Autonomy of 2006[2] establishes an order for judges, magistrates, notaries and registrars to have knowledge of both Spanish and Catalan, a reform of state legislation is required to implement this mandate. Consequently, knowledge of Catalan is only a non-deciding merit for candidates within the legal profession. This is unquestionably a system that favours the majority language, and an unjust situation that is replicated in countries across Europe. Such a structure militates against the expansion of bilingual instruction within law departments, as there is no practical need within the profession for bilingual lawyers.

This is contrasted by the legal requirement in the autonomous province of South Tyrol, that judges, prosecutors, and support staff must prove fluency in both Italian and German, prior to commencing their post. Further, the legal requirement in Finland[3] for the appointment of a specific number of bilingual judges to reflect the bilingual nature of certain areas of the country, creates a specific need within higher education to provide competent bilingual graduates to fill these positions. This reflects the political will to create a truly bilingual community, an attempt to normalise the use of the minority language, and the creation of an effective bilingual legal service.

In order to attempt to engage legal professionals in the acquisition of Catalan, there has been an attempt by the Generalitat of Catalonia to establish policies to encourage the use of Catalan within the legal sphere. Catalan lessons have been provided, along with linguistic support for law firms, free of charge, along with the creation of a linguistic board tasked with the promotion of the minority language. However, such schemes do not go far enough to engage with the central issue of a lack of legal professionals available to practice bilingually. Proposals such as these can only provide support for bilingual provision, but they fail to deal with the reality of the need to train bilingual lawyers in both languages. A catalyst is needed to change current perception within the legal sphere to recognise the need to have fully trained and flexible bilingual law graduates. Such a result requires dedicated legislation requiring solicitors, barristers and judges who

[2] Art. 33 (3), 34, 102 and 147 (1) (a) of the Statute of Autonomy of Catalonia.

[3] Government Decree on the appointment of judges (42/7200) s. 2 (a).

profess to be able to practice bilingually to attain a certain level of fluency.

A system that is devoid of specific requirements has no impetus to enforce the higher education system to increase provision through the minority language. Indeed, one could argue that the opposite is true, and that a persuasive argument to the contrary, in support of the majority language exists.

The ability to speak a certain language is not sufficient in order to practice the law successfully. Law practitioners need specific training in the law through the medium of the second state language or a minority language in order to practice bilingually. As the Galician case study underlines, although a great number of law students are fluent in Galician, the lack of instruction through the minority language results in bilingual candidates becoming monolingual in their use and knowledge of the law.

This practice is perpetuated due to the deficient use of Galician within the law courts. Indeed, this is the field of public service in Galicia where Galician use is at its lowest. The scant use of the minority language by practitioners, influences the medium of provision within law schools across Galicia, resulting in an imbalanced situation that does not develop the already existing linguistic ability of the majority of law students. Indeed, this system differentiates between majority language speakers and minority language speakers.

The legal profession therefore needs to work hand in hand with the higher education sector to ensure the development of a robust and dedicated bilingual legal service, comparable to the system developed in Canada. The linguistic practice exercised by the profession, undoubtedly influences minority or second language provision within higher education, the number of staff available to teach, and importantly, the funding provided for minority or second language provision within legal departments across Europe.

Without doubt, stringent linguistic requirements for bilingual practising lawyers would provide benefits that are twofold, ensuring equal access to justice for speakers of the majority, minority and second state languages, and also a greater provision for law students through the medium of minority languages and second state languages, within higher education.

These are developments that are required immediately, in order to address the second key obstacle limiting the success of bilingual legal provision within higher education.

2. *Resources*

The issue of a lack of resources is often regarded as an issue affecting the higher education sector as a whole, in countries that have no concern with minority or second language provision. However, the chapters included within this volume, almost unanimously identify a lack of resources as a critical impediment to the successful development of minority and second language provision within legal education and training. This is true, whether the case study focuses upon a jurisdiction where a large proportion of the community speak the second language, to case studies where the minority language is recognised as having very few speakers. This issue therefore is not less significant as the number of individuals fluent in the language increases.

Issues concerning lack of resources are three fold, namely a lack of qualified and experienced teaching staff to contribute to minority language teaching, a shortage of materials both for teaching staff and students, and insufficient funding towards the development of new terminology and resources.

Within the Romanian and Welsh examples, as in many other case studies in this volume, the numbers of competent lecturing staff available to teach through the medium of the minority or second language are extremely low.

Typically, the very few teaching staff available to instruct through the medium of the minority language are also expected to contribute to majority language teaching. As the Basque Country case study illustrates, the teaching obligations placed upon bilingual lecturing staff are greater in comparison with their monolingual counterparts. This in turn will limit the number of qualified individuals who wish to contribute to bilingual teaching.

The Basque Country model also expresses concern regarding the age and experience of academics contributing to teaching through the minority language. At the onset of bilingual legal provision in the Basque Country, young and inexperienced staff were expected to tackle enormous responsibilities, with greater teaching obligations than their monolingual equals and the requirement of the translation of materials in a number of topics, without the assistance and encouragement of senior members of staff.

Similarly, from the Welsh perspective, Dr Gwynedd Parry expresses some reservation with the current strategy of appointing very young and inexperienced staff to teach through the medium of Welsh through funding programmes such as PhD scholarships for Welsh speaking candidates, and the appointment of Welsh medium teaching fellowships. Dr Gwynedd Parry perceives this as being detrimental to the development of legal scholarship through the medium of minority languages due to the inexperience of a great majority of the teaching staff. This is replicated by the experience of Dr Arzoz who underlines the lower status given to bilingual lecturing staff in the Basque Country due to their relative inexperience.

The use of young and inexperienced academic staff is however, a medium to long -term strategy, as recognised by Dr Gwynedd Parry. Their typically enhanced position following their initial introduction is emphasised by the experience of the Basque Country, where the situation of, and prospects for, bilingual lecturing staff are improving. There is currently a greater number of bilingual teaching staff across the higher education institutions of the region; they have more experience in teaching through the medium of both official languages, support is also available in the form of experienced colleagues, terminology and teaching materials. Further, following 2007, Spanish legislation has regionalised the process of appointing academic staff. This is turn can allow higher education institutions to appoint bilingual lecturing and professorial staff according to the needs of their establishment.

This in no doubt limits the appeal of minority language provision for students, as learning through the medium of the minority language is seen as a task for which extra commitment is required. Further, the pressure placed upon bilingual teaching staff severely limits their ability to contribute to research within their chosen field. This is turn, constrains their capacity to play a role in the development of terminology, and subsequently, the expansion of teaching materials, and materials for students.

The lack of teaching materials limits the attraction to teaching staff to work through the medium of the minority language. It is perceived as a laborious task, where only very few students undertake the available provision.

However, Dr Suksi raises the possibility that a lack of second language or minority language materials could possibly have a positive impact upon the bilingualism of students. Dr Suksi proposes that the obligatory reading of Finnish legal texts has the end result of Swedish speaking Finns becoming bilingual. However, this is not a reliable foundation upon which to develop bilingualism among law students.

They have no access to correct terminology and no assistance in the development of their bilingual knowledge of the law. Students, whatever their geographical location, and whatever their language of choice require equal access to majority or minority language provision supported by sufficient resources such as materials, terminology and teaching staff.

Inextricably linked to the issue of lack of materials, is the difficulty of a lack of legal terminology available in minority languages. This is an issue that has a disparate effect upon minority language provision within legal education in the case studies included within this volume. Indeed, the Galician case study highlights that minority language legal education depends upon limited vocabulary lists only, with no legal textbooks available through the medium of Galician.

Nevertheless, the Irish example illustrates that when a language is recognised as an official language of the European Union, the issue of creating and modulating terminology within the legal sphere somewhat disappears. Analogous to this is the French language within the Canadian example, where a bilingual legal system has historically developed hand in hand with the development of bilingual legal education, allowing for a well thought through, concise and co-operative development of terminology. However, the Finnish case study stresses that although Finnish and Swedish are official languages of the European Union; their individual legal jurisdictions are not sufficiently alike to allow the sharing of materials for practitioners, teaching staff and students. Official linguistic status within Europe therefore is not always a remedy to the problem of a lack of terminology and materials available for students who wish to learn through the medium of the second state language, or minority language.

The lack of legal terminology available in minority or second languages continues to be a problem across Europe, and as the Welsh and Basque Country examples highlight, a lack of terminology inevitably has a knock on effect upon the development of materials available for teachers and students; and further, upon the number of students and staff undertaking provision through the medium of the minority or second state language. This inevitably leads to a reduced number of bilingual graduates who can work efficiently through the medium of both languages, and this propagates the notion that the majority language is the only language of the law, which in turn influences the language of legal provision within higher education institutions.

The issue of a lack of resources cannot be identified as an issue stemming only from a lack of funding. This is a predicament that will require more than funding alone. Academics must work hand in hand with professionals in order to develop terminology applicable to the workplace. Without sufficient legal terminology available in minority languages, bilingual legal jurisdictions cannot function successfully, thus limiting every minority language or second language speakers' access to justice.

These key obstacles, inevitably lead into the third key obstacle identified within this volume. That is the impact of globalisation upon minority and second state language provision within legal education.

3. *Globalisation*

Globalisation within higher education supports the movement of students across the world to engage in different higher education systems. With the 1999 Bologna Declaration, where twenty-nine countries across Europe are engaged in the development of the European Higher Education Area. Unquestionably, a lingua franca must be found in order to facilitate the mobilisation of the largest number possible of students, and as the papers included within this volume suggests, English is the medium of choice.

Although the example from the University of Maastricht underlines the positive aspects of globalisation upon legal education in Europe, especially the need for a wider European element within legal education, with students being aware of the comparative nature of law and its application across the member states of the European Union. The Dutch example highlights the effect of English medium provision upon both French and Dutch medium instruction in Belgium, where English is recognised as a superior international language in comparison with the other national or regional languages. Europeanisation has led undoubtedly to a vast increase in English medium provision to the detriment of minority or second state languages.

This experience is mirrored in many locations such as the Basque Country, Galicia, Catalonia, and Finland. During the academic year of 2009–2010, the Galician Government recognised the development of English medium provision as a general goal within higher education, providing funding for the expansion of its use as a medium of teaching within masters' and bachelors degrees adapted for the development of the European Higher Education Area. As noted by Dr Arzoz, the purpose of the Bologna process and the development of the European Higher Education Area "...is flexibility, but the result is increasing uniformity".

These developments are extremely detrimental to minority and second state language provision. As Dr Kornet expresses, the law is inextricably linked to a national legal culture that inevitably means the use of a national legal language. In progressing with the ideal of asserting a higher education system which has no barriers or limitations in its point of entry to the student population of Europe, it is acutely important that legal departments do not neglect the importance of their individual legal culture, the legal language connected with that system, and the importance of imparting it to students.

Developments such as the Bologna process encroach upon minority and second state language provision within legal education, by creating barriers for speakers of the second state language or minority language, through the siphoning off of valuable funds, and placing the focus upon the majority language provision, or even English medium provision. Such strategies improve the prospects of the majority of students during their time within the higher education system of Europe, but should these opportunities be available to the detriment of minority languages and their speakers?

This is reflected in the research conducted within law departments across Europe completed through the medium of minority languages. The Basque Country, Finland, Catalonia and Galicia have seen a continued reduction in the number of research theses at all levels being completed through the medium of minority languages, and even through the medium of the majority language, in complete contrast to an increase in the number of research degrees being completed in the English language.

Finland has witnessed a dramatic rise in the number of research and doctoral degrees being completed through the medium of English, as the internationalisation of research has motivated students to choose topics that have an international aspect, in place of more national topics. This experience is replicated in a number of countries such as Catalonia, the Basque Country, Galicia and Wales, where the significance of academic journal rankings, and publishing in the most eminent journals, militates against research conducted through the medium of second state languages, or minority languages.

The case studies within this volume emphasise that there are not many peer-reviewed outlets available for academics to publish through the medium of minority languages or second state languages. Publishing research is key to the professional development of academics, and limiting their output in minority languages or second state languages has a direct effect upon bilingual higher education. It undermines the status of the minority or second state language within that particular area of expertise. Further, it limits the advancement of terminology within the specialised field, thus resulting in a lack of materials being published through the minority or second state language.

In turn, within the legal sphere, this has an undeviating influence upon the use of the second state or minority language within the courts. It limits the reverence placed upon minority or second language speakers within this area of work, and inevitably will limit the number of students aspiring to learn through the medium of a minority or second state language. This in turn will reduce the financial assistance given to the provision within higher education. The consequence of a lack of research outlets for minority and second language research is incessant, and is at the derivation of every limitation that influences the development and normalisation of minority or second language legal education across Europe.

The expansion of English within academia has a direct impact on the belief that minority languages have no standing within this realm. Indeed, as noted by Dr Gwynedd Parry "...this reinforces a perception that Welsh-medium scholarship is marginal and non-essential activity". This is already highlighted in the lack of teaching materials and resources available for students in minority and second state languages, and the number of academics prepared to teach through the medium of minority and second state languages.

There are a number of strategies at work however, that attempt to counteract the influence of majority language and English medium provision within legal education. These strategies are gaining ground in a number of countries, and as a result, the number of students undertaking training in the law through the medium of minority and second state languages, are increasing in a number of locations.

B. Strategies to Increase Minority Language Provision within Higher Education

In order to address the three key obstacles that hinder the development of minority language provision within higher education, a number of policy approaches have been developed across Europe and Canada. These have proven to be very successful.

To counteract the issue of a lack of bilingualism within the legal profession, Finland has implemented a measure of proficiency in each of their official languages, accordingly, perspective lawyers' knowledge of the language can be measured. Subsequently, in providing a bilingual resource, it is known that the service provided is of the highest quality, and provides equal recognition to both languages.

This measure is mirrored in Ireland, with the passing of the Legal Practitioners (Irish) Act (2008), which requires legal practitioners who profess to be able to practice through the medium of Irish to sit exams to measure their individual knowledge of the law through the Irish language. Successful applicants are subsequently enrolled onto the Law Societies 'Irish Language Register' and the King's Inns 'Irish Language Register.'

Such developments allow for a structured framework to monitor the use of the minority language within the legal sphere, it also makes it easier for the public to instruct qualified professionals, proficient in both the majority and minority language. In turn, this creates a need for legal education provision through the minority language, and provides a degree of recognition and respect to the skill of being able to practice the law bilingually. In turn, such a development should allow for an increased uptake in minority language provision, inevitably creating a greater need for the availability of bilingual resources.

Further, the autonomous province of South Tyrol in Northern Italy has developed a *Joint Terminology Commission* responsible for the development of bilingual terminology within the legal field. This measure underpins a successful bilingual legal system, as it allows for the use of the minority language in as many areas of the law as possible. It provides support for legal staff, and ensures that the development of legal terminology is current and in accordance with changes in society.

This strategy has been replicated in the Basque Country with the appointment of official translation staff and the development of *EUSKALTERM*; Catalonia has also implemented the development of *TERMCAT*. This is an official body that works in conjunction with legal departments across Catalonia to correct and update official legal terminology.

Undoubtedly, this allows for a greater degree of development in the number of teaching materials and student materials being made available. Further, this development supports the application of the minority or second language within a bilingual legal system, creating a need for legal practitioners at all levels that profess to have knowledge of the minority language to be able to function in both languages without distinction.

To address the issue of a lack of competent and qualified teaching staff available to teach through the medium of the minority language, the Basque Country has adopted a series of measures to assist teaching staff to learn and develop their fluency in the language. Teaching staff can receive six months paid leave in order to learn the language, and linguistic support is provided for academic staff and students alike within each higher education institution. Within the Finnish case study, teaching staffs are only required to teach through the medium of the language for which they have been employed. This ensures that the quality of teaching is equal whatever the linguistic provision, and that bilingual teaching staff are not overburdened with work. Such a development further allows for the equal recognition of academic staff whatever the language of their instruction. This ensures that whatever the language of choice, students have equal access to a consistent level of teaching, and teaching staff can contribute equally to research in their chosen fields, whatever their language preference.

In order to pool resources within minority language provision in legal education, an attempt has been made in Wales to encourage collaboration between the legal departments of every higher education institution that provide some teaching through the medium of Welsh through the newly created institution, *Y Coleg Cymraeg Cenedlaethol* – a Welsh-medium federal university. Sector groups have been established for each discipline to encourage partnership, and the improvement of minority language provision.

As a consequence of such developments, an on-line resource called *Y Porth* has allowed for the distribution of legal modules through the medium of Welsh across the institutions, which has enabled undergraduate students to access materials available through the medium of Welsh whatever their geographical location. This development has allowed for a growth in the number of students undertaking their legal studies through the medium of Welsh, and has allowed for departments to develop a more strategic framework in order to develop minority language provision. *Y Porth* has also provided the impetus for the commissioning of senior academic staff to begin the process of producing Welsh medium literature to correspond with the development in minority language provision. This strategy has been well received by both students and teaching staff, with the number of enrolments increasing year upon year.

Collaboration has also been witnessed in Catalonia with the development of the *Xarxa Vives*, a network to promote relations between the universities of the Catalan linguistic area. This has enabled the promotion of the normalisation of Catalan within higher education, and collaboration between legal departments to strengthen minority language provision.

Further, within the Basque Country, the Basque Summer University (*Udako Euskal Unibertsitatea*), which was established in 1978, has encouraged collaboration between academics involved in minority language teaching, and has provided the opportunity for minority language academics to publish work through the minority language. The Basque Ministry of Education further provides financial aid for the publication of textbooks and scientific works related to specialised fields through the medium of the minority language. Encouraging public bodies to work together will undoubtedly have a positive impact upon minority language provision, ensuring a more rapid and successful response to the predicament of bilingual provision.

To counter the impact of globalisation upon Basque medium education, the Basque Country has also implemented a strategy that ensures where new degrees are funded by public resources, Basque medium provision will always be required to coincide with each development. This ensures that English medium provision does not supersede minority language provision, and that Basque medium provision is recognised as being of equal value to that of the new international language. Such a strategy has not been implemented in any other case study within this volume, and such an approach highlights the very real threat of English upon minority language provision, and further the requirement to react to its influence sooner rather than later.

The policies recognised within this chapter highlight that the current response to the development of bilingual provision within higher education has been relatively small in scale, and implemented inconsistently across Europe. In order to develop a flourishing bilingual higher education system, particularly within legal provision, the approach must become more strategic, aiming to address every key obstacle that restricts the development of bilingual instruction, with collaboration between the higher education system and the professional legal system at its heart.

The developments mentioned within this section fall behind that of the developments seen in Canada and Switzerland where bilingualism is institutionalised. The position of French within the Canadian province of Quebec is enviable, but this is a situation that many minority languages can strive for, with the development of a bilingual legal system underpinned by a recognition that the majority and minority languages are equal, and are supported by practical application of both languages within the legal system, bilingual terminology, academic publications and bilingual teaching and training.

C. *Conclusion*

It is by learning from each other, that the nations of Europe can successfully compete with the pressures of majority languages; and the processes of globalisation, in order to increase minority language provision within legal education. Political, legal, and financial support are imperative in order to reach this goal, but just as important is the impassioned support of academic and professional lawyers proficient in the minority or second state language. Such support is crucial in order to stabilise the use of state second languages and minority languages within legal systems, and to encourage and strengthen their implementation in an increased number of academic areas.

Lawyers are trained to serve the community in which they live. It is imperative that legal systems recognise the linguistic nature of these communities, and where it is required, acknowledge the need within these communities for a truly bilingual legal service. The legal right to use the second state language or minority language is not sufficient on its own, legal services must also be bilingual in their application.

In order to successfully develop a bilingual legal system, the higher education sector, and legal departments within such institutions play a fundamental role. In order to replicate the success of Canada and the University of Fribourg, Switzerland, educators and practitioners must work hand in hand to create a robust and successful infrastructure to support the creation of bilingual legal education provision, which in turn will provide support for a bilingual legal service. Effective equal access to justice for speakers of majority and minority languages is imperative; it should not only be an ideal to strive for, but should be the norm in each and every bilingual country.

INDEX

www.ingramcontent.com/pod-product-compliance
Ingram Content Group UK Ltd.
Pitfield, Milton Keynes, MK11 3LW, UK
UKHW020132290926
15471UKWH00003B/447

9 789004 209251